FILMMAKERS SERIES
edited by
ANTHONY SLIDE

Reach for the Top

The Turbulent Life
of Laurence Harvey

Anne Sinai

Filmakers Series, No. 99

The Scarecrow Press, Inc.
Lanham, Maryland, and Oxford
2003

SCARECROW PRESS, INC.

Published in the United States of America
by Scarecrow Press, Inc.
A Member of the Rowman & Littlefield Publishing Group
4720 Boston Way
Lanham, Maryland 20706
www.scarecrowpress.com

PO Box 317
Oxford
OX2 9RU, UK

British Cataloguing in Publication Information Available

Library of Congress Cataloging-in-Publication Data

Sinai, Anne.
  Reach for the top : the turbulent life of Laurence Harvy / Anne Sinai.
      p. cm. — (Filmakers series ; no. 99)
Includes bibliographical references and index.
    ISBN 0-8108-4562-8 (hard : alk. paper)
  1. Harvey, Laurence. 2. Actors—Great Britain—Biography. I. Title.
II. Series.
PN2598.H342 S58 2003
791.43'028'092—dc21

                                                          200201298

For Nahshon, Joshua, Domino

Contents

Acknowledgments

I owe a debt of gratitude to Barrie Sumpton of England for his tireless efforts in researching and providing me with materials about Harvey published in England. I thank Dr. Ralph Hardee Reeves of North Carolina for sending me copies of his collection of clippings about Harvey, and Dr. David Parker and Madeline F. Matz of the Film and Television Research and Motion Picture Broadcasting and Recorded Sound Division of the Library of Congress for their always generous advice and assistance.

1

A Lithuanian Childhood

Laurence Harvey was born in Lithuania, but he was not an ethnic Lithuanian. Lovers, wives, and columnists often called him the name he gave himself, Larushka. As he became known, he told everyone—even his closest friends, his lovers, and his wives—that he had been named Larusha Mischa at birth, but this, too, was his own invention. Sometimes admirers called him Laurence of Lithuania and, sometimes, slyly, he would call himself Florence of Lithuania, which, in mischievously self-mocking moods, wickedly amused him. When he died, his obituary, which appeared in *Kaunas Tiesa* (*Kaunas Truth*), a daily published in Kaunas, then still Soviet Lithuania's capital, called him "The famous Lithuanian actor, Larusha Mischa Skikne, who took the English stage name of Laurence Harvey." It named the village where he was born and several of his movies.

Since neither Larusha nor Mischa or Skikne are Lithuanian names, the ethnic Lithuanian readers of *Kaunas Tiesa* could not have been much affected by the news of this Lithuanian's death. In fact, the only person to display excited interest in Laurence Harvey (he had never heard of him as Larusha Mischa) was Idel Marcus, his father's nephew, the only member of a once large clan of Skiknes to have survived the Holocaust. Strolling along Kaunas's Neva River with his family, this cousin's younger son, Hariv, pointed excitedly to the obituary in the newspaper. Their uncle Boris (Laurence Harvey's father) had found his nephew in 1970 after much painful, complicated, and expensive dealings with the Russian and Lithuanian bureaucracies.

Throughout his career, columnists, reporters, and public relations agents invented various backgrounds for Laurence Harvey, and he

1

invented some for himself. With the publicity engendered by his groundbreaking movie, *Room at the Top,* one American critic zoomed into fantasyland by writing confidently that twenty-six-year-old Laurence Harvey (he was thirty at the time) was a Yugoslav who had learned English in South Africa. A publicity release in 1965 claimed that this Lithuanian-born young man "couldn't speak a word of English until he was fourteen." In his *Filmgoer's Companion,* the more careful Leslie Halliwell still carelessly followed the general precedent by giving Harvey's birth name as Larusha Mischa Skikne. To this, the *Motion Picture Guide* adds: "Born Larushka Skikne in Lithuania, he went to South Africa to escape the Nazi holocaust of Jews [*sic*]. When he turned 18, he joined the army and fought bravely until the end of the war. That odd background belied his British upper class accent and he made many films playing roles that had little to do with his real history, a tribute to his acting ability." Another account has it that Jonishik (where he was born) was a Lithuanian town on the Baltic coast. It is not on the Baltic coast and it is only a small village. Plunging further into fantasy, it goes on to assert that Laurence Harvey's father was a well-to-do building contractor, who, fearing a Soviet invasion of Lithuania, took his family to South Africa to begin a new life—on a small farm near Johannesburg. Harvey himself told people that the playwright Moss Hart had declared that his father was a grand duke and that he had been born in an Eastern palace. Adding spice to this story, he told people that Hart had said that his mother was Gladys Cooper, that he had been born in a castle, and had just invented all the rest.

Reality was more mundane. Laurence Harvey never denied that he had been born a Jew but, on occasion, he talked a great deal about his "Russian manic-depressive Slav background." Now and then he said that he had been born Laurence Maurice Skikne. Sometimes he was confidently described as a Lithuanian reared and educated in England. He maintained that the Slav ingredient in his nature loomed very large (no doubt unaware of the fact that the Lithuanians are not Slavs).

Laurence Harvey was born on October 1, 1928, into a Lithuanian Jewish world doomed to destruction, and during his childhood that world was already quivering in anticipation of its oncoming death.

This world was the tiny Lithuanian village of Joniskelis (called Jonishik by the Jews), where his birth was an event of no importance except to his family and their neighbors, who looked forward to a good feed on the occasion of his *brith*. Named in Hebrew, Zvi Mosheh (Yiddish for Zvi was Hirsh), and called, familiarly, the Yiddish diminutive Hirshkeh, he was the third and youngest son of Ber (called Boris and pronounced Baris) and Ella (née Zotnik) Skikne. A sturdy little boy, he was fair haired and gray eyed like his mother, who kept his round bullet head closely shaven to guard against ringworm and lice. In contrast, his older brother by four years, named Yitzhak in Hebrew, whom everybody called Itzkeh, was dark haired and dark eyed like his father, but small and scrawny as a child, while his oldest brother, who bore the Hebrew name Nahum and who was sometimes called by the diminutive Yiddishized Nohumkeh, was eight years old when Hirshkeh was born, and also resembled his mother.

To Hirshkeh, Jonishik represented the whole world. For its Jews, life in the village—in Lithuania as a whole—was brutal, insecure, and dangerous. Little Hirshkeh found the village square a fascinating center where his mother and her sister, his aunt Hava, took him on market days and where he tried to rattle the Lithuanian market women with mischievous little tricks, for which he was soundly slapped and screamed at by his terrified mother. In this square, on a mild summer evening, the young Lithuanian men and women of Joniskelis often gathered to dance and sing. Jews were not welcomed to the festivities, but from the relative security of their homes, strained their ears to listen for the raucous approach of some young toughs made bold by drink and looking for Jews to beat up by way of a lark.

Leading from the village square were modest rows of houses and hovels built of wood and brick planted along twelve or fourteen mud-clogged streets carved out of a clearing in the forest. These streets had names, which distinguished this village from many others: the address of the Zotniks' house, which the Skikne's shared with Ella's father and sister, was 14 Vilnius Street. Joniskelis also boasted a gas pump that had once serviced motorists in the pre–World War I transcontinental race. The gas pump had long since gone dry and rusty, but the villagers regarded it proudly as a symbol of their link with Europe and the Western world. Joniskelis lay some one or two kilometers from its nearest village neighbor. On balmy summer Sabbath afternoons, his mother and her friends would take Hirshkeh and his brothers for a stroll along the narrow, dirt track road to a neighboring village to visit friends and relatives living there. Nor was Joniskelis completely isolated from minor towns. The nearest, Poinevezh, housed several doctors and a cottage hospital. This town could only be reached by horse-drawn cart. Kaunas, Lithuania's capital city at the time, which the Jews called Kovneh, was further away.

When Hirshkeh was born, Kaunas was not just Lithuania's capital, but also its largest city. Though small, Kovneh—at least on the better side of the Neva River—looked much like a Western city, with gracious buildings; pleasant houses; broad streets; a well-run hospital staffed by skilled physicians, many of them Jews, mainly trained in Germany and even England; and a first-rate Academy of Music. Kovneh was said to be a city that seemed almost free of anti-Semitism. It must have come as quite a shock to Kovneh's Jews to find that when Germany marched across Poland toward Lithuania in World War II, German troops had no need to enter Kovneh to slaughter its Jewish population; the Lithuanians themselves turned on their Jewish neighbors and did the job.

But these events were still in the as-yet inconceivable future when the Skikne boys were young. To the Jews in the 1920s music represented culture. Hirshkeh and his brothers were taken to Kovneh once to buy the much-favored Nahum a violin, which he learned to play without much enthusiasm. Hirshkeh had also demanded a violin, screaming for it at the top of his healthy two-year-old lungs, and was roundly spanked by his mother for his tantrum. He had a good ear for music, however, and, as a teenager, took up the bugle.

Hava, their mother's older sister, took charge of the three boys' spiritual and intellectual education. While following the strict rules of kashrut, she was a firm believer in secular Zionist Socialism. Marx, Lenin, and especially Leon Trotsky were her idols. She converted her two oldest nephews to Zionist Socialism. Hirshkeh was too young to care about ideology, yet he was extremely competitive, almost more so than his brother Itzkeh. Both brothers were always arguing and scrapping over something or other, and had to be pried apart by their oldest brother or their mother's shrieks and smacks.

Ella, the boys' mother, was a good-looking woman, giving the appearance of largeness without being overly plump and little more than medium height. Stubbornly willful and uneducated, she could only laboriously read and write Yiddish, but was not altogether unintelligent, and had a talent for getting under the skin of people with biting remarks and seeming to bore into their very souls with a gimlet eye, exposing all their inadequacies. On the other hand, her crippled older sister, Hava, was an acknowledged intellectual. Ella had the strong, broad cheekbones and a small, straight nose that her son inherited, and cut her blond hair fashionably short. Hava had dark brown hair that she rolled severely back on her head in the turn-of-the-century Russian style, a narrow, peaked face with a stern expression, for she was constantly in pain and often out of humor, and large, piercing gray-green eyes, pale and stormy like the waves of the Baltic Sea. While Ella was well built, Hava was painfully thin, gaunt almost, small and hunchbacked, with one sharp, bony shoulder jutting out an inch or two higher than the other. She sewed simple frocks, stuffed comforters with the finest goose feathers, and embroidered monograms on sheets and pillowcases for the wives and daughters of the local Lithuanian officials and minor gentry. Self-taught, she could speak Lithuanian and read Russian. Her Hebrew was fluent, as well as her Yiddish. The whole village respected her and feared her sharp, bitter, and scalding tongue that could slice like a whip when she was aroused.

Hirshkeh's father had very little impact on the boy's early life. He left for South Africa when Hirshkeh was only two years old. The family remembers the uncomprehending complacency with which this small child, trapped in his mother's arms, regarded Itzkeh, who shrieked and yelled and clung to his father's leg and had to be physically restrained by his grandfather until his father had climbed onto his horse and, slapping it into action, disappeared on the first lap of his journey to South Africa.

The brothers and their mother left Lithuania when the youngest was six years old. Until he was six, he lived among cousins and aunts, who later perished in the concentration camps during World War II. His Aunt Hava's bent for what his grandfather called "politics," was instilled in her nephews or at least, into the two older boys. She was extremely proud of the fact that Lithuanian Jewry had been among the first to support the modern, secular Zionist movement, and she herself was the founder and leader of the Zionist Socialist movement (even ten or twelve people constituted a movement) in Jonishik, lecturing to the adults and organizing the children. Zionism was, in her, ingrained. She always reminded her nephews that Palestine was their true homeland and that a Zotnik ancestor, whom she described as "a great rabbi," had made the extremely hazardous journey overland to Jerusalem to study and die there three hundred years earlier.

It was Hava's ambition to become a pioneer, clearing swamps and reclaiming the soil of Palestine, even in her frail physical condition.

The house at 14 Vilnius Street was large by village standards—and owned by their maternal grandfather. It was a two-storied wooden house with six small rooms, built of logs hewn from the abundant trees of the forest surrounding the village, and it had a large yard where chickens scratched, bad-tempered geese fussed angrily, and there was a barn for the cow. An outhouse in the yard served as the toilet and a well, ringed with a stone wall to keep the children out of harm's way, provided fresh water.

Pesah Zotnick, the boys' maternal grandfather, a large, domineering man with sharp gray eyes, a broad, florid blond face, and an explosive temper, was a carpenter by trade and had inherited his house and his trade from his father. He thunderously laid down the law, and his family feared and respected him. Of all his six children, only the last two girls remained at home. Hava, his crippled and passionate-tempered older daughter ruled the kitchen—although not without arguments and violent disputes with her younger sister, Ella. Boris Skikne, the boys' father, was a mild-mannered, gentle man with a thick and wavy crop of black hair, a fashionable black brush of a mustache, and dreamy velvet-brown eyes. His father was the village cobbler and three of his very pretty, unmarried sisters and a younger brother still lived at home. The Skiknes were altogether a handsome family.

Boris was also hardworking, and not unenterprising. Laurence Harvey told everyone that his father had been a well-to-do contractor in Lithuania. Boris was no contractor, but he could do some carpentry and housepainting and such. He was a trader of sorts, exporting eggs and geese on a very small scale, and his petty trading ventures took him as far as Vilneh (then in Poland) and Riga in Latvia. One shining day, proudly remembered by his sons, he actually exported eggs to England through the Lithuanian port of what was then named the German Memel (now known by its original Lithuanian name of Kleipeda).

The two strong Zotnik women dominated Hirshkeh's life. All his cousins were older. Some of them were his brothers' friends, but Hirshkeh seemed to have been born self-contained, and being the youngest, enjoyed special protection when he got into scrapes and was not above using tears and guile to get what he wanted. Itzkeh played football with his cousins. On rainy Sabbath afternoons, or whenever he grew bored with kibitzing and interfering with Itzkeh and his friends, Hirshkeh would go into the house to listen to the conversation of the adults.

The same group of friends—young men and women—would gather to gossip and sing and discuss what they considered were probing questions over tea at the Zotnik's house. Because everyone respected and feared Hava, these gatherings generally took place in this house, where she always presided. Most of the conversation concerned their neighbors' faults and foibles, which the guests were quick to expose and mock, and they were always bubbling over with good yarns and jokes. Everyone was mercilessly mimicked and ridiculed behind their backs.

Hirshkeh absorbed everything. As Laurence Harvey, he knew how to mock and ridicule people; he often set his fellow actors' and critics' teeth on edge and then wondered why they disliked him. He had inherited Hava's cutting tongue and used it indiscriminately all his life. Even under vastly different circumstances, he always loved gossip and relished a good yarn and knew all the Yiddish songs and jokes, in addition to the sometimes witty and more often salacious stories he picked up wherever he traveled.

Every Jew in the village spoke Yiddish. Jews had been living in Lithuania for several hundred years. They had drifted into Lithuania from Turkey, Spain, eastern Germany, and Italy. Useful at first because they were literate, they became despised and abused when no longer needed, and did what they could to keep body and soul together and feed their families, becoming innkeepers, wagoners, peddlers, tailors, bakers, and shopkeepers.

Hava taught the boys that that they were special, for they were Cohens, they belonged to the priestly caste on their father's side, which made them quality. The fact that one of their mother's ancestors had made the hazardous journey to Jerusalem to study and die there added to their prestige. At home, they were regarded as princes. In these little isolated Lithuanian villages, most of the Jewish mothers—unless the family had been reduced to abject ignorance and beggary—regarded their children as princes and princesses, and their children grew up thinking of themselves in the same light. This helps to explain Laurence Harvey's lack of humility and ability to stand up to his scathing critics.

This sense of being special, of being "quality," was indelibly imprinted in the boys.

Hava was especially proud of the fact that the young men of Jonishik—or, at least, many of them—had discarded the *streimel* (the round black hat worn by Orthodox Jews), and many young married women had put their wigs away. Under the spell of the West, many young women bobbed their hair, wore short dresses (the styles culled from some magazine, perhaps sent by an American relative), and powdered their noses, just like Americans. The Orthodox Jews in Lithuania and Poland regarded these young moderns as practically goyim.

Hava was a Trotskyist. She had heard Trotsky speak and she had seen him. The tale of that fateful encounter had been told so many times that the boys never forgot it, not even the inattentive Hirshkeh. It had happened in St. Petersburg at the outbreak of the Russian Revolution. In 1914, the German kaiser's forces had begun moving into Lithuania on their way to what the kaiser expected would be the swift defeat of czarist Russia. Regarding them as traitors and spies, the Russians had ordered the immediate expulsion of all Lithuanian Jews, issuing a decree that those who remained would be shot on sight. The whole of Lithuania's Jewish community ran for their lives. Those who owned horses and carts packed their wives, their children, and whatever of their belongings they could load onto them and fled toward Russia. Others fled on foot, carrying their littlest children on their backs. Like Pesah and his daughters, they bartered clothing, bread, and Sabbath candlesticks for wagon rides, and sacrificed their last coins to pay for rides in overcrowded cattle cars stinking of animal and human excrement. Pesah and his daughters ended their flight in Moscow. His crippled daughter told her nephews that there she had what she called, with flashing eyes, lifting her proud head in a gaze of rapture, and in thrilling tones, "a remarkable experience." One morning, half starved, on her way to the market to forage for stale bread and vegetables for her father and sister, she came upon a crowd of people listening to a speaker on a dais: a thin, intense man with a pointed beard and a shrill voice. It was Trotsky, exhorting the masses. To her, this was an earthshaking event. She felt she had come face-to-face with lofty genius, a true member of the intelligentsia, born a Jew, destined to become one of the leaders of the Russian Revolution!

Afterward, whenever she heard the word intelligentsia, she would toss her head and let her nostrils flare in pride of kinship. In temperament, she was just as volcanic and explosive as her father and sister, and had an unflagging flare for the theatrical. It was a family characteristic.

Boris was hardly the first villager to immigrate to South Africa. His father-in-law had gone there in 1902, only to return extremely disillusioned in 1903. Lithuania had become so impoverished that many young ethnic Lithuanians immigrated to the United States, spending a lifetime of hard labor in the abattoirs of Chicago and the steel mills of Pittsburgh. Lithuania's Jews would literally have starved without aid from the organized Russian Jewish community. In this little country encased between powerful neighbors, suffering under the Russian yoke, young Jews fled to England, South Africa, North and South America. To escape a long and hopeless future of twenty-five years of compulsory military service in the Russian army, the oldest Zotnik son immigrated to America. He left home at the age of barely sixteen, penniless, while Ella was still a baby, and became one of the hope-filled young men walking doggedly across Europe to France and the Atlantic Ocean, somehow finding oases of labor on farms here and there, sleeping in barns or in woods, somehow, half starved and in rags, scraping enough money together for passage in the overcrowded steerage of a barely seaworthy freighter bound for New York. The son was like his father, domineering, volatile, easily aroused to anger, living on his nerves. Like Hava too, he had a slew of strong opinions and stuck to them through thick and thin even as a child. All the Zotniks had the same character.

His father had sailed to South Africa. He arrived at the outbreak of the Anglo-Boer War, and almost immediately scurried back to Lithuania, to the only home he knew, to his wooden house, his log synagogue with its thatched roof, his weekly ablutions in the hot and steaming bathhouse, where, groaning, the men thrashed themselves with birch branches to cleanse their skins on Fridays in honor of the approaching Sabbath; he was full of condemnation for everything in South Africa.

But Jews were also foreigners in Lithuania, as Hava constantly emphasized. Naturally, all her lessons centered around the Jews. To the Jews, she warned, all goyim were dangerous. One had to keep one's distance from them. If one happened to come across a *shaygets* (gentile youth) lurching by after a few drinks at the inn, the safest course was to run and hide. If the *shaygets* felt like picking a fight, only the toughest grown-up could stand up to him.

The Russian Revolution of 1917 had returned Jews to Jonishik. In 1919, after knowing each other all their lives, Boris Skikne and Ella Zotnik suddenly fell in love and married. Ella seemed to have a largesse of life, a verve, that fascinated the quiet, gentle Boris. Their oldest son was born in 1920.

They were both in their early twenties when they married. They were much too unalike but somehow they accommodated themselves to each other. In contrast to his highly strung wife, Boris was a kindly, quiet, gentle man, much loved by his children. He was attracted to her gray-eyed, blond liveliness, her unflagging energy. She found his dark good looks eloquent with charm. He was a decent and honest man, hardworking, able to scrape together a fairly good living. From the outset, Ella was torn between her respect for her husband's virtues and impatience with what she believed was his lack of drive. She was too strong willed for him. He could not satisfy her. In a fit of anger, she would bitingly expose the very core of his weakness to the children. But she was not always at war. Amid the turbulence, there were periods of calm, even of a sort of happiness.

In the early years of their marriage, Ella was a good-looking young woman who liked to assert herself as a leading light in the company of her friends, able to see the ludicrous in people and things, but quick to take umbrage and to think herself put upon when anyone dared to tease her in return. In contrast to the broad-boned, almost Russian fair skin of the Zotniks, which Laurence Harvey inherited, the Skikne grandparents, sons, and daughters had black or dark brown hair and mild brown eyes that faithfully expressed the mildness and forbearance of their natures. As for the family name, Skikne—the boys' paternal grandfather held the opinion that his forefathers had belonged to the estate of some prince or baron from which they had derived that name; the only authentic names they had were biblical, which were useless without a surname. Those who had not belonged to an estate gave themselves second names describing their trades or the towns their people had come from, some in German, some in Spanish.

For Boris and Ella and their children, life was relatively better than for their neighbors—at least, during the first few years. They lived in a decent house, with room enough for a growing family. They had a housemaid of sorts—a Lithuanian peasant girl known as the *shikseh* who came in once a week to light the Sabbath fire and do some of the laundry and housecleaning when allowed to do so by the children's mother and her sister, whose nervous energy encompassed everything. Both sisters cooked rich, marvelous meals for the Sabbath, in which the eternal preponderance of flour and potatoes larded with chicken fat was well disguised.

Thus the Skikne boys grew up in this world within a world, and the two seldom impinged on each other, at least for the children.

Once, years later, in Santa Monica, a Skikne relative met a Lithuanian American woman who boasted that Lithuania had been the only free country in eastern Europe before the Soviet occupation. For the ethnic Lithuanian population, this was true. In 1917, when the Russian Revolution loosened the czarist grip on the country, an officers' coup, led by Anatanas Smetona, declared Lithuania a free republic. Now, instead of Lithuanians having to study their language in secret, Lithuanian became the country's official language.

A new era seemed to have opened up for the Lithuanians.

The Jews had also pinned their hopes on Smetona, but soon discovered that concessions were only for Lithuanians and that further inroads had been made into their precarious livelihoods. The heady days when Boris could export eggs to England ended. Barred from this business venture, he had to turn his hand to painting houses and mending pots and pans. Finally, he was lucky enough to find a relative to sponsor his immigration to South Africa. The unlucky ones, with no sponsors, found themselves increasingly hemmed in and shorn of hope. The Jews of Jonishik and the other villages became families of aged parents, despairing bachelors, old maids, and lonely wives left behind with small children, pitifully dependent on the remittances sent by sons and brothers and husbands from across the seas.

When Laurence Harvey told everyone that he had a Slavic soul this can only be ascribed to fantasy. If challenged by some skeptical acquaintance who knew better, he immediately declared that he did have a streak of gloomy Russian blood, donated to him by some ancient ancestor lost in the clouds of time. He looked Slavic. Tall, with broad shoulders and fair hair like his mother, he could have passed for Russian or, at least, Ukrainian.

Since Hirshkeh was only two when his father left for South Africa, he forgot him almost completely. The separation lasted for four years. It had been universally accepted in Jonishik (Boris's father-in-law's condemnation notwithstanding) that South Africa was a country where gold lay in the streets waiting to be picked up. There were also lions roaming in the streets and, as everybody vaguely knew, there were black people. But imagination ran out at that point, leaving only hope behind. Gold was not lying in the streets waiting to be found—at least, not by Boris. He became a housepainter, a carpenter, a handyman, and he faithfully remitted his pay to his wife, saving a little for his family's fare, for a house to put them in when they came, retaining only a bare pittance to keep body and soul together.

To save money in the increasingly hard times, the house on Vilnius Street was divided into two parts. Hava, Ella, their father, and the children lived downstairs. The second floor was rented to an ethnic Lithuanian family.

For Ella, it was a period of growing bitterness and raw nerves. As the years waxed and waned, she grew increasingly convinced that Boris had a mistress and was deliberately abandoning her and the children. She wrote him letters full of anger and accusations, splotching the ink with her tears, falling into shrieking hysterics each time she heard that one of her neighbors had received the necessary documents to join her husband in South Africa, pouring her heart out in grief and jealousy.

When she fell into these moods, she made her children suffer. They would try to avoid her by running to their aunt Hava, who would regale them with her fine flow of talk about the teachings of Trotsky, or to their gentle Skikne grandparents and pretty young unmarried aunts, who would take the two younger boys into their beds and entertain them with stories and sweet Russian love songs. Sometimes Ella spanked them and yelled at them for some piece of mischief. Sometimes she praised one of them in front of his brothers and told him that he was by far her favorite son, especially endowed with talent and looks, somehow succeeding in driving the other two to jealous despair, thrusting them into competition for her favors. She was not of a saving disposition, but spent the money she received from her husband almost as soon as the remittance arrived. For only the best of everything would do for the children. She did not care about herself.

The two younger children were also swift to do battle for what they wanted, especially Hirshkeh, who grew into a bright-faced little boy and was extremely restless; both were very strong willed. Hirshkeh resisted for days before his mother succeeded in dragging him off to kindergarten. He howled and kicked and had to be dragged out the house. His brother Itzkeh was no less stubborn when it came to food, and most of the time refused to eat anything but dry bread. Both brothers drove their elders practically to distraction. Only Nahum seemed tractable, although he had a stubborn will of his own.

Unlike their father, who had scrambled through some rudiments of education under the strict eye of the rabbi in one of the local *yeshivot*, his sons went to a Jewish school where the language of tuition was Hebrew and the curriculum was Western. At the age of twelve, after graduating from the local Hebrew elementary school, since Jonishik had no Hebrew high school, Nahum was sent to board with a relative living in the small town of Shavel (Saulis) during the week in order to attend the Hebrew Gymnasium there. He joined the young Zionist Socialist group in this town and continued his violin lessons at the local music conservatory. At home, Itzkeh was passionately devoted to playing soccer and, on Sabbath afternoons, went on long walks with his teacher, whom he engaged in what he felt were deep discussions about all kinds of subjects. Hirshkeh, when he was finally forced to attend kindergarten, preferred his own company and, insisting on having his own way in everything, made no friends. Only when the children dressed up in their best clothes during the Jewish holidays and celebrated them with songs to an admiring audience of mothers and aunts and grandparents did he become genuinely interested in participating, and sang all the songs with great enthusiasm. He enjoyed all the biblical festivals, blithely unaware that they were being celebrated out of season.

The sturdy little blond boy with the handsome features and sparkling gray eyes was a precocious child, always getting into some mischief or other, full of pranks, restless and quick-tempered, a born performer, always seeking applause. Now and then he quietly disappeared, making everyone run hither and thither frantically looking for him. Eventually, he would be found, having gone off hand in hand with the *shikseh*, who was fond of him, fearlessly to visit her friends. He would amuse them by singing Yiddish and Hebrew nursery songs and performing little dances. They would give him fruit and cake and call him "little Jew" and treat him like some pet monkey, and giggling, pull down his pants to examine his penis with the "Jew slit in it" and stroke it and ask him whether his mother baked her Passover matzah with the blood of Christian babies, as many believed Jews did. He did not understand what they meant, but he learned the curses they thought it fun to teach him, and they exploded with giggles whenever he lisped them out.

Those visits terrified his mother and aunt. They were deeply convinced that all the goyim wanted to kill all the Jews. However, Hirshkeh was never afraid. Staying close to the *shikseh* he watched the festivities at Lithuanian weddings and festivals, enjoying the ceremonies and the traditional dances from some nook or other, admiring the women's neatly embroidered aprons, their brightly colored scarves, their embroidered white blouses, and pretty headdresses with their flowing colored ribbons worn like crowns on their brown locks, and the virile young men dancing in their colorful costumes.

At home, he surprised the grown-ups with his childish imitations of Lithuanian songs he had picked up in his sharp, clear, piping little voice. He also knew songs in Yiddish, Russian, and Hebrew, many of them American Jewish songs, picked up by some mysterious process of osmosis, since there were no movie houses, no record players, and no radios in the village. Whenever Hirshkeh sang these songs, the grown-ups declared that he melted their hearts. Like his mother, who had a high-pitched, reedy voice, he loved to perform, and exulted in an audience and applause.

Many years later, he enthralled a Los Angeles rabbi who was a guest at his second wife's dinner table with his perfect renditions of these old songs.

Despite the growing hopelessness of the adults, life was not always unpleasant for Hirshkeh and his brothers. In the snow-heaped

winter, they would go on sleigh rides, or Ella would take them, all
bundled up in fur coats and hats and boots, to a solidly frozen lake,
where they learned to skate and exchanged shouts of gleeful exuberance and delight with their school friends and where one morning, Itzkeh fell and broke his nose and his little brother screamed in
sympathy. In summer, when the cooling breeze sighed through the
great trees, the boys, throwing off their clothes, frolicked and
splashed one another in the nearby river. Often, in the company of
their mother and her friends, they picnicked on collations of chicken
and carrots and sponge cake in the forest or on the verdant, lush
green bank of one of the nearby shining little lakes. Afterward they
went sweetly to sleep on the carpet of grass in a meadow or idled
under the cool, green leaves of tall trees where a concourse of flut-
tering birds nested, and the rustling murmur of leaves conversed
with the rippling sheen of a river while the adults gathered daf-
fodils, daisies, azaleas, and lilies to make the Sabbath day festive.

In his father's absence, Nahum became the man of the house,
whom even his mother treated with respect. To Hirshkeh he took the
place of his father. Even in the midst of his complicated and often
wild life as a star, Laurence Harvey respected his oldest brother,
even when he used him. Nahum represented his anchor to an orderly life. Harvey did not want to live an orderly life, but he wanted
to know he had an anchor.

2

Growing Up White in South Africa

Ella Skikne and her sons left their crumbling Lithuanian nest and sailed to South Africa in the summer of 1934. Hirshkeh was not quite six years old. Of this journey, he remembered practically nothing.

Crossing Germany by train through the Polish corridor en route to Ostend, there to board the ferry to England, where the third-class passage was booked on one of the Union Castle Line ships heading for Capetown, the train made its scheduled three-hour halt in Berlin's Stettiner Bahnhof train station. Hitler had already come to power in Germany. Men in Nazi uniform were everywhere to be seen, swaggering down the platform in a self-confident strut, pompously giving orders to subservient porters. Their brutal and smug faces, and the swastikas sewn on their sleeves filled Ella with dread, but the family had visas to South Africa, which lent them immunity. Nazi tanks had not yet begun to rumble across Europe, and besides, the Union Castle Line, which carried immigrants to South Africa, had prepaid their train fare across Europe by agreement with the governments concerned. Fourteen-year-old Nahum was naïvely sent to find a post office in order to mail postcards to his aunt Hava and the rest of the family. With his shock of light brown hair and his gray eyes, he was mistaken for a German—until he opened his mouth. Any plans he may have nurtured to do some sightseeing were abandoned, and fortunately, he came away from the experience unscathed.

Little Hirshkeh wanted to leap out of the train onto the platform too, and catching sight of him, the men in uniform loudly admired

this fresh-faced, well-built young "Aryan" lad. However, they realized their error soon enough when his shrieking and panic-stricken
mother appeared, and their grins turned to muttering curses as she
yanked the child back into the compartment, where Itzkeh was quietly helping himself to some candy.

Glaring at the men from the safe side of their compartment's
glass window hazy with dirt and dust, Ella spat in hatred and fear,
muttering in Yiddish, "*Feh, Feh, Feh,* a vile plague on them." Inured to the vagaries of her non-Jewish world, which might be tol-
erant one moment and turn vicious the next, and despite the
painful cramp in her legs and the restlessness of her children,
she warned the boys to be as still as mice until the train began to
move once more. The two older boys obeyed her and only stared,
open mouthed, at all the fine buildings rising beyond the train station. Hirshkeh became extremely restless and had to be watched
every minute.

"What am I going to do with this child?" his mother wailed, giving him a thorough shaking before settling back in her seat. It was to
be one of her recurrent themes for years.

He took to consoling himself with a handful of nuts and raisins
from the bounty his aunt Hava, shaken with secret tears of grief at
parting with them, joy that they were joining their father, terror for
their safety, and gloom and dread of the nothingness of her own future, had packed for their journey.

In the train they shared a third-class compartment with another
immigrant family. It was uncomfortably crowded with suitcases
and bundles, noisy with the clamor of children, the clatter of the
train's wheels, and the grinding shrieks of the lurching carriage,
and its air was heavy with the scent of the fat roasted chicken, its
skin browned to a crisp and the meat juicy and succulent, that
their aunt Hava, tremulous with nerves and grief concealed behind a mask of impassioned zeal, had wrapped for the journey.
She had packed more than the chicken. Their hamper was laden
with the mouth-watering tang of a largesse of raisins and al-
monds, with *imberlech* (candied gingered carrots) and *pletzlech*
(candied dried apricots) that she had spent countless hours and
nights preparing and had added lest the children grow peckish for
a snack. Boredom had made them eat too much. By the time they
reached Ostend, their stomachs were full to bursting, their legs
were cramped for lack of motion.

Harvey had only faint wisps of memory of embarking on the ship for the two-week voyage to South Africa. But Harvey's mother always said that her restless and inquisitive youngest was everywhere, exploring every corner of the ship, having to be dragged away from the dining room, the deck, the first-class lounge, where he was generally found charming the first-class passengers and accepting chocolates and other goodies. Most of the time confined to the narrow cabin she shared with three other women, the generally seasick Ella had to rely on Nahum to try to control the child.

"Control" was the first English word the children learned. His second brother remembers that this word was constantly being voiced by two of their fellow passengers, an English Jewish couple also emigrating to South Africa. They believed that Jews had to be silent and inconspicuous, traits that were not in the brothers' nature.

Sometimes, as in a dream, the brothers were still on the ship, watching it plunging through the endless, sullen green ocean waves. Toward the end of the voyage—it must have been—there was a ship's party for the children. Everyone appeared in a costume of one kind or another, but Hirshkeh does not appear in the group photograph. He had slipped away to visit his friends and admirers in first class.

And all at once they caught sight of the sudden panorama of land far down below them, which the adults cried was Capetown, a city planted with houses and cars and streets like painted toys, climbing upward toward the grassy, sharp rocks of flat-topped Table Mountain standing guard over the city amid a court of misty clouds. They remembered the wariness with which, upon disembarking, holding tightly onto each other's hands, the two younger brothers looked about for the ferocious lions they had heard prowled freely in the streets of the cities, although they had been assured that there were none.

Only as adults, when they could recall no more than sporadic and isolated fragments like scattered splinters of potsherds of the old life in Lithuania and had come to regard themselves as South African and then had left that country forever, did they learn to appreciate the awesome wonder of South Africa's stark, primeval natural majesty.

"Of course the white herrenvolk mentality is rotten, but nature is absolutely glorious in South Africa," the adult Laurence Harvey used to tell people. "There's nothing like it anywhere." He had seen the jagged ranges of the Drakensberg Mountains turning misty purple with the dawn, the fierce beauty of the Karroo Desert. Privately, however, he preferred the well-groomed artificiality of French gardens, the self-indulgent abundance of Hollywood, the lascivious charms of Nice and Cannes, the humanized polish of Paris and Rome. It was in these places that he spent what little leisure he granted himself.

The two younger brothers had only the blurriest of childhood memories of the thousand-mile train journey from Capetown to Johannesburg.

A relative of Boris's had come to meet the ship, taken the family through customs, brought them fruit and bread and hard-boiled eggs for the journey, and placed them on the train. When he dared to tell Ella to shave the children's heads in order to get rid of lice, her rage at this insult knew no bounds.

She grew more and more hysterical as the train climbed the 6,000 feet to Johannesburg, for she was convinced that Boris had a mistress and would abandon her and the children.

When the train came to its final halt, a stranger with a shock of thick, wavy black hair, black eyes, and a black mustache on a tanned and worriedly smiling face embraced the two oldest boys and attempted to embrace the youngest.

"Who's this man?" Hirshkeh asked Nahum, firmly repelling the stranger, tugging at his brother's arm. He was astonished to learn that this was his not even dimly remembered father.

Ella smothered her anxious and apprehensive husband with hysterical accusations, black looks, unbridled affection, and bitter tears. The two older boys remembered him and almost instantly resumed their former warm relationship with him, but Hirshkeh clung to his oldest brother's hand, refusing even to look at his father.

In Johannesburg, Boris, who was a skillful handyman—a quality none of his sons had inherited—had become a housepainter and a carpenter, in a small way.

Reality and fiction about Laurence Harvey part company at this point. One version asserted that his drive, so evident to anyone coming into contact with him, was the result of his early hardships. His earliest American studio biography brought this even wilder claim:

> Not only did Larry Harvey not have a silver spoon in his mouth as a kid, but in the city of his youth, Johannesburg, South Africa, you counted yourself lucky if you had any teeth in your mouth. . . . Larry had his education pounded into him in a back alley in the roughest part of Johannesburg, and he considered the education for the next few months with his jaw in traction in a South African Naval hospital. He was fourteen. While his peers struggled with Chaucer and Milton in their expensive public schools and universities in England, Larry struggled with life . . . he set out to become something quite impossible considering his background, and he did it.

Laurence Harvey could not discuss his childhood, this studio release continues, "but a friend told the author that he regarded his fame as earned and deserved. . . . He had the most incredible life before he became a success and he did almost everything imaginable in order to survive."

South Africa was, at this time, a society of apartheid. The African majority was hardly considered to exist, except as servants and laborers. The small minority of whites that ruled the country was divided into categories: the Afrikaaners, the English-speaking South Africans, and the Jews. The last had been permitted to immigrate to South Africa to bolster the white minority, but many Afrikaaners regarded them as nonwhites, especially with the rise of Hitler, whom a large number of Afrikaaners admired. In this light, the description of Laurence Harvey's rough childhood bears a closer resemblance to that of a child growing up in the violence of an African township in Johannesburg than to the white experience.

The Skikne's first home was with a relative of their father's, a large, placid, decent, pale widow with two teenage children to support and a large number of entertaining and high-spirited, if somewhat disreputable, brothers. She lived in a large old house and rented out rooms to Jewish traveling salesmen.

This house stood in the white, mainly Jewish, mainly respectable lower-middle-class suburb of Doornfontein. In the days of the Boer Republic, which spread across what became the province of Transvaal, Doornfontein (literally, Thorn Fountain) was once a farm that was purchased from the Boer Republic by Cecil Rhodes and the De Beers Consolidated Mines Company, the world diamond monopoly. Doornfontein was some two miles away from the train station and the center of town. Its streets were filled with mainly small, old brick houses largely inhabited by lower-middle-class Jews and, in some older streets, also large, even stately old mansions. In the time of the newly discovered thirty-mile-rich belt of gold known as the Witwatersrand (White Waters Rand), Doornfontein had been the suburb of the fabulously wealthy gold and diamond robber barons like Barney Barnato and Alfred Beit, both of them members of the De Beers syndicate. Ironically, Sir Alfred Beit, as he later became, was one of the lovers of the English actress Hermione Baddeley, who several years later was to become Laurence Harvey's lover. Rhodes named a country after himself, Rhodesia, which with independence became Zimbabwe. Beit had a street in Doornfontein named after himself: Beit Street, which runs through the whole length of Doornfontein and well into the next suburb of Bertrams. Barnato Park was a high school for middle-class whites. Many of the high-ceilinged mansions where the robber barons once caroused, dousing their whores in champagne, had become boarding houses owned by mainly Jewish but also English South African widows. There were also large and well-kept homes belonging to merchants and their families, some of them Jewish, some of them English-speaking South Africans, some with carefully groomed lawns, fruit trees, flower beds, and tennis courts concealed behind tall, thick flowering hedges.

One room, however large, could not contain the boys. They were quickly acclimatized, learned to ride the tram to the center of town and started going to primary school, which was only a few minutes' walk down the street. Their clothes swiftly underwent a change, too, from eastern European to schoolboy English, which was the South African style. They began to look different, and swallowing the English language almost wholesale, began to think and to dream in English.

One of the first changes was in their names. Their parents consulted an "expert," a brassy young lady who had lived in Johannesburg for at least ten years and had gone through the school system. Without a moment's hesitation, she recommended that Itzkeh be called Isaac, and Hirshkeh, Harry. These names were instantly adopted. Nahum tried on the name Nathan, but swiftly discarded it and stubbornly refused to adopt an English name. He was fourteen years old, and had no intention of remaining in South Africa. Disregarding the fact that the British Mandatory Authority in Palestine had, under acute Arab pressure, stopped issuing immigration visas to Jews, he was determined to leave South Africa in order to become a pioneer in Palestine.

Several months after their arrival in Johannesburg, the family moved into a two-bedroom house in the lower-middle-class suburb of Bertrams, next door to Doornfontein. The house was much too small for three growing boys, and Ella's dissatisfaction was loud and bitter, but the house belonged to them, and it was the best Boris could afford. Adding to the congestion, Boris succeeded in bringing over his pretty youngest sister, and she too came to live in the house—at least, for some time until, made uncomfortable by Ella's moods, she married the young man to whom she had been more or less engaged in Lithuania, thereby facilitating her immigration.

The atmosphere in that house was sometimes stifling. Often Ella was full of bitter criticism of one of her sons and praised another. She smacked them, squeezed large glass jugs of orange juice for them when they caught colds, and cooked their favorite meals.

Most of all, she genuinely admired and loved her husband who, with the help of a relative, had acquired a rudimentary ability to read and write English and perused the daily newspaper to some laborious extent and became, to his neighbors because of his kindly nature, the man to whom many turned for what they considered was reasoned and sage advice on personal matters. Unlike him, while abrasive in her criticisms and condemnations of her friends, family, and neighbors, Ella could also tell a pithy old village joke in a solemn voice. Her youngest son had inherited from her an enormous fund of dynamic energy, but unlike him she had found no creative outlet for it and remained forever unfocused and wild—a frustrated soul.

Doornfontein and its adjoining suburb of Bertrams were in what was known as the Bezuidenhout (familiarly called Bez) Valley. The area had beautiful parkland as well as houses. The two suburbs were peopled, in the main, by middle and lower-income Jews and newly arrived immigrants who had barely managed to escape Hitler's concentration camps. Above the valley was a long hill and on the other side rose the better—and much newer— houses of the middle classes. A kind of snobbery had developed between the top and the bottom of the hill. To those living on the hill and beyond, the inhabitants of Bertrams and certainly of Doornfontein were regarded as ignorant newcomers and low on the social scale.

The Skikne's little house was on Berea Road, in the better section of Bertrams, practically at the foot of the hill. It was separated from its neighbor on one side by a sandy tennis court with a torn and drooping net and a ramshackle wire fence where the boys played tennis. This piece of land was owned by a man who always chased the neighborhood boys out of the "tennis court"—until young Harry boldly approached him and made friends with him. On its other side, the house was separated from its neighbor by a decrepit aluminum shack. From the unpaved sidewalk, a patch of garden, more sandy than grassy, led up three shiny red concrete steps to the house's shiny little red-painted concrete stoop. The ceilings were low. A narrow passage led to the two small bedrooms and a bathroom on one side and to a small living room and dining room on the other side. The passage widened into a sizable kitchen, which housed a coal stove, out of date even in those days. Boris had not been able to afford either an electric stove or a refrigerator.

As a newcomer, Ella hated and loathed everything on sight. She longed for the cool Lithuanian summer and moaned about the strange winter in this new country, which was sometimes wet and often windy and cold yet without a hint of snow, rendering the thick goose-down comforters her sister had labored to make too warm to use. The fact that she now had an indoor bathroom and hot and cold running water did not altogether impress her, though she kept the bathroom, as well as the whole house, ruthlessly clean. In the city, the distant view of the razor-edged yellow mine dumps rising between tall buildings frightened her; the trams, the buses in the paved streets, the swift flow of cars gleaming in the brilliant sunshine under a bright blue sky, the sight of people with black skins everywhere were overwhelming to her. This was so different from Jonishik, or even Kovneh. In her new home, despite its open space, broad streets and wide sidewalks, she developed allergies, headaches, sore throats, sinusitis. Her sons suffered from allergies all their lives. Her bitterness spread fiercely at the sight of her three fast-growing sons forced to share one small bedroom, crowding one another out. There were constant rows. Whenever an evil spirit seized her, she yelled at the boys, berated her husband, cursed her fate. She envied her neighbors, her husband's relatives, even strangers, convinced that everyone she saw was far better off and ridiculing her for her poverty, and wept for her beloved sister, abandoned in Jonishik, for her other sisters trapped in Latvia, for her own fathomless discontents. Sometimes she would smother one or other of her sons with praise, at other times with accusations and blame. From the first, all three of her boys had to learn how to defend themselves against their mother's emotional instability, and each did so in his own way, evading her gimlet glare by slipping out of the house, behaving with seeming callousness when she had one of her frequent accidents, spraining an ankle, or scalding her arm on a pot of boiling water, or slipping on her highly waxed and polished floor. Only her fiery energy kept her family and her house relentlessly in order. "You could eat off her floor" her neighbors said of her. She was proud of that fact.

Finally she hired a servant; a pleasant African woman called Mary, who was paid next to nothing, slept in a frail aluminum shack in the yard and did all the rough work. There was nothing in Ella's Lithuanian experience that could teach her how to relate to Mary. She treated this soft, brown, large-hipped woman, with a

pleasant round face and placid black eyes, aged somewhere in her
late twenties when she first began working for her, not without de-
cency, calling her "mine dear," especially when reprimanding her,
and never screaming at her as some of her neighbors did at their
"girls." To her sons, this woman was merely Mary, the "girl" who
cleaned their bedroom and picked up their dirty clothes to launder.
Having a servant to perform these menial tasks came to seem to
them part of the natural order of things. Nahum removed himself,
mentally, from the scene. He knew he would have to do menial labor in Palestine. Only later, did the two younger brothers come to
learn that the Africans' lot under white rule was not part of the natural order of things. Ella was quite unable to resist cleaning all
over again what Mary had cleaned only moments earlier, and
much to her neighbors' chagrin, she also swept the wide, still unpaved sandy sidewalk outside the house, which no other white
housewife dreamed of doing, and not even their houseboys who
lived in rooms in the backyards and did the rough work like polishing the teak floors and mowing the lawns. In other respects, she
seemed to have made up her mind to overlook and to accustom
herself—if never quite adapt—to certain things that were different
in South Africa. She learned to use the tram, no longer to be intimidated by the rush of traffic in the city streets, to make herself understood in English. Only her cooking never changed. Ignoring the
difference in climate, she prepared the same meals that she and her
sister had cooked in Jonishik, and this food, in the vastly different
environment, lay heavily on her family's stomachs. Like his brothers, Laurence Harvey always remembered these meals with pleasure, yet he later came to believe that they must have begun the de-
terioration of his health.

   The two younger boys speedily adapted to their new environment. They went to school, and considered themselves white South
Africans who liked swimming and tennis and played cricket, soccer,
and rugby. Nahum condescended to go to school for two years and
his English became fluent, but he always averred that his two years
at the gymnasium in Riga had given him a far superior educational
lift than his two years at the Johannesburg school.

As she had done in Lithuania, Ella continued to push and prod her husband to earn more. He added repairing houses to his work as a painter, and hired a gang of three African laborers to do the rough work. Initially he attempted to enlist the help of his sons. After school, they were supposed to supervise the workers while he was occupied elsewhere. It was a hopeless endeavor. Nahum became absorbed in a book. Isaac read comics. Harry simply wandered away and did not reappear for hours. Their father reacted with anger and resignation and gave up on them. All the same, and even though he was left to himself, Boris's new enterprise did not do badly, but because Ella was not of a saving disposition, the additional money was spent as soon as it was earned.

The long separation from her husband burned and smoldered forever in her heart and burst into wild flame now and then. To her, drama was everything, and she indulged in at least one tempestuous performance each day. Usually, this took the form of shouting at her two younger sons for some prank or other, and warning them, "Just wait till *papeh* comes home!" and marching the miscreant like a righteous sentinel to the front door the minute her husband reached the front steps and demanding that the offender be instantly punished. Then and there Boris, sighing with heavy weariness, would reach out and deliver a smack on the boy's buttocks. For, despite her nagging, he respected his wife's recommendations and, as a father, felt duty bound to enforce his authority over the children. He did not spank them very hard, and they always forgave him and continued to love him. "My three princes," Ella still proudly called them to her neighbors. But all too often she was berating them and screaming at them, making the small house a maelstrom of turmoil whenever a dark mood struck her.

All three brothers sought, somehow, to defend themselves against their mother's explosive moods. Harry was restless and rebellious from the start. One memorable Saturday morning, shouting that he had been spanked for nothing, he packed a sandwich in one of Ella's kerchiefs, tied it to a stick, and announced that he was leaving home forever. Seizing the sharp bread knife lying on the kitchen table, Ella clutched it to her bosom and shrieked, "My husband and my children hate me. I'll kill myself. I'll kill myself." "Stop!" Isaac yelled, and grabbed the knife out of her hand. Too numbed with shock to react, Boris could do no more than rumble, in his throat, "Ach, *die ideneh!*" (the woman!) as he always did during one of her hysterical tirades, and Harry ran, crying with rage and bitterness to the bedroom, his flight to freedom postponed, if not forgotten.

When her three sons grew up and led their own lives, the memory of their mother's destructive impulses kept them cautiously out of her reach.

If she was not belittling him for his failure to earn as much as her neighbors' husbands did (or thought they did), or at times falling into fits of hysteria, reviving her accusations that he had kept a mistress while she was languishing in Lithuania, Ella had great respect for her husband. And she impressed upon her sons that their father had to be respected. She was always complaining about being unable to buy the nice dresses other women bought, yet the boys never lacked for anything they needed. Nevertheless, they grew up with a sense of poverty and deprivation, and this sense never left them and was especially ingrained in the two younger boy's subconscious. "Money," Laurence Harvey said in a 1968 *Esquire* interview, "is only a medium of exchange, so I spend it before somebody steals it." He could lavish thousands upon clothes and antiques without a second thought and yet skimp on pennies. And however much he earned, he still complained in his letters to his parents that he never earned as much as the newspapers claimed he did and that most of what he made went on taxes.

He inherited his mother's obsession with spick-and-span tidiness and also his parents' sociability, or rather, his mother's craving for admiring audiences. Both Ella and Boris enjoyed the company of friends and relatives. When they were not yet teenagers, the two younger boys used to have to accompany their parents to the frequent family gatherings. Ella had no relatives of her own in South Africa, but the Skikne clan was numerous, and its members were scattered like pebbles in towns large and small. Mainly they were a colorful lot, including professional gamblers who played the horses and were frequently in and out of jail, womanizers and neurotic businessmen with all kinds of quirks. They were likable and jolly, most of them, with a sense of fun and full of jokes and easy laughter. "If you find yourself in jail," a good-humored gambler advised, "make friends with the jailor!" This was a lesson Laurence Harvey remembered when the need arose.

Another bachelor relative warned the boys to avoid having a relationship with women, because, as Laurence Harvey later explained, putting his own interpretation upon the warning, it was like having a relationship with a known thief. In a dark mood, Harvey would describe some of his female costars in unprintable language. On the other hand, early in his career he gushed in an interview with the London *Times* that women were divine and mysterious, capricious and unpredictable. He did not know how their minds worked, but he could never do without them. Their greatest gift, which he eternally envied, was their ability to give birth to a child. He would love, he often gushed, to creep into a woman's skin for a day to understand how her mind worked. And then, his self-deprecating sense of humor appearing, he would add wistfully that he would probably find that he had chosen the wrong day.

Ella loved the excitement of entertaining friends and relatives at Sunday afternoon teas, where the cheesecakes and apple tarts and pastries and sponge cakes were baked by her own skillful and nerve-racked hands, and a large bowl of fresh fruit salad, consisting of sliced pawpaws (papayas), melons, bananas, pineapple, and peaches bathing in a lake of freshly squeezed orange juice held pride of place. She stuffed her guests with the largesse of her table, and worked herself into a rage if, after they had left, her hospitality and her culinary art had not been praised to the skies, in which case she accused her guests of jealousy and deliberate spite. From her Laurence Harvey inherited his love of parties, but he entertained his guests with the finest wines and gourmet dishes.

The passing years thickened her body. She grew larger, dyed her graying hair blond, then let it grow white under a blue rinse, then dyed it blond again according to the passing fashions. Her face grew lined and her skin wrinkled, although her gray eyes, reddened by the sun and her resentful tears, probed everyone's failings to the quick as skillfully as ever, while her large hands became tremulous. She was full of nervous tension, like a wire ready to snap. "The Skikne women age quickly. The men stay as good looking and young as ever," she would say with an unexpected touch of wry, philosophic humor. And this was more or less true. The years seemed to sit far more lightly on Boris than on Ella, yet his dark eyes had become bloodshot, his skin had roughened, his breathing had become sonorous and his shock of thick black hair had turned gray.

From her nervous tension, her rages, her disappointments, she found refuge in sleep. The whole family adopted the same habit. Coming home after work, or after a heavy Saturday and Sunday lunch, they took to their beds. It became a routine that Laurence Harvey and his brothers somehow managed to follow all their lives, although not always at the same hour. Sleep was precious to Laurence Harvey. He was not to be disturbed while he slept. And when he went to sleep, he fell into the deepest sleep, from which it took some minutes to awaken fully.

In Jonishik, Ella's father died—she sighed, but he had been over ninety. Her sister's letters became more and more frantic and despairing as the certainty of war moved closer, for it was all too clear that she had been caught in a trap with no hope of escape. All of Ella's and Boris's families remaining in Lithuania cried out to be rescued, and all their neighbors and friends in Johannesburg had the same sorrowful tale to relate, reading to one another extracts of letters from sisters and brothers pleading to be saved from starvation and certain death, to be brought to South Africa. The borders of Lithuania were shut tight, trapping them. From their fading world of plaintive songs of deprivation and loss, their cries rang in their South African relatives' ears day and night and filled their lives with tears.

Life was different for the boys. The two younger ones sloughed off their old life without a backward glance. Almost before they could speak English, they discovered the movies. There was a movie theater (called a bioscope) in Doornfontein. It was grandly named The Alhambra, although everyone called it the Bug House, a name well deserved. Some thirty years old, its facade had been designed to ape, in miniature, the splendid thirteenth-century palace and fortress built by the Moors in Granada, but it had fallen into third-rate shoddiness. Many of its once-plush velvet seats were broken, but this bioscope always housed an audience. On Saturday mornings there was a feast of American serials and cowboy movies starring the likes of Tom Mix, Gene Autry, and John Wayne. There were comedy features with Laurel and Hardy, Charlie Chaplin, Harold Lloyd, Buster Keaton, W. C. Fields, the Marx Brothers, among others, and the local school children packed this bioscope to bursting, yelling and shrieking and hooting with excitement and glee, heedlessly throwing peanut shells and chocolate and chewing gum wrappers on the floor at their feet. The Saturday matinees showed movies starring Fred Astaire and Ginger Rogers, Ronald Colman, and Buck Jones. Years later, Laurence Harvey said that their glossy images used to confront him, as if to say, "You are the chosen one."

When he was younger, he never missed a performance, wheedling the necessary small admission fee of sixpence out of grown-ups everywhere. His mother always shooed him away, declaring that they could not spare the money for such frivolities, but then he would go to his father, for whom he had developed a great affection, behind his mother's back, and begin to cry, and his father would slip him the sixpence surreptitiously, and murmur, "Don't tell *Mameh*," and sigh into his mustache.

Harry cried easily in those days, a weakness Laurence Harvey never quite outgrew.

In their new environment the boys grew tall and strong, even Isaac, who had been so small and skinny in Lithuania. But while Isaac and Harry had so easily changed with their new environment, Nahum absolutely refused to change anything except his European clothes. The two younger boys had begun speaking English with the proper rough South African drawl almost within a handful of weeks, and would no longer speak Yiddish. Nahum's accent retained a slightly eastern European flavor, and although he read books and magazines almost exclusively in English, he regarded English as ranking second in importance to Hebrew. The fact that his classmates called him "Bolshie" (short for Bolshevik) because he came from eastern Europe only made him all the more stubbornly resolved to emphasize his superiority to them. Quitting school at the legal age of sixteen, he became apprenticed to a printer, nursing some expectations of working for his Zionist Socialist party's newspaper as a member of a kibbutz in Palestine. In Jonishik, he had belonged to *Hashomer Hatzair* (the Young Watchman), the radical Zionist Socialist youth movement. He devoted himself to creating this movement in Johannesburg, and dreamed, upon settling in Palestine, of becoming a leader of *Mapam*, the political party to which his youth movement belonged—naturally as a Trotskyist. Neither the fact that *Mapam* in Palestine followed the Soviet Communist Party line and its leader, Stalin, the man who had been Trotsky's greatest enemy and had succeeded in having him murdered in Mexico, nor that the British Mandatory Authority in Palestine restricted Jewish immigration deterred him from his goal. He was determined to reach Palestine, there to fulfill his destiny.

Meanwhile, well read in Zionist Socialism, his shock of wavy brown hair, well-cut features, humorous gray eyes, and the fund of amusing Yiddish anecdotes he could readily serve up, made him an attractive personality at meetings of the organized general Zionist community. To these well-to-do businessmen, in the later 1930s, by far still former immigrants from all the villages and little towns of Lithuania, most of them conservative Zionists, he talked of Jewish-Arab cooperation and friendship, and they found it inspirational, at least while they listened. But he felt much happier as the head of the local *Hashomer Hatzair* that he had organized. He was rather pleased than otherwise to know that *Mapam* had already threatened to expel him from the party, but he blithely intended to change the party's political direction as soon as he reached Palestine.

In young Harry's eyes, his oldest brother was a wise intellectual and a matchless idealist, in character the epitome of moral integrity. He admired him tremendously, although he felt he could never live up to Nahum's lofty standards and was not really interested in politics. Even when, as Laurence Harvey, his life became vastly different from Nahum's and he knew that his oldest brother would find much of it shocking if he ever discovered how he really lived, he still regarded Nahum as almost an icon, to be cherished and admired, like some precious object, if also to be used to shield him from their mother.

At primary school, called the Jewish Government School, where some 80 percent or more of the students were Jewish, both brothers became proficient at tennis, football, soccer, rugby, and cricket. Although he liked rugby, Harry did not fully share Isaac's passion for these sports; he was too restless and impatient, and never joined a team. There was an untamed and untamable wildness in him, an ebullience of energy that consistently led him into mischief and trouble.

Nahum and Isaac, who also belonged to *Hashomer Hatzair*, and other senior members of their group used to take twelve year olds, to whom they taught the tenets of the movement, camping for two weeks during the summer vacation—theoretically, to ready both themselves and their charges to live on the land as farmers in Palestine. The camp was near a shallow stream on land owned by a compliant Afrikaaner farmer who was only too happy to know that these young Jews wished to leave South Africa. Jews were suspect, communists, troublemakers; the Afrikaaners wanted no interference by outsiders in their relations with those they called the *volkies* ("the little people"—i.e., not quite human)—the Africans who labored for a pittance on their land and lived in smoke-filled kraals (huts).

At Ella's insistence, young Harry was always dragged, however extremely unwillingly, to spend the two weeks at the camp with his older brothers. In general, he was inattentive, restless, rebelliously uncooperative, disruptive and teasing, and got into everyone's hair. Yet there came one memorable evening when he startled his brothers and all the other campers. While they were sitting around the campfire singing Hebrew songs, a stunning vision suddenly appeared. It was Harry, costumed as Carmen Miranda, the popular American movie star and comedienne of the time, known as the Brazilian Bombshell. Somehow, he had dragged together a colorful few kerchiefs filched from the girls and wrapped these round his body as a tight fitting gown, bare at the midriff. He had filched a bunch of bananas and several oranges and apples from the camp kitchen and tied them onto a towel in the style of Carmen Miranda's famous "tutti-frutti" turbans. Having helped himself to a morsel of scarlet lipstick from his mother's dressing table, he used it to daub his lips a violent red. Suddenly making an entrance out of a tent, he moved forward with swaying hips, singing "I, yi, yi, yi, like you ver-rry much . . ." in perfect imitation of Carmen Miranda's mellifluous gestures, warm voice, and heavy Brazilian accent. He looked like a pretty little girl and a handsome little boy all rolled into one, and his performance drew hilarious applause.

After taking several bows, he slipped away as unobserved as he had been when he made his entrance, careful to avoid what he expected would be a scolding by his oldest brother. But Nahum had been extremely amused and was full of admiration for his talented little brother.

In an interview years later, when it was fashionable for stars to speak of their poverty-stricken childhoods, Harvey told reporters that his family had been so poor that they could not afford his bus fare to high school, and he had to walk for miles. This was quite untrue. His high school, which he had entered at the standard age of twelve, was a ten-minute bus ride away from his house and he was always given the fare.

Athlone High School was a coeducational day school (for whites only, as was the rule then) run according to English public school principles complete with school uniforms and prefects. Needless to say, Harry and Isaac's school uniforms were kept in immaculate condition by their mother.

At school, sports were emphasized and sportsmanship considered the ideal. Harry could have participated in any he chose. The school contained a fully equipped gym, and there were swimming lessons at the Olympic-sized local municipal pool close to home in Doornfontein.

Athlone High School was not in the First League in (white) school sports in the Witwatersrand—then only thirty miles, and in later years extending to sixty and more miles of gold-rich underground rock on which Johannesburg stands. Still, Athlone's sports record was not to be sneered at. Harry played rugby for half a season, tennis for rather longer, went to cricket matches, and learned to swim, but was interested in none of these activities. He did become a member of Athlone's Cadet School Band, however, and this band was the best of all the (white) school cadet bands in the Witwatersrand. He played the bugle and was universally acknowledged as the finest bugler in all the high school bands. Smartly turned out, its members wore the full khaki uniform, including the regalia of a regular South African military band. The bugle was his greatest love, and he practiced assiduously on the steps of the red stoop of his house, much to the despair of all the neighbors.

It came as no surprise to those who knew he had been a bugler in his high school band when, in 1964 as Laurence Harvey, much to the astonishment of his host, he suddenly brought out a bugle on a BBC talk program and played it perfectly.

At thirteen, for his bar mitzvah, which his mother insisted had to be celebrated with the full pomp and circumstance of the attendance of the crowd of relatives at the well-accoutred large synagogue in Doornfontein and, following that, at a great food feast at their house, Harry had grown so tall that she had to buy him a regular men's suit. This was in contrast with his brother Isaac, who had to wear short pants at his bar mitzvah four years earlier because his mother could not find a suit small enough to fit him.

Harry was almost fourteen when he discovered the stage. When one of the teachers organized a dramatic society, he was one of the first to join it. A fast learner when it came to a subject he liked, he took direction without much argument, and loved every moment he was on stage. Later, he always hinted that a certain teacher—he called her "divine"—had shown him his true vocation.

The founder of the dramatic society, being quite enterprising, also organized social gatherings in the school hall that came to be known as after-school "Tickey Drive" dances. (A tickey was three pennies.) These dances were supervised by prefects (girls from the senior class, placed in charge), and a gramophone provided the dance music. One classmate remembers that Harry was one of the boldest participants. Physically, he looked far more mature than the much smaller boys of his own age. He had grown tall and well developed and was cocky, self-confident, and precocious. While his still quite puny little classmates were too gauche and timid to ask the girls to dance, Harry always headed straight for the prefects and asked one of them to dance with him. None of the other boys would have dared to do that.

This was, in later years, to become a habit of his. Laurence Harvey always headed for the "prefects."

Yet there came a time when these activities appear to have begun to pall. He took to playing truant from school and disappearing, often for hours on end. Where he went remained a mystery to his parents. Ella shouted and ranted. Sighing and breathing laboriously through his mustache with sun and weariness, Boris growled his reprimands, but nothing helped. Sometimes Harry did spend an hour or two at home after school playing tennis with his older brother and some other boys in the unused tennis court with a torn net next door to their house, but these games usually ended in fierce arguments.

For a time, following Isaac's lead, he joined an American-inspired physical fitness club whose motto was *Mens Sanum in Corpora Sana* (a healthy mind in a healthy body). Its leader also preached the benefits of good sex. Both boys exercised assiduously and became very fit.

One afternoon, Harry brought a dog home, telling his mother, vaguely, that a friend had given it to him. It was no more than a mongrel, with terrier ancestry, perhaps less than a year old, a white and black dog with a comical black ring around one eye, very wiry and good natured. He named him Rexy and Harry spent hours running with him, chasing him, playing wild games with him in the old tennis court. There is a small, faded photograph of Harry wearing his khaki school band uniform, sitting on a patch of lawn outside his house with his legs to one side and his arm round the lively mongrel on the other. The dog is cocking an ear and looking puzzled. Harry is looking into the camera unsmilingly but somehow, as always, self-contained.

Years later, Laurence Harvey acquired two beautiful pedigree dogs and gave them handsome names. Rexy was only his first love.

All three brothers, in their own ways, were rebels. Nahum found love with a girl in his movement, an immigrant from Lithuania like himself. Not surprisingly, Ella loathed her. She became almost hysterical every time Nahum left the house, would not allow the girl to come into her house, and when she saw her on the stoop, banged the front door shut in her face.

No girl was good enough for her beautiful and brilliant son, her noble oldest prince.

Both his brothers felt ashamed of their mother and pitied Nahum. Their father, sighing into his mustache, rumbled and shouted admonitions, but nothing could stop her.

Henya worked as a seamstress in a factory and earned more money than Nahum, who gave half his pay to his mother. Harry found his way to Henya's house, tears starting in his eyes and sobs choking his throat, begged for and received sixpence from her for the bioscope.

Defying his mother, Nahum married his girl. Isaac and Harry accompanied their father to the wedding. Scandalizing everyone, Ella adamantly refused to attend, or to recognize the marriage. It was 1940. Still not twenty-one (his father, defying his wife, signed his consent to the marriage), Nahum and his wife left for Palestine despite the war, taking advantage of the immigration certificates issued by the British Mandatory Authority that should have gone to Jews in Europe, but could no longer reach them and would otherwise have been wasted.

Shooting up at fourteen to five feet eleven inches, Isaac lost interest in sports and began avidly reading Marx, Lenin, and Trotsky. He also discovered that everything he had accepted as normal in South Africa was false and wrong and that the Africans were savagely exploited as workers, and agreed with Nahum that socialism and Trotsky's theory of the permanent revolution would solve not only the Arab-Jewish conflict in Palestine and the African problem but all the world's problems. Harry had no interest in ideology. He took to playing truant from school with increasing frequency and disappearing every evening after dinner, and no one could fathom where he went. His second brother maintains that Harry never seemed to have any friends, and never invited anyone to their house. His only visible activities were playing tennis with Isaac and Isaac's friends, swimming, and playing his bugle.

Instead of going to school, he spent his money, begged or borrowed, on the continuous shows at what was known as the "tea-room bioscope." This was a musty hall at the top of a flight of stairs adorned with glossy stills of American movie stars in a row of old buildings facing the tram terminal and the town hall where mainly old cowboy movies were screened. The price of admission included a soft drink of choice, dumped by careless usherettes wearing black dresses and frilly lace headbands like French maids, on a wooden ledge fixed to the backs of the row of seats in front of the one where he was seated. There, Harry spent the greater part of his school day, and since he looked sixteen, no one questioned him.

Later, his arena widened to include the two handsome new bioscopes in town—which were for whites only. One of these belonged to Twentieth Century Fox. Its facade was modern and its interior was handsomely upholstered with red velvet seats and wine-red carpeted floors. Although it featured mainly movies produced by Twentieth Century Fox, it also showed the better class of English movies produced by J. Arthur Rank and Alexander Korda. The theater was air-conditioned and the decor was vaguely art deco Egyptian and considered quite spectacular for Johannesburg. During intermission, between the commercials and cartoons and the featured movie, a Wurlitzer organ rose to the stage from the pit, and an organist sporting a thin Royal Air Force mustache and a toothy smile played a medley of popular jazz melodies.

The second bioscope, called the Coliseum, was even larger. On a lofty round ceiling, as the lights dimmed, a misty dark sky seemed to appear, where languid and smoky clouds floated and tiny stars twinkled. Intermission at the Coliseum was a show in itself. Rising from the pit came an orchestra billed as Charles Manning and His Band of Renown. Charles Manning, its conductor, was a small, middle-aged man with a mane of white hair that he tossed into pandemonium as he conducted, beginning with his signature tune, "Espagna," running through a repertoire of mainly Strauss waltzes, and then turning to face the audience and bowing fervently and grinning breathlessly and panting, "Thank you. Thank you," and tossing his white mane again and again to the giggles and generous applause he received.

Harry soon learned to mimic him to perfection.

The bioscopes changed their programs every week. Among American movie stars, suave Fred Astaire was his favorite. In private, he tried to imitate Ronald Colman's aristocratic British accent. The movies he loved best were British, because being bred at school in the English tradition, he felt closer to Britain than to America. Like all English-speaking South African whites, both he and Isaac had been educated to think of Britain as "home," although, like the former, they had never lived in England.

Soon enough, Harry began dreaming of becoming another David Niven as the mischievous and charming *Raffles,* or a sophisticated Rex Harrison, or George Sanders as *The Saint,* or a clever Michael Redgrave, coolly outwitting the Nazis. He also admired American stars like Mickey Rooney in *Boys Town,* and the swashbuckling Errol Flynn, and visualized himself in their roles, or singing the latest American and British pop songs, costarring with Judy Garland and Deanna Durban. Through them, he began living in a different world, dreaming of a scintillating future as a movie star.

This dream was suddenly and rudely shattered when his mother discovered where he had been spending his evenings and swiftly put a stop to his moviegoing. Brutally torn from his delights, he felt devastated. His parents could not understand him. He could not understand himself. "I'm going to kill myself one of these days," he told Isaac moodily. "I feel so empty inside. Like an empty peanut shell. Life has no meaning for me." But his brother did not take him seriously.

Now he hated school more than ever and was always up to some piece of mischief or other. One of his pranks almost had serious consequences. Johannesburg, in those days, boasted of its first three department stores, called bazaars. On a dare, in one of these—the O.K. Bazaar—Harry and two other boys in his class at school challenged one another to filch a pair of socks from a number of them lying on a counter. The other boys hesitated. Harry coolly picked up the nearest pair of socks, but one of the assistants spotted him, and just as he approached, Harry, in a panic, tried to stuff the socks into one of the other boy's pocket.

Fortunately for him, one of the store's managers, a compassionate soul, let him go with no more than a stern warning.

Then he found a new solution to cure his restlessness and unhappiness.

At the outbreak of World War II, despite the weighty Afrikaaner Nationalist Party's opposition, the United Party, which ruled South Africa under the leadership of Prime Minister Jan Smuts, declared war on Germany. Although it could not introduce conscription, since the nationalist opposition was too strong, the government had been sending volunteers to North Africa to fight with the Allies. As a Zionist-Trotskyist, Isaac opposed the "capitalist-imperialist war." Harry was still only fourteen when, in an act of desperate rebellion, he stole away from school one morning, went to the nearest recruiting office, and enlisted in the

South African navy, coolly stating his age as eighteen and giving his name as Harry Hopkins.

He was provided with a uniform and sent to Capetown by train, there to embark on a ship for training, but his period of service lasted no longer than a week or two, for his mother speedily discovered his whereabouts, bravely made the thousand-mile train trip to Capetown alone and, with her limited English vocabulary, succeeded in persuading his commanding officer that her son was only fourteen and dragged him back to Johannesburg, though he strenuously denied ever having met this strange woman, or knowing who she was.

Harvey had several different versions of his stay in the navy. One is that being such an excellent bugler, he was immediately entrusted with the duty of sounding reveille each morning. Twelve years later, he was telling interviewers that he had blown the "bloody reveille" every morning in the navy and the army, and that had accustomed him to army discipline. "Actually, army discipline got used to me," was how he expressed it. Getting up early when working in a movie did not present a problem for him, he boasted.

While in the navy, he told some interviewers, he got himself assigned to a minesweeper, a converted whaling ship. The ship was so overloaded that it started sinking soon after being put to sea. Fortunately, the crew was rescued and returned to base. There his mother appeared to claim him. In another interview, this version was embellished with the assertion that the vessel was so old and decrepit that when it began to sink at sea, he and the rest of the crew barely escaped drowning.

When Ella returned home with her errant son, he was forced to return to school. Filled with despair, he wrote a bitter letter to Nahum. "Dear Nahum and Henya," he began,

> I hope you are all well and happy. I am well as far as health is concerned, but sick as far [as] life is concerned. I will be gone away by the time the next letter comes so don't bother to write but I will write separately to you wherever I will be and you can write to ma. After [I] returned to JHB from [the] Cape life was so monotonous and with no meaning. Please

forgive me about not taking your advice [i.e., to finish high school] but somehow I think there is a better life waiting for me. I have nothing more to say so GOOD-BYE . . . and may God bless you. *"Chazak V'Ematz"* [Be Strong and Courageous, the *Hashomer Hatzair* greeting].

He did not tell his second brother what his plans were; he was afraid his brother might stop him, but he did ask him for a loan, and bought a train ticket to Durban. Alerted by her brother, his father's sister found him at the train station in the small town where she was living and pleaded with him not to run away. He loved this aunt. She had given the younger boys the kindness and affection their mother had been unable to give. Heartbroken, he came home.

The war had brought not only refugees from Europe and Asia to South Africa but also such exotics as the shah of Persia; assorted members of European royalty like the former king of Yugoslavia; artists; Frenchmen married to women from the Philippines, Burma, and Hong Kong; and others (instantly categorized as nonwhites). There was also a small collection of performers from England who had either been stranded in South Africa by the war or who had managed to escape its clutch. Several of these were more monied than talented and lived in Johannesburg's luxurious, newly con-structed blocks of flats in the city. They sneered at those they termed "boring provincials"—Johannesburg's white community and, above all, at those, especially Jewish, families who lived in what they called the poverty-stricken and ragged suburbs of Bezuidenhout Valley. Self-indulgent and filled with self-congratulatory petty snobberies, they much impressed their naïve admirers in this wealthy provincial backwater of Johannesburg. Chancing to come across "a bit of rough stuff"—young Harry cutting school—they drew him into their Bohemian lifestyles of easy sex with men and women. He proved vigorously adept at both and admired their chatter about art and the theater. To impress them, he adopted an American accent and told them, coolly, that he was an American sailor who had jumped ship in the port of Durban. He did, in fact, know a young American—one of Isaac's friends—who had jumped ship in Durban in order to find a way to reach Palestine, and had studied him carefully, imitating his accent, his slang, his rolling sailor's walk, the way he used his fork with his right hand, and his performance was so good that his new friends really believed that he was an authentic American. They made much of him. He reigned among them. But a handful of weeks later he was unexpectedly exposed by a chance encounter with a neighbor as just a poor boy from the lowly suburb of Bertrams and, much shaken, never went back to his snobbish new friends.

His parents knew nothing about this escapade, but faced the inevitable: Harry would never remain in Athlone. His father insisted that he complete his high school education, and on the advice of a relative, sent him to Mayerton College, a private boarding school for difficult boys. There he remained until he turned sixteen and graduated from high school. Acting upon the sage advice of another relative, he was then apprenticed as a draftsman in an architect's office.

For a time he liked the work and even thought of becoming an architect.

Years later, as Laurence Harvey, he told interviewers that he had studied architecture and designed a unique toilet seat. He also boasted to several friends and told his third wife that he had met Krushshev at a private reception during the latter's 1960 visit to the United States, and when Krushshev boasted about his humble beginnings he had slyly told him that he too had started at the "bottom"—by designing a toilet seat!

His stay in the architect's office was not a long one, but for the rest of his life he claimed to have a professional knowledge of architecture, and (with the help of an expert architect) planned and designed all his homes.

During his brief friendship with his pretentiously snobbish new friends he had discovered the theatrical company run by the British actress Gwen Ffrangcon-Davies, which was producing a play at the Standard Theater, Johannesburg's largest theater at the time. He auditioned unsuccessfully but hung stubbornly about until, almost by chance, he was given a small part in a play, *The Man Who Ate the*

Popomack, by W. J. Turner. It was not a very good play, or particularly well directed; the actors sat in a circle and talked—but he loved the greasepaint he rubbed on his face, the garish costume he had to wear as a Chinese mandarin. He loved every moment he appeared on stage, the polite applause of the audience, and could quote his lines from the play all his life. These had, not surprisingly, to do with women:

"You can go to bed with a woman, you enjoy her, but as you lie in bed beside her, you say to yourself, 'Is that all?'"

Suavely, he claimed to have spoken these lines with a Chinese accent, and to have received the play's only good review in his truly authentic portrayal of an old man.

In an interview with *Family Weekly* five years later, he provided a different version of the experience. Despite his apparent self-assurance and confidence, he said, he had always been terribly shy. As a result, his first appearance on stage had been a near disaster. When he came on stage with his one-line role, he froze. "Except my knees," he said. "They were knocking like the chains of an impatient ghost." A long silence had followed. The actor he was to address covered for him, and his only alternative was to walk offstage. Only gradually did he learn to subdue his shyness. "It's all in the stomach," he explained.

However, all brother Isaac (who had naturally come to root for his little brother) and the rest of the audience saw were actors dressed as Chinese noblemen seated on the floor in a circle and speaking their lines. He was clearly recognizable among them.

After his theater experience, Johannesburg became too constricting to contain him. He told his parents firmly that he was leaving for England to become an actor as soon as the war ended.

Ella was appalled. Actors were gypsies, akin to beggars.

He said that he was going to become a big star, and would support her and his father in great luxury for the rest of their lives.

Isaac backed him, but he was a disappointment to his parents.

At sixteen, Harry looked eighteen. He was bored, angry, restless, humiliated by his exposure as a fraud to his rich artistic friends, afraid of his bisexuality.

"I'm suffocating here," he told his brother. "Can you understand that?"

His brother did, all too well.

The next morning Harry went to the nearest recruiting office and enlisted in the South African army. He was still some months away from seventeen. Despite his father's efforts to restrain her, Ella ran to drag him home. This time, however, Harry told her firmly that he would only run away again and would keep on running away to enlist however often she dragged him back. If she persisted, he threatened, he would disappear forever.

He proved too strong for her. Even her husband sided against her. Curiously resigned, she let Harry go without a fight. She had fought so hard over the years to make her sons conform to her wishes, and had been defeated so often. Outside their home, they ate ham and all kinds of other nonkosher foods. There was nothing she could do to stop them, to bring them back to conformity. Sometimes she was quite guiltily glad that her father had never learned of his grandsons' falling off before he died.

In uniform, Harry looked eighteen at least, tall and blond and well built. His mother could not help admiring his good looks, and felt immensely proud of him. At the recruiting office, he had lied about his age, but he was obviously too young to join a fighting unit. Questioned about his background, he played up his experience in the theatrical company to the hilt. The South African military theater of operations was "up north" (in North Africa). He was placed in the army's Entertainment Unit and sent up north to join the unit that sent companies of performers to entertain the troops.

3

The Youngest
South African Soldier

He never regretted his decision to enlist. It freed him from the en-
cumbrance of his mother, his fear of wounding and shocking his
beloved father and his brothers if they found out about his true nature, and his growing frustrations with his life in South Africa. All
he now wanted was to become a professional actor. He could conceive of no other ambition, and no other future. Fame, fortune, and
certain success seemed to lie within clear sight. For the first time in
his life, it seemed to him, he felt truly happy.

In North Africa his audition was conducted by Sid James, an actor from Johannesburg who had "joined up" and become a sergeant
in the Union Defense Forces Entertainment Unit and the associate
producer of its concert parties, which consisted of companies of actors who staged shows wherever troops were based. At his audition,
the young new volunteer appeared so self-assured, cocky, and confident that this almost disguised his flagrant amateurishness. He
looked deceptively older than his age, but his feet were too large, he
flailed his arms, and his speech, when he was told to drop the American accent he had used to impress his artistic friends in Johannesburg, had the clumsy, South African English drawl typically full of
rough edges hewn by Afrikaans. Still, he could carry a tune, his
voice was not displeasing, and he had invented an amazingly agile
jitterbug act, which he performed with hilarious gusto. Added to
these advantages were his good looks and his ardent determination
to succeed.

It was the second half of 1944. With the war moving violently
toward its close, he was one of the South African Defense Forces'

Entertainment Unit's last volunteers. Sid James had accepted him in the unit, but had not taken a liking to the brash young newcomer. Nevertheless, James, a short, plain actor with a humorous smile who came from a South African Jewish showbiz family and was to star as the cockney rogue in many British "Carry On" movies, grudgingly approved of retaining him although the unit's producer and choreographer complained that he had two left feet and would never learn to dance. It was the rule that if the performer was approved, he had to enlist in the regular army before he could join the Entertainment Unit. This young Skikne did. Then came a hitch. In South Africa, he had enlisted in the infantry, giving his age as eighteen. Now when he signed up for the regular army, his true age was inevitably revealed. He could have been sent home, but since the Entertainment Unit was not a combat unit and, physically, he looked eighteen and was moving toward that age, he was permitted to stay.

He was assigned to a concert party named The Bandoliers. There, considered gauche, brash, a terrible actor, and an even worse dancer and singer, he was deliberately excluded from appearing on the stage and made to carry bags and props. Rebellious and refusing to take insults quietly, he irritated Sid James to such an extent that James threatened to "punch his lights out," according to James's biographer. Later, however, he was given a pink zoot suit and an enormous clown's bow tie and performed his jitterbug act singing "Hey, Mabel. Wait for Me," making it sound so lewd and comical that it drew uproarious laughter, according to several ex-soldiers, both male and female, who remembered his act. In fact, as actor Micky Beresford who was in the same concert party at one stage commented to journalist David Clayton, "Larry would never have been a vaudevillian. He specialized in invective. He always gave as good as he got in down-to-earth soldiers' talk." On the other hand, at least one admiring young woman declared that he had been a fine—and certainly one of the most handsome—of all the performers she had seen in the army.

Laurence Harvey always claimed that he had seen action in North Africa, Italy, France, Germany—in fact, in every military theater of the war. Now and then, fantasy taking precedence over fact, he appeared to imply that he himself had, practically single-handedly, "helped to kick Rommel out of Africa." (Notwithstanding the fact that Rommel had been driven out of North Africa before he arrived!)

His unit, he claimed in *Queen* magazine in 1962, was its own United Nations, "spreading goodwill among the armed forces of the world so that when they came home they could beat up their wives. . . . We took them . . . right up to Cloud Nine, so that later on they could become the first astronauts . . . we helped pioneer the whole new marvelous jet age." It would be more realistic to say that the theatrical company to which he was attached staged shows in North Africa, Austria, and Italy. He sang, jitterbugged with a female partner, and performed his solo jitterbugging act, flattening the top of his hat Mickey Rooney style, wearing his zoot suit and ballooning bow tie, and cavorting about the stage with indefatigable energy.

His American accent, which he had been ordered to drop, actually proved useful to his unit on several occasions. Whenever the Bandoliers needed supplies, he donned a U.S. Army uniform, compiled a shopping list, and ingratiating himself with the people in charge and using his broadest American accent, picked up whatever supplies were needed at the local PX.

He did not boast about his exploits at the PX, but he did claim that he was entertaining the 34th U.S. Infantry when they were stationed at Monte Casino, and by imitating them learned how to speak with a Southern accent—an invaluable asset for his roles in *Summer and Smoke* and *A Walk on the Wild Side.*

On stage, he threw himself into his act with such fervor and verve that his wild gyrations earned him roars of applause from the sand-infested soldiers in the camps. Offstage, he was a loner, as always, and although he tagged along with some of the others, had no close buddies. His chief fault, which tried the producer's patience, was his habit of crawling under tables and benches and falling asleep, generally at the wrong times, when needed for rehearsals. In general, being extremely competitive, he was quite disliked, especially by the lazy and the incompetent.

"That fucking little bastard's just *too* bloody competitive," one of the performers still remembers the others grumbling over their beers in the canteen, forming little pockets of camaraderie that Harry Skikne was seldom invited to join: "He isn't a team player. He's a son of a bitch who'll do his damnest to upstage you whenever he goes on. You never know how he'll shit on you next."

This was true enough: he was afraid of being eclipsed, and generally went about inventing wily new efforts to upstage everyone in his fierce perennial need to shine. To this fear of losing the spotlight was added the fact that he soon learned to tell the filthiest jokes and to use the foulest language, which he unhesitatingly employed against anyone who annoyed him, and larded everything he said with curses. At seventeen, he still had the softest baby down on his face. Because of this, he was constantly being teased. Worst of all, he showed no interest in any of the girls—or at least, if he did, no one knew it—and this was considered highly aberrant behavior. Also, unlike most of the men, he was always nattily turned out and kept his uniform spotless, and except for his hair, which he refused to cut in the army style, had an obvious flair for fashion. These "oddities" set him apart from the rest, and he was labeled effeminate. Gossip and innuendo reached such a peak that, at one point, he was sent to a session with a bored and overworked army psychiatrist to whom he explained, coolly, that the girls in the company were not to his taste. Perhaps remembering this episode, he said in a London *Times* interview in 1971 that there had been a time when "he did not care for very young women because he thought they were too busy thinking and talking about themselves to hold an interesting conversation." To the company, he seemed an oddball in many ways: quick tempered, argumentative, ready to hurl vituperative insults at those who offended him, mocking, and swift to take umbrage. The most insignificant incident might set him off; it all depended on his mood of the moment. "Go dip your head into the shit hole in the latrine," he would yell. He was always fiercely scatological. And as for army discipline, he claimed, years later, that got used to him, not he to it; he had been the one to blow "the bloody reveille."

Yet he was not always at war with his comrades. He had admirers and was bedded by a few, including, some remembered, a sergeant and a colonel. Sometimes he went to visit places with several men—to the Pyramids of Giza, where they shared ribald jokes about the motives of the unknown, drunken British soldier who was said to have shot off the Sphinx's nose, and felt secretly awed by this enigmatic man-beast crouching in stone in the sand. The highly unpopular King Farouk was still on the Egyptian throne and the Allies had imposed a form of calm and order that had not yet been smashed. For the soldiers, Cairo offered a welcome break from army food. There were delicious meals of large shrimp from the Nile, or chicken cooked to shreds and made tasty with spices in a restaurant on an island on the Nile. One could drink afternoon tea like the prewar British colonial officers and their spouses, lounging in the old, broad wickerwork armchairs on the long, dusty veranda of the once elegant Shepheard's Hotel, or sip dark, bitter coffee in the V-shaped cafe where two sharp streets met and crossed, and dusty pastries were served at little tables where men waited for men. Here the soldiers exchanged leers with their friends, and winked and made lewd comments watching these men, sipping coffee, hungrily waiting for love, and taking in the sight (and this was not infrequent) of two young men walking side by side with their fingers closely intertwined in friendship or love, encased within their own intimate silence.

His letters home and to his brother Nahum in Palestine were brief, written in his large round schoolboy hand saying bland nothings, stressing how hard he had to work, how much he enjoyed what he was doing, and how successful he was, and, in general terms, that he was making plans for his future once the war ended. He stressed his absolute determination to become a professional actor and to star on the mighty English stage. Somehow, because habit so decreed, it was still always England, and not America, that figured in his ambition, although he meant to star in American movies too, after achieving fame in England.

If he told anyone about his ambition—in some accidental moment of confidence—and was greeted with astonishment or skepticism, he became filled with bitterness. He felt he was being hounded by enemies, people were doing their darnedest to strangle him and hold him back.

He could not remember when he first realized that some people, like a pack of snarling wild hounds, were eager to nip away at his flesh, and determined to drag him down to their level, that all too many people hated him and would do anything to destroy him. Years later, as Laurence Harvey, he believed this more firmly than ever. Asked in a 1968 interview with *Esquire* why so many people hated him, he said he was really pleased to know they did; one's importance could be gauged by the number of one's enemies. And, with his typically grandiose exaggeration, added, "Not since Billy Graham has there been a religious revival of such magnitude and scope, because people of every denomination are packing the synagogues and mosques and churches [sometimes he used the Dutch word *Kirks* for churches] praying for my downfall."

Although his company performed throughout Europe, their base remained outside Cairo. He was promoted to corporal. Waiting to be sent home, he obtained a week's leave of absence and set out to pay a visit to his oldest brother, who had just settled in his newly established kibbutz in Galilee, in the northern hills of what was then part of British Mandatory Palestine.

He found a place on a ship northward bound through the Suez Canal and this voyage influenced him deeply. As he stood at the prow of the war-weary freighter steaming through the narrow blue watered ribbon of the Suez Canal, he saw how this ditch sliced like a wound through the vast body of the desert. On his left, concealed beyond a mantle of blazing gold sands, lay the invisible, people-clogged city of Cairo and the narrow, silver streak of the Nile running through it. On his right he saw the soft, sifting layers of blazing golden sands that was the Sinai Desert and, above these sands, the clear, pale blue dome of the sky encasing the golden expanse with a heavy rim, as if nothing existed beyond this finite, enclosed womb. The silence, the emptiness, had a hypnotic effect on him. To be alone in a solitary universe enclosed by sand and sky was a sensation he remembered all his life and sought to reincarnate. People used to wonder why he would lock himself away, why he chose to spend hours in his narrow toilet, or in his tiny, luxurious bedroom, the only bedroom he had built in his twelve-room mews house in London, and later in his large house in Los Angeles and excommunicate himself from the world. Was it a driving wish to return to the security of the womb—the womb of existence, where fear and pain were unknown and a golden comfort reigned?

Then, hypnotically, as the freighter steamed ever forward along the narrow blue ditch of water slicing through the intractable sands, the water suddenly widened, the sands all at once fell apart and rushed away as the freighter entered the wide and radiant waters of the Mediterranean and he returned to himself.

Nahum was waiting for him amidst the noisy burst of life in the then still crude and small port of Haifa, which formed a messy nest of concrete and sand at the foot of Mount Carmel looming sharply toward the heat-soaked blue sky. Harry had grown since he had last seen him, and had matured so much, it appeared to Nahum, that he almost failed to recognize his little brother in the tall, well-built soldier with his air of self-containment. It may well be that Harry's first impression of his oldest brother, whom he had grown up practically venerating, was one of secret dismay—at least he hinted at this to his second brother when they met. This was not the Nahum he remembered. He seemed smaller, more foreign looking. Nahum's pronounced accent, his lack of polish, shocked him. He had locked the village of Jonishik and his childhood there firmly out of his mind and, in South Africa, had grown up thinking of Palestine rather disparagingly as some third-rate Middle Eastern Jewish village, while he himself belonged to the great English-speaking empire.

Yet the very next moment, he grew ashamed of his prejudice. His cool English handshake turned instantly into a warm brotherly hug. This was Nahum, his beloved oldest brother.

As the sclerotic and frail elderly bus climbed laboriously up and circled the hills of Galilee on its way toward Nahum's kibbutz, the old warm feeling of respect and admiration for his oldest brother overwhelmed him. Chameleonlike, he adopted the hue of his immediate environment, almost becoming, again, the baby brother whose oldest brother's wisdom and idealism evoked his deepest awe.

Kibbutz Ein Dor lying at the foot of the biblical hill where the Witch of Endor had predicted the death of Saul, Israel's first king, was still in the throes of creation, as Nahum carefully explained to his brother. A row of prefabricated rooms served as living quarters for married couples, while the unmarried members had more humble accommodation in the form of aluminum shacks. There was a nursery for infants. This was by far the most permanent, best built and equipped structure. Ringed by the living quarters was a long, rectangular wooden prefab that served as the communal dining room and was furnished with several rows of long, rickety steel trestle tables with accompanying wooden benches on either side of a broad aisle. A smaller aluminum shack that served as the communal kitchen was annexed to the dining room. Unpleasantly near the kitchen was the old cowshed, which, Nahum humorously and not without pride, complained had been an original mistake, now rectified. Yet, if the cows had been removed to more sanitary quarters, bunches of the flies had remained to plague the kitchen staff. Completing the structures was an aluminum shack situated near the living quarters, housing two communal shower rooms separated by an aluminum wall, one side serving the men and the other, the women. Another shack served as the communal laundry room. Adjoining it were the kibbutz offices.

It was late afternoon when they arrived. Nahum took his brother to his own room, which he insisted was Harry's as a privileged visitor. Both he and Henya, his wife, had moved into one of the shacks reserved for visitors. Henya was pregnant, a small young woman, very blown up, and laughed at her brother-in-law's embarrassment.

Dinner, served on tin plates in the dining room, was a festive meal prepared in Harry's honor. It consisted of small helpings of boiled chicken and vegetables, with stewed fruit for dessert, and cups of weak tea served in tin cups out of large tin beakers set on the long tables. It was an unappetizing meal; the helpings were smaller, but in quality and taste not much worse than army fare.

The membership of Kibbutz Ein Dor consisted of young Americans and young Hungarians. Nahum and Henya were the only South Africans. Everyone worked hard, at all kinds of jobs, living in the makeshift quarters that formed their first collective settlement, pooling their wages before getting their land. Henya had washed clothes, Nahum had been a cleaner and performed other menial tasks. Now they were their own masters, on their own kibbutz, working harder than ever, but for the kibbutz, which they owned collectively.

After dinner, when the tables had been cleared, and because even the Europeans knew some English and certainly Yiddish, Harry entertained those kibbutz members who wanted to stay with jokes in both languages, vibrant imitations of American comedians whose movies most of them had enjoyed watching in the movie theaters of Haifa and Tel Aviv, and comical impersonations of Hitler, Mussolini, and Hirohito. They laughed and applauded, filled with astonishment at the amazing richness of his repertoire, making Nahum extremely proud of his talented little brother.

Nahum was to take a two-day break to be with his brother. Since he was on the kitchen duty roster for breakfast, Henya entertained her brother-in-law. She talked about the baby that was coming, fretful that it would have to live in the children's house and not with her, and about the hard life on a collective farm that was just beginning to take root. One month after her baby's birth she would have to return to work in the chicken house, amidst a hundred cackling hens. The noise was deafening, she said, and she emerged covered in chicken feathers from head to toe. She longed to have a little house, or even an apartment, in Tel Aviv. She was not an idealist like Nahum.

Her complaints bewildered her brother-in-law. Most disturbing to him was her attitude to the "Tommies," whom she said she loathed. The Tommies, she explained, were the British soldiers who came searching for hidden caches of arms, turning the kibbutz upside down, refusing to let desperate mothers take their sick babies to the cottage hospital in the nearby small town.

He could not associate the "Tommies" with Englishmen and dismissed this problem from his mind, as he did most things that did not immediately concern him.

She was deeply worried about the future, when, with the war's imminent end, the British Mandate for Palestine was also due to end and the British troops would be withdrawn, leaving Palestine in turmoil. The British supported the Arab side. An Arab invasion was threatened the moment the British left. Impulsively, he vowed to return to Palestine to fight if this happened. Later, he announced this resolution to many of his friends, with the greatest sincerity, and they were convinced that he meant it. He was given to making impulsive promises all his life but not always of keeping them.

Nahum was a great believer in maintaining family ties. He dragged his brother to Haifa to meet a cousin of their mother's—a tall, heavily built, well-muscled, red-faced man, a pioneer who had participated in the construction of Haifa's roads, and bore some resemblance to Harry's vaguely remembered grandfather. The next day their groaning bus climbed up toward Jerusalem and the procession of flowing hills at the crest of this city, whose hills moved as he moved, accompanying him like a living presence everywhere. In the Old City, as it was then called, they visited the "Wailing Wall," and he saw, with disbelief, the notes penned to God by young and old squeezed between the narrow gaps in the wall's great stone blocks. The wall rose on one side of a dirty, narrow old street—a lane more than a street—where Arabs and Jews brushed against one another in a bustle of noise, street vendors, burdened donkeys, frenzy, and prayer. Later, Harry confessed to his second brother that he had felt quite moved, but also too South African, too English, to share Nahum's feelings.

He never did get to see where their mother's sixteenth-century ancestor had been buried. Nahum had no interest in this. He merely pointed to the still visible outlines of the Second Temple's once great doors still dominantly facing the Mount of Olives on the opposite hill and said, carelessly, "Over there, somewhere. Who knows?"

Before returning to Cairo, he told his brother that he was absolutely determined to go to England.

"Have you told the parents?" Nahum asked shakenly.

"Not yet, but I will. They think I'm going to study architecture. I know pa will understand. But talk to ma? I love her, honestly, but trying to reason with her is like sticking your head into an active volcano." Nahum had to agree.

Turning passionately to face his brother, Harry cried, "If I don't succeed in going to England and becoming a star, I'll commit suicide, because my life won't be worth living."

Although the two brothers parted affectionately and corresponded frequently, Harry had an acute sense of rejecting everything Nahum represented.

In Cairo, as soon as he received his discharge, he conned an officer into assigning space for him on a plane to Johannesburg. He had discovered the beauty and ease of flight, and in later years always chose to travel by plane, always urgent to rush from country to country, from location to location.

At home, his mother received him with surprising placidity. In truth, she was rather proud of him. Mostly, her mind was fixed on the horrors being revealed in eastern Europe, and thoughts too terrible to contemplate about the fate of her family. She had heard nothing of them. Neither had Boris about his many brothers and sisters. They could only conjecture that no one remained alive.

Harry tried to distract his mother with the gifts he had gone out of his way to buy for her. In Italy, he had found two handsome cups of Murano glass, wine red in color, their rims ornately adorned with a cluster of grapes embossed in gold, on a silver plated tray. She was quite in awe of this exotic acquisition, and though he assured her that Italian princes drank their morning coffee out of such cups, she never dreamed of using them for so mundane a purpose and placed them carefully on the dining room sideboard to display to marveling neighbors and relatives. The brooch of blue Hebron glass he had chosen for her in the Jerusalem *suk* she did, however, wear, and fingered with some awe the short, royal blue nylon scarf with the slogan "Oui Oui," twice repeated embroidered on it in red, which General de Gaulle was using in his election campaign for the presidency of France. But when nothing further appeared, she whispered fiercely in her son's ear, "And *papeh,* didn't you get anything for *papeh*?" and looked highly gratified when Harry produced a tie pin he had bought for his father as a last minute thought at the Al Kahzar *suk* in Cairo.

She did, grudgingly, ask after Nahum. "I hope the baby won't take after *her* family," she sniffed disparagingly.

There was no pleasing her on that point.

She grunted her discontent. Mainly, she hated having to become a grandmother at her age. She was only fifty. It did not seem fair, somehow. Her feelings were torn between fond pride and offended sensibility. Boris was in regular correspondence with Nahum, who wrote an excellent Yiddish, and she always crossly consented to listen to what her son had to say—his letters always presented everything in the best possible light—and when her husband was out of the house, surreptitiously labored to read the letters herself, and boasted about his pioneering hard labor and self-sacrifice to all her neighbors and relatives, practically sneering at their children, who preferred making money to idealism.

Harry took several days off to regain his bearings before breaking the news to his parents that he was going to England. When he did, his mother seemed devastated.

"You *really* want to become an actor? Is that how you want to waste your life?" she cried. But his father nodded, looking bright and prescient, and said, "You must do what you must do. Naturally. I expected it," and looked his wife sternly in the face to silence any symptoms of hysteria she might decide to display.

Boris was not well. His wife worried about his health. When Isaac left, what would become of him? Harry wondered in despair. He looked at his father's beautifully shaped hands; his own hands were so ugly, he thought. None of his sons had inherited his hands. Or his rich and wavy crop of hair. Laurence Harvey cultivated a cowlick that enchanted his female fans.

He had already quietly formulated his plan of action. In Cairo, waiting to be sent home, he had told no one of his future plans, but he had learned that grants were available to ex-servicemen and had applied to study at the Royal Academy of Dramatic Art (RADA) in London. Though his application was unusual, his credentials were legitimate. In single-minded pursuit of his goal, he spent weeks shuttling by train between Johannesburg and the military authorities in Pretoria, then South Africa's legislative capital, filling out innumerable forms and finally succeeding in obtaining a grant and a six-month loan of £717.2.

He was the first South African to be granted a loan to study at the RADA, as he wrote proudly to Nahum. The *Rand Daily Mail*, Johannesburg's English-language daily, published a news item about it. This was his first press clipping.

In his letters to Nahum he exuded determination, optimism, and confidence in the certainty of his future success. He planned to work and study in England for only three years and then also to act in films in the States. To his second brother he explained how hard he would have to work and how demanding his work would be. Isaac, in turn, told him that he, too, had resolved to leave South Africa. He had spent a night in jail for participating in an African workers' strike and was under police surveillance—a fact of which he was extremely proud— but had clearly come to perceive that whites had no place in the African struggle for power, which had to be fought by Africans. Harry said he was glad that Isaac (who now called himself Robert) was to come to London. Then he would not be isolated and friendless.

In later years, Laurence Harvey told interviewers (and also his wives) that he had arrived in London with only a sweater, a couple of shirts, his army uniform, and his army greatcoat. That was not totally correct. It is true that he wore his army uniform as long as he could; he looked so much more mature in it, as a girl who had been a schoolmate of his remarked to his brother. Seeing him in the street, she had called out to him with a smile, but he had wheeled sharply round to face her with total hostility, then unbending a little when he recognized her, returned her greeting and spoke to her for a minute or two before wheeling away. She never could understand why his reaction to her greeting had been so hostile.

He always claimed that he arrived in England wearing his army uniform and duffel coat, which he had dyed navy blue. It is true that he had outgrown all his civilian outfits, and he may have *wanted* to keep wearing his army uniform, but his mother—and his father, too—would never have permitted him to leave for England without being decently outfitted. Ella dragged him, practically by force, to one of the better men's clothing stores, where, under protest, she insisted on buying him a good wool blazer, flannel pants, woolen socks, shirts, a sweater, and underwear. He loathed the blazer and the pants. They were too conservative, made of excellent English cloth but far inferior in style to anything he had seen in the newly published fashion magazines arriving from France and the United States. He absolutely refused to allow her to buy him an overcoat.

Only a handful of months after being demobilized, he was set to leave South Africa. On the Sunday before his departure, Ella invited all the friends and relatives to tea. On this guest-packed afternoon, Ella was too busy serving the delicious repast she had prepared, too boastful, too excited and nerve-racked to weep.

But the next day brought a different scene.

He was to travel by train to Capetown, and there board the Union Castle Line ship that would take him to England. At the train station, where his brother and a horde of relatives had gathered to see him off, knowing what to expect, he pleaded with his mother not to make a scene, but of course she did, the moment the train rolled silently in, weeping and wailing for all to hear, wringing her hands and screaming, "My little Hirshkeh, my little boy. I'll never see you again. My heart's burning. I'm dying."

Everyone tried, in vain, to calm her.

He tried to remind her of his promise to take care of her and his father as soon as he became a star, to shower her with gifts and support them both.

"Just get onto the bloody train, or she'll keep you here forever," his brother said, trying hard to keep his excitement and anxiety in check.

"Quite right," said his father heartily, his eyes too bright to disguise his real feelings.

Planting a final kiss on his mother's tear-swept cheek, he dragged himself out of her clutching embrace and sprang nimbly onto the train as it began, stealthily, to move.

4

The Scorned Alien Learns His Craft in England

Watching his ship steal into the dock at Southampton, Harvey found the English shoreline disappointingly dismal on that morning in 1946. On board, he had been the life of the party, a witty English-speaking South African with a great sense of fun and a bundle of salacious stories inherited from his army days. Handing his documents to the customs officers, he later told his brother, he had been acutely aware that everyone would now know that he was a state-less person born in Lithuania and only residing in South Africa, traveling on a certificate issued by the South African government entitling him to remain abroad for a period of six months, with permission from the British government to stay in Britain on condition that he remain at RADA for this period and he did not enter into any gainful employment in the country.

For the first time since immigrating to South Africa as a child he felt like a foreigner. It was a deeply humiliating experience. His father had never become a South African citizen. He could not have applied for citizenship himself because he was underage. Though he spoke English, thought in English, and had served in the army, the rigid bureaucracy in South Africa had dubbed him a Lithuanian, and its British counterpart had tamely followed suit. "What do I know about Lithuania, except that it was the charnel house where Aunt Hava and the others lie buried in mass graves?" he asked his brother Robert when they met. But he was young—not yet nineteen—and hopeful as he boarded the train to London, and reaching Waterloo Station, was immediately engulfed in the city's huge gray, cold clamor of grime and motion. Before disembarking, he had changed into his army uniform, perhaps as a symbol of his defiance. Nineteen forty-six was the cold-est winter in memory. In the streets, he had noticed how gray and dreary the pedestrians looked. He had known no one in London, he told his second brother, but he had heard that he could rent a cheap room in Chelsea. In this disheveled and, at the time impoverished, quarter of London, which he described to his brother as quaint and ex-otic despite its crowd of ugly three-story buildings and its dilapidated, musty, and threadbare postwar flavor, he had inspected the handwrit-ten cards pasted on the dusty windows of the dark and narrow little tobacconist and newspaper shops proliferating everywhere, advertis-ing rooms for rent. He climbed many flights of stairs, he said, before coming upon a room that passed muster. It was small and narrow. Against one wall, a gas heater turned a rosy blush of genteel red to provide a morsel of heat when a coin was dropped into its meter. A single gas ring fixed in the wooden floor and resting on the room's meager brown carpet heated a tea kettle and, from the only faucet above a small dull white sink came a thin spurt of cold water for tea and a wash. An iron cot covered with a frugally skimpy gray blanket stood against the wall opposite the window. The rest of the furniture consisted of a narrow, old-fashioned wardrobe with a creaking door and a small, low chest of drawers, drooping from much use. The pas-sage between the three rooms contained the communal toilet, and the only bath was in a narrow bathroom in the basement, where, re-sponding to a coin, a modest flare of gas filled the bath with an inch or two of lukewarm water or, if one wanted a hot bath one could, at a small price, visit the public baths nearby.

In Johannesburg, he had triumphantly informed his family that he would be receiving an army grant and loan of £717.2 ($2,868). Years later, in a *Cosmopolitan* interview, he said that he had received £4 ($16) a week and the sum was even quoted as being only $10 per week by other journalists. In any event, he had next to nothing to live on.

London was only just beginning to recover from the horrors of the devastating German bombing attacks and was still years away from normalcy. A dingy dreariness enveloped it. Decaying build-ings, once haughty monuments of an empire, gaping wounds where houses and shops had stood met the eyes, worn buses creaked down drab streets filled with cheerless passengers, store windows seemed to have lost their luster, and a sense of general drabness seemed to have descended upon the men and women

everywhere under a melancholy sky. There was nothing but gray-
ness; weary housewives in dull kerchiefs and characterless coats,
with the family ration cards in their purses, lining up patiently outside the food stores for their family's weekly food rations, with traffic splashing through wet streets.

Still, there was the thrill of being in London, he told his brother,
of knowing he was walking down streets within sight of famous
landmarks and monuments, near the great theaters where so
many famous actors performed, and where one day he too would
pound the stage to the tumult of enthusiastic applause, knowing
that he had taken the preliminary steps toward the realization of
his burning ambition.

He had to apply for his ration cards so that he could buy the meager weekly allowances of meat and butter and eggs to which he was
entitled. Making a mental inventory of the things he had to do, he
realized, he told his brother, that Johannesburg existed on a different
planet. The war, from its beginning to its end, had been an impene-
trable distance removed from South Africa. Returning to Johannesburg after being demobilized, he had found the city looking more
prosperous and handsome than ever and growing ever more beautiful from the profits it had made as a consequence of that far-off
war. Luxurious skyscrapers had sprung up like gleaming gigantic
hills, dwarfing the razor-edged golden sand of the mine dumps. The
whites were well dressed, if not in the height of fashion, and well
fed. A flood of Africans had entered the city to work in the bur-
geoning industries and they, too, looked different; they were no
longer peasants.

His grant was pitifully small, but he felt ready to starve if he had
to, in order to achieve his goal, he told his brother. He had granted
himself six months in which to achieve it, he said. He had not
wanted even to harbor a fleeting thought of failure in his mind. He
had *known* he would succeed.

Fastidious in his person, he had an obsession with cleanliness that
was every bit as unyielding as his mother's. Before taking any other
steps, he said, he had gone out in search of necessary toiletries like
soap, a washcloth, and a towel. Then he had purchased a broom and

a scrubbing brush and a bucket with which to clean his room and, after an hour of industrious scrubbing and sweeping, had the room looking—almost—spick and span.

To his brother when they met in London, he described what he said was his first day. There was a fish-and-chips shop round the corner. He had to stand in a line of shivering, unwashed men and women smelling of old clothes and grime for at least twenty minutes before receiving his helping of steaming fish and chips wrapped in separate sheets of newspaper. The fish was succulent, greasy, and very hot, and the chips greasy and limp. He ate his swiftly cooling bounty standing over the sink in his room to avoid soiling his uniform and, after a careful wash in icy water, threw his army greatcoat over the blanket on the bed, and flinging himself down on it, fell instantly asleep.

He told his brother the story of his first morning with wry amusement. His alarm clock, a cheap, old-fashioned, round circle with a loudly ticking face, shrilled seven o'clock and he woke up with a start. It was still dark. Was it really morning? Cautiously he had stuck a forefinger out from under his blanket, licked it and tested the air in order to ascertain that morning had indeed arrived. So accustomed had he grown to the strong morning daylight of Johannesburg and Egypt that he had completely forgotten the dark winters of Jonishik. "That is how you know if it's morning," he laughed, but he was semiserious too. "You stick your forefinger out of the blanket to find out which way the wind is blowing!" The sky—what little he glimpsed of it in the gaps between buildings—was dark and gloomy that day. Shivering in the chill air, that the pale glow of his gas heater failed to warm, he boiled a kettle full of water and shaved—he had, finally, grown facial hair, which he had assiduously nursed out of its adolescent down into the makings of a beard—and washed himself as best he could in the sink.

The clouded mirror above his sink allowed him a hazy glimpse of his light brown hair, which he combed back, and his neat cowlick (which was later to become so familiar to his fans) perched saucily above his forehead.

He spent that pitch-black afternoon touring the streets where the best theaters were, staring at the thrilling posters advertising performances by such great stars as John Gielgud and Ralph Richardson, touring the larger movie theaters featuring the great stars of the day: the dashing Stewart Granger; the young sophisticate, Rex Harrison; the newcomer at the time, Michael Redgrave; the popular Robert Donat; the fine character actor, Robert Newton; and, towering above them all, the incomparable Laurence Olivier. These were his heroes, his rivals.

The next morning, putting on his army greatcoat (in some versions he was seen wearing a duffel coat, either begged or borrowed, and his army uniform dyed black), because he could not afford to spend anything but the barest minimum on food, he told his brother, he tried to quiet the growling in his stomach with a stale sweet bun—available at half price, he said—and made his way to Bloomsbury and the building on Gower Street housing the Royal Academy of Dramatic Art (RADA).

Of the 374 applicants auditioned at RADA that semester, only 139 were accepted, and one of them was the raw young man still called Harry Skikne. RADA's entrance office has a record of his payment of the cost of auditioning—one guinea—and of seventeen guineas for the eleven-weeks autumn term. Mysteriously, according to RADA's records, he registered as "a draftsman," and provided what appeared to be the address of a friend, or an office. Since RADA had a full curriculum, from ten in the morning to five-thirty in the evening, it is hardly possible that the new student, Harry Skikne, had the time to do anything else.

RADA's records state that Larry had registered for the autumn term (Term C) which began on October 2 and ended on December 17, 1946. The record states that he participated in the two plays staged during this term. In the first, he played Camillo, one of the four lords of Sicilia—a minor but substantial part, with several weighty speeches—in Shakespeare's *The Winter's Tale*. The second was Oscar Wilde's *A Woman of No Importance*. According to the record he had indicated his intention of taking the University of London Diploma in Dramatic Art. The record also confirms that his grant was paid by the South African government and includes a letter of recommendation from a Mr. Arthur Penley of African Consolidated Theatres, Ltd.

During his term at RADA, he was described, disparagingly, by some of his fellow students as "frivolous," "cheeky," and able to con people into giving him what he wanted. From the very outset he was regarded as the outsider, the gate-crasher, poaching on others' preserves. He must have antagonized many of them with his sharp tongue, and yet at least one young woman student remembered him as a talented actor, and he must have shown talent or he would not have been encouraged to continue the course. One of his fiercest detractors was Sid James. After the war, Sid James, himself an outsider, but with more experience as an actor and not a student at RADA and therefore less challenging to the hopeful English students, had arrived in England from Johannesburg armed with an army grant and an actress wife who was also the recipient of a grant. Young Skikne, blind to James's intense dislike of him, showed up at his mews home to invite him and his wife to tea. On their visit to Skikne's flat, which James's biographer writes, he was sharing with a homosexual classmate, Sid James and his wife found it gaudily decorated in red and gold velvet with gilt trimmings.

Ever oblivious to James's contemptuous dislike (as James's biographer was told) young Skikne (as he referred to him) would sometimes arrive at James's door with his arms draped either about a young woman or, more often, a young man and flaunt his behavior so brazenly that James could scarcely restrain himself from beating him up. The aspiring young actor had guts, no one could fault him for that, and was not afraid to take chances, and this, James's biographer concedes, was often misinterpreted as arrogance.

"Humility," Laurence Harvey declared many years later, "is so bourgeois. One must avoid it at all costs."

Perhaps his "arrogance" was only a shield he had constructed to conceal his insecurity and loneliness.

That he had not merely been frivolous in this period is clear. He had been reading plays and with his retentive memory knew passages from many of them by heart. This facility was, in fact, one of his problems. He absorbed things quickly, without pausing to analyze them. At his audition at RADA, he had appeared self-possessed, brash, and confident while he was inwardly shaking with nervous tension. Waiting for their auditions, he always said, most actors had butterflies in their stomach; his were iron butterflies—the most painful of all. Only his strong will and ambition, he said, had carried him through.

He did not notice his auditors expressions of astonishment at his murderous enunciation. Still, they must have seen some merit in him. He was a good deal better looking than most of the other students, had grown to six feet in height, was lithe and well muscled, had an attention-getting personality, and he knew what he wanted. What he primarily needed, he was told, was training in elocution—hours and weeks, and undoubtedly months and months of training to rid himself of his colonial and clumsy drawl. Actors, he came to learn, had to speak the King's English, or better still (since the king stammered) BBC English, which was as lucid and succinct as a bell, and had to learn to project their voices, although in this respect he had a natural gift that needed only to be groomed. RADA, in those days, was criticized for primarily concentrating upon diction, but it certainly paid off (in its time). The ideal was the dulcet charm of Laurence Olivier's voice, the crystal clarity of Ralph Richardson's, the fluid tones of John Gielgud's, and others like them. Cockneys, Welshmen, the Irish, North countrymen, Scotsmen—those who could not, or would not learn "the King's English"—seemed doomed forever to be relegated to playing character roles in second-rate movies and plays.

RADA's intensive training gave Laurence Harvey's voice the fine clarity it might otherwise have lacked, although he sometimes sounded as if he were treading on glass.

Within days, he had dropped much of his rough South African English drawl for well-rounded, cut-glass clear BBC English. With his keen ear, ability to imitate, and an almost photographic memory—talents he had never before realized he possessed—many South African pronunciations were soon crushed. He learned to speak clearly and developed a love affair with the English language, even when the words he recited sometimes puzzled him and their meaning was beyond his comprehension. He found a kind of excitement and exhilaration in every passage he recited. Then he marveled at himself for having found his English classes so boring at school, and condemned his teachers for failing to inspire him. The language of the plays he read—not only the language of Shakespeare's plays, but all plays—became, for him, poetic, romantic, beautiful. He loved to hear himself recite.

At RADA he became convinced that only the stage was worthy of a true actor, and that acting in movies was an achievement of lesser value. So influenced was he by this early conviction that, in later years, he always felt secretly guilty and rather ashamed of himself when he chose to act in a movie instead of a play. He did so only for the lure of the money, he liked to confess.

He was assiduous in courting his teachers, asking them for advice, listening to them with close attention. And he collected, if not exactly friends, at least cronies among the students. Later, he described his time of hardship and deprivation to his brother. Sometimes he had gone with some fellow students to a local pub for a glass of beer and gossip. He had not been able to afford the greasy steak and kidney pies, or the unappetizing ham or stale cheese sandwiches on dead white bread, or the tasteless, heavily bread-filled pork sausages the pub offered, let alone the awful whale steaks on the menus of the cheaper tearooms and restaurants. Once or twice a week he had treated himself to his scant, weekly eggs ration and boiled an egg for his breakfast. Now and then he had been invited to dine by some well-to-do patron of the academy whom he had deliberately set out to court, or by some wealthy homosexual would-be sponsors who found him very attractive and offered to set him up in luxury had he been willing to pay their price of becoming their kept lover, which he was not. He did not tell his brother about the company he kept, but said—and this was true—that his basic diet had consisted of stale bread or buns and jam and tea—a diet that he later claimed started him on the road to his physical ruin. Pride alone had prevented him from writing home for money, he said, although he knew that his brother would unhesitatingly have sent it. His letters to his parents were full of omissions—for how could he tell them the truth?—and expressions of high-flown optimism, telling of vastly exaggerated triumphs and successes at RADA. He wrote in English, for he had been too young to learn to write in Yiddish and Hebrew in Lithuania. And he wrote as simply as possible, for he knew how laboriously his father toiled to read English and how valiantly he struggled to write to him in this language. Harry Skikne penned all his personal letters in the same round script of a primary school student and this remained Laurence Harvey's unchanged script for the rest of his life.

Only to his brother, when the latter came to London, did he confess to what he called the dire poverty of his early days, and when Robert asked why he had never written to ask for money, he reminded him that he might have been more forthright had not Robert written to warn him that their mother found ways of ferreting out his letters and commandeering a neighbor to read them to her. He was generally cautious about what he wrote even to Nahum, whom his mother could not reach, and only once, at his lowest ebb, after enduring grueling criticism in one of his classes, his stomach growling with hunger following a supper of weak tea and a bun, loathing the shabby little room he lived in, dashed off a letter to his oldest brother in which he confessed how miserable he was feeling and how desperate, vowing to commit suicide if he did not succeed in becoming a star within three months—the time he had allotted to himself to succeed. Despite his claims, his grant was not to last for more than six months. Three of these months were looming to a close. And he had been so confident that he would work in England for three years and then set out to conquer Hollywood.

Unexpectedly, his most despairing moment became one of thrilling afflatus. Talent scouts and agents were at times permitted to attend RADA's productions in their quest to seek out new talent to harness to their stable of clients. During his class production of Oscar Wilde's *A Woman of No Importance,* he was noticed by Gordon Harbord, then one of Britain's top theatrical agents, who assumed at first that this tall, handsome young man with the good physique and the fresh face was an American. Harbord's office was in St. Martin's Lane, close to Trafalgar Square. His wife, Eleanor, worked with him and they had a smart flat above their office. Young Harry was only too eager to put himself in their professional care, not only for the sake of his career, but also because he could get a good feed whenever they invited him to dinner without being owned by anyone.

The agent's first step was to cable Boris, formally requesting permission to manage his young son's career. Trembling with nerves and trepidation, Boris spent a hectic and exciting day consulting a lawyer recommended by his Skikne relatives, and cabled his reply granting Harbord power of attorney on behalf of his son, Harry M. Skikne.

It was about this time that the name Harry, which he hated, was sloughed off, unofficially, in favor of Larry, a name with which he felt far more comfortable and which, in fact, far better suited his personality. At school, his middle name Mosheh had become Morris. Now that was dropped and he used the initial M as simply a letter of the alphabet. Americans, he once explained, liked having a middle initial.

With his acquisition of an agent, he began to crave the good life, which, in due course, meant spending lavishly. At this stage in his life, it was only a pipe dream. But he did make one change, and that was to move. Refusing to live in digs in Epping Forest or Kendal Green, where most of the students lived, he had been moving from room to room in and around Chelsea—he had moved at least sixteen times, he boasted with his usual flair for exaggeration—when he learned from a gossiping fellow student at RADA that rooms were available in Shepherd's Market, which was still, despite some war damage and neglect, a placid little nook on the rim of Mayfair. Abandoning what he came to see as his latest hideous room in Chelsea, he moved into a room in one of the three-story buildings there.

Shepherd's Market was, in those days, a relatively inexpensive (although very expensive, initially, for him) little pocket of London. It was certainly Bohemian and some have sensationalized it as a red-light district. He had moved, he said in a 1962 interview in *Queen*, into this red-light quarter in Mayfair into a room in one of its three-story houses with a fishmonger's shop on the ground floor, his room on the second, and a whore "on top of me." The smells emanating from the fishmonger's and the whore's room literally drove him away. He moved into the house next door, into a room above a bookshop.

His new room was actually a tiny flat according to the two pretty young women who rented it. He had asked the young women if he could have a bed and a base with them and they had agreed to let him, provided he cleaned the bathtub, washed the dishes, and made the large double bed, the only one there was, every morning. Half starved, with no room he could afford any longer, he accepted their conditions. All three of them slept in the bed, the women with their heads resting on the pillows, while Larry slept in the opposite direction. Larry, one of them years later reminisced, was totally consumed by his ambition to become a professional actor. He was determined to let nothing stand

in his way. Either stardom or wealth, however it was gained, she told
Queen in the same interview, was his goal.

In his virulent attack on Laurence Harvey in *The Great Movie Stars,*
David Shipman allows the actor not one iota of talent—Harvey
owed his success, he writes, solely to his ability to deceive the producers and the public with his forceful self-salesmanship—and
states flatly that Laurence Harvey was a male prostitute in this red-
light sector of Mayfair, but offers no proof for this contention. In fact
it was Harvey himself who blithely boasted to his interviewers that
Shepherd's Market was a red-light district.

At RADA he had another stroke of luck. Sophie Rosenstein, a
Warner Bros. talent scout attended the RADA students' end-of-term
performance of *A Woman of No Importance,* and liking the looks of the
young student, offered him an audition, and if that was successful,
a seven-year contract starting at $100 a week.

Warner Bros. had entered into a long-range coproduction deal
with Associated British Cinemas, Ltd. in which Warner Bros. owned
considerable stock. In awe of the exalted company of stars he might
be joining, the still rawly inexperienced young Larry was reduced to
quivering nerves—with iron butterflies in his stomach, as he described his bouts of nervous tension. Years later, he told an interviewer that on the day of his test, dazed with excitement, and half
starved, in his anxiety to impress he decided that a decent luncheon
would bolster his morale and give him the stamina to go through
with the test. After swallowing a tasteless luncheon of the then-
popular whale steak larded with stomach-turning sauce, he told his
brother, he had to rush to the nearest men's room to throw up, and
made his film test with a deathly white face and herculean efforts to
appear composed. Greatly aided by an excellent and sympathetic
cameraman and a technician who knew how to light his face to its
best advantage, he said, his test was successful. Besides, he had the
kind of face that the camera liked. The promise of a six-month contract

at $100 a week (once he went to Hollywood) turned him dizzy with excitement and disbelief. He hardly knew how he reached his flat, where he depressed his tongue with his finger and he threw up the remainder of his meal. That evening, he wrote to his family in a delirium of happy exultation and, the next day, headed straight for Savile Row, the small, insignificant-looking street where England's finest tailors have their genteel establishments.

He knew precisely what he wanted: a beautifully cut, handsome gray suit with the fashionably wide lapels of the day and—his own invention—revolutionary narrower trousers than was de rigueur at the time—and was eager to discuss every minute detail of the tailoring. But there were several obstacles to overcome. One was the fact that, much to his disappointment, the establishments he visited were not impressed by his credentials and would not be persuaded to make up a suit on credit. The other was that material was strictly rationed, and even the more sympathetic of the tailors informed this earnest fledgling young actor that he did not have enough clothing coupons for a suit.

Finally, he found the means to resolve both these difficulties. How he came up with the requisite clothing coupons remains a matter of speculation, but one tailoring establishment, he said, was persuaded at least to agree to make up his suit within three months, provided he pay £10 per month toward the cost, which would be £27.10.

In later years, Laurence Harvey told the story of the suit with insouciant pride. It may be, as he related, that the tailoring establishment sensed the public relations potential that a Savile Row suit worn by a handsome actor would bring their establishment. And, as to not having any money: "It's natural to owe one's tailor," Laurence Harvey often drawled, like some full-fledged English aristocrat.

He had no choice but to agree to their terms, and apparently blithely relied on the glamour of the promised Warner Bros. contract to meet the monthly payments—or found a willing "friend" to pay it. As, years later he explained in a *Cosmopolitan* interview, "I learned early in life that it was much better to have one good thing than a lot of cheap things. And that is the way I have tried to live." He had been abysmally poor when he first came to England, he told another interviewer, but had done everything to conceal it. "I was determined not to let my poverty show like some frayed cuff," he declared. "I never belonged to that school that believed scruffiness was next to stardom." Someone had told him that a prominent personality had declared that in England a man was measured by the cut of his clothes and his table manners. However brilliant he may be, if he was poorly dressed and lacked good table manners, he was judged to be a man of no importance. The young actor made certain that his clothes and his table manners were perfect, although, at the height of his fame, he developed some disconcerting table manners. His clothes, on the other hand, remained impeccable all his life. Whether he wore Savile Row suits or jeans, when it became fashionable to wear them, everything had to be cut just right, and he unfailingly supervised the design of every suit he ordered, instructing his tailor as to precisely how he wanted each one cut. "I guess you might say I'm madly Savile Row," he told his interviewers, not in the least modestly.

He developed a new ambition. Sauntering along Oxford Street one evening, his eyes unexpectedly encountered the fabulous Rolls-Royce that had been custom built for Nubar Gulbekian, a Middle Eastern millionaire, gliding past. The sheer ostentation of this vehicle, its golden splendor, its two shades of bronze, its electrically operated windows—the first of its kind in Britain—dazzled him. He began dreaming of owning his own Rolls-Royce, only his would be black, with a narrow gold stripe down the middle. Meanwhile, he sank deeply into debt by purchasing a small used car and using his ration coupons to buy an expensive shirt.

Iron determination and daring chance-taking played a great part in this early stage of his career. With a loan from his agent, he was able to move into his own tiny flat in a corner building near the one he shared with the two young women. The flat was only superior in comparison with the rooms he had lived in. It was, by his later standards, quite spartan, yet he loved it, for it made him his own master. It consisted of a narrow bed/sitting room, furnished with a green carpet, an army cot, and a closet. A toilet, which he painted pink, was neatly tucked into a little nook in a wall. There was a narrow sliver of a kitchen with a high, modest little window. Attached to the wall beside it was a small box of a cupboard in which to store food, hopefully out of reach of ever-hungry, ever-foraging mice. A two-plated gas stove replete with a small hood of an oven stood under the window and, on the opposite wall, there was a flaring gas heater, which, prompted by a coin, spluttered several inches of lukewarm water into a narrow bathtub. The rent was, for him, exorbitant, but he managed it somehow, perhaps engaging in modeling or other occupations. This private little nook, within walking distance of Oxford Street and Hyde Park, was worth every penny it cost him. Here he could cook his own meals and store his bread and weekly egg and margarine rations. Often enough, he returned to his diet of bread and jam and tea, but he became a highly proficient cook— preparing not his mother's fulsomely rich dishes, but recipes with mushrooms and carrots that he gleaned from magazines found here and there, or invented himself, and sometimes, in a moment of affluence, buying fish, which was not rationed.

His rent, when paid, left him just four shillings a week for food. He yearned for fruit, especially apples. They were not rationed, but he could not afford to buy any. Walking home from RADA late one gray afternoon, he exchanged jokes with a barrow boy peddling his favorite shiny green Granny Smith apples heaped in neat pyramids on his wooden barrow on a street corner. On the strength of their camaraderie, this young cockney fruit vender began generously supplying him with a free apple whenever he passed by. Through him, the young actor came to know spivs, teddy boys, and other barrow boys, and discovered these lively sections of the working-class community. They were the people he used as models to create his character as a spiv in his role in the 1952 British movie, *I Believe in You.*

He had another lucky break. Deciding that he needed more acting experience, his agent introduced him to André Van Gyseghem, one of the dignitaries who had attended the performance of RADA's production of *A Woman of No Importance.*

Van Gyseghem was a highly regarded actor, director, and producer, who had recently founded the Manchester Intimate Theatre Company. Its first performance was scheduled to take place in February 1947. The Intimate Theatre was connected with Joan Littlewood, who ran a Theatre Workshop Company that gave acting courses to promising young actors and actresses who served as "apprentices" and trained them by giving them the experience of

acting in front of an audience. Despite its many flaws, the performance of the young South African actor had impressed Van Gyseghem. In his eagerness to acquire acting skills, young Harry
Skikne had practically swallowed wholesale everything he had
been taught at RADA. His accent was carefully good, yet a rawly
South African usage would slip out now and then. For example, in
casual conversation, he would pronounce "bloody" as "bladdy,"
but acutely aware of his mistakes, would speedily correct them. He
had other flaws. Clearly, he had not really understood the character
he was playing. His feet were too large, and he had not yet fully
learned to project his voice properly. But he was graceful and athletic, and he was handsome. There was something dashing about
him. He had natural stage presence.

Letters were exchanged between Van Gyseghem and Kenneth
Barnes, RADA's principal, reinforcing Larry's obligation to return
to RADA after Manchester. He never returned and in a 1962 *Queen*
interview gave this ungenerous reason for quitting: "I reigned at
RADA for three glorious months, where my greatest feat was to be
listed among Sir Kenneth Barnes' 'people I never thought would
be stars.' It was so claustrophobic: Sixty people in a class. There I
was, stuck between debutantes and dilettantes, learning to intone
'He jests at scars that never felt a wound' in exactly the same low
timbre as 59 others." In an interview with the American columnist
Hedda Hopper in 1960, he called the students "older men." There
had been seventy of them in his class, he said. Many of them had
been ex-servicemen much older than himself. It had been impossible for him to learn much. Yet one fellow student had been the
young Robert Shaw, an excellent actor who became a star in England and the United States in his own short life, and there were
several others who became fine actors.

On another occasion, he gave an interviewer his own version of
how he became a member of Van Gyseghem's company. Offered
the chance to go to Hollywood for Warner Bros. or to join the company performing at the Intimate Theatre in Manchester, he said, he
had deliberately chosen the latter. He wanted to learn more about
the "fundamentals of acting." Money—real money—would come
later. He had an instinct about that. One suspects, also, that like
many colonials, he thought of the United States as rather wild and
foreign territory. Or, as an unknown and on his own, he might
have been afraid that he would be lost in the crowd among the

powerful Hollywood stars and felt still too uncertain and inexperienced to take the plunge into the turbulent waters of the studios.

With the exception of Larry Skikne (as he now officially called himself) and other apprentices, Van Gyseghem and his actress wife, Jean Forbes-Robertson, had put together a company of experienced players. The company rehearsed in London for three weeks prior to traveling to Manchester. During rehearsals, the actors were paid £4 per week. When actual performances began, their salaries increased to £8 per week.

The three weeks of rehearsal took place in a large room in a Soho pub in London. They passed swiftly, as in a dream. A quick learner, with a retentive memory, the untried young actor soaked up everything he was told. After rehearsals, he would go home and rehearse his lines every night. Exhausted and exhilarated, he would get up early to rehearse his lines once again, then sweep his floors, dust and polish what little furniture his flat possessed so that everything looked as neat as a pin, then bathe and shave to the uncouth snort of the gas heater while the kettle steamed on the gas stove, prepare some tea and bread and jam, wash and dry every plate, and rush to catch the crowded and rumbling underground train to the pub for rehearsals.

He wrote letters home ablaze with thrilling expectations and received replies that were paeans of confidence in his certain future success. Ushering in the four months of the season, he wrote, he was to play the tragic young hero, Constantine Gavrilovitch Treplev, in Chekhov's *The Seagull.* This "difficult and wonderful part," he wrote enthusiastically, kept him working night and day. He identified with Treplev, the doomed young poet who strives to explore new forms of artistic expression, to climb out of the muddy bog of humdrum existence, out of the doom of the passivity and the empty yearnings of his seniors. Somehow, he felt that he *was* Treplev, and that his whole previous existence had been as wasteful and meaningless as was this character's. He practically lived in the theater and loved every minute of it. "I wish I could sleep here, I love my role so much. I'm so busy, I can only find a few minutes to write to you between rehearsals," he wrote home. ("Chekhov! its no small matter," his father said proudly. "My poor boy!" his mother cooed.) He loved the paraphernalia that activated the scenery, the costumes, the makeup, the very smell of everything backstage.

The Seagull was followed by bit parts in *Amphitryon 38* (in which he played the Warrior), *The Kirby Fortune* (he played Lieutenant Commander Tim Kirby), *The Beau's Strategem* (he played Thomas Aimwell), and *The Circle* (he was Edward Luton).

He was enthusiastic about his work in Manchester. "These are all works of the highest intellectual quality," he wrote to his brothers, as if indicating that he was now a member of what he earnestly regarded as their exalted intellectual company. He did not mention that his parts were small, although he did get some good reviews, and those he made much of. His plans for the future, he wrote in grandiose terms, were to attain the highest form of achievement in the theater and films, as an actor and producer and possibly a writer. He was setting himself the task of absorbing as much knowledge about the theater as possible.

He had told his family that he had the leading role in *The Seagull*, but this play has a number of important roles, played by older, more seasoned actors, and his name appeared not at the top of the program but in order of appearance. He was listed as "Larry M. Skikne (By kind permission of Warner Bros.)." In this way, he could prove to the authorities that he was still a student, while his connection with the American Warner Bros. enabled him to get paid.

His largest and most important role was in *The Seagull*, and this role filled his head with questions as to how Chekhov had envisioned this character and what Stanislavsky had demanded of the actor who played him. It was only when he appeared alone on stage that he received his first staggering sight of a hushed and expectant audience and was seized with nausea and trembling. The theater was full. Every seat was occupied, filled with men and women waiting to be entertained. They seemed to him like an inhuman mob, waiting, like a pack of wolves, to tear him to shreds, to howl abuse, to mock and jeer at him the moment he began to speak. He had not felt this sense of terror in the army, where his function had been merely to entertain and the soldiers forming the audiences had been only too indiscriminately eager to laugh and applaud, or during rehearsals in the reassuring company of the experienced actors in Manchester. Public speakers like his brothers must have a far easier time of it than actors, he later told his brother. They needed only to be themselves and devise their own scripts, while an actor had to woo and charm people through the characters he played and the lines he was given by the playwright. That was so much more difficult. And acting in a movie must be even harder, he thought. On stage, one could see what one was up against. Before the cold, impersonal lens of a camera, one had to woo vast, invisible, unknown audiences.

In Manchester, on stage, alone, in *The Seagull,* he sensed the eagerness of the audience to fall under his spell, and it lifted him out of himself and he only returned to reality when he heard the crash of their applause.

It was freezing cold that winter, almost as cold as it had been the winter before, damp and miserable, with frozen water pipes. Hot water bottles were a rare luxury brought to the lucky and the rich by American friends, and two years after the war's end, rationing was still in full force and unrationed goods were priced beyond his reach. The demands of his family irritated him. He begged his brothers to try to reason with their mother, who kept nagging him to write more often and in minute detail about his life. Since he was in Manchester, Nahum asked him to take out a subscription in his name to *The Manchester Guardian* and some other papers, which in Palestine were priced too high for his pocket. Then Nahum's letters began taking on an increasingly ominous tone, telling of the growing tensions in Palestine and accusing the British of supporting the Arabs against the Jews. There were terrorist attacks by both sides. Britain's League of Nations' Mandate for Palestine was about to end, the British troops were due to pull out of Palestine on May 16, 1948. Nobody knew what would happen when the British left, but people generally predicted a bloodbath against the Palestinian Jewish community by the Palestinian Arab community and their allies. The newly created United Nations was to discuss the problem of Palestine and attempt to find some solution before that day came.

Larry did not like reading about these things. They made him feel acutely uncomfortable. Despite all the admiration and enthusiasm he had displayed during his visit to Palestine, he thought and dreamed in English and longed, above all, to be regarded as an Englishman, yet knew that he was regarded as a foreigner. These contradictions tore at him. He loved his brother and he had vowed to come and fight at his side in the advent of a war. But his ambition was to shine on the English stage, to be an Englishman.

As tensions in Palestine increased and the British Mandate for Palestine neared its end, he could not help smelling the growing stench of anti-Semitism in the air, the false accusations that Jews were black marketers who profited while the true English people had to live on meager rations. But he chose to ignore these mean comments; they had nothing to do with him. In Manchester he also discovered that the rich lived well under every circumstance. Invited to dinner at their houses, he heard nothing but complaints from the well-fed, highly respectable Manchester manufacturers and their guests, consuming large helpings of black-market prime English beef, about the outrageous inroads the Labor government was making into their legitimate profits. The working class was called cheeky and lazy. The trade unions were accused of ruining the economy.

He would try to get him a subscription to *The Manchester Guardian* as soon as he could find the time, he wrote to Nahum. To his brother's plea that he get in touch with his relatives in Sheffield, stressing as always, the importance of family ties, he wrote that he had received a note from their English relatives who had driven in from Sheffield to watch him perform and, out of deference to their dear father, had invited them backstage during intermission and had been gracious to them, but really did not have the time to spare for visiting relatives. And on the other topic, he responded coldly, that as far as he was concerned, he had personally had no experience with anti-Semitism. He had made up his mind to believe that everyone accepted him as English, if of colonial origin. At this stage, he was signing himself "Larry."

If Van Gyseghem may have had a qualm or two about engaging this inexperienced young actor, these were speedily allayed. Larry's fresh and attractive looks, his ability to learn his parts quickly, practically devouring his lines, and to take direction without argument or question made life a great deal easier. Theoretically, at least, members of repertory companies are supposed to consider the play first and their egos last. In practice there can be very few actors who bear this precept in mind. As a young and untried newcomer, Larry

Skikne became what others found particularly obstreperous, attempting to milk everyone for advice and especially praise, boring them into impatience with his incessant questions. Savagely competitive, convinced of their superiority to this foreign novice, they were unwilling to give away any of their secrets or techniques, and ended by disliking him. Worse still, he talked solely about his own performance, which antagonized everyone.

This was also true of his relationship with the directors. When praised, he was happy, but wanted to know why in minutest detail. If criticized, he immediately interpreted it as unjust and deliberately destructive, and sank into rebellious misery. It was as if, in some secret recess in his mind, he was terrified that one day, inadvertently, lurking beneath his self-confident exterior, he might expose the ignorance, confusion, fear, and insecurity lurking there.

The audiences loved him, even if the actors did not. He became the matinee idol of young women and middle-aged wives of successful local businessmen. Copies of all his notices and reviews, generally good ones, published in the local papers, were carefully clipped and mailed to Nahum and his parents. From Nahum he received fulsome and unstinting praise, and his reply was warm with gratitude. Nahum's letters, he wrote, were to him "really a source of inspiration." He was proud, he wrote to both brothers, "to be part of a family who have each taken upon themselves work of the highest possible ideals, and although our paths are somewhat different, there is a bond which links us together which can never be broken." "I am so proud of belonging to such a talented family," he wrote in another letter. "We three are indissoluably [sic] bound forever, not alone as brothers but also in our quest to reach the holy grail of the highest ideals. I am determined to test my powers in many directions. In addition to acting and script writing, I am going to start my own company one day, and produce, direct and star in my own plays."

Self-contained, eager, and hardworking, he moved from one role to the next. Chekhov's "passionately ambitious artist" (as he interpreted Treplov's character in *The Seagull*) was, as he put it, "akin" to himself. His role as Aimless in the Restoration comedy *The Beaux Strategem* transformed him into a quite different character, whom he played with equal enjoyment. There came a sour note, nevertheless. Playing the young Edward Luton in Somerset Maugham's *The Circle*, he was startled to hear from Eric Uttley, a small-time playwright who was directing this play, that although he was playing a very English character, he did not look terribly English. Everyone knew he was a "bloody foreigner," therefore he would have to buy a blond wig.

When they met, he told his brother Robert about this incident.

"Apparently, all Englishmen are blonds!" he scoffed.

The young actor weathered the insult in his own way. Instead of buying a blond wig, he appeared on stage the next day with his hair dyed orange.

This was called an example of his "arrogance."

Like grains of sand rubbing against a sensitive skin, these and similar incidents may indicate why he began calling himself a "Lithuanian," a "Slav," and spoke of his "Slavonic" moodiness. It constituted a form of defiance. He was deliberately emphasizing his "foreignness."

None of this appeared in his letters to his parents. He wrote how remarkable it was that someone of his age had been given leading roles, and how hard he had to work. He claimed that he intended to outclass Laurence Olivier and John Gielgud and that he was going to act in Shakespearean roles at Stratford-upon-Avon one of these days, "which was the greatest honor in the world," no matter what hardships he would have to suffer to achieve this goal, such as starvation and dire poverty and living in a garret for years while perfecting his art.

The promise of a Warner Bros. contract had been useful; it had served to list the American studio as his official employer, thus skirting the law that stated that aliens could not be gainfully employed in England. But after six months, this contract was to wither on the vine, for he did not go to Hollywood. Before that time, he had another lucky break. On his tour of the provincial repertory theaters, Robert Lennard, the casting director for Associated British Pictures, saw Larry Skikne's performance and liked his looks and his stage presence. He was offered a seven-year contract with the Rank Organisation at a starting salary of £20 per week. The snag, however, was that there would be months of negotiations before the contract would be signed.

When the season in Manchester ended, an interesting item appeared in the Manchester *Evening News* of June 12, 1947. "Larry M. Skikne,"

was to go on to the South Seas to star in a beautiful new picture called
The Blue Lagoon.

He may have planted this item himself. He appeared to have believed very strongly that he was to be offered the starring role in this
picture. Perhaps he had heard a rumor about his being considered
for the part. But he did not get it.

He was practically broke when he returned to London and would
have starved and been thrown out into the street by his landlady if
his agent had not saved him by granting him a loan. It began to look
as if his promised contract would never come through. Nevertheless, he felt convinced that work would flow in a torrent toward him
because of his great success in Manchester. But this did not happen.
There was nothing. Once again, as when he was at RADA, he had
less than the barest minimum to hold body and soul together; to
make some extra money by modeling, or by photographic assignments found for him by his homosexual friends, or by finding tiny
walk-on roles in plays here and there. He took to haunting the casting offices with his clippings from Manchester and making himself
visible to directors and producers, and still there was nothing. He
was not a member of the right set; they disliked him for what they
termed his cheeky arrogance, or perhaps he was excluded in revenge for his rejection of some powerful sponsor.

This was a period of acute misery and despair.

With no work in sight, feeling the heavy breath of failure on his
back, he dreamed of sticking his head into the narrow little oven of
the gas stove, which he kept impeccably spotless in his spotless
kitchen/bathroom, and may even have made a few trial forays into
doing so without turning on the gas. If he could not act, he felt that
life would not be worth living.

He told the story of this "suicide attempt" many times in several
versions to various interviewers and friends. His third wife
recorded in her book the version he told her, with all its elaborate
trimmings. As he was placing a cushion inside his oven to rest his
head on, he saw that the oven was thick with grease. Refusing to
be found dead in such filth, he spent the whole afternoon cleaning
the oven until it was spotless. By that time, the whole idea of suicide disgusted him.

There is no doubt that he was deeply depressed and even, perhaps, contemplating suicide, yet reality does not quite mesh with
fantasy in this case. The oven in his Shepherd's Market flat was far

too tiny for his head. All the same, it made a very effective story, and reveals his rather macabre sense of humor.

Hollywood had its casting couch on which many a budding female movie career was made or squashed. London's casting couch was where male talents—"stud boys"—were tested for roles in the theater. Added to this was Britain's show-business snobbery. It was deemed impossible for "foreigners" to be able to play authentic Englishmen in the drawing-room comedies that were favored on the London stage. No foreigner (or, for that matter, no one who did not have a BBC accent) could understand a proper Englishman's manners or behavior. "I was looked on as a cocky intruder," Laurence Harvey often reminisced, with the bitterness, pain, and anger still evident in his voice. Added to which, he was legally an alien in Britain. All this may well serve to explain his facade of arrogance, his extravagant exhibitionism, his filthy language, his whole behavior that was meant deliberately to shock.

London's biggest impresario was the much-admired extremely powerful, unabashedly homosexual Binkie Beaumont, who with H. M. Tennent, controlled some dozen theaters, and encouraged talented actors while paying his stars mere pittances. Besides Binkie Beaumont, there was also a network of lesser homosexual impresarios and producers who were always on the look out for talent. According to Melvyn Bragg in his biography of Richard Burton, an ambitious newcomer did not have to be homosexual, although it eased his way if he was one. Young Larry Skikne understood that this lifestyle could open doors to stardom and found it not unattractive. It was not unusual for actors to prefer same-sex partners, but in those days these were deep secrets that no one divulged. There was the increasingly popular and handsome Dirk Bogarde, who made women swoon; the classical actor John Gielgud, whom they worshipped; Michael Redgrave, a family man with a wife and children, but secretly bisexual, to cite but three. Even a womanizer like Richard Burton revealed to Melvyn Bragg that he had tried "it" once, but had not liked it. Laurence Harvey, later to become the dream lover of women fans everywhere, was surely acutely aware of the risks involved for him if he were publicly exposed even as bisexual. The law was very strict and the penalties, for those who were caught even soliciting men to engage in homosexual acts in public, severe. If caught, as a "foreigner," permitted to stay in Britain on a study scholarship, it would have meant at the least deportation to South Africa. As still a minor, he would, at best, have been returned to the care of his father, never to return to England.

Putting stud boys and casting couches aside, even in the best of circumstances, as an alien, how could he get any gainful employment in England? He found the newspaper reports about the very simple step the Greek-born Prince Phillip had to take in order to become a British citizen particularly ironic. Before becoming engaged to Princess Elizabeth, the British-educated prince applied for British citizenship and received it upon payment of the requisite fee of £10.3.6.

After deadly months of negotiations, young Larry Skikne finally succeeded in signing a seven-year contract with the Rank Organisation at a salary of £20 per week. He was elated, although he knew that to begin with he would be lent out to small movie companies producing B pictures. If he was lucky, he would star in some of them and would have to repay his agent for the money that had been lent to him as well as his agent's fee.

To the young, untried actor, a steady income seemed like a fortune. "I've sold out!" he wrote exultantly to Robert, half ashamed of his decision. What he meant was that he had "sold" himself for "filthy lucre" to the inferior movie industry—instead of struggling, living, half starved in some attic to attain the higher goal of becoming a classical stage actor.

The men behind his first film were demobilized friends from the same regiment eager to make their fortunes in the postwar world. One of them, Kenneth Villiers, who had some experience in making films, had talked two friends from his regiment into backing him in his plans to produce B movies and also beguiled Douglas Sutherland, a Fleet Street journalist and another friend from his regiment, into becoming the chief publicist of the new enterprise.

In his book, *Portrait of a Decade: London Life, 1945–55,* Sutherland writes that their first film was to be *House of Darkness,* "a powerful drama" (he was told) with a script so strong that the film would instantly break open the closed doors of the distributors, that it could be made on an extremely low budget and without big and expensive stars.

In reality, *House of Darkness* turned out to be an insignificant, low-budget Victorian melodrama directed by Oswald Mitchell, who had already made several third-rate movies, but it gave Larry a starring role, albeit as the villain, a megalomaniac and murderous pianist. If he overacted, he nonetheless stood out strongly against the rest of the film's competent if uninspired cast. They did their jobs. The pretty female star had only signed on to make enough money to afford to have a baby. The film's opening credit misspelled his name. It reads: "Introducing *Lawrence* Harvey."

Almost as soon as shooting began, it was discovered that he was an alien and not entitled to work for pay in England. Instead of firing him, the irate studio gave him two weeks' leave and his agent advanced the fare for his flight to Johannesburg to help finalize his father's naturalization as a South African citizen. Since he was underage, he would then automatically become a South African citizen himself and, because South Africa was still, in those days, a member of the British Commonwealth, he could be eligible to work for pay in Britain.

5

Becoming Laurence Harvey: The First Films

Apart from the acquisition of his passport as a South African citizen, his only purpose in making the trip to Johannesburg, he did not look forward to the visit. He had grown too different and he would have to convince his parents—and especially his mother—to accept him on his own terms. Angrily suspecting that she had probably summoned every relative to greet him at the airport, he readied himself for the worst, visualizing how she would dominate the scene with her dramatic cries and copious tears, turning the whole airport into a stage.

He had nothing but a few publicity stills of *House of Darkness* to bring with him to Johannesburg, but these represented a major achievement for a beginner and a foreigner to boot. Generously, he planned to buy his mother a diamond ring in Johannesburg with money he had borrowed (he told Robert) from a rich friend. It was important to him to give his mother this gift. In one of her gloomy moods, she had often bitterly complained that she possessed no jewelry except her gold wedding band—and that, he had come to learn, was no more than nine karats in gold, as much as the average Jew in Lithuania could afford. In South Africa most of her neighbors (she claimed) had diamond rings.

In the plane, watching the winter gray skies of England transform themselves into balmy blue above the mountains of clouds and, hours later, watching the descent into the bright sunlight of a Johannesburg summer day, he thought how far he had traveled from his former self. He could not sleep for thinking of it, and only dozed off now and then out of sheer exhaustion, only to wake up imagining the worst. Wanly, he hoped that his brother would be there to rescue him from their mother's smothering embraces.

And yet he loved her, and when his plane landed and he saw her frantic face and his father looking flushed and struggling to conceal his excitement, he knew how much he loved them both.

They looked older, he thought, and perceptibly crumbling into dry husks. His father, still a handsome man, had kept his head of thick and wavy hair, but it was turning from its original glossy black to white. In addition, his father's face looked worn and his dark eyes bore the stigma of a recent illness. He had been shocked, he later wrote to Nahum, to see how much their father had dete-riorated. His mother looked a great deal older, too. Wanting to look her best, she had paid a visit to the hairdresser and freshly dyed her hair blond, but the fingers of her large hands quivered with nerves. She was her usual neurotic self, he wrote, half in res-ignation, half in despair, to Nahum. He had almost forgotten how tense she always was. And oddly, for he had always considered her a woman of good taste—or at least, she had convinced her family that she had the very best of taste—she was wearing an ugly brown straw hat with a brown plastic rose pinned on its rim above her forehead and a brown moiré ribbon tied in a bow at the back. Her dress, which was of shining cotton, had a pattern of large green leaves and red flowers on a white background and was obviously quite new, specially purchased to impress him. It was fortunate that she could not read his mind, for he found it horribly dowdy, as were the locally manufactured brown shoes on her broad feet.

"How wrinkled she's become," he whispered to his brother.

At home, in her nervous state, she had sprayed the Attar of Roses perfume, which she always used a little too freely on her neck and chest. Her white skin, as pallid as death, had grown lined and was caked with the powder she used, which she proudly told everyone was Coty, imported from England, and bright red Max Factor lip-stick spread like a slash on her thin lips. She was aging, and not well, her skin wrinkling and pallid, and yet she exuded a certain wild dy-namism, a kind of fierce energy that drew him, as in the old days, into her maternal net. His brother looked different too, somehow, more mature, and though his eyes sparkled and his narrow face, so unlike, and yet in its expressions so like his own, seemed to reflect an only temporarily subdued frustration.

"My God, your accent is awful," he said accusingly to his brother. Robert had the standard South African English accent. Like the one he had worked so hard to squash in himself.

Robert had married several months earlier. His wife had left for London to continue her studies. Her winter term started on December 15. Robert had remained behind in order to apply again for citizenship so that they could settle in England. Larry had generously offered his sister-in-law the use of his flat in Shepherd's Market while he was in Johannesburg.

Much to his relief, Robert and his parents were the only three people to greet him at the airport. Both his brother and their father had seen to that. And amazingly, his mother seemed shyly subdued, as if overawed and almost respectful in the face of what she appeared to consider his great achievements. At first, she hardly dared to touch him, but, growing more familiar, stroked his arm and said, in her splintered English mixed with Yiddish, "My little boy, mine prince, I thought I would never see you again in this life, how beautiful you look! What a beautiful suit!" and in Yiddish, "*Oi ich starb avek!* ("Oh, I'm dying!") meaning that she was bursting with pride and amazement to see how handsome he looked, and how well dressed.

She clung to his arm and would not let him move, though his father, a valiant failure, commanded her sternly to do so, muttering in a mixture of Yiddish and South African invective, "Ach, this woman! Ach, this woman!" and shaking his head and puncturing the air with snorts of irritation.

"My son is a famous actor in England!" she boasted.

As her family expected, her lofty remark did not fail to draw the interested glances of the passengers waiting for taxis.

"You see," Robert murmured to Larry, "when it comes to hogging the limelight, she's the expert."

Larry had always known that.

When her first rapture had exhausted itself, Ella pushed him into a taxi and climbed in after him.

"What a waste of money!" she took a moment to snap between transports of exaltation as she seated herself on Larry's right. "Boris, why didn't you ask your cousin Natie to drive us here and back in his car?"

"He said he didn't want nobody but us at the airport," his father exonerated himself, still striving valiantly to hide his excitement, and squeezed himself into place on Larry's left.

"Poor *papeh*," his mother whispered in Larry's ear, "he's been so sick. It breaks my heart."

Larry's heart sank when they reached the house. He felt no touch of sentiment about his youth there, but rather disgust at the sight of the broad and unpaved sidewalk, the dusty trees lining it, the sandy old tennis court with its broken net and enclosing wire fence where four young boys were playing tennis, the brick house with its shiny red stoop and scratchy green lawn. The house appeared to have shrunk while he was away, and the room that he had to share growing up with his two brothers looked incredibly small. He would infinitely have preferred to have stayed at the Carlton, the best hotel in town, but he knew that his mother would never have tolerated that.

The house smelled deliciously of the fresh cheesecake that his mother had risen at dawn to bake and that now rested grandly on a cut-glass platter on her best damask tablecloth on the dining room table. She hastened to the kitchen, where Mary had set the kettle to boil on the coal stove. Larry followed to say hello to Mary, who looked quite pleased to find that he had not forgotten her.

On Sunday, his mother beamingly announced, all the relatives were coming to greet him. "The whole family's proud of you!" his father said sternly. While she busied herself with the tea things—she had also made a large fruit salad of sliced oranges, bananas, papaya, and peaches, to be eaten with large dollops of rich ice cream, he slipped into the bathroom—"it's the only decent room in the house," he told Robert, looking approvingly at the ruthlessly clean white bath, sink, flush toilet, and the hot water faucet that provided instant hot water and was so different from the grunting gas-metered monstrosity in his own kitchen.

In his next flat, he resolved, he was going to have a real bathroom. He made up his mind to move as soon as he returned to London.

From the bathroom he went to the bedroom with its teak beds that his father had bought for his family upon their arrival in Johannesburg and had never been changed. He took his new summer suit out of its garment bag and put it in the narrow, old-fashioned teak wardrobe the boys had used, and brought out the gifts he had brought: cashmere sweaters for his parents, a small gift for Mary. How, his mother asked naïvely, had he managed to buy all these expensive presents despite the rationing and the shortages? In fact, the gifts had plunged him deeply into debt, he told Robert in confidence. He owed money everywhere. Yet he did not seem too concerned about that.

For dinner, she had prepared what she fondly imagined was Larry's favorite meal: a huge *pirogen* with savory chicken soup swarming with islands of chicken fat, a whole, large roasted chicken with roasted potatoes, and a salad of the freshest lettuce and tomatoes and cucumbers, and for dessert, the fruit salad once more, but without the ice cream, for she prided herself on keeping a strictly kosher house.

"You're so thin," she cried, watching the tiny bites Larry took. "My poor little bird. Dear God, you must be starving there, in London. You've forgotten how to eat. I saw how you hide the food in your napkin. They say everybody's starving there. They have nothing to eat."

"She certainly knows how to get under one's skin," Larry muttered to Robert. In vain, he tried to explain to her that he had to maintain his figure, since people always looked much heavier on the screen.

"Nonsense," she cried. "My food will not make you fat."

Later that night, in their old bedroom, Larry wondered bitterly why their father had not become a citizen years earlier.

The basic reason, Robert explained, was that the Jews of eastern Europe spent their lives trying to keep out of sight of the authorities. Their father had brought the same mentality along with him to South Africa. Tragically, while herded together in the frail shelter of their villages, trying to be meek and inconspicuous, the Jews had only made it all the easier for the Nazis to pick them out and destroy them. They had no rights in Lithuania, no vote, no say in its government, and believed that was a natural state of affairs. This was the mentality their father had brought with him to South Africa.

As was the case while he was growing up, Larry's admiration for his brother's intellect was boundless. Robert's great intellectual abilities, he later wrote to Nahum, would carry him to great heights one day.

At this point, their whispered conversation was interrupted by the timid creak of the door to their bedroom and their mother, in her nightgown, peeped in. Inured to such interruptions as teenagers, both brothers pretended to be fast asleep. She tiptoed to Larry's bed and hovered admiringly over him. When he showed no sign of waking, she tiptoed away to her bedroom with a sigh, and they heard her low, high-pitched moan as she settled back in the double bed she shared with her husband.

The two of them waited until they heard the little moan and the low snort that indicated she had fallen asleep

"Is Dad really ill? What's wrong with him?" Larry asked.

"Arteriosclerosis, the doctor said," Robert replied. "He had an attack and can't work as hard as before."

What would become of them, all alone, when he left too, Larry asked?

Robert replied that once the situation in Palestine stabilized, they could settle there. Nahum would look after them. They could live in his kibbutz. Parents had that right.

But, Larry worried, wasn't there sure to be a bloodbath in Palestine when the British left?

That, Robert assured him, was pure British propaganda. The Jews would fight. Even in the ghettos of Lithuania, there had been fierce pockets of resistance against the Nazis. The Jews of Palestine would fight and win.

Much relieved, Larry was immediately convinced by his brother's argument. When the relatives flocked to the house that Sunday afternoon, he patiently endured what Robert called their "moronic village provincialism." In the warm glow of the Johannesburg summer, having slaved half the night at her hot stove in the kitchen, his mother treated them to tea and cakes, bursting with pride, and his father, putting on his spectacles, gravely showed them glossies of the plays his son had been in and read aloud from reviews in the Manchester press.

Much to his surprise, however, they were curious, not about his work, but about his clothes and how much money he made. Now he was a rich boy, they said admiringly, no doubt informed of this "fact" by his doting mother. The young unmarried girls devoured him with their yearning provincial eyes. The men informed him that they knew all about the English. The royal family had paid a visit to South Africa. The queen had fat cheeks, they said, but the princesses had a lovely English bloom. Not that the Afrikaaners cared about the British Royal family. Only the English did, for if they did not they would become rootless. And as for the Africans, Robert added, why should they feel any love for the British royal family! The visit had not even done very much for the English-speaking South Africans and Prime Minister Smut's United Party, which was sure to lose the coming election to the Nationalists.

The men fingered his jacket, asking how much he had paid for it, paying lip service to its admirable cut, but obviously found the style much too extreme for their self-contented vulgarity and cast their critical eyes over his shirt and his tie and his shoes, speculating about the price of every item. How much was he getting paid for a film he was making? they asked. Was he going to make a lot of money? they wanted to know. To Larry they seemed like a horde of vultures pecking at his flesh, howling in his ears, not really interested in him or his work, soon turning to gossip about their own concerns.

"South Africa has degenerated to an inexplicable degree of laziness, exploitation and has now even lost any foundation of culture and art it might have had, and the mad scramble for financial power and wealth has more than ever become the chief object in people's lives," he wrote to Nahum. He was not unintelligent and had grasped some of the essentials of his brothers' philosophy, which he interpreted in his own way.

To escape them and his mother's boasts and high-flown exaggerations about his prowess, he slipped away to the stoop with Robert for some much needed air. On the sandy sidewalk, the small horde of neighborhood children, who somehow seemed always hovering there, had collected, filled with curiosity to see "the film star." The day was balmy, the sky cloudless and blue, and the sun pleasantly hot. Shooing the children away with a threatening gesture, the two brothers began, unthinkingly, to walk in the direction of their old high school. It was a good two miles away, but the walk was beautiful, for the sidewalks were green with large old trees and shrubs of great red hibiscus flowers and soft blue morning glories dividing the spacious gardens of large old houses from the sidewalks, and the air was scented with grass.

When they reached the high school, it was still as they had known it, the same large three-storied brick building, clean swept and neat, surrounded on three sides by well-tended lawns. The same rocky kopje faced the school's front entrance across the street, and they stopped to reminisce about the fun they used to have climbing it with their friends during the school lunch hour. Much to Robert's amusement, Larry confessed that he had more than occasionally felt compelled to climb down the other side and cut classes, and Robert joked, "So that's where you went when you used to disappear all day!"

But he was not told where Larry had gone or what he had done when he cut classes and came home late at night.

The playing fields sloping downhill across the street behind the school attracted them next. Larry said he had never heard of such large school grounds anywhere in England except in the great public schools. Once they had played fierce games of tennis here, and languidly paced cricket matches.

"Let's face it," he said, "we had a bloody privileged youth"— although this was a fact he soon forgot in his mythmaking about his past—"I'm sorry I didn't take full advantage of it and stay on at school. You know, sometimes I feel so uneducated."

"Well," Robert said, "do it on your own. I did."

And his brother reminded him that the African majority had only the most meager school facilities—if they were lucky enough to get even these and that their Lithuanian cousins may have had decent educations, but went to their deaths in the concentration camps all the same.

"You mean we were lucky. I know," Larry said. But he looked quite impatient with his brother's preaching.

On the way back to the house he said that his real ambition was to become the greatest Shakespearean actor in England, regardless of what sacrifice this cost him, and then to perform in musicals and afterward to go on to Broadway and then on to produce, direct, and star in films in Hollywood, where the sky alone was the limit.

The two brothers felt very proud of each other, and very close. For the sake of his ambition, Larry said, he had suffered horribly those first few terrible months in London. He had been isolated and half starved, living on bread and jam and tea, freezing in a bare room in a shoddy old building. Why hadn't he written him the truth? Robert demanded, horrified. He would have been helped. Stubbornly, Larry shook his head. He had been, he said, determined to suffer in silence, because he always knew he would succeed, although some people had done their best to destroy him.

His father became a naturalized South African citizen on December 17, 1947. Larry received his new passport the same day and booked his return trip to London. In a flare of impulsive generosity, he told his parents on the evening before he left that he would begin sending them at least some money every month, and that this would be only the beginning. He reminded them that he had promised to support them before he left for England the first time and would keep his word.

They heard him out with astonishment and joyous pride. Far surpassing his brothers, he became the most important of their sons, and he knew it. Yet, somehow, he always felt inferior to his brothers, however famous he became. "Tell him I read a lot," he instructed a mutual acquaintance to relay to Robert. He had to impress him.

"He means he's sending the money to me," his mother snapped at his startled father, "not to you." Too accustomed to her spasms of moodiness, he let this pass in silence.

As a parting gift, Larry took her to one of the handsomest jewelry stores in town in order to buy her the diamond ring she craved. Instead of the modest diamond ring he tried to persuade her to accept, her eyes were attracted to a large rectangular ring and a matching bracelet of large, rectangular-shaped amethyst gemstones, each framed in gold-dipped steel with a large diamond zircon set at either end.

At the airport his mother was surprisingly subdued. Her fortitude collapsed at the last moment however, and her tears flowed, and she clung to Larry until he broke away by force to walk to the waiting plane.

Mulling over his visit in the plane, he decided that she was impossible, that he had to keep her at a safe distance, or she would smother him, but he felt ineradicably bound to her all the same, and loved her despite everything she did and said.

All the same, the flight from Johannesburg to London relieved him from the cloying grip of his past and his mother, with her raw, emotional outbursts and frenzies, and sent his spirits soaring. When the plane plunged out of its blanket of bright blue sky and penetrated the gray storm clouds of England to land in the cold of the dark London winter afternoon, some of his exhilaration gave way to the grimy prospect of having to play minor roles in third-rate films, perhaps for years to come. Clenching his fists, he vowed that he would never let this happen, come what may.

In later years, he claimed that he had been tested for the male lead in *House of Darkness* at the J. Arthur Rank Charm School (a training ground for the clerks and high school dropouts who became "gentlemen") and that he had been one of thirty actors being tested for the part. "It was like a mass execution," he said. Yet he had won the part, although why, he declared, he could not imagine. All the charm school had done for him was to teach him to be a mannequin.

The set of *House of Darkness* was a large unfurnished house that had been converted into a studio. It was obvious from the first that "Lawrence Harvey" had a very different acting style than the staid and competent rest of the cast. He was, in fact, a stage actor. In his autobiography, *Caught in the Act,* John Stuart, a stage and screen actor prominent at the time who was also in the movie, comments that Oswald Mitchell, the movie's director, had told him, "Watch this young man—he's going to go a long way. "And how right he was," John Stuart comments. John Stuart came to know the young actor well, for later that year, he played a fellow detective in *Man on the Run* and after that, in the film *The Man from Yesterday.*

His role in *House of Darkness*, on which he resumed working immediately upon his return to London, gave young Larry invaluable experience as a movie actor and, above all, an acute awareness of the camera and what it could do for him. He had an intuitive sense of the needs of the camera, and knew instinctively that he had to win the special and sympathetic attention of the cameraman, who could highlight the best angles of his face. Forever afterward, his first act when beginning a new film was always to establish a special rapport with the lighting cameraman, for the lighting had to be imaginative; a "love affair" between the actor and the camera could transform the actor into a star. He always made a point of establishing a good relationship with the film crew on every film he made, and he was always generous, thoughtful, and well liked by them.

In *House of Darkness*, basking in the camera's penetrating gaze, learning how to use his assets to his greatest advantage, deeply engrossed in his role, he became totally blind and deaf to his surroundings, he later told his brother. In one scene, he was supposed to kick a heavy glass door with his foot. So ferociously did he hurl himself into this scene, he said, that he smashed his right foot through the glass without even being aware of it until the fiery pain, the blood spurting over his shoe, and the shattered glass told him what he had done. Rushed to the nearest hospital, he had to have the shoe cut open and needed several stitches on his foot. From the hospital, he took a taxi straight back to the studio and, gritting his teeth to conceal his pain, striving not to limp, insisted on continuing the scene.

The whole cast and the crew had marveled at him for his fortitude, he told his brother when they met in England. He declared that the mishap, as he called it, did not altogether displease him, for it demonstrated how seriously he took his work. Not even acute pain could stop him. Only the fact that he had ruined his shoe really annoyed him.

On the set he did not mind the long hours, the waiting, the constant repetition of a sentence or a scene. He had a genuine passion for the work. Between takes, he rehearsed his lines and practiced how he was going to say them; he teased the girls and told the filthy jokes that he was always picking up. On weekends, he began exploring flea markets and antique shops, feeding a developing hunger for fine—which he translated as expensive—things he could not yet afford.

Feeding this hunger, he had paid a visit to St. James Palace where the royal wedding gifts had been on display to the public before the marriage of Princess Elizabeth and Prince Phillip. There was a record player encased in a walnut cabinet, a gift of the marquess of Milford Haven, which had caught his fancy, and a Fabergé silver box and, above all, the fabulous wreath of diamond roses sent by the nizam of Hyderabad. One day, he resolved, he too would be able to possess if not an identical, at least a similar record player to the one given to the royal couple by the marquess of Milford Haven as well as Fabergé boxes and diamond jewelry. He understood the purpose of this exhibition, and of the lavish wedding—lavish, at least, in those lean days. They had brought a ray of sunshine into the gray, bleak lives of people. The glittering life of a film star did that too.

The studio gave a reception to celebrate the completion of *House of Darkness*. It was attended by the producer and various other movie industry dignitaries. "You're going to be a big star," everyone told him. Naturally, he relayed this prediction and faithfully sent copies of publicity stills from the movie to his overwhelmingly proud parents, who exhibited them to all their relatives and friends, and to the much edified Nahum, who showed them to all his comrades.

In his book, *Portraits of a Decade: London Life, 1945–55*, Sutherland provides a glimpse of what the stars were like on the set of *House of Darkness*. The very pretty leading lady baldly told everyone that she was only interested in earning the money in order to retire and have a baby. How young Larry had arrived in England from "Yoniskis" and South Africa and got himself enrolled at the Royal Academy of Dramatic Art, Sutherland writes, "was never very clear. . . . He seemed . . . to be entirely on his own in the world. . . . He was a mixture of aggressive independence and quite ruthless ambition, using anybody he could to claw his way to the top." He was not even sure, Sutherland comments, whether Larry's single-mindedness was limited to succeeding as an actor. Had he been able to find a more immediate way to satisfy his lust for fast cars, great clothes, and luxury, he would probably have taken it, in Sutherland's opinion—"although he was undoubtedly very talented." He was not a "nice" young man, but he was streetwise and given to immense bouts of agonizing, thinking nothing of telephoning Sutherland at all hours to discuss whether he should have his picture taken for the casting directory, *Spotlight*, or let his hair grow, or style it differently, or consult a doctor about the spot threatening to appear on his chin. And he had a childlike belief that Sutherland's wife Moyra, an actress with a mounting reputation, knew everyone and everything, from the rumor of a part that was to become available to some gossip about a coming new production, and he was forever telephoning her.

This seems more to define total self-absorption than ruthless ambition.

Out of pity, perhaps, the Sutherlands took him to one of Hermione Baddeley's informal Sunday brunches at the actress's house on Chester Square. Hermione Baddeley, at this time, was a leading musical comedy stage star and also a screen actress. The two of them got along so well that Larry was still chatting enthusiastically with Hermione when the Sutherlands departed. He was talking about himself—naturally—and Hermione, Sutherland writes, seemed flushed with excitement.

In the course of filming *House of Darkness*, the distributors voiced their objections to the name Larry Skikne, criticizing it as not commercially attractive, and quite unsuitable for a British movie star. His first name could easily become "Laurence" in place of Larry.

Laurence was an honorable name, made resplendent by Laurence Olivier. But Skikne was meaningless, not even remotely Russian or Lithuanian. His agent had renamed several stars and it had helped to make them famous. Larry was quite ready to change the name Skikne to something far more attractive. But naturally, Sutherland claims, he agonized over the problem.

Here, the story undergoes some variations. One version has it that it was his agent who transformed Larry Skikne into Laurence Harvey. Another is that, riding on the top deck of a red London bus with Sid James on their way to the Hippodrome, where James was to open in a play and had promised to put in a good word for young Skikne, their discussion turned, inevitably, to finding a suitable name for the aspiring actor. As the bus passed streets and stores, they tested the names to judge if these were suitable. Could he be called Laurence Oxford? Laurence Willis? Laurence Woolworth?

Finally, as the bus stopped opposite the Harvey Nichols store, Sid James cried, "It's either Laurence Nichols or Laurence Harvey." Larry Skikne chose the latter.

Laurence Harvey's own version has several variations. The producers were threatening to call him Jock Strap or Bang Cock or something like that, he averred. "I was walking past Harvey Nichols's store one night, and saw in enormous letters and red lights, 'Harvey.' It seemed dignified, good, apt, Laurence Harvey. Laurence Harvey. . . . I was mesmerized by it."

The more general version, which he related in several interviews, was that, knowing he would have to change his name, he was walking down a street in Soho deep in thought when he suddenly looked up to see a sign outside a liquor store reading 'Harvey's Bristol Cream.' He liked the sherry and the name, and became Laurence Harvey.

Apparently, he mulled long and hard over his decision to change his name. He consulted Sutherland, his agent, others. He had, for some reason, qualms of conscience about the change and wrote to Nahum that the change was "regrettable" and that it was, like being forced to act in another bad film, something over which he had no control, for he was obligated to act in this film because of "the sheet of paper known as a contract."

"Oh, this too, too unfortunate society!" he exclaimed. He had, perhaps, been attending a performance of *Hamlet,* and added, "I dream and long for the day when I can break these chains which bind me to a society which through its own folly and stupidity is heading slowly to destruction. This pseudo world of art and culture is so heartbreaking that I am more determined than ever to work and learn and then guide and teach the true principles of art and culture." All this seemed aimed at impressing his big brother with his "intellectual" grasp of political and social realities. Still, he dimly realized how half-baked and adolescent he sounded, and felt rather dissatisfied with himself.

There is no explanation of how "Maurice"—his new version of Morris (Mosheh)—became "Misha."

Much to his astonishment, Nahum replied that he, too, had changed Skikne, Hebrewizing it into the biblical "Sneh," meaning "the Burning Bush" (where Moses had received the Ten Commandments on Mount Sinai). Several years later, Robert transformed Skikne into Sinai. Perhaps their father, when told of these changes, was a little saddened, but he wrote to say, staunchly, that he understood the need for the change where his sons were concerned, but would not, for the sake of his family slaughtered in Lithuania, change his own.

After *House of Darkness* there seemed to be no other role in sight. Like some hopeful supplicant, he roamed the casting offices looking for work, accepting a minuscule role in a play in which Sid James was one of the featured actors, later returning the favor when he could. Like hungry dogs, they scrambled to get bit parts and boasted of their achievements.

6

A Biting Tongue, Adoring Fans, and Trips to Paris

In *Man on the Run*, his second picture, shot in the new Rank studios at Elstree, he played a police detective. His lines were few but his presence was overwhelming. As was de rigueur for men in those days, he wore a hat fashionably tilted to the right and made his face look large and plump with baby fat. He had come to know several policemen and emulated their blunt, gruff manner and their clipped, formal way of speaking. But he looked too large for the cheaply built set representing the house he supposedly entered, too tall for the front door he opened, too heavy for its narrow entrance hall, which seemed to threaten to collapse at his touch.

By this time his voice, which some had criticized as high, had dropped an octave.

His performance was judged satisfactory. But if he believed that this less than indifferent picture had launched him on the road to stardom, he was sadly disappointed. There followed a long period of waiting, a kind of restless limbo, during which he returned, filled with anger and pessimism, to acting in bit parts wherever they were available. He was twenty years old, an actor with a goodly amount of experience and no stage for his talent.

That year, his brother Robert arrived, traveling as a stateless person on a six-month travel visa issued by the South African government. His application for naturalization had been rejected again, and the South African police had sent a report about him to Scotland Yard, labeling him an inflammatory and dangerous revolutionary. This he discovered two or three months later, when a sympathetic Labor member of Parliament took the trouble to investigate his case.

The report, when he learned of it, shocked him, but with the ebullient confidence and naïveté of youth, he felt convinced that Britain's Labor government, which ostensibly opposed apartheid, or at least paid lip service to this opposition, would shrug it off as wildly exaggerated. His article on segregation in South Africa had been published in French translation in Jean-Paul Sartre's prestigious journal, *Les Temps modernes.* On the strength of it he set about meeting with leading Labor Party personalities, hoping to find a place for himself as a journalist and, thereby, to gain permanent residence in England.

Initially, his presence in London was a great boon to Larry, for Robert had an unswerving faith in his younger brother's future as a star on stage and screen. They met, not all the time, for both had their own interests and activities to pursue, but quite frequently. Larry never talked about his personal life and Robert never questioned him about it. To Robert, Larry was still his fresh-faced kid brother, more grown up, a lot quieter, who always wore a tan-colored corduroy jacket and gray flannel trousers whenever they met and looked so innocent and self-contained.

One evening, they went to a performance by the superb American dancer Katherine Dunham and her company. The sensuous Caribbean music, the sinuous dancing, the women's brightly colored costumes trapping their bodies from naked golden brown shoulders to bare feet, the male dancers, graceful, slim and lithe, their golden brown chests exposed in the flow of their shirts, stirred Larry to confess that he had experienced eight orgasms while watching them.

"Eight!" Robert exclaimed with amused skepticism.

He attributed this boast to his brother's youthful exuberance.

"No. Really!" Larry claimed with disarming frankness. "I counted them."

He had moved into a larger and more expensive flat in Shepherd's Market with a living room, bedroom, kitchen, and a separate bathroom complete with a bathtub, toilet, and running water. One Saturday evening, he invited Robert and Anne to dinner there. Living in one room where they were crowded out with boxes of books and his wife had an old-fashioned, wholly inadequate closet, they were extremely impressed with this new flat, even though the only furniture in the living room consisted of gray wall-to-wall carpet, a couch covered in gray velvet, and a low coffee table around which they dined sitting, for lack of chairs, on the carpet in Japanese fashion.

He showed them an eight-by-ten glossy of a handsome young woman wearing a turban and a fur coat.

"I was in love with her," he said. "She treated me bloody badly. I did so much for her. When her boyfriend let her down, I comforted her. She was pregnant and needed my help, but she used me in the most bloody and callous way. I did everything for her. I cleaned up the mess in her house after her abortion. I'll never let anyone use me like that again."

To their young, startled eyes, the young woman looked old—at least thirty.

"Wasn't she a bit too . . . sophisticated for you?" his brother asked, meaning, "too old."

Larry frowned.

"I'm not exactly a country bumpkin," he returned coldly.

She may or may not have been the first "prefect" whom he had spunkily approached after graduating from the "tickey dances" at school. Or she may not have existed at all. He never spoke about his male friends.

For their dinner, he had prepared a perfect asparagus soufflé, a dish at which he excelled. Where he unearthed all the eggs for it, so far exceeding the miserly prevailing weekly ration, they would neither guess nor question. What they found surprising, however, was his mania for neatness and spick-and-span cleanliness. When, accidentally, his sister-in-law dropped some ash from her cigarette on the carpet, he instantly strode, long legged, into the kitchen to fetch his broom and his dustpan and she watched in silent amazement as he stooped to brush the ash off the carpet.

"That's so much like your mother," Anne said when they left. "Why aren't you as tidy as that?"

"Nahum is. It's a family trait I never inherited," Robert returned smugly.

As soon as they discovered that *House of Darkness* was showing at the local cinema, his brother and sister-in-law descended upon it with trepidation and enthusiasm. Armed with notebooks and pencils, they planned to pass themselves off as reporters asking people what they thought of "the new star, Laurence Harvey." The cinema reminded them rather too depressingly of the Alhambra in

Johannesburg, the "bughouse" in Doornfontein, although this one was much larger and its seats were in somewhat better condition. Eagerly, as the film began, they readied themselves to be thrilled and entertained, but they could not help noticing that the rest of the audience seemed indifferent to what they were watching, as if they had merely come to the cinema in order to spend a few hours away from their cold houses.

The two watched the film with affectionate pride and determination to admire, but they had to admit that the film was mediocre—in truth, far worse than mediocre—and that Larry's theatrical style clashed with that of the rest of the cast, although he made the others, all of them competent if uninspired actors, look quite pedestrian. They constructed excuses to conceal their disappointment. Their judgment was flawed, they told each other, because they knew Larry too well, and saw, not the character he was playing, not the airy illusion on the screen, but the flesh-and-blood reality. This was a form of myopic vision from which they suffered for years, until they learned to look at the character he was playing objectively and only then could they appreciate his work.

With their notebooks and pencils poised at the ready, they hurried to meet people streaming out of the foyer, accosting everyone who chanced to notice them with the same question: "We're doing a survey. What did you think of this new actor, Laurence Harvey?"

Under the lights, dazed and puzzled, good humor taking the place of reflection, most of them responded generously, "He was quite good. We liked him."

A light rain was falling. The two of them might have remained to question every one in the audience, but people speedily scattered. Wet through but glowing with exhilaration, they hurried back to their room perhaps, without admitting it even to themselves, rather disappointed by the milksop reaction.

"Well, the English are so phlegmatic," his sister-in-law said.

His brother agreed. He was absolutely convinced that his kid brother had the makings of a brilliant actor.

One evening it became clear that the two brothers had come to inhabit different worlds. Impulsively, Larry had invited his brother and sister-in-law to a buffet supper in the private dining room at one of the grander hotels. For Larry, this was an important occasion. He had been to several such receptions, arranged to entertain a particular producer who was the guest of honor and whom the actors were expected to charm. This, Larry failed to explain to his brother and sister-in-law, no doubt taking it for granted that they would understand, but the whole evening rather puzzled them. Where Larry saw a potential investor for a film in which he would play the lead, they saw a heavy-set, hard-drinking businessman whom every guest fought to court.

In this time of austerity and still-strict rationing, the guests faced an elegant cold repast of smoked salmon flown in from Scotland, Beluga caviar, and a mountain of the finest homegrown roast beef. Vodka accompanied the caviar. Champagne and imported red wine they were too inexperienced to identify accompanied the beef. The dessert was a superb chocolate creme. French cognac was served with the coffee and afterward, Scotch whisky.

They ate and drank in silent wonder, but what marked the dinner most in their minds was the appalling lack of intelligent conversation. Underlying the jovial laughter, an intense internecine warfare seemed to be going on among the guests. Several very pretty, newly sprung young actresses with complexions like delicate English cottage roses, soon to be ruined by late nights, alcohol, and sex for the sake of ambition, twittered, birdlike, competing for the investor's attention. Almost in unison, the aspiring young actors laughed at every inept joke he made in a voice like a coarse bellow. The way everyone fawned on this loud and vulgar man, hoping for a crumb of recognition was, to the outsiders, beneath contempt. They were sickened by his half-smug, half-suspicious acceptance of the subservience he was offered, by his recognition that he could plant his boot firmly on their willing necks.

Larry alone seemed aloof from this orgy of lackeydom. Seated on the investor's left, facing his brother and sister-in-law across the long table, he looked neither ashamed of the company he was keeping, nor in the least apologetic. Rather, his demeanor, so self-contained and cool, seemed wordlessly to be stating: "Don't expect *me* to be humble in the idiotic company of this rich nobody. I'm here because this is where I choose to be."

He had this quality, as a young man, always to seem self-contained and cool, as if existing in his own space, which no one

else could penetrate or touch. All the same, he seemed rather annoyed when his brother, engaged in conversation with one of the
guests without a touch of awe. It was as if his brother was poaching on his preserve, and he did not like being deprived of the
limelight.

Cockily, he interrupted Robert's flow of talk with a vulgar and
suggestive joke that set the investor bellowing with laughter.

At least a week or two passed before Larry seemed able to collect
himself enough to visit his brother and sister-in-law. He came because he was lonely. Because, acknowledging his own abysmal ignorance in a secret enclave in his mind, he did not want people to
think him shallow and empty-headed, and needed the intellectual
stimulation he felt Robert could provide in order to appear greater
and smarter in the estimation of those he wanted to impress.

"They're such disgusting people," he said, referring to the
guests at the reception they had attended a fortnight earlier. "I just
wanted you to see what awful people I've got to deal with.
They're a true reflection of the society we live in. A society
doomed for destruction. The most ruthless, crude and base and
untrustworthy moguls have combined their weight to crush us
and make all the decisions in our present world. It's absolutely
disgusting. They buy everything and everyone, and we're forced
to compromise and bow down to their shitty ideas. They've got
the money, that's why, those ruthless, crude and base moguls. . . .
When I'm famous, I'll show them up for the rubbish they are. I'm
going to leap over all their irrelevant and trivial ideas and all the
conventions and idiocies they believe in, and kick all that rubbish
out of my way. The cinema is the greatest cultural and artistic
medium of the future. I intend to learn everything about making
films and acting in them and then I'll be able to serve as a model
to others. It's the only way we're going to achieve true art and culture in this lousy world."

But even at the height of his impassioned diatribe (and he spoke
with fervent intensity) he knew that he would not include his
brother and sister-in-law in his world. He was convinced that they
did not fit into that sphere. They had looked so grossly out of place
and sounded so wrong with their rough South African drawls. Without consciously acknowledging this, he longed to outshine his
brother intellectually, to be the cynosure of all admiring eyes, to put

his own stamp on all the company he kept, and be the sun around which everything revolved.

The emotional strain between the two brothers remained volcanically underground. Robert and his wife moved into the second floor of a house in Finchley. Larry visited them there, but they were never invited to his flat again. Having made the decision to avoid exhibiting them, he felt secure enough to resume his pattern as Robert's devoted and innocuous youngest brother. On their wedding anniversary, he surprised them with a small chocolate cake made with real butter and eggs and cream, covered in a chocolate crust, odoriferous and redolent of vanilla, and crowned with two candied pink roses. He did not say how he had come by it, and only smiled modestly when they marveled at this spectacular acquisition when even the plain Cadbury chocolate bars that used to be available in slot machines in the underground stations were rationed and almost impossible to come by.

He had also brought a bottle of wine. They drank toasts to their future greatness and laughed a good deal, but a serious note also sounded throughout the evening. The news from Palestine worried them, and what might happen to Nahum and his family. The Arab states had rejected the UN Partition Resolution for Palestine of November 1947, which was to divide Palestine into two states, one Jewish, and one Arab. Everyone—even Nahum, in the most sanguine of his letters to his brothers—knew that war between the Arabs and the Jews was inevitable. Fighting had broken out on May 14, 1948, the day the British forces sailed for home, David Ben-Gurion declared the existence of the State of Israel, and the armies of seven Arab states invaded the newly created Jewish state.

"I feel so helpless in my desire to participate," Larry told his brother and also wrote to Nahum. And thinking, no doubt of the blood being shed between Muslims and Indians in India, declared that he condemned the British government for "their policy of starting chaos and destruction wherever they leave," and declared that he found himself in such a state of anguish that he wanted to leave England and move to America as soon as possible.

The battles between Israel and the Arab states continued for months, interspersed with UN-negotiated truces. Both his brothers knew that Nahum was holed up somewhere in the south, fighting with his unit, and worried about him. The letters they received from their father reflected his worry too, though he must have had a great struggle, they knew, in trying to keep their mother's hysteria in check.

This was a period when the brothers felt very close and had long and earnest discussions.

Larry liked to listen to his brother, despite Robert's lecturing manner, which he deeply resented while absorbing everything Robert said in order to impress people with his understanding of political issues. They discussed the rise of anti-Semitism, fueled by shortages and the dwindling of the British empire. Larry would have liked to believe that some of the casting directors who did not give him leading roles were deliberately discriminating against him because he was Jewish, but he knew that this was not true. They were just unimaginative incompetents who would never rise above making B films. Besides, they did not know he was Jewish—not that he ever tried to conceal this fact, it just never came up.

He developed an interest in Britain's nineteenth-century prime minister Benjamin Disraeli. Although, as he now learned, Disraeli's father had converted to Christianity, and Disraeli had been a practicing Christian, he had never quite been accepted by the British establishment. He had been far too exotic for the staid English taste. Disraeli had been exaggeratedly flashy, wearing his hair in ringlets across his forehead, adopting special dandyisms and gorgeous embroidered waistcoats. All acts of defiance, it seemed to the young actor.

To be conscious of never being fully accepted, however brilliant one was! It was a lesson brought home to Larry and it must have sunk deeply into the budding new star's consciousness. Flamboyant by nature, to behave outrageously became to him an act of defiance. If he was to be regarded as an outsider, then he would become an outsider with vengeance. It was then that he began, still dimly, to conceive of a different origin; that he began to become "Larusha," the Lithuanian, the Russian, the moody Slav. With his fair coloring and broad cheekbones, he looked Russian. People always asked him whether he was Lithuanian or Russian. Never English.

Weeks passed. His career seemed to him not to be going anywhere; he was terrified of having to face a future of getting only insipid parts in insipid little movies.

He complained bitterly about this to his brother and sister-in-law.

"I think," his sister-in-law said injudiciously, "you'd make a fine romantic hero."

"What do you suggest?" asked Larry, narrowing his eye in sudden speculation.

She practically worshipped Balzac, particularly his novels in *The Human Comedy*, which she devoured in what was, in those days, encased in volumes in almost unintelligible English translation and said,

"I think the role of young Calyste in *Béatrix* might be perfect for you."

Larry had never heard of Balzac, but he was immediately attracted to the character that was sketched out for him and instantly saw Calyste as a romantic figure, dashing, bold, and heroic, a youth adored by women.

"Write the script and I'll sell it," he said, his eyes a shrewd and speculative gray and his whole demeanor expressing a burning determination.

But when she came to confront the task, she found herself out of her depth, for she entirely lacked the knowledge to tackle so daunting an enterprise. Also, a careful rereading of the book made it very clear that it described strong-minded women and their willful manipulation of a charming but naïve young man whose only talent was for loving. This was not the image Larry should want to project at the very onset of his career, she considered.

In later life, she always felt a spasm of guilt for abandoning her efforts to write the script. She suffered from bad timing and wrong judgment. Unlike Larry, she never knew how to seize an opportunity, or to be ruthless in pursuit of her objective.

Extremely disappointed by her defection, Larry visualized himself all the more romantically as the dashing leading man of this novel. Quite unable to believe that the character would be wrong for him—and, in fact, with a little imaginative editing he could have emerged as the kind of young man women loved for his vulnerability as well as his strength—he set out to write the script himself, employing, as he explained with innocent simplicity, the technique of copying all the dialogue and assigning it to the characters. Modestly, upon being questioned, he told his brother and sister-in-law that he had submitted the script to the BBC and that they had liked it very much. Only, they claimed that all the rich costumes of the period, the vast cast of characters he had included, and the ornate sets would make it too expensive to produce.

When their visas expired, his brother and sister-in-law had to leave England. Frantically, Robert pleaded with Larry to use his influence with people he knew to find him some kind of job that would keep him in England, but Larry protested that he knew no one. Determined never to return to South Africa, where the new and fanatical Afrikaaner Nationalist government was waging a fierce campaign against all those who opposed apartheid, they left for France. A British Labor member of Parliament had asked a French diplomat to grant them temporary residence as stateless persons. They moved to Paris, with dwindling funds, hoping for some miracle, perhaps.

Despite his affection for his second brother, Larry felt as if a weight had been lifted from his shoulders.

"Robert is so self-centered and impractical," he complained bitterly in a letter to Nahum. "He is so domineering and made my life impossible. I can't help him. I can barely survive myself. I don't know any influential people."

Nahum replied that he sympathized with his struggling little brother.

The American movie companies were now making a number of movies in Britain. This relieved some of the pressure on Britain's dollar shortage, but did little to provide employment to British actors— the number of unemployed actors in Britain had risen to 12,000 by 1950—since the American companies imported their own stars. In August 1949, Larry was still waiting for a part in a picture and expressed his feelings of frustration in his response to a sympathetic letter from Nahum,

> you have already expressed my feelings for me, however, I should like to add that in spite of the fact that one finds oneself surrounded by crude, base, unreliable and completely ruthless moguls—(the combined weight is by no means an easy burden) I have nevertheless sufficient energy and strength left in me to continue to fight for what I believe is a true expression of one's feelings, in this particular field. That the medium of the film is an art is an undisputable [*sic*] fact, perhaps one may readily say that it is probably the greatest form of expression the world has ever known, but for the present and from a practical standpoint I have had to compromise and accept (reluctantly) certain ideas and forms which is so manifest within the industry.

But, before he mailed this letter, he had a triumphant achievement to add. He became one of the few British actors to win a part, however minor, in one of the American movies made in Britain. This was in the handsome film made by Twentieth Century Fox titled *The Black Rose*, starring Tyrone Power and Orson Welles. The film was made in Britain to enable the studio to recoup some of the $5 million Britain owed and could not repay.

The story is set in thirteenth-century England, when the Saxons are still defying their Norman conquerors, and later in China. Larry plays Edmond, the cowardly Norman younger brother who has inherited the property and rights of the rebellious Saxon played by Tyrone Power.

Still youthfully fresh faced, Larry looks slimmer in this film, somewhat dandified, a gentleman, cynical rather than cowardly as his role demanded; he does not quite fit into the character, and his appearance in this film is brief. Much to his disappointment, he had no scenes with Orson Welles, whom he met for the first time and greatly admired.

"I have just completed a small but important principal role in . . . *The Black Rose* with Tyrone Power and Orson Welles," Larry wrote to Nahum. "The company as you are no doubt aware is a Hollywood Unit who are over here making films. The experience has been invaluable and who knows—it may lead to bigger things and eventually America—I play the part of Ty Power's brother, cruel, jealous and a coward (character part, of course). Ty is really a very charming person, whose only talent lies within those two qualities and Orson is a completely brilliant character on his own."

If Larry was sanguine about this movie leading to bigger things and a triumphant flight to Hollywood, this did not happen. Mainly, the movie was a vehicle for Tyrone Power, whose handsome features and fencing abilities had cast him as the romantic hero in many similar movies. Adored by women everywhere, admired and envied by men, he was one of the top box office draws of the time. Good natured and popular with the crew, he had only one detractor: the young and still untried Laurence Harvey. "Ty's very nice and charming, but his only talent lies within those two qualities," he repeated blandly to one and all. This was among the first of his putdowns of his fellow actors. He repeated it several times in public, at least once within hearing of Power's wife at the time. It did not serve to get him liked.

In England, the public was beginning to take notice of Laurence Harvey. The British movie magazines had kept reiterating that the British film industry was down in the dumps and asking rhetorically whether it would ever find another James Mason or Wendy Hiller, advising producers to get rid of actors with superior accents for "real flesh and blood people." With the advent of Laurence Harvey, the popular *Picture Post* was quick to call him a "New Star." The tabloids described him as "the stuff that stars are made of." The financial director of Capitol Film Productions declared that his face was a new type for the screen. His picture appeared in movie magazines. Fans wrote to the studio requesting signed photographs. He went out of his way to charm tabloid journalists and cameramen, made himself readily available to them, and studied how to get himself into print. He made good copy and the tabloids faithfully printed his increasingly uninhibited remarks. Why had he wanted to become an actor, he was asked by one interviewer. "I wanted a profession where I could start at the top," he replied cheekily. The tabloids faithfully printed this statement and his admiring fans lapped it up.

He was cast as Cassio in Shakespeare's *Othello* and one or two other small parts—the kind of roles he had been drilled at RADA to play—on BBC television. These were extremely important parts, he wrote to his brothers modestly. At this time, British television technology was quite far ahead of its American counterpart, but television sets were exorbitantly expensive and this limited the number of viewers.

Whether on the screen, in the tabloids, in movie magazines, or in his appearances on television, his face was becoming widely known. The tabloids labeled him romantic and dashing, and he suddenly found himself the target of dozens of mushy notes from young women hungry for love.

One of them actually succeeded in picking the lock of his flat while he was out and stealing into his bed. Returning to his flat quite tipsy that evening, having imbibed too much at one of a producer's boring receptions for a wealthy businessman he hoped to win over, throwing off his clothes without bothering to switch on the light, and climbing naked into bed, he felt the soft touch of the warm, firm body of a girl pressing against his own. Lips plugged onto his, strong, smooth knees pried open his legs. His stomach was pressed down on the mattress and a determined hand reached for his penis.

Trembling with terror and desire, he had barely managed to summon the strength to throw her off him and switch on the light. The girl in his bed—she was no more than fifteen or sixteen, at most, he said—seemed to him pathetically vulnerable. She was obviously working class, even her loud sobs, arising in snorts of misery, revealed it. Her body had the shape of some classical Greek Venus, like those he had seen in books on art, which he had begun to collect without reading them, with full, firm, high breasts, hips broad and curving like melons from a small soft waist. Her stomach was flat and her legs long and well muscled, though her features were coarse and her hands red and rough, amateurishly manicured with peeling blood-red nail polish.

Weeks later, he described the encounter to his brother when he saw him in Paris. By then he had taken to making quick weekend trips to that city.

He mimicked the girl perfectly.

"Oh, Larry I love you so much, I dream about you every night," she had wailed, vainly attempting to cover her breasts with her arms and trembling with misery, "won't you make love to me, you're so wonderful, I hate the bloody boys I got to go with, honestly, all they want is a bloody beer and a fuck, I'm so miserable, you don't know. Me bloody Dad beats the hell out of me when he gets drunk and says I'm a fucking whore, which I am not, honest, and me mum gets drunk and cries. Larry, I'll be so good to you, honest I will. . . ."

"Put your clothes on, for God's sake, and get the hell out of my flat, or I'll call the police," Larry said he had rasped, sobering up.

Sobbing heartrendingly, she had put on her clothes and, resignedly, left.

"My God" still trembling at the memory, he told his brother. "What would have happened to me if the police found that girl in my flat! I'd have been charged with rape, with corrupting a minor. That would've put a dandy end to my career, it would! Of course I had no intention of telephoning the police. That would only have led to scandal and trouble for me. Luckily she was stupid enough not to know that, and got shakily into her clothes and slunk out of the door, trembling with tears. I changed the lock to the front door after that. Not that it helped. . . ."

But he never succumbed to that kind of temptation, he said. Never. He simply did not feel attracted to that kind of thing, and knew enough beautiful girls to be able to pick and choose. He did not talk about his male friends. His brother had no inkling about his dual nature. It was only gossiped about in the world of the movie industry. Mainly, he was photographed in the company of some pretty young actress at a premiere or nightclub.

The experience with the fan was nightmarish to him. More young girls appeared at his door at night. He moved to a larger flat in a more expensive neighborhood—in fact he had wanted to move even before the incident with the young fan—changed the lock on his front door frequently, and became extremely vigilant and incessantly on the watch to avoid a repetition of it. Publicly, he seemed perkily untroubled and posed for glossies immaculately dressed, sometimes with his unruly clump of hair falling cockily over his forehead and a mischievous grin lighting up his features, sometimes looking suave and sophisticated, sporting a cigarette in the long black holder that he had begun to use.

He had good parts in two more B movies: *The Man from Yesterday* and *Man on the Run*—neither of them requiring much effort on his part—and he looked handsome and spoke his lines well. The Rank conglomerate was still paying him no more than £20 a week and hiring out his services to various companies, making healthy profits from his work. He could afford very little, but all the same, he began spending his money on practically everything his hungry gaze encountered. New clothes, made to his minute and strict specifications, were his passion. Above all, he was determined to be visible, a "man about town," and went to nightclubs and fashionable restaurants. He had debts. Living expensively, he was forced to supplement his income by modeling and posing for tailors' advertisements in addition to his occasional adventures with rich older men. At the same time, he made good his promise to his mother and sent his parents a check every month—not always for the same amount; this depended on his expenditures at the time.

Whatever he sent was received with overwhelming gratification by his mother. His parents were immensely proud of him, dazzled by what seemed to them his swift success. Sure of his genius, his mother, clucking, "Poor boy!" like a fretting hen anxious to protect her brood, boasted to all the relatives and neighbors about how hard he had to work and how his remarkable talent was universally recognized. She had reached the stage where she believed everything he wrote and was thrilled by everything he claimed he had achieved.

His brothers were also grateful to find that he had taken on the responsibility of supporting their parents, which they were incapable of doing. Nahum practically revered him. As a result of his military service during the War of Independence, he had developed a chronically bad back that caused him a great deal of pain. Once the fighting had more or less ended in the Negev, where he was stationed, he had returned to his kibbutz where, in his free time, he began collecting press clipping about his brother, which were translated from English and American gossip magazines and published in local Hebrew gossip papers, and he carefully preserved his brother's letters, which he kept under lock and key.

In *Cairo Road*, his next movie, which premiered in 1950, Larry costarred with Eric Portman, a leading British actor of the period. Filmed in black and white on location in Cairo, Port Said, and Suez, the movie was produced by Rank's Associated British Cinemas.

Cairo Road was about the flow of hashish from Asia being smuggled into the West via Egypt and the Eyptian effort to put a stop to it. The highly regarded Eric Portman plays an Egyptian colonel battling the worldwide smuggling ring, and Larry plays his lieutenant. As Portman's sidekick, he appeared with Portman in almost every scene and stood his ground well against the star of the movie.

Portman at the time was forty-five. His performance was, as always for this experienced actor, predictably good, his pout was, as always, prominent, his wavy blond hair slicked back, and his classical profile proffered to the camera on all occasions. By contrast, Larry looked young, virile, forceful, handsome, and tall. He was, director David McDonald said, pliable material that could easily be groomed. Grown more familiar with the camera and the technique demanded by acting in movies, he created a character for himself. In contrast to the straight-arrowed Portman, he played Portman's rather bumbling, earnest sidekick and invented poses, glances, gestures, and intonations of speech that appeared to him suited to this character, lending him extra dimensions. This violently displeased Portman, who publicly raged that Larry kept deliberately upstaging him and that he would never again make a movie with "that little shit." It was true that Larry was fiercely competitive, and perhaps Portman felt insecure when confronted with so young and good-looking a costar. Larry was not yet twenty-one, less than half Portman's age, and he also had the movie's only love interest, in the form of a beautiful Egyptian star who played his wife.

Surprisingly, despite Portman's dislike, Larry liked this star and even admired him, calling him an excellent actor whom he valued as a teacher who taught him a great deal about acting in movies.

He was also enthusiastic about his role, which he declared was his best yet. It was exciting, authentic, and dramatic. He described his part as quite strenuous and said he was trying hard to make the character interesting and realistic. Determined to prove his mettle, and against every drawback imposed by the script, he succeeded in endowing his character with a sympathetic and very human dimension in making him more than the script decreed.

He also succeeded in winning the homosexual star's friendship.

In the course of the picture, growing ever more confident, the smell of his makeup became a piercing delight to his senses. He tasted the sheer thrill of being under the glaring scrutiny of the brilliant lights, of feeling at home on the soundstage in a film studio, where walls and rooms were painted illusions. Above all, the realization that he was the focus of cameras expertly manipulated by professional camera-men intoxicated him. The long waits, the rehearsals, the retakes, did not try his patience. Instinctively, he understood the need for them. He found himself in the center of attention, and he loved every mo-ment he appeared before the camera. It gave him an exhilarating sense of purpose and of self-esteem, as if on the set he became sud-denly transformed into another person.

While on location in Egypt, he had only one disappointment, his in-ability to fly over to Israel to pay Nahum a visit or, at least that is what he wrote to Nahum after returning to London. In distance, Cairo was only a relatively short flight from Tel Aviv, but politically the two coun-tries inhabited different worlds. Egypt was ruled by President Colonel Mohammed Nagib, a leading participant in the Officer's Coup that had toppled the country's King Farouk and his family and sent them into a luxurious life of exile in the playgrounds of Europe. Run by the officers who had engineered the coup, Egypt was still at war with Is-rael and refused to recognize its right to exist. Communications be-tween the two countries did not exist.

In his letters to Nahum, he complained bitterly about how help-less he felt because he was unable to visit him. His only recourse, he explained, would have been to fly to Italy and from there to Israel, which he could not do. For how would he then—apart from the ex-pense of this trip—have received permission to return to Egypt to complete his role in the movie?

Several leading movie reviewers, dubbed his performance in *Cairo Road* "poor"; some of them even called it "awful." This appeared to be the beginning of the internecine war of scorn and disparagement several influential critics waged against him on both sides of the At-lantic throughout his career. On the other hand, the movie was a fi-nancial success and popular with the audiences, and his perfor-mance was praised by the fan magazines. As one wrote, he was in no danger of getting a swollen head over the generous press and the popular acclaim because, as he told everyone modestly, to him it was just another performance. "As yet, he hasn't the touch of the film star about him," this magazine gushed. A whole new herd of fans flocked to see the picture and wrote away for his autographed photograph.

He took to dining at the Caprice, a most fashionable restaurant, or lunching on lobster and champagne at Claridge's, and the Savoy, having gone out of his way to make great friends with the maître d's ("always make friends with the maître d' and the cook," he used to say). Consequently, he was always ushered to the best table, where he could be the most conspicuous and allow himself to be displayed and admired.

Although feeling the pinch engendered by his extravagances, when his mother wrote expressing a wish to visit Nahum in Israel, he somehow scraped together or borrowed or charmed the money out of a wealthy patron to buy her plane ticket. Thrilled, she prodded Boris to respond that she would also love to visit him in London on her return trip to Johannesburg. This news horrified him. He responded immediately, providing all kinds of frantic excuses, telling her that although he would have been delighted to see her, he was extremely busy, having to get up at five every morning, and not returning home before at least eight at night. All he could manage was to have a bite to eat, learn his next day's lines, and then fall, exhausted, into bed. Nothing must distract him from this routine if he wanted to become a success.

Besides, he added as a clinching argument, his flat was far too tiny and unfurnished to put her up and, financially, he could not afford to put her up in a hotel.

He would make every endeavor to visit her in South Africa, he assured her, and as soon as he achieved what he was aiming for, all the barriers to their reunion would fall.

Ella felt deeply disappointed, but she had the insight to understand that he really did not want her to come to England, and with heavy sighs, forgave him. What alternative did she have? Boris was not well. They were both becoming more and more dependent on him.

As a result of his careless extravagances, he really was strapped for money. His rent fell into arrears and he owed some £100 to his landlord without much hope of paying it. To Nahum's letter asking him (at the nagging prompting of their mother) about his financial situation, he replied that he was flat broke, and working extremely hard, and to cap his miseries and difficulties, whether well or ill, had to do everything himself: act as his own mother, wife, and secretary, spend all his time at social functions, meeting with important people, and spend vast sums of money to look good, which his profession demanded.

His next movie was a minor whodunit shot in black and white on location in Cambridge. It so happened that *Cairo Road* came to one of the local movie houses while he was shooting this movie. In a grandiose gesture, he invited and paid for a crowd of "friends" to come to watch the film, and basked in the glow of success, seemingly without a care in the world.

The film he was shooting in Cambridge was *The Scarlet Thread* and was pretty insipid. In it he plays a small-time American crook who participates in a bank robbery and falls in love with the daughter of a man who is accidentally shot during the robbery. Released in 1951, this British Nettlefold-International Realist production was directed by Lewis Gilbert, a minor British director, and was based on a play by A. Rawlinson and Moie Charles. But the movie was distinguished only by the fact that, much to his own amusement and professional pride, Larry played the part with an American accent.

Again, the film gave him more recognition and increased his fan mail, but after that there seemed to be nothing. He felt he had reached a dead end, acting in insignificant little movies that would get him nowhere, doomed to scrounge for money to suit his lifestyle. Anxiety and restlessness clung to him with invisible chains, heavier than the thick chain of gold links he now wore on his right wrist.

In despair, he demanded a raise, but was told that he was lucky to be earning anything. The film industry's financial woes had brought the production of British films almost to a halt. Far from alleviating the dollar drain as had been hoped, Hollywood was spending its frozen dollar assets by importing its own stars, leaving only tiny parts available to British actors.

He felt he had touched bottom. The end of his life.

He could not bear it. On his way to his agent's office, desperately to offer to do any kind of work, he happened to see the headline on the front page of a newspaper. It shook him to the core: the Rank Organisation had earned £2 million in pure profit during the past year.

Far from being bankrupt, as he had been assured it was when he asked for a raise, it was wealthier than ever.

"What the bloody hell goes on here?" he cried, storming into his agent's office and pointing to the newspaper headline. Angrily, he threatened to walk out, to tear up his contract.

Faced with the loss of an actor who brought in money, the studio decided that it needed him after all; lending him out to various companies was a lucrative business. His contract was renewed at £35 per week.

He professed himself grudgingly satisfied—for the present—and took off for Paris, there to visit his brother and the newfound delights that city had to offer.

He took to "hopping over," as he termed it, to Paris whenever he had a free weekend, or felt the need to unburden himself of some grievance, real or perceived, and he knew that he could always count on his brother's ready sympathy. How he got the travel allowance—British citizens were allowed no more than £10 in foreign currency at the time—they neither knew nor asked.

"So it seems I've made some enemies among the film critics," he told Robert, referring to some of the critics' snide comments about his acting in *Cairo Road*. "I can't think why. What are they scared of? I suppose I terrify the shit out of them."

"They'll respect genius—if they haven't succeeded in dragging it down into the mud! But they prefer the second rate," replied Robert, cynically, quoting Balzac.

Larry liked that.

"That's right," he cried. "They can't stand anyone with talent. The minute they see someone with talent they rush to cut him down. Hell, I'm just a bloody commercial commodity, something the greedy money moguls make money out of. They can pick you up and drop you, just like that. I don't have anything in sight right now, but I refuse to make any more rotten and stupid films. I mean, I wish I could refuse to make them, but I'm tied hand and foot by that damned sheet of paper they call a contract. I've got to do what they tell me to do."

He had a room in the Georges V hotel on the Right Bank. They did not even wonder how he managed to pay for it. That evening he invited his brother and sister-in-law to dinner at an elegant little restaurant he had discovered, or been told about, near Avenue Foche. Traveling by Métro from their flat on the still, in those days, inexpensive Left Bank, they arrived a little early. The restaurant was very Parisian. It had a row of tables along the walls on either side of the room, leaving an empty space in the center where the waiters could move with their trays. The clientele was upper-middle-class French, very fashionably dressed, and the atmosphere was elegantly subdued.

They had already been seated when Larry made his own dramatic entrance, appearing like some vision, tall, broad shoulders, handsome, gray eyed; a young god, as one admirer had dubbed him. Stationing himself languidly in the middle aisle left vacant for the waiters, poised, statuesque, and with cool deliberation, in a single grand gesture he unbuttoned his beautifully tailored navy blue cashmere overcoat. All conversation came to a halt. All eyes were transfixed upon him. A wave of admiration flowed across the tables as, with suave nonchalance, as if wholly unaware of the sensation he was creating, he parted his overcoat carelessly to reveal its bright crimson Chinese silk lining.

He ignored, or rather, seemed superbly to rise above the diners' admiration, granting himself only a tiny inward smile of pleasure and, seating himself, occupied himself and the hovering waiter with the great task of ordering the meal. The preliminary cocktails, the mixing and presentation of which he carefully supervised, were served in prechilled glasses capped by a garland frosting of coarse salt. He prepared the correct amounts of coarse salt, the cocktail itself, and demonstrated how to sip the liquor in precisely the proper manner. The chateaubriand was prime and delicious. It was accompanied by the perfect red wine and later he ordered a green and yellow Chartreuse. He had acquired his knowledge about wines by making friends with Rudolph, the head barman at the Georges V hotel.

Compared with still grim-faced London, Paris in those days was, especially for the young, filled with charm. The Left Bank intrigued Larry, but he did not feel altogether at home there, as his brother did, for he felt much more attracted to the cafés and restaurants frequented by well-dressed men and women and the expensive shops on the Right Bank. From his room at the Georges V (he absolutely rejected his brother's suggestion that he stay at the

Lutécia off the Boulevard Raspail, which was handsome but far less showy, and also far less expensive), he strolled to one of the large cafés and drank his cognac and his café au lait there in the morning. Splendor and wealth won his instant approbation. Adopting an air of amused cynicism, he would take out his ivory cigarette holder and light an English cigarette, showing off in the process his impeccably tailored jacket. Determined to be seen and admired, he admired in turn the modish affluence of the women chatting idly at the tables or walking their neat little poodles down the street, the elegant, light tread of the beautifully shod men.

Dreaming, perhaps, of being eyed as a tantalizing aristocrat, perhaps a prince of mysterious and formidable heritage, sitting in a popular café on the Right Bank one afternoon, he told his brother, he had a strange experience. He became aware of a handsome, impeccably dressed man sporting an eagle eye and a slim black mustache—someone in the style of Proust's French aristocrat, Baron de Charlus, he thought, about whom his sister-in-law, who also admired Proust, had told him—sipping a glass of golden cognac two or three tables away, and surveying him through heavy-lidded, veiled eyes. Those eyes resting upon him had brought a flush of heat to his cheeks and sent a quivering excitement and discomfort tingling through him. A glaring, challenging inspection of the stranger's long, narrow face showed him to be in his fifties, if not more, of a sallow complexion embellished by rouged cheeks, thin, painted red lips, and an aquiline nose.

Shakily, he had left the café, practically escaping from it, he said.

He preferred the sixteenth arrondissement, but he stored enough of the mannerisms of the Left Bank to claim a familiarity with it, and this earned him the reputation, among actors, producers, writers for fan magazines and the women's weeklies of being alluringly cosmopolitan.

Sometimes when, always unexpectedly, he appeared at his brother's door, he wanted to have lunch at a traditionally Jewish restaurant on the still medieval-featured Rue Vieille-du-Temple. Over a delicious soufflé, which, they grinned, must contain kosher ham to make it so good, and in order to divert attention from melancholy topics, the two brothers talked about their mother, and laughed at the memory of her outbursts and foibles with great affection and despair, reminding each other of what a marvelous cook she was. They claimed they missed her cooking, and exclaimed, jokingly, and without nostalgia, in the next breath, "Thank goodness, no more. It would have killed us!" Yet they claimed that nothing compared with the dishes she made. Nothing in this Parisian quarter had even remote pretensions to her Lithuanian Jewish cooking. Nostalgically, they talked of her Passover *kneidlach* as large as tennis balls, fluffy and light, each concealing a brown "soul" of matzah and cinnamon and a dash of sugar in their center. The matzah meal for the *kneidlach* was made of regular matzah boards that she crushed between her palms, careless of the sharp fragments that scratched them, making them sting with pain for hours afterward, for nothing else, she claimed, could produce the right consistency. And after describing several of their favorite dishes in mouthwatering and nostalgic detail, they broke into laughter in the middle of the clamorous, winding, and narrow old street, reminding each other that they were in Paris, the culinary center of the world, and yet were talking exclusively of their mother's cooking.

One evening they went to a crowded Russian nightclub on the Left Bank, where the chicken Kiev they ordered swam in a sea of butter, and a soulful Russian baritone strolled from table to table, singing of loves lost and heartache to the romantic strumming of his balalaika. All at once, the mournful refrain became wild and joyous. Beautiful Russian gypsies appeared, black tresses flowing about their necks, shoulders pulsating and weaving to the rhythm of their dance. Then came the cossacks, clad in loose coats and astrakhan hats and boots, arms folded across their chests, hurling themselves zestfully into their crouching kicks with yells of joy as the music grew louder and wilder.

The performers had suddenly metamorphosed from soulful and romantically melancholy to unrestrainedly wild.

"At least, they're Russian. What are we? Not Lithuanian, not South African," Anne said.

"Tonight," Larry proclaimed "I'm Russian."

Throwing off his jacket, loosening his tie, tousling his hair so that his cowlick fell rapturously over his forehead, he suddenly shot up out of his seat and joined in the dance, squatting like a cossack, kicking and singing with the best of them, until he collapsed in helpless merriment on the floor.

The audience, the dancers, the musicians went wild. They thundered their applause.

"A true Russian soul," they cried, and toasted him with vodka, sending bottles to his table.

Robert, though he could not participate in the dancing, could share in the vodka. The two brothers became thoroughly sloshed.

7

Averting a Potential Scandal

In London there followed a period of gnawing boredom, with no work in sight. One morning Larry suddenly appeared at his brother's door with three friends. All were actors like himself, at least one of them already quite well known, none of them leading-man material, all of them resolved, like himself, to rent a car and drive across France into Italy, where they had heard that Orson Welles had sequestered himself. When they learned that Orson Welles had removed himself to another country they flew tamely home.

The next trip to Paris almost culminated in scandal. Totally unexpectedly, Larry knocked at his brother's door early one Sunday morning and, without removing his beautiful overcoat, slumped down on the hard camp bed that, with a small round table and two chairs, was all the furniture their single room contained, methodically emptied the contents of his pockets and threw them on the scruffy wool blanket— his wallet, his keys, several coins, a small bundle of francs, his cigarette case, and his ivory cigarette holder—almost as if these articles were symbolic of his confession, and unburdened himself of his story in a calm, if almost apologetically low voice.

That previous night, he said, he had attended a reception given by a very rich potential investor. Food and drink had been abundant. Extremely bored, he had drunk too much.

Even whisky had not helped to alleviate his restlessness and boredom, or his contempt for the "shitty money bags" as he privately (and sometimes not so privately) labeled his host and his friends. Glancing gloomily about, his bored gaze had rested speculatively upon the features of a pretty, petite young woman he had never seen before. He was told that she was the practically newly married latest wife of Robert Newton, a brilliant actor whose work everyone knew and admired. This actor was away on an American tour with the Old Vic, and since she had recently given birth, his wife had not accompanied him. That she was more than a little drunk was obvious, and also that she was feeling forlorn and abandoned, knowing that her husband was whoring and drinking in America. He had a great reputation for doing both, and people often speculated as to which activity he indulged in the most.

Larry winked at her conspiratorially. She smiled. Impulsively, he leaned over toward her and mouthed the words: "Let's get the hell out of here." Her eyes shone with excitement. She had practically thrown herself at him, he said.

That same evening they caught a flight to Paris and he took a suite for the weekend at the Georges V. They made love in a halfhearted and desultory way, for she did not appeal to him much, and he had only been excited by the glamour of bedding the wife of one of the most famous actors in Britain. Mostly, they had lain in bed drinking champagne and cognac.

In the middle of the night, he said, "she got the D.T.'s." He was terrified. She started shrieking and shuddering and vomiting. He did not know what to do, except that he could not abandon her in that state, and rushed her to the English hospital. "Thank goodness I had the wits to take her through the servant's entrance and pile her into a taxi to avoid being recognized by some prying English tourist. I'm not ready for that kind of publicity," he said, with a shudder. At the hospital, the doctor told him that she would have to remain there for at least a week. Well, he said, that was out of the question as far as he was concerned. He absolutely positively had to be in London on Monday morning. This meant that he absolutely had to be on the flight from Paris that afternoon. Luckily, she did not know anyone in Paris—except the couture houses, of course, but they did not count. But if some bloody reporter were to come snooping around, the scandal would be too ghastly. Newton was known to have a terrible temper. There would be a hideous divorce case and he would be named corespondent. He could not afford that. Not at this early stage in his career.

"Christ! What a bloody mess," Robert exclaimed.

"I know," said Larry. "I can't think why I had anything to do with her in the first place, that nasty, boring little bitch. Don't think I had such a great time in bed either. She's as frozen as a block of ice."

He shrugged, as if dismissing the whole experience, and looked at his sister-in-law speculatively. If his voice, when he spoke, held some appeal in it, his expression did not. He seemed coolly confident that she would do anything he requested.

He desperately needed to return to London immediately, he said. The woman would have to return to London by Wednesday at the very latest. Her husband was due to return to London on Wednesday night. He had tried to get a plane reservation for her on Wednesday morning, but unfortunately there just weren't any seats available before Thursday. So he had booked a first-class cabin for her on the Tuesday afternoon ferry. He wanted his sister-in-law to see to it that she caught the boat train to Calais on Tuesday morning.

It was impossible to refuse his request. Tamely, she accompanied Larry to the hospital. What followed seemed to her like some play she was watching.

Lying on her bed in her private room, for which Larry had paid, encased in the flowers that he had ordered, the woman looked wan and ill and very young and vulnerable. She could not have been more than twenty-five or twenty-six, and had the English prettiness of a country rose, yet it seemed to be a stagnant kind of prettiness that would not bloom for long, but would dry out soon enough. Her hair was long, extremely fine, and a naturally wavy brown. Her eyes, though reddened and dulled with pain and fright, were hazel and round, and her mouth was childishly petulant.

Pathetically, she pleaded with Larry not to leave her. Each was stubborn and petulant. The "darlings" with which they addressed each other flew about the room like feathers from a split cushion.

He was adamant. So was she. But he won in the end and left.

The moment he left, the "darlings" that had flown back and forth between Larry and the young woman turned into wasp's stings.

"Is he a faggot—a homosexual?" the young woman asked angrily.

His sister-in-law was extremely startled by the question.

The next day she accompanied the woman on the boat train to Calais. There the young woman made quite a scene, demanding that she accompany her to England, which the latter could not do without a visa. Waiting to embark, beautifully dressed in a flared chocolate brown Dior coat and matching fur hat, soft brown leather boots, her pretty hands encased in a fur muff, the young woman became all the more wobbly and hysterical as the minutes passed. When a stout, middle-aged North Country businessman with a florid complexion and calculating gray eyes approached and asked whether he could help her, she introduced herself as the wife of the famous actor and, almost sobbing, told him how very ill she had been in Paris. He offered to take care of her—provided she have a drink with him, leaving no doubt that he meant more. She readily agreed. He put his arm about her waist and they walked off to the ferry.

Filled with shock and bewilderment, his sister-in-law wondered why the young woman had asked her whether Larry was homosexual. "It's out of sheer nastiness and jealous gossip, that's all," she thought, dismissing the notion. She counted several homosexuals in Paris and in London among acquaintances, and Larry did not seem to her in any way like them. They were as fragile as blades of grass in a puff of wind. Larry was not like that, not nearly as vulnerable. At least, that was how she saw him then.

She found herself wishing that the channel would be choppy and the young woman would throw up all over her escort and her Dior coat.

They did not hear from Larry for several weeks and assumed that he was working on a new film. Then one morning, they were astounded to receive a postcard from him, dated the previous day and bearing a French postage stamp.

"The little bastard," Robert grinned affectionately, "Just look at his address: Maison d'arrêt, Grasse. That's on the French Riviera. I'll bet he's staying at some fancy hotel. Would he be staying anywhere else! What's he doing in France, I wonder?"

The contents of the postcard soon enlightened them.

"I've been arrested and flung into the jail here," it read. "Can you get me out?"

Robert knew a publisher who was a friend of one of the ministers. A telephone call made by the minister's office provided the assurance that Larry would be released in his brother's custody.

He caught the night train to Nice and from there took a bus up the steep green-grass hill at the crest of which perched the lovely little perfumed town of Grasse.

He found Larry still incarcerated in the local jail. It was lunchtime. He occupied a private cell, where he was enjoying a thick and juicy *bifteck*, a fresh green salad, and a bottle of *vin de Provence* served to him on a silver tray at a clean, white-cloth-covered table by one of the guards.

"*Salut!*" Larry cried with a laconic grin, raising his glass in a toast. "*À la Santé. Tchin-tchin.*"

He had become great friends with one of the local Mafia heads who was serving time in the same jail for robbing a bank of several millions of francs, which he had stashed away—somewhere—while serving out his sentence, after which he intended to pick up his loot and live the good life. In jail, he was jovially enjoying every good thing—excellent meals, visits from his wife, his children, his mistress, and his thugs—that money could buy, except freedom. He had taken a fancy to Larry from the first, for Larry knew how to ingratiate himself and to assert his charm when he wished to impress anyone, and kept the man in stitches every day with his comic impersonations of grave magistrates and whores, and his fund of lewd songs and jokes. These were funny even in translation, for he knew next to no French, and he had topped his performance with a crass, suggestive, and filthy imitation of an Englishman trying to solicit a very proper Frenchwoman whom he mistook for a prostitute.

The telephone call from the minister had worked like a charm. Larry was released upon the payment of a token fine.

"*Laurence Harvey, bonne chance!* We shall miss you!" his Mafia friend cried heartily in a low, thick, rough rumble reminiscent of the popular French actor Jean Gabin when Larry went to say good-bye. "Will you not consider joining my little company? *Zut alors!*" I can make you a millionaire. . . ."

Politely, Larry declined the offer, explaining that his ambition lay elsewhere.

Even the warden watched him leave with genuine regret. He had been an amusing diversion from the tedium of prison routine.

Rudolph showed up just as the two brothers were leaving the jail. He too had been summoned by Larry, who had recruited all the help he could get.

This was not the first time that Robert had met Rudolph. In an impulsively generous mood, Larry had taken his brother and sister-in-law for drinks in the bar of the Georges V on a previous visit to Paris and introduced them to Rudolph. Rudolph, in a gesture of shyly ecstatic courtesy, had invited them to sign their names in his official visitors' book under, he said, the signature of the Duke of Windsor who he said was a frequent patron. The two of them found this signal honor highly amusing, for growing up in South Africa, they had seen him in the newsreels as the Prince of Wales and briefly as king, and knew all about his naïve visit to Hitler.

Rudolph was a man perhaps in his early fifties, a Hungarian from Budapest who had been living in Paris since the mid-1920s, a loner without close friends or relatives. Having learned his profession in the bistros and the minor and then major hotels of the city, he had graduated to the position of head barman at the Georges V some ten years earlier. A shy and lonely man, in appearance tall and gray haired, with diffident pale blue eyes, often downcast, and a pale, wan look, who spoke French with his native Hungarian accent, he had instantly been fascinated by Larry when, one evening, the latter had shown up in the bar of the Georges V. Larry had been in one of his most expansive and happy moods. Lusting to be among the wealthy, he had landed in the bar of the Georges V, and there, finding himself in the presence of a company of well-tailored men and women sparkling with diamonds, had swiftly moved to dominate center stage, giving one of his most gallant performances, commanding everyone's admiring attention and greatly impressing Rudolph, with whom he had become instant friends.

Ever since that evening, Rudolph had practically worshipped him and would have done anything for him and his approbation extended to Robert. He could come and have a drink on the house whenever he chose. Rudolph was always shyly delighted to see him, and sometimes, to save money, Robert would lunch on a cognac and the bowl of peanuts at the bar under Rudolph's benevolently approving eye.

Instantly, upon receipt of Larry's postcard, Rudolph had driven down to Grasse to rescue him from jail. To him this had been only the least of the services he could render his young idol.

The complicated business of extricating Larry's rented car from the authorities took up most of the afternoon. Toward evening, the three men—Larry, Rudolph, and Robert—drove down to Nice for dinner.

Rudolph knew Nice well, and also all the head barmen in the great hotels everywhere in Cannes, Menton, Monte Carlo, Cap d'Antibes, and as far as Saint-Tropez. Diffidently, he asked where they would like to dine, suggesting the grand Hôtel Negresco facing the promenade in Nice, where he knew Albert, the head barman. Instead, Larry chose an exquisite seafood restaurant he had heard someone describe, at the very water's edge in Nice. Over freshly caught fish, so fresh that the fragrance of the sea still clung to them, with the sea breeze rustling the white tablecloth and gently ruffling their hair, and the sight of distant yachts like motionless toys lying in port in neighboring Cannes, Larry told them how he had come to land in jail in Grasse.

It began, he said, because, sick of the measly parts he was getting, tired of being just a workhorse minting money for others, he had decided once and for all to go in search of Orson Welles, who, he had learned, was now actually making a film in Italy. Driving his rented car through Grasse (he had made the detour to Grasse out of sheer curiosity to see it, he confessed) rolling down the steep road out of Grasse, he had been forced to—had almost smashed into, but definitely barely touched, he swore—the bumper of a large limousine bearing a French license plate and driven by a man in uniform whom he described as "some vicious French bugger of a chauffeur."

The limousine had forced him to stop. Leaping out of it, the chauffeur, releasing a battery of French curses ("I assume they were French curses," Larry said, "they sounded like French curses, and pretty filthy ones, describing the anatomy of foreigners, especially Englishmen in graphic detail") had come flying at him with his fists clenched and at the ready.

"You bloody fucking fascist," Larry said he had yelled.

"Bastaard," the chauffeur had yelled back, finding this an unbearable insult, "English pig!

"Nazi Schweinehundt!"

The next thing Larry said he remembered was seeing "the damned French bastard" heading for him with his right fist swinging. He had swung back with his own right fist. A policeman appeared. Unfortunately, Larry said, as he swung his fist landed on the policeman's chest.

"Being a foreigner, I was the one who landed in jail," he explained morosely.

The three of them could not help laughing.

Abandoning all hope of meeting Orson Welles, Larry decided to drive his rented car to Paris, where he had to return it before taking his flight to London. Rudolph wished to remain in Nice for several days. The two brothers drove back through the night, stopping only at dawn along the road for breakfast where, in a tiny café in a village, one or two early risers were already enjoying their traditional glass of cognac, knocked back in one gulp, it seemed, and a café au lait slowly sipped out of a wide cup.

They felt very close that morning, telling each other all their hopes, dreams, and ambitions. Robert told Larry that he meant to continue to write and that, fortunately or otherwise, his language was English and that was why he wished to live in England. For, not unlike many brought up within the fold of the former British Empire, he had the deepest admiration for English culture and English civilization, and felt that he was part of it as, in his own way, Larry did too. Even Nehru, India's first prime minister and disciple of Gandhi, although he had fought the British tooth and nail and had been jailed for his views, Robert told him, had confessed to a secret longing to have been a British member of Parliament.

"Damn it, Larry," he pleaded, "you *must* be able to get me *some* kind of lousy job. Don't you realize my terrible dilemma? If I were in South Africa, I'd be in jail, just for opposing apartheid. Now I'm a stateless alien. Not even a Displaced Person. I'm not Lithuanian. I'm not a South African citizen. I'll take any job. I'll do anything. Besides, I could be of some use to you, too."

Larry promised fervently to do what he could. Then he talked about his own future.

"I'm going to learn as much as I can in England, gain more experience on the stage and screen there. Then, when the time's ripe, I'll try to make my way to Hollywood. I'll never settle for less than the best," he vowed. "It's going to be all or nothing for me."

"Quite right," Robert agreed heartily. "Never compromise. But you absolutely have got to cultivate your mind. You absolutely must develop a broad intellectual background. In other words, read, read, read and think."

Larry said, irritably, "I haven't done so badly, considering how hard I've had to fight for everything I've achieved in this vile culture where the moguls rule everything."

It was obvious that he felt deeply wounded by what seemed to him to be Robert's lack of respect for his intellectual grasp and his talent. It was as if his brother still viewed him as the empty-headed schoolboy who was always playing truant.

They reached Paris in silence, each encased in his own reflections.

Larry caught the next flight to London, filled with refreshed resolve and determination to succeed and holding an uneasy grudge against Robert for appearing to denigrate his intellect. He resolved to live his own life in his own way, and to let no one tell him what to do, as he told one of his cronies, without explaining why he had come to this conclusion. Paris meant, to him, good food and the presence of beautiful things, so different from drab old London, but London represented his real life, the actor and maverick he really was, without the need to pretend that he was anything else.

When the studio offered him a part in another B film, he almost threw the script in the producer's face. Chafing and fuming with frustration, he hardly knew what to do with himself.

"This ugly world has really got me in its grip," he wrote to Nahum. He felt certain that he could rely on Nahum always to have faith in him. "Robert keeps breathing fire down my neck, demanding that I help him settle in England. How can I? He has become completely irrational. I myself am being exploited to the hilt. I have no idea where my next role is coming from. So far, I've been cruelly and disastrously treated by this exploitative system we all live in, and I can see no end in sight."

To make matters worse, he was threatened with eviction from his flat for failing to pay his rent.

He had begun smoking a joint every now and then. It gave no comfort and he did not much like it, but preferred his cigarettes held in his sophisticated new black holder.

In the midst of his despair, he was unexpectedly offered a good part in a film called *There Is Another Sun*. He was thrilled. For Hermione Baddeley was included in the cast.

8

Enter Hermione Baddeley, "A Rather Splendid Old Girl"

"She's a rather splendid old girl," was how Laurence Harvey defined Hermione Baddeley. He called her "Totie," as all her friends did.

He was often quoted as saying that he had a "mother fixation." Hermione was not much younger than his mother. She took him under her wing and was good to him as Ella Skikne, his real mother, had never really been able to be.

His relationship with Hermione Baddeley was sexual, but they also needed each other for many other reasons. Born in 1906, one of four daughters of a French singer and an English composer, Hermione Baddeley made her acting debut at the age of twelve and became a leading comedy star at the age of sixteen.

Rather on the plain side, but fun loving and lively, the young star had married and later divorced the rich but philandering David Tennant, the younger son of Lord Glenconner, the head of Imperial Chemical Industries. In her London mews house, during her marriage, she had met leading poets and entertained the Prince of Wales prior to his torrid affair with Mrs. Simpson. At one stage, she double-dated with Lady Elizabeth Bowes Lyon, with whom her brother-in-law, the reigning Lord Glenconner, was very much in love. Lady Elizabeth married the duke of York and became queen.

Among the people she knew were the writer Virginia Woolf and Unity Mitford, the eccentric English aristocrat who fell in love with Hitler. She met the Nazi businessman Von Ribbentrop who was later hanged as a war criminal, and the British fascist leader Sir Oswald Mosley, to whom, unaware of his activities, she had almost lent two cars to transport his thugs to a fascist rally. One of her friends was

Rosa Lewis, reputedly the mistress of King Edward VII, who ran an exclusive hotel, called The Cavendish, dramatized in the very popular BBC series *The Duchess of Duke Street*.

Though Bohemian and pleasure loving by nature, Hermione returned to the stage after her divorce. A hardworking, consummate professional, a comedienne as well as a dramatic actress, and a musical comedy star, she was much sought after by directors and producers. Always active, she had entertained the British forces for ENSA during World War II and was briefly married to a war hero.

The irony of having kept company, socially at least, with Nazis and Nazi sympathizers, and, a few short years later, taking a Jewish lover seemed not to have occurred to her. As a further irony, Sir Alfred Beit, the neurotic robber baron who had, with Cecil Rhodes, founded the De Beers consortium that has ruled and exploited the diamond and gold output of South Africa, was her admirer—perhaps even her lover—and wanted to marry her.

Following her brief second marriage, Hermione fell in love with Francis de Moleyns, a handsome, alcoholic, totally indigent and totally irresponsible Irishman, the younger brother of the very wealthy Lord Ventry, who had given up helping his hopelessly impractical brother. Full of bright ideas, de Moleyns had proposed opening a mussel and seafood bar shortly after the war's end, with Hermione as the chief investor. Initially, the enterprise was very successful. In grim postwar London, the mussels, not rationed, particularly delicious to eat because they were kept in brine and fed on oatmeal, attracted London society and kept the seafood bar profitable and humming. Or, at least, it would have been, except for the fact that de Moleyns kept taking money from the till. What was the point of making money, he said, if not to spend it?

When the young actor now familiarly known as Laurence Harvey appeared in her life, de Moleyns had gone to Ireland to establish the Irish Tie Company, later to be expanded, its founders hoped, into the Acquaintance Tie Company, in partnership with Douglas Sutherland and Hermione Baddeley and mainly to be financed by the actress. If any ties were actually manufactured, they were never sold. Mainly, in Ireland, de Moleyns went salmon fishing and drank.

After *House of Darkness*, Sutherland and his wife Moyra continued a relationship with the young actor they called Larry, who seemed so lonely and friendless. Out of pity, and because he appeared to cling to them, they took him to one of the luncheons Hermione loved to give at her house. Engrossed in discussing the tie business, they did not notice the spark of mutual interest and excitement ignited between the two.

Hermione was living in a charming jewel of a house she owned off Chester Square—her pink house, she called it—and de Moleyns was still doing—nobody quite knew what—in Ireland.

The very young actor and the much older woman began their affair practically on the first day of appearing in *There Is Another Sun*. In this film, Hermione Baddeley plays a fortune-teller at a fairground, while Laurence Harvey, who has the second lead, plays an innocent and trusting young boxer who almost ruins his own promising career to help his criminal friend, played by Maxwell Reed.

To Hermione working in this film meant the chance to make some quick money. She had just been starring in a revival of Noel Coward's *Fallen Angels*, a comedy playing at the Ambassadors Theater in the West End. It had become a smash hit, breaking all previous box office records, with every seat booked for years ahead, but its run ended abruptly when her costar, Hermione Gingold, decided to quit and no replacement was available.

The film was shot at the studios at Shepperton, a pleasant area not far from London. Harvey made it his business to seek out Hermione Baddeley on the very first morning on the set. He found her in a tent trying on wigs for her part as an amusement park gypsy fortune-teller. On his best behavior, acting very much the suave gentleman, he stood at the entrance to the dressing room, coolly watching her.

She saw his reflection in the mirror. The studio's new hairdresser arrived with wigs for her to try on. He did not know who she was.

The lady, Harvey sternly informed him, was Miss Hermione Baddeley; one of Britain's finest comedians.

Brushing the dazed hairdresser aside, he strode forward, offered her his arm and the two of them strode off together to get a drink at the local pub.

Hermione was a small woman, a great deal shorter than Larry's lofty six feet. He made her feel quite tiny, she writes in her autobiography, *The Unsinkable Hermione Baddeley*, as, confidently, he took her arm and marched her forward at his side. This, she writes, was how they always walked together.

Throughout the film he paid scant attention to Susan Shaw, the pretty young actress who played his leading lady, but spent all his free time with Hermione and the older members of the cast. She found him good company and very sophisticated for a young man of, she assumed, twenty-six, but in reality was twenty-one. Not only was he extraordinarily good-looking, but also, she noted, star material and on his way to the top, a very good actor, much too good to be acting in an insignificant B picture like *There Is Another Sun*. He was a hard worker and always gave his best, never holding back, never succumbing to boredom; playing the naïve innocent working-class youth, soaring far above the usual reach of a B picture star.

Sutherland claims that Larry moved into Hermione's house two days after their first meeting. This is not what Hermione asserts in her autobiography. When filming ended for the day, she writes, he fell into the habit of driving her home, dismissing her own chauffeur and car, helping her into his small Morris saloon car, which he treated like some precious object. Outside London and its traffic, speeding dizzily, full of laughter and teasing fun, he took corners on two terrifying wheels, but she always delighted in what she called his high spirits. Often they dined together, either in some fashionable nightclub or at her house. On his paycheck of £35 a week, he could hardly have afforded to dine at some expensive nightclub himself, let alone pay for her dinner, yet he told several interviewers that the generous manager of the ultrafashionable Caprice, ever ready to assist aspiring actors, was so impressed with him that he allowed him credit for months and even years. More realistically, Hermione Baddeley writes that in her usual careless way she always signed the checks, and did not mind doing so because she was accustomed to paying the check for indigent friends. She does concede, however, that when they began living together he contributed what he could for household expenses out of his meager paycheck. He was also, as she seemed not to know, sending a little of his pay to his parents, together with regular letters, a habit he continued all his life.

The first act in their intimate relationship began, she writes, after they had dined at Les Ambassadeurs, a popular nightclub of the time. Escorting her to her door, he told her, ruefully, that he had locked himself out of his flat and could not find his key. Whether the story of his missing key was true or false, or they were just playing a little game of seduction, it is a fact that he had been threatened with eviction from his flat for failing to pay his rent. Her son was away. She claims that she invited him to stay in her son's room for the night—she often had people staying for the night, or the month—and that later he slipped into her bedroom and literally flung himself onto her. She was feeling too warm and cozy to resist and they became lovers. Almost immediately, he proposed marriage. He seemed to have the old-fashioned notion that if a gentleman seduced a woman he had to marry her. He was convinced that he had seduced her, and he was in dead earnest. She merely laughed at the notion. However, she let him move into one of her bedrooms, although they spent most nights in her bed. Another bedroom was given to his stand-in.

Everywhere they went, she writes, they had fun. She introduced him to all the many influential people she knew, and he began to copy their habit of greeting men as well as women with fluttery kisses and in language speckled with "darlings." Yet their fights soon began. In the flighty thespian world they inhabited, he sometimes took her to parties where all the men were gay. Once, having drunk a great deal of brandy, he struck her in a fit of jealous rage for flirting with a sailor. She fled from the party, but he followed her home and beat her up. Sobering up the next morning, seeing the bruises he had inflicted on her face, he begged her forgiveness and sent for three (!) doctors to patch her up.

They reconciled and, for a while, were happy. But not for long.

One evening a quarrel began as they were leaving her house to go out. He climbed into his car, which he kept parked in the mews beside her house, started the engine and headed straight for her. He might have injured her seriously if she had not leapt out of his way.

She attributed his black moods and his bouts of violence not to frustration and rage against his dependence on her, or the fact that she was old and plain and he had nowhere else to turn unless he chose the path of male whoredom, but to what he had told her was his "Slavonic" heritage. He had told her he was a Slav, and she believed him. His youth and good looks enchanted her, as did the power he seemed to exude over young women who flocked to him at parties and stared them out of countenance in restaurants. In the face of this keen competition, he had chosen only her. She seems to have loved the fact that he was so possessive, that his nature was so volatile, pouring out energy, that he was so easily aroused to explosiveness, especially, she believed, when drinking brandy. She was not even disillusioned when he antagonized her friends or called her filthy names or mocked her for being old and ugly. There are men and women who are never disillusioned by the most dreadful behavior of their lovers, and Hermione appears to have been one of them. She seems to have accepted being physically abused by him with some resignation, even with pride, for it seemed to make her more desirable and she writes that she enjoyed being good to him, and that it gave her pleasure to learn that, years later, he told one of his wives that she had been the first person in London who was kind to him. Generally, however, they seemed to have gotten along quite amicably. Even her son, who was in the army at the time, got on well with him whenever he came home on leave.

He did not strike her as being in any way English, however, but she decided that he had a continental style, and therefore that he was authentically European, although she provides no evidence for this assumption. Her attitude could only have reinforced his decision to be flamboyantly different. Yet to her he confessed much of the truth: that he had been born in Lithuania and was brought to South Africa as a child, about his army service, and how passing the Harvey Nichols store in Knightsbridge he had been inspired to change his name to Harvey. This change in name, he explained, was made only because no one could pronounce the name Skikne.

Only, he told her that he had changed the name Larushka, given to him at birth, to Larry, short for Laurence.

This was the first time the name Larushka made its appearance.

Clearly, the fact that he had been born in Lithuania—by sheer accident of birth—lay on him like a shroud, sometimes smothering him and weighing him down. Sometimes he felt like a fraud, but he knew that the British film and stage establishment, however grudgingly, accepted him only on condition that he label himself a foreigner. To be Lithuanian was not altogether exotic, but he tried to make it so, to use it to his advantage. If he was not going to be accepted as an Englishman, if he was going to be called "foreign," he was going to rename himself and push his "foreignness" to the utmost limit.

He appeared not to have told her much about his childhood, but while showing her some of his glossies one evening, a family photograph chanced to fall out of the pile. It was a posed old studio photograph of two very pretty young women stationed behind an older, rather plump blond woman in a dark dress and a fashionably short, straight haircut seated with three little boys clustered about her. The youngest was a young, bullet-headed, sturdy blond five year old.

Angrily, Larry had snatched the photograph from her and, in a rage, almost struck her. She realized, she wrote, why. The women looked foreign, poor, probably Jewish. In fact, they looked much like the denizens of villages anywhere, circa 1932.

Yet he relied on her friendship and almost confided in her—at least about his brother Robert. Shortly before Robert left England for France, Larry had introduced Hermione at a pub. All Larry had told him was that she was a good friend. At forty-four, she looked, to Robert's twenty-four-year-old eyes as practically an old woman and Larry did not possess the artfully dependent manners of a gigolo. At that meeting, Larry had complained that his life was so unsettled that he could not give him his own telephone number—he was rarely at home. Instead, he gave him Hermione's telephone number, saying that in the event of any emergency, Robert could call this number and Hermione would relay his message. Later, this was to have its repercussions. Rumors of Hermione's new liaison had filtered through to Ireland and de Moleyns returned unexpectedly one Sunday morning to confront his two-timing mistress. Larry and several guests were in the house drinking gin and tonic when, totally sloshed, de Moleyns suddenly appeared, headed straight for Larry and dealt him a punch that sent him reeling. His second blow hit one of the guests. Undeterred, he picked up a full bottle of whisky and headed for Larry again. This time, however, Larry was ready for him and landed a blow that knocked the Irishman senseless for a time. When he recovered, he picked himself up and departed with, to Hermione's regret, his family's silver, which he had left with her for safekeeping. Thus ended the great venture of the Irish Tie Factory.

After that incident, Hermione Baddeley's life underwent a radical change. Despising the puppy fat clearly evidenced in his pictures, Larry had taken to strict dieting, and he made her throw her chocolate cakes, trifles, and cream out of the refrigerator and, by his decree, eat chicken, fish, and burned toast, and sip dry white wine with her meals instead of other fattening beverages. Her figure underwent a sea change, from flabby to sleek. This pleased her very much.

Burned toast and blackened potato skins were Laurence Harvey's favorite hors d'oeuvres. He loved good (expensive) things and worked hard in order to acquire them, and these included gourmet foods. At this stage he had not yet become a stringent dieter living, as he did later, on practically nothing—once on a diet of lemons and water—and made a determined effort to learn about delicacies and cooking and the finest wines. Above all, clothes were becoming an abiding passion: the perfectly tailored suit, the finest custom-made shoes and shirts and ties. Without being a dandy, or devoting himself to gazing at his reflection in the mirror—he seemed to take himself for granted as he was—his apparel had to be perfect.

What both he and Hermione most shared in common was a love of parties, and they were invited everywhere. One memorable weekend was spent at Megginch Castle, the home of her friends. Despite her trepidations, Larry appeared to feel quite at ease there, melding so well with the wealthy guests that he seemed to the manner born. There was a grouse shoot, which he was invited to join. Coolly, he did. She was certain that he would miss his grouse and hit his host or a beater instead, but she had not counted on his experience; he had learned to shoot in the South African army, and more than passed muster in the field.

There Is Another Sun was a quirky little film that did surprisingly well at the box office, but after it there came no other offer of work. It was a terrible time for him. He developed stomach problems, complained of relentless constipation, and took irrigation treatments every week with his agent paying his medical bills. He ran up alarming large bills at his tailor's and for wine. When the publicity department of Associated British organized a cocktail party to introduce the organization's chief executives to their contract players, Larry tried to calm his nerves with so many vodkas that he was too sloshed to be introduced to the chairman and fell flat on his face on the carpet at his feet. At least, that is what he *said* happened!

He was not the first actor to get sloshed, although perhaps one of the very few to fall flat on his face at the chief executive's feet. If this in fact happened, this may also have done him some harm, for he was next cast in another insignificant B picture titled *A Killer Walks* in which he tries to frame his brother for murdering their grandmother, a crime he himself committed.

He was miserable, getting nowhere, he felt. To make matters worse, Associated British Pictures again threatened to drop the option on his contract and, in a pique, he tore up his contract, determined to make it on his own. In order to make a splash in the tabloids, he bought a white Chrysler with borrowed money, and drove it about ostentatiously with its top down while smoking a long cigarette fixed to a long holder. Waiting for the good parts to come, he suffered his third bout of flu that winter, which left him extremely weak, and he might not have survived but for Hermione's nurturing care.

Then in May 1951 he chanced to read a report that Basil Dean, still a leading producer, was planning to stage a revival of *Hassan* by James Elroy Flecker, a play he had produced in 1923, and Larry became frantic to win a part in it. Hermione Baddeley knew Basil Dean well. He had made her a star when she was still only fifteen. This new production was to be a contribution to the Festival of Britain.

Hermione introduced them and Dean consented to audition Larry. Taking his audition extremely seriously, he memorized a chunk of the play's sentimental, romance-drenched dialogue. Years later, he still remembered how nervous and drained he had felt at his audition. This, he said, had gone almost as badly as his first audition in Johannesburg. Basil Dean, he explained, was considered the "Frankenstein" of the theater. It was one of those rare days of sunshine in London when he entered the Palace Theatre for his audition, and he was blinded by the darkness inside. Groping his way to the stage, he tripped over an ashtray, which rolled down the stage over the footlights and into the orchestra pit with a tremendous crash. Basil Dean was not visible, but he kept mumbling apologies until commanded to shut up. Then a voice from the gallery told him to get on with the audition. It was almost, he said, like hearing the voice of God.

He had rehearsed the role of Rafi, king of the beggars.

"Now that the night before our day is ending, and the Wolf's Tail is already brushing the eastern sky; now that our plot is ready, our conspiracy established, our victory imminent . . . ," he intoned in a voice barely rising above a hoarse croak. He had rehearsed the lines a million times, but was so shaken with nervous tension that he forgot them and had to recite them from the script (he said). When he finished, he heard a curt "Thank you very much" from the invisible man in the stalls.

Yet perhaps things were not as desperate as he described them, perhaps his account was somewhat embellished, for the audition was judged very successful and he was given the choice of one of two parts. He chose the part of Rafi.

The play was staged at London's Cambridge Theatre. Unfortunately, what had charmed the audiences in 1925 failed to stir the audiences of 1951. The play was a flop and closed quickly, but the critics were kind, especially to him. William Glynn Jones wrote of the young actor's appearance with his leading lady: "And Rafi and Pervaneh, the lovers doomed to a day of bliss and protracted torment and death at the end of it, yearn and suffer with a white-hot brightness. . . . Laurence Harvey and Hilda Simms are superlatively good as these two characters who usurp the interest in the second half of this strange, disturbing, voluptuous, intense, and at times heart breakingly beautiful work."

Good reviews notwithstanding, he could find no work except now and then in tiny bit parts, and this must have contributed to his black moods, his excessive drinking, and his bouts of uncontrollable violence against Hermione.

Eager to snatch at any straw, he gladly accepted a small part in the play *Uprooted*, directed by Eric Uttley, who had worked with him in Manchester. The play was staged in a "Sixpenny Theatre" (the audience paid sixpence per person) outside London, and the actors were paid eight pounds a week. The Sixpenny Theatre featured experimental plays by both unknown and relatively new playwrights and did attract an audience, but the play Larry was in closed quickly.

Uttley, who was one of the directors of this theater, offered him another part in a new play. The cast included several influential homosexual actors who, pretending friendship but bent on revenge because the handsome young actor was too obviously ambitious or had rejected their advances, kept feeding him drinks every night. As a result he was always half sloshed at rehearsals the next morning and they complained to Uttley that he did not know his lines.

He had shot headlong and heedlessly into a group of homosexual men whom he openly scorned as inferior as actors and paid for it by being dropped. Tearfully, he pleaded with Uttley to give him back his role, and although Uttley knew how he worked—that he needed to feel his way through the lines until they flowed from him naturally and that he would have been word perfect when the curtain went up—the opposition against him was too strong. Harvey felt extremely dejected. Since he had given up his contract with Associated British, he had counted desperately on the £8 per week the play would bring him. In a moment of confidence, he had told Uttley that he was Lithuanian (and Slav). Lithuanians, Uttley decided, were too emotional. So were actors. In his totally inexperienced eyes, Larry personified a combination of both.

Now Harvey felt certain that the whole world was against him, and that only Hermione believed in him.

The first months of 1951 were as empty of promise as had been the closing months of 1950. He was back in London, in Hermione's house, almost totally dependent on her, drinking and sleeping most of the day when the telephone call came from Robert in Paris. Hermione answered the telephone. Would she call Larry to the telephone, Robert demanded. No, she replied coldly, he was sleeping and could not be disturbed. But, Robert said, this is an emergency. At this point, Larry, who was not sleeping, picked up the receiver. Frantically, Robert told him that they could no longer remain in

Paris. Could Larry make a last-ditch effort to ask someone he knew to give him a job in England? "Leave Larry alone," came Hermione's cold command. She had been listening in to their conversation and had taken the receiver out of Larry's hand. His temper flaring, Robert cried, "Fuck you, you stupid old hag." He heard the click of the receiver being banged down and the line went dead. Hermione was not, it appears, as frivolous or carefree as she presented herself to be in her autobiography but, rather, steely willed and ruthlessly possessive. Larry was totally dependent on her and she let him know it in no uncertain terms. Besides, surrounded by hatred and envy everywhere, as he felt he was, he saw her as the only person who believed in his talent and was good to him. He may also have had a deeper motive for his passivity: he did not want his brother to know how he lived. He did not want his family to know. In his regular letters to his parents he played the earnest, devoted son, struggling to earn a living and promising to support them in great comfort all their lives as soon as he was able. And he *was* that character, too.

"Robert is absolutely impossible," he salved his conscience by writing to Nahum. "He doesn't understand that I am powerless to help him."

And Nahum replied, "I understand what you mean."

The brothers, when tempers and heated feelings cooled, maintained a tenuous correspondence through the years, but never met again.

Larry's dismissal from the play at the experimental theater and total lack of prospects left him feeling so low that to console him Hermione took him to Cornwall for a vacation, letting him drive her expensive Chrysler at his usual breakneck speed through the narrow and winding roads. They settled in an old house in the little seaside resort of Par and there, by sheer chance, he saw Eric Portman, with whom he had starred in *Cairo Road*, and with whom, after their initial friction, he had become fast friends. Portman happened to be spending his weekends at a house in the village where, much to the villagers' disgust, males spent their weekends consorting with males, and Larry took to staying there, although never abandoning Hermione, whom he kept lovingly entertained with stories and jokes.

But he was broke, forced to rely solely on Hermione's generosity, unable to control his extravagance, and feeling so desperate that he had dark thoughts of selling his car and trying to get into the States with the meager proceeds. Short-tempered and nasty when his evil mood descended, he lambasted everyone with his sharp tongue. Yet in what seemed to him to be his darkest hour, an actor whom he had once angrily called a beat-up old ham (although he apologized for this later) recommended him to his wife, who happened to be the head of one of London's leading theatrical agencies. He arrived at her office with a bundle of his clippings, which he always displayed to everyone, and was rather miffed when she refused to look at them. Still, she liked his good looks, and his determined ambition, and arranged for a five-year contract for him with one of Britain's top agents.

This resulted in his role in *I Believe in You,* featuring Joan Collins, then a new young actress, also a RADA student who had left without waiting to graduate. In this movie, she plays a working-class girl gone bad and Larry plays her spiv boyfriend. Both received accolades for their performances. The film made Joan Collins a star. Harvey was especially praised for his authentic portrayal of a sensitive and yet tough working-class teenager who was a petty criminal. The lean days when walking back to his flat from RADA he had been given free Granny Smith apples by the barrow boy and had come to know the neighborhood spivs had paid off.

Joan introduced Larry to her parents who, she writes (at least in her first autobiography) "adored" him. He knew how to conduct himself when he wished: he was polite, gentlemanly, told extremely witty, if dirty, stories, and was (initially) considered a reliable escort for young Joan.

Larry—he had told her that he was Lithuanian and that his Lithuanian birth name was Larushka Skikne—dazzled her with his elegance, his jokes, bad language, the exotic cigarettes fixed in his long cigarette holder he chain-smoked, the vodka he endlessly drank, the dashing cars he drove, and the handsome and expensive suits he wore. She yearned to attain the lifestyle he personified. Patronizing but kind, he promised to educate her and take her under his wing, and this, she writes, he endeavored to do, for living well, he declared, was his credo: the best revenge. He tried to teach her how to dress, took her to the finest dressmakers, selecting beautiful dresses she could not afford, insisting she invest several hundred pounds that she did not possess on clothes, advising her, scornfully, to borrow the money, for she had to look soignée. She also provides a glimpse of the way he dressed at this period. The lapels of his suits were wide-shouldered and his shirts (undoubtedly silk) were pastel colored. He taught her about fine wines and how to translate a menu from the French and how to smoke and swear, but he would not physically touch her, although she appears to have wanted to lose her virginity to him. He told her that plumbers were more important than actors and that the best actors were children, who possess the secret of truth and honesty that adults cannot have. He took her to glamorous restaurants like the Caprice, and to Les Ambassadeurs, a private gambling club, where they dined on his favorite caviar and baked potato and danced all night. He knew everyone who was anyone. At La Rue, another club, he pointed out a notorious gangster who was also dining there.

No one had told her that he was living with Hermione Baddeley. Only when he invited her to a party at her house did she learn the truth.

That evening, Hermione, she writes, was drunk and practically accosted her at the door with biting sarcasm, literally tearing apart her looks, her dress, denigrating her talent. Scornfully inspecting her makeup, her own head of dyed red curls swaying drunkenly and a cigarette suspended from her painted red lips, she launched into vehement insults about the young actress's gauche appearance and lack of talent. When Joan Collins fled from the house in tears, she called raucously after her, yelling that like the rest of the young people she had no guts. Larry came running after her, assuring her that Hermione did not mean what she said and that he wanted the two of them to be friends. When, in tears, she refused to return to the house, he put her into a taxi, gave the driver a pound note, planted a kiss on her forehead and returned to the party. There, when Hermione taunted him for his bad taste in girls, he hit her with such ferocity that the other guests were riveted with shock. Yet everyone chose to ignore the incident, and went on talking and drinking as if nothing had happened.

Joan Collins concluded that Larry would never love her, that he loved no one but himself.

While dining at La Rue, they had been spotted by Maxwell Reed who callously abandoned his date, strode to their table, and asked to be introduced. Maxwell Reed, then a top star and idol of the young women in Britain, had been the star of *There Is Another Sun*. Growing up, Joan Collins had idolized this dashing Irishman. Unfortunately, the introduction led to unhappy consequences. Taking her to his house on some flimsy pretext, he gave her a large scotch and coke, which he had drugged, and a book of erotic drawings to look at while he went off to take a bath. She awoke to find that she had been raped. The relationship led to a brief, unhappy marriage.

She blamed Larry for failing to warn her against Maxwell Reed.

In her autobiography, Hermione Baddeley provides her own fairy-tale version of the first meeting between Joan Collins and Maxwell Reed.

Joan Collins was a young actress who had a crush on Larry. He did not reciprocate her feelings and wanted to find a good man for her. After consulting a sweetly sympathetic Hermione, both settled on Maxwell Reed and organized a party at Hermione's house at which the two young people were introduced. They got along splendidly that evening. When the two married, everyone was happy. The fact that the marriage quite speedily failed was not, she claims, due to any fault of Larry's or her own. They had arranged that first meeting meaning to be as kind as possible.

She did not mention—or chose to overlook—the abuse to which she had subjected the young Joan Collins at their first meeting.

9

Enter James Woolf, and Fame, Fortune, and Friendship

In the final months of 1951, fame and fortune made their entrance into Larry's life and stayed at his side for years. Their incarnation in the flesh was James Woolf.

James and his older brother, John, were the sons of C. M. Woolf, one of the shakers and makers of the British film industry in the 1920s and 1930s. He had formed General Film Distributors, which became the nucleus of the Rank Organisation. John, who had been educated at Eton and in Switzerland, joined his father's company in 1946 at the age of seventeen. James joined his father's company at fourteen, working in the publicity department. He moved to Hollywood, where he worked in Universal's publicity department and then served in the RAF during World War II. With his brother, he created Romulus Films and Remus Films, and both were the financial backers of Alexander Korda's London Films after his British Lion was placed in the hands of receivers. John was financially shrewd and had the brains for business. James (Jimmy, as his friends called him) was artistic and a man of exquisite taste and judgment, exceptional among producers in his love of craftsmanship, and ready to support a director instead of attempting to suffocate him. In appearance, he was less than plain; he was downright ugly. He had a harelip and he was also openly homosexual. Above all, he suffered deeply because he lacked the talent to write or direct. However, he had served his apprenticeship with the best—at Columbia in Hollywood—and had studied Columbia's production techniques. An obsessed moviemaker, he loved everything involved in moviemaking, from the wheeling and dealing to create a movie to the selection of the right actor to fill a role, and his greatest pleasure lay in spotting potential young protégés and furthering their careers, savoring their success and popularity as solace to his essentially solitary nature. He had marvelous taste in furniture, paintings, antiques, and filled his exquisitely appointed houses with Queen Anne chairs, Lutyens paintings, and other beautiful things. Fair and straightforward in his dealings, he was universally respected by actors and directors and everyone connected with making movies in England and Hollywood. People laughed fondly at his idiosyncracies—his suits were always rumpled, and he stubbornly wore heavy tweed in all climates, including that of Los Angeles in the summer. Acutely aware of being physically ugly, he once confided to a friend that he saw himself as Quasimodo, the deformed bell ringer in *The Hunchback of Notre Dame.* Yet, despite his physical handicaps, which might have destroyed a lesser man, he had great taste and faultless instincts in his judgment of talent and screen scripts. In the course of his life, he was to further the careers of Michael Caine, Terence Stamp, and Sarah Miles, among others. For this sad and unfulfilled man lived his life through the triumphs and glamour of his protégés.

None of them seemed to be as precious to him or as adored as Laurence Harvey.

As its first filmmaking venture, Romulus Films had produced *Pandora and the Flying Dutchman,* starring James Mason and Ava Gardner. This movie had been an artistic success if not financially ultraprofitable. Its next film, directed by the great John Huston, was *The African Queen,* with Katherine Hepburn and Humphrey Bogart.

James Woolf had just returned from Africa, where he had produced *The African Queen.* He was to go on to produce other beautiful films like *Moulin Rouge* but, in this period, Romulus Films' next venture was an unpretentious little movie titled *Treasure Hunt.* As a promotional gimmick, the Woolf brothers organized a well-publicized treasure hunt for easy-to-find goodies concealed all over London. Only film and stage stars were invited to participate. They went out in groups, or as couples, with a journalist from a popular newspaper accompanying each group, thus ensuring publicity for both the film and the participants. As a top star Hermione, who knew both Woolf brothers, was invited to participate, and when she asked whether she could bring her unknown friend Laurence Harvey along because he was so entertaining, the invitation was extended as a matter of course. The two of them were joined by a reporter from the *Daily Mirror.*

They had a great deal of fun catching up with the clues—one of them being to produce a hair plucked from Tallulah Bankhead's head. This reigning American star was appearing in a play in the West End.

As the first to reach the Caprice, where the treasure hunt ended, with all their loot, Hermione and Larry were named the winners. James Woolf was there, waiting to congratulate them with an embrace, a jeroboam of champagne, and a slew of photographers. Later, they dined with Woolf, and Harvey positively sparkled with witty remarks and spicy jokes. Stories, dialects, mimicry, jokes flowed in a sparkling torrent out of his mouth. "This guy came on like an absolute dynamo, telling stories marvelously as he does, doing impersonations, making wisecracks," Jimmy Woolf reminisced. He was enchanted, overwhelmed, enthralled.

Hermione writes that she does not believe they became lovers. Larry was always effusively kissing and hugging people—kissing the maître d's on both cheeks, flinging his arms around the managers of nightclubs, et cetera. This he did for fun, to amuse himself and to tease and shock the onlookers, she maintains. On the other hand, many people have claimed that the two men became lovers from the first day of their meeting, that it was reminiscent of, although not precisely like, the writer Oscar Wilde and his young protégé, Lord Alfred Douglas. Only, Harvey was talented, hardworking, and fiercely ambitious to succeed in his profession, whereas Lord Alfred had not been much more than a beautiful, indolent young man who triggered Wilde's public humiliation, imprisonment, and exile.

It is a fact that Jimmy Woolf was forever giving Larry gifts: a new car, an expensive ornament, a fine painting. He was a prodigious spender, a very witty conversationalist, who loved fine furniture and objets d'art and entertained lavishly in his magnificently accoutered flat in London's exclusive Grosvenor House. It is also a fact that they rented adjoining flats there, one in the name of Laurence

Harvey, the other in the name of Larry Skikne. It was obvious to all who knew him that Jimmy Woolf idolized Larry from that first meeting. He practically worshipped the young actor and offered him a contract before he had seen anything he had done.

Always looking for talented newcomers, Jimmy invited Hermione and Larushka Harvey, as he was now universally called, to the star-studded premiere of *The African Queen,* where he introduced them to older brother John. By this time both brothers had seen *There Is Another Sun* at a private viewing and recognized the young actor's star quality. They were also highly amused by his comic takeoffs of some of the leading film producers. Over their supper of smoked salmon at the Caprice, Jimmy Woolf offered the young unknown an impressively lucrative five-year contract, later to be succeeded by an equally impressive seven-year contract.

Naturally, Harvey was overjoyed. However, now a new wrinkle appeared. Hermione's brother-in-law Glen Byam Shaw had been appointed, with the actor Anthony Quayle, as codirectors of the Shakespeare Memorial Theatre at Stratford-upon-Avon. Curious to watch Hermione's new lover prove his metal as an actor, Shaw and his wife, Hermione's sister, Angela, also a leading actress (she appeared as the cook in the television serial *Upstairs, Downstairs* and also as a duchess in *The Buccaneers*) had been in the audience on the opening night of the ill-fated *Hassan.* Shaw had been impressed by the young actor's performance and now offered him a season at Stratford.

To act at Stratford-upon-Avon! It was like a dream come true. Shaw had been highly praised for his work at Stratford. Every actor would have given his soul for the opportunity to work under his direction. The fact that he was Hermione's brother-in-law, and that Hermione's affair with this young man had prompted her brother-in-law to see *Hassan* did not appear to count.

At Stratford, Larry's pay was to be a paltry £50 per week—no one was paid more, not even John Gielgud or Laurence Olivier—but he was quite ready to give up James Woolf's offer of a highly lucrative movie contract for the sake of playing on the most prestigious stage in the world. There was no money in that, James Woolf snorted upon hearing Larry's decision. Yet, as an artist—even an artist manqué—he understood. Instead of abandoning the young actor in a huff, as some other producer would surely have done, he offered to augment Larry's salary with money from Romulus. Af-

ter a successful season at Stratford, he told his highly practical
brother, the young actor would be worth a fortune.

Laurence Harvey, as he was now generally known, enjoyed a
hugely successful first season at Stratford. He played Tullus Aufid-
ius in *Coriolanus,* Malcolm in *Macbeth,* Castro in *Volpone.* His first,
and most notable role, however, in which *his* youth and freshness
could be exploited to the full, was that of Orlando, playing opposite
Margaret Leighton as Rosalind in *As You Like It.* There was chemistry
between the two of them from the start.

In this 1952 season at Stratford, he was especially singled out for
praise by the acid-tongued Kenneth Tynan, doyen of critics, whose
reviews could make or break an actor. James Woolf brought director
John Huston to see his performance as Orlando. In a happy haze of
success, Larry wrote to Nahum that his days were completely taken
up with the theater. He lived, ate, breathed, and slept Shakespeare,
he wrote, and the experience was invaluable. He had already been
approached, he boasted, to make a film with Katherine Hepburn, to
be directed by John Huston. And, torn between working at Stratford
for the next three years—he had been offered a three-year contract
there—or making films, he had shamefacedly chosen the latter because of his enormous debts, which had to be cleared. "Being from
a family of idealists makes one rather regret this course, because to
be the ideal and great actor it has been proved that Shakespeare and
playing Shakespeare is the only way," he wrote to his brother. Then
he made a strange admission: "I must confess I have had my moments of loathing it, but when one thinks about it one finds what a
great source of inspiration and truth there is in his writing."

His temperament and his extravagance pointed toward making
movies and money. His brothers had instilled in him an admiration
for culture, but he lacked the necessary will to sacrifice money for
art. Instead, he wrote proudly of his commitment to make a movie
titled *Beat the Devil* with Humphrey Bogart on location on the Island
of Capri. The movie was made, but not with Laurence Harvey.

"He was then the darling of the highbrows," Woolf enthused.
"They were all urging him to sign a five-year contract at Stratford
and telling him he could be the greatest young actor on the English

stage. And at that time he was terribly torn between doing that and acting in movies, and he debated with himself for five months before he signed our contract."

Hermione had asked her sister to look after him at Stratford—or perhaps to see to it that he did not stray too far from her. At first, he made a friend, Siobhan McKenna, another newcomer to Stratford, but a well-known and highly regarded actress of stage and screen. She was one of the very few women he respected in his life. While at Stratford, they often had dinner together. The rules at Stratford were strict. There was to be no drunkenness, no late nights, and behavior had to be exemplary and moral.

She said she felt like a schoolgirl at her Irish Catholic school again.

Nobody paid any attention to that rule, Harvey taught her with a cocky grin.

He was well aware that he was regarded as a newcomer, surfacing out of nowhere, and that the rest of the company hated his guts. How were they to know that, after a full day's intense rehearsal, he often spent hours into the night rehearsing his lines, quite belying the flamboyant image he cultivated of himself? When that image needed polishing, he did what he loved best, drinking to excess, living it up. He took the flame-haired Siobhan to restaurants where he taught her how to savor wine and they bought a loaf of bread, dug out the soft inside, fed it to the swans on the River Avon, topped the crust with butter and ham, and feasted on it, washed down with a bottle of wine.

At restaurants, he always tipped the waiter *before* being served, so as to ensure, he taught her, "marvelous" service. Impressing the wine steward was, he said, essential. One sent back the wine if one did not approve of its bouquet.

At Stratford people observed how much he adored showing off in public. One bright morning in June, clad in white trousers and a pale blue sweater, as reported in *John Bull*, he breakfasted on champagne at Stratford's oldest hotel, and relished every moment, not alone because he liked drinking champagne, but because he loved watching the tourists' faces when he ordered it. In those days, he served as his own public relations agent. He posed for his tailor's advertisements and received a discount for it. He wore elastic-sided boots (they were, he held, more elegant and comfortable than laced shoes). He bought embroidered waistcoats, silk shirts, drainpipe trousers. One producer told him, bluntly, that he was too good an actor to have to show off the way he did, but he would not have been Laurence Harvey if he had not shown off. It was not ambition alone that drove him. This was his personality.

Whenever he had a free day, he took off for London—and Hermione. Once, with what seems to be totally blinkered vision, he brought Siobhan along with him. They were not having an affair, he may have reasoned, they were just good friends. Hermione, however, thought differently. Who was this woman, she demanded, made coldly haughty with jealous rage. It was almost like a repetition of her first encounter with Joan Collins.

It appears that Hermione was ready to tolerate Harvey's sexual encounters with young men, even his violent rages and his beatings, but treated any friendship he enjoyed with young women as intolerable treachery.

In London, he was still tied to Hermione. He still allowed Hermione casually to pay the check when they went out nightclubbing or to suppers at the Caprice. Then he developed a new twist. Now and then his behavior became erratic, especially when he had drunk too much. She had been asked to bring him along to a dinner party at one of her influential society friend's houses because of his growing reputation as a brilliant young man. After a rather dull dinner, the guests had begun telling mildly risqué jokes, when Harvey, quite sloshed by then, broke into their tame anecdotes with a radiant grin and an outrageously filthy story.

Did he deliberately intend to shock them, or, feeling ignored, childishly attempt to assert himself, or was he drunk or, as Hermione seemed convinced, quite mad?

All the dinner guests walked out of the room. Their host threw Hermione and Larry out of his house.

She could fill the Café de Paris every night, but he could clear out a dining room in three minutes flat, Harvey grinned contritely on their way home.

She noticed a change in him, a new concentration on his appearance. He bought new suits, tailor made, naturally, to his detailed instructions, shirts of sheer silk, Lobb shoes, carefully selecting the proper ties to suit each outfit. He was still witty and fun to be with, and worried about her, unless he was drinking brandy. She believed it was the brandy that made him dangerous, wildly jealous, volcanic.

Following a quarrel in the car one night, realizing he had drunk too much brandy, she hurried out of the car to her back door, but just as she inserted her key, heard his car revving up and saw the car's headlights focused on her and the car heading straight at her. Shrinking back against the door in terror, she saw his face contorted in an awful grimace, and heard the screech of brakes as the car struck her legs.

She fainted. When she came to, he was holding her in his arms, his face wet with tears. He had gone mad, he wept, he had not known what he was doing. It had been due to his insane jealousy.

This time he called two doctors to examine her bruises and the injuries to her legs, and swore he would never do her any harm again.

He did not keep his promise. Drinking brandy at a party one night, he saw her talking to one of her men friends and brusquely interrupted their conversation. Fearing a scene, she hurried home in her car. But she was furious. Seeking revenge, she went to the bedroom, took his beautiful brand new suit out of the wardrobe and dropped it out of her window. It landed on a tree top and looked like a figure dancing in the breeze.

Highly amused, she picked out another of his suits and threw it out of the window. It landed on the lawn. Then she caught sight of Harvey standing in the doorway, his features distorted with rage. The suits on the lawn stirred her to laughter, and she beckoned to him to look at them and share her amusement. He approached, and she saw that he was beside himself with fury. His hand struck a blow across her face. Another sent her reeling back. She tried to escape. He caught her and threw her onto the bed, kneeling over her and beating her on her face again and again. His hands were on her throat. His eyes glittered. He was going to kill her for that, he hissed; this time he was going to kill her.

Fortunately, as he squeezed her throat, her hand grabbed his beautiful new, monogrammed shirt as she tried to tear off its very expensive buttons. Unwilling to ruin it, he let go of her throat. She managed to slip off the bed and run to his stand-in's room. Staggering drunkenly after her, he broke into this room, but was too drunk to resist his stand-in, who succeeded in pushing him out of the room and locking the door. He tried to break the door down. Eventually, his stand-in succeeded in calming him down, and he went away. She spent the night in his stand-in's bed.

Harvey spent the next day feeling full of remorse, pleading that she did not understand what love was, that he would go mad with jealousy.

Hermione was in the midst of making a movie. Her face was so swollen and bruised that the makeup man had his work cut out, and in addition, she had to wear a veil. Her humor never deserted her, however. At a girl guides' rally some days later, she thought her face had been well disguised until a fellow actor whispered that some of his boyfriends knocked him about too, but that he quite enjoyed it. She, it appears, did not enjoy this kind of treatment.

Perhaps, unwittingly or even deliberately, she egged him on to do violence. Perhaps she wanted this violence, wanted to be punished or abused, although this is no excuse for his actions. They were both artists, both unconventional, although this does not necessarily lead to physical abuse. But he had unbridled fits of violence when he was with her that were not repeated with any other of his women. Or, at least, there is no evidence of it.

She writes that she knew, after that night, that he could never make one woman happy for very long. He had his dark, dangerous side and if life was exciting and fun, he was hungry to have everything, fame, wealth and all the riches life could offer. It was as if he knew that there was only so much time allotted to him, she writes perceptively.

They remained together, even after the last, bruising battle. She needed his advice, daring, and courage. Taking over from the brilliant comedienne Bea Lillie at the last moment (Lillie had lost her voice) as the star of the famous Café de Paris, where Noel Coward and Marlene Dietrich also performed, she made her grand, hilarious entrance wearing an elegant black velvet gown and stiletto heels and trailing yards of scruffy white fox fur stitched together. The whole hilarious costume had been Larry's idea and chosen by him.

She would never have had the guts, she writes, to go on at such short notice if Larry had not practically forced her to do so. He had selected her gown, called her accompanist, rehearsed her dramatic entrance with her, ordered the half-dozen white fox furs that had been hastily stitched together in her dressing room.

For all these things, she writes, she felt grateful to him. Her performance scored a dazzling success.

The rift between them—in the sense that their relationship cooled and he moved out of her house—came with two events. One was her meeting with the playwright Tennessee Williams, who offered her the lead in his play *The Rose Tattoo,* to be staged in London.

Lady St. Just who, as "Little Brit," had once shared a flat with Hermione and was now Tennessee Williams's mentor and guardian and finally heir, had brought the playwright to Hermione's house. Hermione had been dressing for a date with the maharajah of Cooch Behar, who was waiting to take her to a polo match and a picnic lunch. In her drawing room, the maharajah was getting along famously with Tennessee Williams when Larry unexpectedly arrived wearing an exquisite white silk shirt and insisted on accompanying the whole party to the polo match.

In the maharajah's limousine, a quarrel broke out between him and Tennessee Williams, and the playwright, ordering the chauffeur to stop, got out of the car and took a taxi home.

Hermione appears to have blamed Larry for the quarrel. One senses her resentment, and the growing estrangement between them. *The Rose Tattoo* was not staged in Britain at this time. Binkie Beaumont told her it would never pass the British censor.

Later, Hermione did play the lead in Tennessee Williams's *The Milk Train Doesn't Stop Here Any More,* and he swore that he had written it just for her.

The second strand in the estrangement between Hermione and Larry was the growing attraction between Larry and the actress Margaret Leighton, who was also, at this time, playing in her first season at Stratford. In *As You Like It,* she played Rosalind, niece of the wicked duke who had exiled them, to Larry's Orlando. On stage, the chemistry, the attraction between the two of them was palpable, obvious to all. It was obvious most of all to Hermoine Baddeley, who had gone up to Stratford to see the play on opening night.

Once more, with his curious lack of sensitivity, he asked Hermione if she would mind inviting Margaret to dine with them.

She had met the young blond star before and thought her lovely, but too perfectly dressed, too coldly beautiful. Were Larry and Margaret playing lovers in private life, too? she wondered. Her brother-in-law complained that Margaret *had* fallen in love with Larry. He would only make her unhappy, he told Hermoine. He was not good husband material.

Hermoine agreed.

To his parents, who, with his increased support, had moved up the hill from Bertrams to the better-class suburb of Yeoville in Johannesburg, Larry wrote, " I am snowed under with work, and all one's energies are concentrated on one's job."

It appears that not quite all his energies were concentrated on his job. As soon as the Stratford season ended, on November l, he wrote to Nahum, he was going "straight to Hollywood for a few weeks before starting on my film [*Beat the Devil*] which is to be made in Italy on the island of Capri." He hoped, he wrote, to be able to fly over to Israel from Capri for a visit.

After Stratford, Hermione and Larry maintained a friendship—of sorts. She declared that she had spent a fortune on him, that he had almost bankrupted her. He gave her minor roles in two of his movies: as the tragic heroine's best friend in *Room at the Top* and as a streetwalker in *Expresso Bongo*. Her Irish lover came back into her life. Her tumultuous relationship with Laurence Harvey occupies some twenty-two pages in her autobiography.

10

Shakespeare and Margaret Leighton

Margaret Leighton, the daughter of a master steelworker, was born in Worcestershire in 1922. The acting bug had infected her early in life, but her strict and religious father did not approve of a stage career for his daughter. She went to a religious school until the age of fifteen, but, fortunately for her, an aunt encouraged her to study acting. While still living at home, she became a full-time student at the Hicks-Smale Drama School in Birmingham run by a relative of her mother's, enrolled as a ballet student at the School of Dance run by a private teacher, and took elocution and singing lessons. Without her father's approval, she joined the Birmingham Repertory Company while still only fifteen, and became brilliantly successful almost immediately.

"Maggie . . . when I first knew her, was the most beautiful woman in England," Laurence Harvey said in a 1971 interview with the London *Times*.

She was very beautiful, tall, blond, very slim, and as fragile looking as a porcelain doll, with a milklike complexion and a perfect, willowy figure. Draped in chiffon, she looked helplessly feminine, but there was, beneath that seeming fragility and a sensitivity that moved her easily to tears, an ironlike will. Her charming blue eyes were a little too close set and she was very shortsighted, giving her a distant look that people who did not know her mistook for coldness, yet she stubbornly refused to wear glasses.

Scouting for fresh talent in the provinces, Laurence Olivier and Ralph Richardson saw her in *Laugh with Me*, her first starring role in Birmingham, and, going backstage, invited her to come to London to perform with the Old Vic theater company, which they were reforming. She left almost immediately. Playing modest parts, she would linger in the wings watching Olivier on stage thinking, enviously, "Men have it all." Bursting with ambition and energy, in those days she considered the fact that men dominated the stage extremely unfair. "But that's the only time it has crossed my mind," she told Hedda Hopper in 1960. "I'm glad I'm a woman."

She had burning ambition and energy despite a chronic nervousness —the legacy of her repressed childhood—which kept her alarmingly thin. She had developed other symptoms as well: an abysmal inferiority complex, a fear of seeing herself without makeup, a sense of looking perpetually bedraggled. She was never happy, she told people, unless there was something she could worry about—and she always found that something to worry about, she liked to say. What saved her from abysmal depression, she believed, was her wry sense of humor and her love of parties and social life.

At the Old Vic she enjoyed a personal triumph in a minor play, *The Sleeping Clergyman*. A series of stage successes followed.

In 1947, she married Max Reinhardt, of the prestigious Holt and Reinhardt publishing house. She made her movie debut in 1948 and became one of Britain's most accomplished and popular stars.

When she met Laurence Harvey at Stratford in the 1952 season, she was already a famous film and stage star. They were introduced when the cast assembled prior to rehearsals. He struck her then as a fresh-faced, good-looking "teddy boy" who smiled all the time and looked brash and overconfident, as if determined to prove that he was as sophisticated and clever as anyone else in the cast. What he did not know (Margaret told an interviewer years later) was that he had only been invited to Stratford because another actor had pulled out and he had been brought in to replace him. Behind his back, everyone mocked his naïve assumption that he was at Stratford on the strength of his genius alone.

That same morning he sent a note to Margaret's dressing room inviting her to lunch. When they met, she noticed that his hair was the color of marmalade. He had dyed it that color when Eric Uttley had said that he did not look English when he was cast as young Edward Luton in Somerset Maugham's *The Circle* in Manchester and kept the color, probably deciding that it suited him. Arriving to take her to lunch she thought he looked very grand in the blue cotton pants he always wore at rehearsals at this time, smoking a cigarette fixed to a cigarette holder.

"What an extraordinary young man!" she remembered thinking.

Quite astoundingly, his opening gambit, she told Hedda Hopper, was, "We nearly played together once before. I was up for *The Deep Blue Sea* [ultimately titled *The Blue Lagoon*] and you were suggested for it, but they said you were too old for me." Neither of them won the parts.

Did she feel she had to prove that she was not too old for him? the famous Hollywood columnist queried. "Perhaps," she laughed. "When you really know him, you find something vulnerable and perhaps a bit naïve."

Curiously, she had laughed off the gauche comment he made when they met. He was incredibly naïve, she thought. Later, it became quite fashionable among some of her friends to laugh at him behind his back. Sometimes he made what they called the silliest comments, and they quoted him mockingly and giggled in the privacy of someone's home.

Yet Margaret Leighton found a vulnerable core in him that endeared him to her and charmed her from the start. Beneath his brash exterior she discovered that there dwelt a surprising lack of confidence and fear of rejection and failure. His sense of fun led to outrageous behavior. He was the life of every party and spoke his mind quite freely where others hesitated, did impressions, and told dirty jokes, but he was also totally dedicated to his work.

She was quite fiercely competitive and always determined to outshine her male costars, and her leading men not infrequently became her lovers. Because Harvey was, at this time, very friendly with Siobhan McKenna, Margaret believed, quite mistakenly, that they were having an affair and this stirred her to begin an affair with him. Ralph Richardson, who was also performing at Stratford that season, was in love with her, but she chose the still raw, young Larry Harvey, thereby upstaging (as she mistakenly believed) Siobhan, who happened to be happily married. "It certainly was an interesting season!" Margaret commented years later.

As lovers, they were superbly well matched in *As You Like It*. What gave their stage romance an added fillip was the flirtation, swiftly turning into the affair they began offstage. This was well publicized in the gossip columns and added to the play's smashing success.

Larry had very little money (or so he said, failing to mention the allowance he received from Romulus Films). Either for show, or by design, he drove a very old car that kept breaking down. Impulsively generous, he spent whole evenings baby-sitting for one star and helping others to practice their lines. She wanted to help him, she said, just as he wanted to help others. They grew, she felt, very close.

Did he take advantage of their friendship? as some critics accused him of doing. This Margaret firmly denied. Whenever his car broke down, which was frequently, he would call her and she would always pick him up in her Jaguar. By the time they both appeared in *Macbeth* their love affair had grown so evident that they became the subject of gossip everywhere.

His stay at Stratford was, for Harvey, a period of happiness. He savored the membership it gave him in this great theatrical establishment, even if he was openly and vociferously critical and disdainful of some of its reigning stars' acting talents. All too often, he leveled open and embarrassing criticisms of the greats in the theater world. Margaret Leighton would never have ventured to do such a thing, but she admired his spunk for doing it.

She must have personified, to him, the "prefect" par excellence of his school days, the high school senior no one but he had dared to invite to dance with him at the tickey dances. This elegant and beautiful woman, this provocative and desirable lady, this great star whose picture appeared in all the movie magazines, this gracious older woman was in love with him!

Yet Margaret was only six years his senior and looked very young. A natural blond, she must have reminded him of his mother, in coloring at least, which Hermione, short and plain, did not. In his memory of her, however, his mother seemed old and vulgar, while Margaret was refined and lovely. She was not good to him like Hermione, but she was charmed by him and, at that stage, undemanding. There was a problem, however. Her upbringing and her early struggles to survive on a pittance had made her frugal. He liked her style, but not her fashion sense, and soon began severely criticizing the clothes she wore, which he condemned as old maidenish. Determined to change this, he took her to the most stylish London dressmakers and began selecting everything she wore, down to the buckles on her shoes. She fell head over heels in love with him and, as she told a friend, was dazzled by the thought of all the marvelous plays and films they would be able to star in together.

Privately, Margaret had a reputation of behaving like a hellcat to the men in her life and treating them very badly. Her marriage to Max Reinhardt appeared to have permitted each of them to have affairs, at least as long as these did not provoke any scandal. Also, her profession—and she was a dedicated actress—kept them apart a great deal.

Though officially registered in different hotel rooms, Harvey and Margaret Leighton had come to share her bed. One morning her husband came to Stratford, officially to host a party for the company, and arrived earlier than expected. No doubt he had heard some gossip about their affair and wished to surprise them and discover the truth. In the midst of lovemaking, hearing his knock on Margaret's bedroom door, Harvey made his swift escape through a window and after a bath and a change of clothes, appeared boldly at the party as one of the invited guests.

What Reinhardt noticed—or guessed—is not recorded. If he did, he had the good taste to rise above pique. Under his auspices, Reinhardt published a beautiful volume of photographs and accompanying text in 1953 titled *Shakespeare Memorial Theatre, 1951–53: A Critical Analysis* by Ivor Brown, which included photographs of Ralph Richardson, Michael Redgrave, Anthony Quayle, Margaret Leighton, and Laurence Harvey among others.

After Stratford, their separate commitments kept the two stars a great deal apart, but the gossip about their affair kept appearing in the British tabloids and gossip columns. Finally, Max Reinhardt instituted divorce proceedings. Devastated, Margaret swallowed a large drink and several sleeping pills—something she had never done before. What saved her life, she later said, was being awakened by the ringing of the telephone. It was Noel Coward calling, asking her to star with him in *The Apple Cart*. He became her friend for life.

If she had not taken her affair with Harvey too seriously, he had, and asked her to marry him. As with Hermione Baddeley, he believed this was the honorable thing to do: in these cases he was an old-fashioned romantic. The newspapers and gossip columnists kept declaring that they were planning marriage, and asking them to "name the day." But his career had taken off after Stratford and the sweetness she had discerned in him seemed to fade. He became more self-centered and vain and worried about his looks and his figure, he dieted. They saw each other very rarely because of the demands of their separate careers, but when they met she noticed that his confidence had increased and that he had become domineering. She saw the change in him, but she was in love and that was all, to her, that mattered.

Many of Margaret's friends and worshipful fans were, on the whole, unkind. What was a refined lady like her doing with this shady parvenu, they asked? She had disgraced herself, touched dirt. Even in faraway Rangoon where Robert was assigned for a two-year stay at the time, he was startled to hear the second secretary at the British Embassy there confess, with a flushed face and an apologetic air, that one of his school friends, a very proper lower-middle-class Englishman who had worshipped Margaret Leighton practically as a saint among women had been shocked and heartbroken to read about her romance with Laurence Harvey—a foreigner, a disreputable nobody, as he had considered him. How this man's idol had fallen! Robert responded with an icy rejoinder, but it brought home to him Larry's real standing in Britain.

For Harvey, the years between 1952 to 1959 marked steadily increasing recognition as a rising actor, yet many of the string of films he made in those years, under the watchful eye of James Woolf, both for Romulus and on loan to other companies, were second rate or less. Clearly, his mentor and guardian was grooming him for better roles and Harvey was willing to be groomed. He had a small part in *Landfall*, about an RAF pilot wrongly accused of responsibility for sinking a ship in the English Channel, but tackled it seriously and acquitted himself well enough to be noticed. In *Twilight Women*, another small film about an evil landlady who practically owns her helpless young women tenants, he was the only male, a nightclub singer, a small part to which he lent a little dimension. In *Innocents in Paris*, he plays an amorous Parisian who charms the inexperienced Claire Bloom. His part was so minuscule that in 1955, when it was to be shown on television, James Woolf cut it out of the film, declaring that a star of Laurence Harvey's stature should not be seen in a bit part.

Although only a few of the films he had made were distributed in the United States and in only a handful of cities, James Woolf had negotiated a deal that put the young actor under contract with Warner Bros. to make one film a year in Hollywood. He accompanied his favorite protégé to Los Angeles, where they shared a bungalow in the pink Beverly Hills Hotel, a situation that speedily became the source of gossip in the film community. Harvey was twenty-five, tall, slim, and debonair—he had learned this deportment by keen observation of socialites in London and Paris—but he was a completely unknown quantity in the Hollywood world, even with a season at Stratford behind him.

He was tested for various small parts. Preparing for his first interview, he repeated the mistake he had made prior to his first test for Warner Bros. in London: he ate a huge breakfast at the elegant Beverly Hills Hotel coffee shop and then rushed to the men's room, put his finger in his mouth and threw up everything he had eaten. Socially, he did rather better. Woolf, admired and respected everywhere because of the success of *The African Queen*, introduced him to screen celebrities. As Woolf's protégé, he was invited to all the best parties. In those days, a favorite form of entertainment was a party around the swimming pool. All the guests wore swimsuits and splashed about in the pool. Food and drinks were served on special floating trays. "Not my idea of fun—I found myself drinking wine AND pool water," he commented. The only intelligent person there, he said, was Humphrey Bogart, who sat by the pool fully clothed, sensibly drinking unadulterated whisky. It must have cut the raw newcomer to the quick to see that people were not interested in him; they seemed hardly to know he was there.

Marlon Brando, Montgomery Clift, Richard Burton were the current rage, all of them young, bright, different, and wildly successful. But James Woolf had unwavering faith in him. He talked John Huston into promising to give Harvey a part in his next film, though this came to nothing, as did his attempt to arrange a four-picture deal with Fox, or win a starring role for him at M-G-M.

Miffed at being still ignored, the eternal, untamed adolescent in him made him hit on several pieces of maverick behavior. At a "Come as Your Favorite Person" party given by Marion Davies at fabulous San Simeon, at which all the guests had to come wearing makeup and costumes as their favorite characters, Harvey showed up wearing his designer slacks, a silk shirt, and a beautiful Italian-made cashmere sweater. "If one is truly honest," he informed his hostess blandly, "one turns up as oneself. I am my own favorite person." Later he said that he had not had the time to change.

This comment did not go unnoticed and boosted his reputation as a swollen-headed egoist. At another party he stunned everyone with his

burlesque rendition of a nun doing a striptease while singing "My De-
fenses Are Down" (in a later version of this story, he said that he had
burlesqued *an American* doing a striptease). Even Hollywood was not
yet totally cynical then, and the air was thick with outrage and shock.

When Woolf berated him in the privacy of their hotel bedroom, he
apologized for his unbridled behavior. It did not improve matters,
however, when in the next breath he added that he had not known
he was attending a Sunday School retreat.

The most impressive party, he seemed to feel, was the farewell party
(primarily for James Woolf, although he did not say so) given by
Humphrey Bogart in his new house in Bel-Air. There was champagne
and dancing to an all-African American band in the hall, which was
paved with black-and-white marble squares, and everyone was
there—Judy Garland, the Van Johnsons, the Sam Goldwyns, the James
Masons, the Rex Harrisons (all of them later divorced), and Zsa Zsa
Gabor escorted by her lover at the time, the notorious South American
playboy Rubirosa, who later blackened one of Zsa Zsa's eyes and went
off to marry, briefly, the much-marrying Woolworth's heiress, Barbara
Hutton. As he was leaving the party, Harvey said, he saw the glamorous Rubirosa silently popping balloons with his lighted cigarette in
an adjoining room.

He had much more to criticize Hollywood for, providing at the
same time a highly embellished portrait of that city's cultural facilities, or rather, lack of them. He accused its film community of having no legitimate theaters, only rows and rows of burlesque theaters
on Skid Row offering "a dreary diet of strip-tease—a flimsy substitute for drama." And if one is a bachelor in Hollywood, he said with
a bored yawn, and regarded as eligible, this could be tiresome. During his first visit, the studio's publicity department had paired him
with actress Terry Moore in an effort to promote both their careers,
and the gossip columnists had immediately labeled them a "two-
some." It was disillusioning truths like these and worse, which he
never hesitated to express, that made him so intensely disliked.

Back in London for a short break, he was packing (with a great
many sighs, he informed an interviewer) to return to Hollywood to
play Paris in *Helen of Troy* when he received the telephone call he

had eagerly been awaiting. Italian producer Renato Castellani informed him that he had won the part of Romeo in the joint British Rank Organisation-Italian Universalcine production of *Romeo and Juliet.*

He had been aware, of course, that James Woolf had been negotiating with Castellani to get him this role. But, as he dramatically explained, like many important phases of his life, this one began with a phone call—from Renato Castellani himself, who declared, "I am going to make MY version of Shakespeare's Romeo and Juliet—and I want you to play Romeo." Shirts, socks, et cetera, were all swiftly unpacked. His delight was evident. In Hollywood, where he was to have gone on loan from Romulus, he had been given major roles in three films at a reputed $25,000 per film, plus expenses. ("Bear in mind the fact that the money-chucking days are gone and you get some idea of Hollywood's high assessment of Harvey," *Picturegoer's* interviewer, David Marlowe, commented.) It was a wonderful opportunity, but Hollywood could wait, Larry responded. Given the chance to play Romeo in Castellani's film, "I forgot Hollywood—but don't think I did it because the money was better. It wasn't. *I have only one ambition. To be a full-blooded and serious craftsman.*" And, he added, he also had a purely personal reason—to be closer to Margaret Leighton. They had seen very little of each other for months because of their work, only managing to spend an occasional weekend together. From his tone his interviewer gathered that he had no doubts about his ability to succeed in Hollywood when the time was ripe. Was he overconfident? No, was the interviewer's comment. He just happened to be frank about his increased market value.

In this interview, having said all that, lolling in a chair, his fashionable stovepipe-trousered legs draped over one of its arms (he had introduced the "stovepipe" trousers fashion), Harvey returned to his favorite theme:

"I'm so keen on perfection," he said. "Never am I satisfied with what I do. I must do better all the time. . . . I want to do so well. . . . But mind you, I've learnt my job before the cameras. Fourteen British films have shown me the way. I'd call it my film repertory. It was very useful. But I couldn't go on trying to lend perfection to imperfect parts, could I? . . . Truth is, I've discovered as I've gone on that I just don't know anything. Nothing at all. One dies without reaching the true heights in drama."

He was, his interviewer comments, perfectly sincere.

Writing from Italy, his letter to his brother Nahum positively glowed with excitement. Shooting on location in Venice and Verona was difficult, he wrote, hard work. He was up at four-thirty in the morning and worked until eight every evening. The three days off he had been given were spent in England, where he had signed a contract to return to Stratford for ten months the following year, and after Stratford he had to go on to New York for four months on a tour that included cities in Canada and the United States. Stratford's directors, he wrote enthusiastically, "want me to go back there as the STAR and leading man of the season, which is a great honor as they believe in me to the extent of following in the footsteps of Laurence Olivier and John Gielgud." Because of his commitment to Stratford, he had been forced to sacrifice his Hollywood film contract and to suffer a great personal financial loss, he grumbled. Yet, "I know I have done the right thing because I do not want to be just another film star, but a great and distinguished actor with a classical background which I can only get in the theater, and now that I have reached a position where I am in demand in both spheres, I want to maintain it on the highest possible level."

At Stratford, he wrote, he was going to play Romeo again, Oberon in *A Midsummer Night's Dream,* and Troilus in *Troilus and Cressida,* parts that "no other actor of my age has ever been asked to do before, here or in America. If I am a success then there will never be any dispute as to my position as one of the leading young actors in the world today."

But money—or rather the lack of it—troubled him. Or at least, he said it did. He would do his best to maintain the regular allowance he sent to their parents, as he had promised, but really could not do more. In the next two years he would be earning very little money, he predicted. He had sent his father on a trip to Israel to see his sons and grandsons. Robert had immigrated to Israel in 1950, and their father was staying with him and his family in Tel Aviv. Nachum's wife had given birth to a baby girl who died. This was one of the chief reasons why Nahum and his wife made the decision to leave their kibbutz with their seven-year-old son and settle in the southern town of Beersheba, in those days still a hot and sandy desert outpost, called a "development town." Yes, Harvey wrote, he would love to come and see them all, but "I am afraid I will have to disappoint you."

Many months later, after finishing *The Talisman*, his first American film, lunching in a quiet midtown Italian restaurant in Manhattan, sporting a luxuriant blond mane plus a mustache, a goatee, and a splint on an index finger, the result of an accident on the set, he told journalist Howard Thompson in an interview that he was still on tap for *The Talisman* retakes until plane time the next day. "This I got during a fight scene," he explained, tapping the wire brace on his index finger and smiling—he was prone to injuries throughout his career. "That's CinemaScope for you. All that leeway to leap around in during those sustained long shots. I'm all for CinemaScope, by the way." Then he launched into a critique of the people who sneered at Hollywood. "You always hear people sneering at the place," he declared. "No art, they say. Well, the only reason they don't go there is because they're not invited. True, you have this box office standardization. But take all those amazing technical facilities, those immense hangars equipped from top to bottom." Here he tested his finger again. "Another thing I like," he continued, "is their general enthusiasm. They do talk in superlatives and it may seem false. But they're really enthusiastic. I'd say what the place really needs is creative vitality."

His real stamping ground, he declared, was the stage, "so I signed with Romulus Films for a whole batch [of films] that weren't so hot. Castellani saw one test and that led to Romeo."

In this interview he also offered an insight to his approach to acting. "I've always believed that adherence to set theories and techniques, other people's, is the wrong approach. . . . Life teaches enough, for instance, for a villain role I did once, I tried to think of one who was real different. I based him on a certain chap I know in London. He wants money, claps you on the shoulder: 'Hallo, old boy.' Then his hand slides into your inner pocket and he takes $25,000. Those are the ones, you know."

Asked whether he preferred the stage to the screen, he immediately murmured "Both. I mean it, too. This I like about pictures, though. You do something, finish it, and have it catch up with you all over the world—Bangkok, London or Pittsburgh, Pa. It's like being chosen all over again." (This was a reference to his boyhood in Johannesburg, when films first fascinated him and called to him, saying, "You are the chosen one.")

He talked of working in *Romeo and Juliet.* That, he reminisced with a mischievous grin, had not always been without its merry side. Lovely young Susan Shentall, as Juliet, was a complete amateur, engaged to be married and not interested in becoming a professional actress. She had been spotted by Castellani while dining with her parents in a restaurant and he had instantly determined that she was, visually, the perfect Juliet.

Harvey had resigned himself to playing opposite Shentall, he said, although he called it an axiom of the business that a professional will always suffer as a result of playing with an amateur, and he was no exception. Nevertheless, he said, he did not blame her. She had "terrific guts." Still, he had not been above teasing her. At dinner, she was usually chaperoned by her parents, but one evening the two of them happened to dine alone. They went to a restaurant that served "the most exquisite roast chicken. . . . Determined not to miss those juicy bones, I picked them up in peasant style and commenced to gnaw. . . . Giving a gasp of dismay, Susan said, with a grimness that was really quite charming, '[that] is NOT done in the best circles.' Wiping the grease from my chin I grinned—and replied that some of my pheasant-hunting aristocratic friends in Scotland ALWAYS chewed the bones. Susan was not convinced."

He recounted what he termed "another amusing experience on location." Generally working in ancient palaces, they nearly always found themselves near some antique Roman lavatory. "These palaces bristled with them. . . . I laid a bet with my make-up man that we'd finish up by using one for a dressing room. Sure enough, I won my bet—but this one was quite modern and we used the seats instead of chairs. I wondered what Shakespeare would have thought."

Toilets were one of his lifelong obsessions.

Romeo and Juliet was bitingly criticized as well as praised. Shooting entirely on location in various Italian cities, Castellani had spent months in museums, designing the sets, studying the clothes worn in the fifteenth century, basing the costumes designed for this film on the paintings of such magnificent artists as Fra Lippo Lippi and Botticelli. The film was a feast for the eyes and the ears. Of the many reviews, the most perceptive was by Bosley Crowther who wrote in the *New York Times* that it was like looking at a whole gallery of Italian Renaissance paintings and that Castellani was less interested in the lyrical language of Shakespeare than in creating visual images and a film drama in the "violent, smashing, uncompromising style of the Italian neo-realist school." He found Susan Shentall's performance "quiet, dignified and yet aglow with the warmth of youthful emotion," while Laurence Harvey's Romeo was "handsome, nimble, hot-headed and eventually rent in mad despair."

Nonetheless, this film was, on the whole, a failure. Harvey's performance was generally judged as wooden and stereotyped. Yet, at Stratford, during his first season, he had been praised for his imagination and intelligence. He moved and spoke with authority, the critics had said, and his virility had been tempered with grace. He had the personality of a thinking actor, they had said, nervous, sharp edged, electric. Talking about this film, he revealed his habitual tendency to blame others for his failures. Castellani had been to blame for his disappointing performance, he said. The director had appeared determined to make a superb travelogue of northern Italy and had ignored all his own attempts to interpret the world's greatest love story.

The film was nominated for the Venice Film Festival's Grand Prix, but lost out to Fellini's *La Strada.* It did not even receive mention at the Academy Awards.

For his role as Romeo he was paid £30,000 plus expenses, hardly starvation pay, but next to nothing by present-day standards.

Although some of the finest of Shakespeare's poetic dialogue was cut to make way for action and the film was visually beautiful, its static quality did not attract large audiences, and it made its way to the art theaters quite soon after release.

The meaner wits in the world of actors and journalists held that Laurence Harvey had wanted to play Juliet as well as Romeo—and every other character, his ego was so large. For his seemingly overwhelming egotism he was now openly hated; his ferocious displays of self-confidence made people bristle. "I'm so very keen on perfection," he informed everyone. There was the initial shock, as Peter Hammond pointed out in *Photoplay* in meeting a newcomer who saw himself as a future Olivier, Gielgud, and Richardson—all rolled into one. Clearly this actor did not believe in hiding the light of his undoubted talent under a bushel. Besides, he knew he had charm and looks. He had made up his mind as to where he was going, and he was not going to let anyone stand in his way. And if he was so ruthlessly ambitious, the same critic asked, why then had he turned down

Hollywood to take on the difficult part of Romeo for Castellani? Because, Hammond believed, at heart Harvey was an idealist. He felt that Castellani was offering him the chance to succeed as a really great actor. Many Harvey haters had rejoiced and predicted that Hollywood would never give him another chance. But, said this critic, if one had the makings of a great actor and was bold enough to kick Hollywood in the teeth and get away with it, he felt certain that Laurence Harvey could do it. He had the talent—and the impertinence.

It was in reference to this film that one critic wrote that Laurence Harvey was a "Yugoslav born actor who mastered English in South Africa."

After finishing the film, he had meant to relax for a short time in Italy, but was summoned to London to start work in *The Good Die Young*. This he did the day after his return. Margaret was also in the film, and they had a brief reunion.

The Good Die Young is the story of four men who plan to rob a mail van. Harvey plays an upper-class scoundrel who organizes them. They use the different skills they learned in the army to carry out their plan, but their efforts end in failure and death. Margaret Leighton plays Harvey's wealthy wife, who pays his gambling debts. Joan Collins is also in this film, playing the wife of one of the men. The film had a mixed contingent of English and American stars, including Canadian-born John Ireland. While working together in this film, a close friendship developed between Harvey and John Ireland, who became one of his most devoted admirers. The film was a box office success and was released in the United States under the auspices of United Artists.

After this film, he starred with Margaret Leighton in the television production of *A Month in the Country*, the first full-length, made-for-television film in Britain.

For this brief period, they were together.

During that interview in the midtown Italian restaurant in Manhattan, he also talked about Margaret Leighton and how he had first met her during his first season at Stratford, where, he said, their successful partnership on stage had drawn them into a very close friendship. "Since then," he said, "Margaret has been a great help to me in everything I have done. . . . She has been and is still my dearest friend. I have enormous love and admiration for her both as an actress and as a woman. It is my greatest hope that we shall be able to work together a great deal more in the future as this would be the supreme contribution to our lasting happiness."

Ironically, all this love and admiration did not serve to persuade him to propose that they marry immediately, though she was desperate to have him marry her. Her husband had named Harvey as corespondent in his divorce action and neither of them had contested this claim. She was living in scandal-riddled discomfort, unable to turn the pages of any popular newspaper or magazine without finding some reference to the ugly details of the affair.

While almost pathetically claiming that he had very little money and very large expenses, Larry had grudgingly subsidized his mother's trip to Israel to visit Nahum and his family in early 1950, and his father in 1953. His parents had come practically to depend on him for support. Ever the dutiful and affectionate son, he wrote to them regularly and after his father's return to South Africa, he began, with his two brothers, discussing the possibility of their parents settling permanently in Israel, for there was nothing left for them in South Africa. "Find a small villa," he wrote to Nahum (houses, in Israel, were called villas). Despite what he called his chronic shortage of funds and the severe restrictions placed on exporting British pounds, he would just about be able to afford to purchase one for them, he wrote.

Of his own work, he wrote to his parents in glowing terms about his splendid successes on stage and in his films, and how very hard he worked, with long hours and little rest. Several of his films had reached Johannesburg. During the premier of *Cairo Road* his mother had summoned four rows of beaming relatives to the movie house, and the film had opened to a packed house. The exaltation of his proud parents is visible in every picture published in the local press. The fact that his wife, in this film, was the beautiful Egyptian actress, Carmelia, was a source of genuine wonder: a Jew and an Arab acting together! Ella Skikne boasted that she went to see his films every evening while they were showing and her dedication was the talk of all her neighbors. A veteran member, since the mid-1940s, of the Jewish Ladies' Choral Society, her high, reedy voice was often featured in their performances; she was, after all, the mother of a famous star.

The prospect of relocating to Israel was not altogether pleasing to her. It was hard for her to have to consider giving up all the prestige and glory of being the mother of a "South African film star" (as the local press called him).

According to the agreement that James Woolf made with Warner Bros., Harvey was to make one film a year for that studio. The first film he was contracted to make was *The Talisman* (also titled *King Richard and the Crusaders*) costarring three famous and popular actors: Virginia Mayo, Rex Harrison, and George Sanders, and the as yet unknown quantity, Laurence Harvey.

The Talisman, when released, was panned by the critics as a poorly directed and edited, crude adaptation of Sir Walter Scott's classic novel.

Morale among the cast was not good. Manic-depressive George Sanders, as his biographer writes in *An Exhausted Life*, spent the time between takes during this slow-paced production composing limericks about the cast. His nastiest was about Harvey, whom he dubbed a mixture of Shakespeare and Madame DuBarry who could be had by either sex.

That Laurence Harvey had affairs with both sexes was known to most people in Hollywood. Margaret Leighton was well aware of it too, but, like Hermione Baddeley, knew many actors who had the same proclivities, and viewed it as the way of the thespian world. Perhaps it may almost have seemed to them a safety measure; if their lovers liked men they would be easier to hold.

The antipathy between the stars was palpable. In her first biography, *"One Lifetime Is Not Enough,"* Zsa Zsa Gabor claims that James Woolf despised George Sanders, to whom she was married at this time, and always referred to him as "that bastard." Unlike George Sanders, she writes that she herself considered Harvey a genius.

She was not, all the same, above enjoying the tricks the other stars played on him. In one scene, she records, Rex Harrison enlisted

George Sanders's aid in deflating Harvey's ego, which she terms "outsized." Since Harvey, she claims, regarded himself one of the world's best actors, Harrison slyly asked him to teach him how to play a certain scene. Apparently quite unruffled, Larry replied, seriously, that he could not teach him how to play it, but he could give him some good advice. In one scene, Harvey had to lift up Sanders's "dead" body and carry it away. Much to his surprise, he discovered that try as he might, he could not budge Sanders when the cameras began rolling, despite the fact that the scene had been thoroughly rehearsed. The entire cast and crew burst out laughing at Harvey's embarrassment. It then appeared that Sanders and Harrison had surreptitiously placed weights in George Sanders's pockets.

The critics called *The Talisman*, "A droning, static, conversation piece." The film was a critical and commercial failure and closed three weeks after its Hollywood premiere. Warner Bros. lost nearly a million dollars on the film. It had cost $3 million, a princely sum in those days, to make and still had not recouped its investment thirty years later.

Harvey himself had much to say about this film:

"I will not pretend that Don Juan had nothing on me. I am not quite so conceited as my critics maintain," he said in an interview with the Johannesburg *Star* several years later. "But, nevertheless, I may say in all modesty that, as a lover, I considered myself no slouch." He had made love to some of the screen's loveliest women, he reminisced, and their kisses had been ardent, while the camera watched every move. And he confessed that his temperature had risen a little then, and he had enjoyed those moments. Yet of all these women, only Virginia Mayo had called him a cranky lover.

She had been quite right, he admitted wryly. Filming on location at the Mexican border had been a hot and uncomfortable experience. He praised Virginia Mayo who, he said, was a "very lovely girl" for whom he had a great regard, and who had "the most terrific screen technique and always [took] a highly professional attitude toward the job in hand." Only, he was wearing chain mail (weighing no more than three pounds, as he did not say) in the fierce heat, while Virginia wore "diaphanous gowns which stirred provocatively with every puff of the hot desert air." The result was that his fierce embraces left indentations on her body where his arms had pressed against her. Being a very passionate girl, he said, Virginia responded warmly to his embraces. "How I cursed that armor!" he reminisced. Finally, however, this awkward lovemaking proved too painful for her, and she threatened to soak him in oil if he did not do something about the creaking chain mail. She had never heard Harvey's version of this story.

On another occasion, he reminisced, a dog was supposed to leap onto his shoulder and lick his face in excited recognition as he returned to the crusaders' camp after a long absence. Two dogs were trained for this scene. Initially, nothing would induce either dog to leap on his shoulder. He said, "either I am not attractive to dogs or those dogs were just plain mean. Nothing would persuade them to kiss me. At least, nothing except a thick and rather smelly hamburger strapped to my cheek beneath my helmet of chain mail. That proved so attractive that the only difficulty was to prevent them from eating me completely."

His own account of the trick played on him by George Sanders and Rex Harrison differed substantially from Zsa Zsa Gabor's. The armor all three stars had to wear, he said, led to all kinds of incidents. George Sanders was a large, heavy man. Larry had to lift him, heavy armor and all, from a chair and place him on a couch. During rehearsals, George Sanders cooperated by evenly distributing his weight and Larry was able to lift him without too much trouble. "But during the take he mischievously sagged like a sack of spuds. I dropped him sharply. There was a yell from George—and the next time he DID cooperate!"

The animosities between the stars only helped to make a bad movie worse.

When the film was wrapped up, Larry threw a lavish party for the crew at a Mexican restaurant, a generous gesture that earned him a great deal of good feeling. He was always good to the crew when making a film, always thoughtful and generous, and he was well liked by them.

The tabloid reports about the money he had made in Hollywood troubled him; he was afraid that his parents might ask for a larger allowance. "All the talk about my contracts and fabulous earnings and millionaire talk," he wrote to Nahum, asking him to relay what he wrote to their parents, were "slightly palling." His income, he explained, had to be split between the Chancellor of the Exchequer and himself. Ten percent of his share had to go to his American agent, 10 percent to his London agent, 50 percent of the profits above his basic salary had to go to the company to which he was under contract in Britain, in addition to the salaries of the million and one people whom he had to employ. Britain's super tax took nineteen shillings and sixpence out of every pound, leaving him with next to nothing, and he had to pay that tax again for every pound he sent to their parents. He was not, he admitted, poor, but was also not in a position to produce any cash. Then he had to pay a fine of £10,000 to Stratford, he claimed, for his release from his contract to perform in *A Midsummer Night's Dream* because of his commitment in Hollywood. He would now be working for nothing for the next few months, he complained dolefully.

Perhaps his financial situation was not as dismal as he described. As the stalking horse of the critics, however, it had been, for him, a bad year. When he returned to Stratford for the 1954 season, they denigrated his performances, envied the money he had made in Hollywood, told him to go to Hollywood if he would not learn the discipline of acting on the British stage. He wrote to Nahum that the critics' condemnation unnerved and upset him, but that he was determined to survive and fight back. He was a public figure, he wrote resignedly and, like all public figures, had to take the good as well as the bad.

11

Romeo and His Juliet

Upon his return to England, the tabloids had a field day describing his luxurious, Regency-style flat next door to that of his mentor and lover, James Woolf, in Grosvenor House on London's exclusive Park Lane. Deliberately, defiantly, he had shown some of the journalists his rooms filled with antiques and paintings, all of them "rather val," (valuable and expensive) he told people. Woolf had taught him about art and luxurious living and he had proved to be an ardent student. They wrote about his gold cuff links, his marvelous clothes, his ultra-expensive gold watch, his Jaguar. Warner Bros. had wanted him back to play the lead in *The Silver Chalice* (the film became the starring vehicle of the young Paul Newman) and *Helen of Troy.* He told one journalist, whom he had invited to his flat, that he had firmly rejected these and two other film offers in order to fulfill his prior commitment at Stratford for another season of Shakespeare (and perhaps to get out of having to pay Stratford the £10,000 he owed them). In Hollywood, he said, they had politely referred to him as "the new Shakespearean thesp"—but now "I'm known as the knight in shining armor."

When the journalist arrived at his flat, Harvey was wearing a bathrobe and looked weary, troubled, forlorn. "I'm so tired, I just don't know how to stand," he said. "I think I shall collapse," and threw himself wearily into one of his expensive brocade armchairs.

He had been giving interviews all that week, and now he lashed out at his critics. Journalists, he said, had been falling over backward to spotlight him, and yet, only a handful of years earlier, they had totally ignored him. Now that he had a half-million-dollar contract with Warner Bros. to make one film a year and another contract

with Romulus, and in addition, a permanently open door at Stratford, "They come to see me in droves," he said of the journalists,
with a thin, contemptuous smile. "They try to be smart and catch
me out. . . . They want me to say unpleasant things about Hollywood. . . . They don't succeed. . . . I love making films there and say
so. I adore the people. . . . They make cracks in print about this"—
here he tugged at the blond beard he had kept from his role in *The
Talisman*—"and because my hair is still blond [from the film]. But I
don't care. They don't worry me."

"I shall always be a discontented person," Harvey said, slithering
around his flat in leather slippers, rummaging in the cocktail cabinet, pouring himself a Campari and soda, serving his interviewer a
whisky and ginger ale. "Of course, it's nice to know one has got
somewhere," he added, churning the ice in his glass. "It's all been
done by sheer hard work. No one helped me. I did it on my own.
You don't think I could stand in front of a camera all day long and
say my lines and not be conceited, do you? I wouldn't be an actor at
all if I lacked ego."

He never had been an easy person to get along with, the journalist
recalled. He was always moaning and groaning, forever needing bol-
stering up and praise for qualities he profoundly believed he had,
draping himself disconsolately on chairs in the London Screenwriters
Club, elegantly clad in his Edwardian-type suits, wearing his hair long
and showing off his flamboyant cuff links, full of condemnation for
British directors and producers whom he accused of not knowing their
job, scornful of the journalists who showed no interest in him.

His other grievance was about money. He never had much money.
It went, he said, to support his family and friends who had to be
looked after. Then there was the flat. Everything was expensive. He
received excellent service, but he paid for it in heavy tips—he tipped
all his servants, all the time, for every service, great or small. Of the
extraordinary help he received from his intimate friend, companion,
and sponsor, he said nothing.

And now, he said, he would have to act at Stratford for nothing,
because *The Talisman* had overrun its schedule.

At Stratford, his salary was still £50 a week (now and then he told
his interviewers that his salary was £30 a week). In Hollywood, he

said, two of that town's top producers had seen his work at Stratford during his first season there, and had offered him £6,500 for a two-picture deal that would have taken only six months' work. "No," he told journalist Howard Thompson, "it didn't turn my head, although it was something of a jump from my thirty pounds a week at Stratford. In fact, I didn't take it! Because having virtually settled the deal and taken an apartment, I made a quick trip back to England . . . to run into yet another offer." [This had been the one made by Castellani to play Romeo.] "I forgot Hollywood—but don't think I did it because the money was better. It wasn't. *I have only one ambition. To be a full-blooded and serious craftsman.*" But, he added, he also had a purely personal reason—to be closer to Margaret Leighton. They had seen very little of each other for months because of their work, he said, and had only managed an occasional weekend together.

Rejecting the fleshpots of Hollywood, he had gone to Stratford with no break after his film and television work. This was to be his pattern for the rest of his career; he was a glutton for work and could not bear to be idle. Besides, he told another interviewer, "I was certain that at that stage of my career I would be better working at Stratford and improving my acting than filming in Hollywood, though it meant a considerable financial sacrifice. . . . In Hollywood, I could have made around 2,000 pounds a week. . . . Still, Stratford gave me so much valuable experience and I saw this despite the mixed reception by the critics for my performances."

At a salary of only £50 a week, one did nine performances a week after only four weeks of rehearsal and while a play was running at night, he explained, the actor had to rehearse a second one in the daytime. "But if one wants to develop as an actor as opposed to being a personality, one must learn one's job."

Films required a different technique, he told the *Los Angeles Times* in 1954. In film, he pontificated (and he was still, at this time, a relatively unknown newcomer in Hollywood), one wanted to create a personality *for* the actor instead of drowning the personality *in* the actor.

Before the season at Stratford ended, Sir Anthony Eden, then Britain's foreign secretary, came to see his performance as Troilus in *Troilus and Cressida,* which was one of his favorite plays. Visiting Larry backstage after the performance, they chatted amiably for a good half hour he told *Everybody's* journalist David Clayton in 1957. To Eden, rather than discussing his role, the young actor complained about Britain's heavy taxation, and then could not resist talking about himself and what he termed "my two pet peeves." The first—and the greatest—was his complaint about the newspaper columnists and critics who kept chronicling his flamboyance, his offstage extravagances, his friendships with older actresses. They had even unearthed the fact that he had a brief fling, in the United States with the beautiful and very famous Anglo-Irish import, Greer Garson, whose classic films had won her stardom on both sides of the Atlantic and who, it appeared, had a penchant for much younger men. His second peeve was that, despite all his excellent work, the dramatic critics refused to take him seriously.

Sir Anthony, too, had been accused of being too "elegant." As he turned to leave he said: "I shouldn't worry about the Press, if I were you, old boy. You should see some of *my* notices."

"This put everything into the right perspective for me," Harvey grinned.

There was no relief in the criticism he had to endure that season. His Romeo was called "a mechanical clockwork lover crying crocodile tears," and his Troilus, "dim, brash, shallow." Responding to the lambasting that he received, he coolly gave interviews explaining why the critics had misunderstood his performance. He had, as he explained in his letter to Nahum, given his Romeo a strength and Latin excitement and madness that had never been seen on any stage before, and as for his Troilus, he portrayed him as a disillusioned young man who mocked love. The audiences loved him and flocked to the theater. The critics called his attitude "arrogant," and, as he perceived it, only succeeded in adding themselves to his list of "enemies," as he began to label those critics who disliked him. After all, as he philosophically reminded people, John Gielgud himself had been lambasted for his production at Stratford several years earlier.

It marked the beginning of the strange dichotomy between the enchanted audiences filling the movie houses and the theaters and the devastating opinions of the critics both in England and the United States, who wrote that nobody watched his films or went to see his stage performances. Still, the reactions of the critics must have upset him more than he admitted. He became subjected to spasms of violent behavior. At the end of a performance of *As You Like It*, as the audience filed out of the auditorium of the Shakespeare Memorial Theatre, Harvey was suddenly seen, dressed as Orlando, walking jauntily onto the stage in front of the safety curtain. All he had intended to do, he claimed later, was to try to move from one side of the stage to the other, because the scene shifters were at work behind the curtain.

A very irate house manager, Harvey said, "rudely and boorishly told me to get backstage where I belonged." Infuriated, Harvey leaped from the stage and began chasing after the house manager, who fled for safety. In hot pursuit, Harvey knocked over an usherette and reached the house manager's office just as the door was slammed in his face. Dragged away, protesting, by the theater's staff, he was summoned to the business manager's office the next morning and was threatened with the cancellation of his contract.

That was the kind of behavior that labeled him emotionally unstable, said a friend. As reported by Francis Hitching in *John Bull*, Harvey conceded that he was in the wrong, but claimed that he just could not help it.

That season he was responsible for a tragic accident. Speeding to the theater from London in his Jaguar to be on time for his performance as Romeo on May 4, 1954, he accidentally ran over and killed a cyclist named Patrick Moore, a fifty-nine-year-old Ministry of Civil Aviation policeman. Although badly shaken when he left the police station after his interrogation, he nevertheless insisted on being driven to Stratford, changing into his costume and going on, telling his understudy, who was dressed in costume ready to go on, "Relax, dear heart. Romeo is here."

There was another death, this time not of his doing. As soon as he learned that his dear friend Rudolph, the head barman of the Georges V hotel had fallen victim to cancer, he immediately brought him over to England, kissed him tenderly at the airport, and placed him in an exclusive clinic in London. He wept when Rudolph died and sent his coffin back to France, to be buried where Rudolph had wished to lie.

The tabloids had gleefully printed every detail of Margaret Leighton's "misconduct" with Laurence Harvey as specified in Max Reinhardt's divorce suit, and Harvey was made to pay costs, which constituted a further drain on his financial resources. Margaret was now free, but she and Harvey did not live together. Their work—with increasing frequency, on different continents—kept them apart.

They saw each less and less frequently as they pursued their separate careers. For Margaret Leighton, the ugly tumult surrounding her divorce soon died down and she became the toast of London (and later, New York) as the star of the stage version of Terence Rattigan's *Separate Tables.* Two days after the final curtain descended at Stratford, Harvey went to work on his new film, *I Am a Camera.*

This film, put together from Christopher Isherwood's *Berlin Stories,* felt the whip of the censor—a problem that began even before John Collier, the scriptwriter, began writing the screenplay, as Harvey later told Hollywood columnist Sheilah Graham. The British film censor read the play and instantly ruled that the film could only receive an "X" certificate—and then only that if its dialogue was handled in a "most adult fashion," in other words, without talk of sex. Avoiding mention of sex was not easy, he said, since it constituted the theme of the story. However, he insisted, this film dealt with sex that sprang from *wholesome* love, and not the vulgar kind (he did not elaborate what this might mean), and the censors, he hoped, would therefore treat the film more leniently. Could he say something controversial, he asked the interviewer? He did, without waiting for a reply. "American actresses are much more willing to take off their clothes if the script calls for it than the British actresses," he grinned.

The film was turned down for the American Motion Picture Association's Seal of Approval, but did moderately well nevertheless. Today it appears rather staid. If this film, with its hints of homosexuality as well as promiscuous behavior was shocking in 1955, *Cabaret,* its musical successor might, at the time, never have been able even to set a foot in the censor's door.

The film, produced by James Woolf, was introduced with much fanfare.

"I think he's too good looking to portray me on the screen," Christopher Isherwood said when he met Harvey. Scrawny and very plain himself, an entry in his *The Diaries of Christopher Isherwood* reads: "I always thought the part should have been played by a character man. No author should be portrayed by a romantic leading actor, with the possible exception of Lord Byron."

Nevertheless, he admired Harvey, loved his performance, and they became friends. Harvey, he wrote in his diary, was an unusual man. In his April 1960 entry, he described a party Harvey had given at Chasens. Harvey had stood up and embraced him in front of everyone. That, he wrote, was the kind of thing that set him apart from most actors. Laurence Olivier might have done the same, but almost no American.

This film was the screen adaptation of the Broadway play. Apart from Laurence Harvey, who portrayed Isherwood, it also starred Julie Harris, who had created her role as Sally Bowles in the Broadway play, and also Shelley Winters, who portrayed the German-Jewish girl.

In her first autobiography, *The Best of Times, the Worst of Times,* Shelley Winters provides a vivid sketch of her first meeting with Harvey. Arriving in London which was wrapped in thick fog that day, she writes, she was met by the producers, Laurence Harvey, and the film's famous director, South African-born Henry Cornelius. Settling down at the Dorchester Hotel, she was told that a teacher who worked with the Royal Shakespeare Company would arrive the next day to begin coaching her to speak with the very difficult German accent.

Harvey, whom she had met several years earlier at an engagement party given by John Gielgud for actor Farley Granger and herself (they never married) telephoned her to say that he would take her to the studio for wardrobe fittings, since he lived nearby at Grosvenor House. With his usual exaggeration, he called the fog terrible, and said that people were "literally expiring" from it.

Picking her up in his chauffeur-driven Rolls-Royce—he had bought his very fancy Rolls-Royce a year or two earlier, for how could *anyone* exist without a Rolls-Royce, he had argued—he arrived with her teacher in tow. He had also come provided with a thermos flask of coffee and a picnic basket filled with egg sandwiches and scones, and said, in his clipped, upper-class British accent (she writes) that he also had whisky and beer in the "boot" [trunk] of the car. The fog was so bad, he explained, that it might take them till lunchtime to reach the studio at Shepperton and if the fog got any worse they would have to live at the studio.

They drove through the fog at about twenty-five miles an hour, and the chauffeur had to stop every few blocks to inspect the road for the presence of craters that had been made during the war and

Mrs. Skikne's three princes: Nahum, Isaac, and Harry.

The family in Johannesburg.

Harry and Rexy, his
first dog.

The cadet bugler.

The schoolboy, 1941.

The soldier, aged 17.

The army entertainer.

In England: Larry Skikne, first publicity releases.

With Margaret Leighton Harvey. (*Courtesy of Photofest*)

With Joan Cohn Harvey.

Paulene Stone Harvey with daughters Domino and Susan.

Harvey and daughter Domino.

With good friend Elizabeth Taylor in *Butterfield 8*. (*Courtesy of Photofest*)

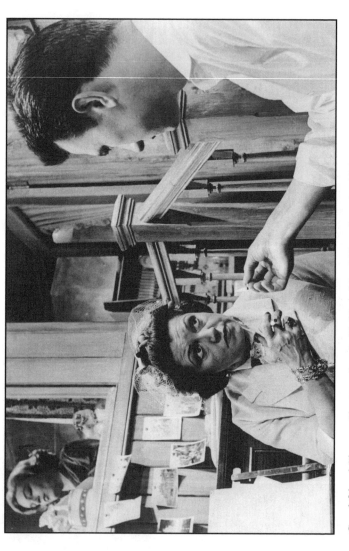

Good friend Simone Signoret (top left). First friend Hermione Baddeley. (*Courtesy of Photofest*)

With adoring mother, beaming father (far left), and fans in Johannesburg, 1956.

First screen nudity. In *Room at the Top*. Laurence Harvey and Simone Signoret. (*Courtesy of Photofest*)

Richard Widmark, Laurence Harvey, and John Wayne in *The Alamo*. (*Courtesy of Photofest*)

In Renato
Castellani's
*Romeo and
Juliet*, 1958.

In *I Am a Camera* with Shelley Winters, Julie Harris, and Anton
Diffring.

With Frank Sinatra in *The Manchurian Candidate*. (*Courtesy of Photofest*)

With Angela Lansbury in *The Manchurian Candidate*. (*Courtesy of Photofest*)

Harvey as Henry V in the Old Vic's tour of the United States with
Judi Dench. (*Courtesy of Photofest*)

Harvey was to be Cary Grant's successor as spokesman for Arpege.

King Richard and the Crusaders, 1954. Harvey and friend.

had still not been repaired. Larry drank warm whiskey and soda. Over hot coffee from the thermos, Shelley Winters and her teacher began working on the accent. This was, apparently, highly amusing to Harvey, who kept teasingly deriding Shelley Winters's efforts until, exasperated, her coach told him to stop. She could still hear his Lithuanian sibilants and the South African twang in his speech, she said. The coach, who was also a don at Oxford, did not, apparently, know that Harvey had never learned to speak Lithuanian (either with or without "Lithuanian sibilants") and that South African speech patterns (whether black or white) do not contain any twang. As a further irony, Shelley Winters writes that she burst out sobbing in her dressing room during the filming, thinking of the hopeless search her uncle was undertaking to find missing relatives who might have survived the Holocaust. She was not alone. Laurence Harvey, too, had relatives who had been murdered in Lithuania, however dimly he remembered them.

Harvey enjoyed working with Julie Harris. They developed an instant and long-lasting friendship and rapport. She became one of the less than a handful of actresses for whom he had a true affection and whom he genuinely admired. "She made *I Am a Camera* an exciting experience for me," he told journalist Ivy A. Harding in 1955. "She acts at breath-taking level." They had long scenes together, and their rapport is clearly evident in this film. Still a busy actress, reminiscing in 1998 with all the vivid enthusiasm of youth, she told this biographer, "He was an elegant actor, skillful and dedicated to acting. A big smoker and drinker, but a charming man. And very romantic."

She was a great admirer of Margaret Leighton, whom she termed "one of the greatest actresses of our time."

While they were filming *I Am a Camera,* Margaret Leighton was starring in Terence Rattigan's *Separate Tables* on the London stage. On opening night, Harvey took Margaret to the theater while John and James Woolf escorted Julie Harris. They had insisted, she reminisced, on having the studio design a special and quite wonderful dress for her to wear, and lent her the most marvelous jewels. The added responsibility of wearing all that heavy finery had given her a painful headache, but it was a wonderful evening, she laughed.

When Harris and Harvey were lunching once at a theatrical restaurant in London and having a great time a friend said to her, "Don't try to get him away from Margaret!" She thought that a great joke; Margaret and Larry, she said, were so much in love.

He was not, she noted, a cautious man. Driving her to Stratford after a very hearty lunch (he was still able to consume big meals at this stage), he became quite sleepy but insisted on driving at his usual top speed.

They starred together in a second film, *The Truth about Women,* and later, in the Broadway production of *A Country Wife.*

Praise for his work as Romeo in the film version of *Romeo and Juliet* had appeared in the American media. During the filming of *I Am a Camera,* he kept all the clippings with him, prepared to exhibit them to all who asked to read them. All this praise had—comparatively—subdued him. Thomas Wiseman wrote in *The Evening Standard* that arriving at the studio at Walton-on-Thames to have lunch with him, he found Harvey dressed for his role as Isherwood in high-necked monogrammed Russian pajamas, smoking a long cigarette through an even longer holder. Harvey compared himself, the interviewer noted, not without humor, only once to Sir Laurence Olivier and not even once to Sir John Gielgud!

The director had appeared. It was his mission, he said, to get "all that Shakespeare stuff" out of Harvey. His role as Romeo had given him an artificial veneer, he complained, and now he had to "come down to earth."

But Harvey said that he did not want to be "un-Romeo'd."

Harvey, the interviewer conceded, had "panache—and a sort of naïve ostentation." An exhibitionist he might have been, the interviewer commented, but he also possessed a personality to exhibit. There followed an intriguing glimpse of his ostentation. He had, he boasted, a closet filled with some thirty suits—"I value luxury only less than acting," he explained. He had always, from the very first, been a big spender, he said, choosing only the best—or at least, the most expensive. He kept a Cadillac in the States. ("I would have felt conspicuous without one.") In England, he had got rid of his Rolls-Royce as too impractical but owned a Jaguar and was planning to buy a plane—"you do not have to have one that goes faster than sound," he said, sounding unexpectedly frugal. One costing a modest £5,000 would do. Not, he said, that he ever had much money in the bank. This was because he liked to live to the full every hour of the day. "I can't grieve over what impression I give to other people. The things I say are not liked, I know. I can't please everyone. First they boost you up—and then, when you are up there, they say: 'Right, on top now? O.K. Shoot him down.' I am very restless. But I intend to be a great actor. Nothing less would satisfy me."

He was expressing himself, his interviewer notes, with unusual restraint. In a previous interview with the same journalist he had said, "I have been bashed, battered, mutilated, decapitated and massacred by the English critics. And I do care. I am deeply hurt. But it is better than being ignored. At least they can't ignore me. It was the same with Olivier. He was 45 before he was recognized. His Romeo was also damned."

Statements like these had earned Harvey a reputation for "lack of modesty." There was no reason why he should not think highly of himself, his interviewer commented, but there was every reason not to say so in public. To this Harvey replied that he knew he was outspoken and that it got him into hot water, and it was also true that he was flamboyant. He had been flamboyant in his cradle, but in relation to his art, he was very humble—or at least, there were degrees of humility.

I Am a Camera had loomed as a challenge: "Two of the easiest tasks you can assign to an actor," he told American reporters, "is either to cast him in a picture as the sole star, where he is boss of the roost and doesn't have to vie with any other top names, or as a supporting player, where he can let the star carry the ball and all the responsibilities." He had neither of these easy tasks, he said, for he had been pitted against two of the most talented and clever actresses in the business. "I had to hold my own against the keenest competition I had ever run up against," he declared. Not that he would have missed that opportunity for the world, but with two such scene stealers as Julie Harris and Shelley Winters as competition, he had to fight if he wanted the audiences to know he was even in the film!

Here, again, he provided some insight into how he worked.

Wearing the right clothes helped to fit him into a character, he had found. He was conscious, too, he said, that the static nature of his role made it essential that he play it with minute timing. One source of inspiration in this respect, he claimed, was the shabby clothes he had to wear in this movie. He infinitely preferred these to the elaborate costumes he had been wearing in *The Talisman* and *Romeo and Juliet* at Stratford. On the other hand, even shabby clothes could be a trap. When the stage wardrobe is too drab and informal, one unconsciously tended to relax too much. It was only Cornelius's genius that had steered him right.

This film was not, for him, accident free. In one sequence he had to
fight six Nazi thugs. Henry Cornelius had demanded such total real-
ism that Harvey had to take to his bed and x-rays revealed that
he had suffered a cracked rib among other injuries. As a result, he became the envy of all the other actors in this film. Shot during one of
the worst and bleakest winters in England, Julie Harris had to dress
in revealing and flimsy evening gowns for her routines as a nightclub
performer while the thermometer plummeted to four degrees below
zero and the heating unit broke. Harvey's accident occurred after the
heating unit was repaired and, confined to bed, he spent three shooting days luxuriously covered with heavy blankets and surrounded
by hot water bottles. In fact, he admitted, he had been so warm and
comfortable that he kept falling asleep during shooting. Finally, the
director had assigned a stagehand to lie under the bed and prod Harvey awake whenever the director gave him his cue.

It was during the making of this film that Harvey revealed his ambition to appear in a musical comedy and, introduced to a Hollywood correspondent who had been assigned to London, instantly
struck a deal with him. The correspondent had happened to mention that he had to rent a flat in London while still maintaining his
apartment in Hollywood because he had a long lease. He would let
anyone take his Hollywood apartment at half the rent just to get rid
of it for two years, he said. The actor, who was planning to fly to
Hollywood later that year in order to do a film for M-G-M instantly
took up the offer and signed the sublease.

What he looked forward to most, he said, was returning to working out in Hollywood's health clubs. He wished he could import at
least one of these to London. While filming *The Talisman* he had
worked out in a gym for two hours after shooting ended each day.
His role in the Castellani's *Romeo and Julie* had called for so much action that it had served as a good workout. *I Am a Camera* had very
little action, and he complained loudly about his lack of physical activity. To placate him and keep him fit, director Cornelius installed a
miniature gym in a room off the studio floor complete with barbells,
high jumping equipment, leather horses, and a punching bag. Harvey worked out there every day.

Life was not always harmonious on the set, however, mainly due to Harvey's temperamental outbursts. During one freezing day, while the actors and the crew were plodding through a particularly difficult scene, Harvey, irritated by some minor setback, clouded the cold air with his heavy smoking. Angrily, Cornelius shouted at him to stop smoking. How could he expect to give a good performance if he kept smoking all the time instead of concentrating on his lines? "I can act with or without a cigarette," Harvey snapped back. "But I can't act for a man who makes such futile remarks about my behavior," and stormed off to his dressing room.

James Woolf was telephoned and rushed to the set. During a forty-five-minute conference, the director and the producer discussed how to get Harvey back. Finally, the director, his ruffled feelings soothed by the very diplomatic Woolf went to his dressing room to ask his star to return to the set. Harvey yelled out his refusal and threatened to punch Cornelius on the nose. Not until the following morning did he cool off sufficiently to consent to return.

In another show of temperament, he accused Shelley Winters of trying to dictate camera angles. Having listened to an argument between Winters and Cornelius, Harvey told her acidly, "Miss Winters, there are other stars in this picture besides yourself, and life would be a great deal easier if you stopped making interruptions." If she had answered back, one of the technicians said, there would have been an awful row. "Harvey was in the mood for a row." Sensibly, she did not.

By way of apology, Harvey claimed that his tantrums sprang from nerves and deep-seated insecurity. "One tries not to show one's innermost emotions," he explained. People who knew him well agreed that he was naturally shy and tried hard to attempt to subdue this character trait. On the other hand, John Woolf called him "refreshingly extroverted," and Harvey himself reminded people that he was—unfairly, he claimed—known as the most conceited actor in England.

His basic conflict, a friend explained, was the sharp contrast between his determination to achieve fame as an actor and as an internationally famous and glamorous playboy, with all the appurtenances that great wealth can provide. Perhaps he nursed dreams of becoming another Rubirosa.

There may well have been moments when he might have wished he had been a playboy instead of an actor. Attending London's famed annual film ball during the filming of *I Am a Camera*, he was mobbed by a small army of screaming teenagers who began pulling at his tie and coat buttons. His workouts at the studio's gym stood him in good stead. Vaulting a bar he managed to hold the screaming fans at bay until a group of uniformed attendants came to his rescue.

Within hours after the last shot was taken of *I Am a Camera* he was on a plane bound for Khartoum, where he was going on location to make *Storm over the Nile*.

12

Coming Home
to Mother—Briefly

Storm over the Nile (also titled, *None but the Brave*) was the fourth re-make of *The Four Feathers*, a saga of the Victorian upper classes and their codes of honor, self-sacrifice, and courage for the glory and the preservation of the British Empire. By 1955, when the film was re-leased, the British Empire no longer girded the globe and the impe-rial army had become a relic of the past. Nor did the film pay too much attention to historical accuracy. It was Britain's first venture into CinemaScope and its goal was to dazzle audiences with the Su-dan's spectacular landscape, its blazing desert, the dashing uni-forms of the old British imperial army, with swords flashing in the sun and cannons roaring in the clash of battle. This was American-based Zoltan Korda's version of *The Four Feathers*, which his late brother, Sir Alexander Korda, had produced two decades earlier. In the studios' determined battle to compete with television, the new film possessed all the superior technical advantages of Cinema-Scope and Technicolor and was even more spectacular, bigger, and more skillfully produced than the first film. It had only one disad-vantage: it made use of the older film's backgrounds. Korda com-plained bitterly that stretching these backgrounds to fill the new screen created so many distortions that the camels looked more like greyhounds.

Harvey costarred with Britain's popular Anthony Steel and Mary Ure, one of the most talented and delicately lovely actresses briefly to illumine Britain's stage and screen. She went on to play Richard Burton's long-suffering wife in *Look Back in Anger* and died while still very young.

Harvey plays the soldier blinded by exposure to the blazing sun. Always seriously bent on authenticity in his roles, he told interviewers that he had to master a difficult new technique in order to make his character believable. It had been one of his hardest assignments. In order to learn how to play this character believably, he said, he had spent long periods of time in a London hospital studying exactly how someone blinded by the sun and heat would look and how he would adjust to blindness.

As soon as his part was wrapped up, Harvey flew down to Johannesburg to visit his parents. Getting off the plane he was swamped with reporters and relatives whom his mother had liberally invited to come and greet him, and whisked away for a radio interview immediately after embracing his parents. Ever dramatic, his mother instantly collapsed with excitement and, when she recovered, begged everyone not to tell her son, since, she declared, his career came first and she did not want him to abandon his interview in order to fuss over her. Naturally, she had spent the whole day prior to his arrival preparing the gefilte fish and the *kalfleis* that she fondly believed were still his favorite dishes. Knowing that she had undoubtedly spent hours in her kitchen preparing these dishes, he was fulsomely complimentary. There was not a single restaurant in the world, or another culinary genius who could make these dishes so marvelously delicious, he told her. Speaking of cooking, he said, he was no mean cook himself. Once he had decided to cook an early Christmas dinner at his house for friends. As luck would have it, he had broken his right arm a little earlier. Undaunted, he had cooked his turkey with his left arm. Unable to cook vegetables, or make stuffing or sauces, he had served his friends "Turkey Solitaire."

Mrs. Skikne (as everyone called her) was no longer slaving over that hot coal stove in their house on Berea Road. Their new home possessed all the modern conveniences she had always longed for, but was too small, rather to her disappointment, to house her famous, beloved youngest son. He had, of course, seen to it that he had been given the use of a luxurious flat owned by one of his friends ("my very good friend and boss," the very wealthy theater owner John Schlesinger).

His mother was far too excited to protest. His father told reporters that he was in a constant daze. "What with the doorbell and the telephone constantly ringing: I've hardly managed to have a cup of tea in peace." He had his own take on his son's talent. Even as a small child, he told Hilda Schaffer of *The Zionist Record,* Larry had always been spunky. At the age of four he had wanted to dress up as a devil at a Purim festival in Jonishik. And even Mr. Skikne, as he was known to everyone, although the soul of integrity, was not above inventing a story or two himself on this exalted occasion. He said that his two younger sons had inherited his own wanderlust, for in Lithuania he had only rarely been much at home. He had traveled so much around Europe "to gain experience." As a lad, his second son had told him one day that he planned to go to the Far East. He called his eldest son a Hebrew teacher as well as a pioneer. It was his way of saying that he was equally proud of all three sons.

At dinner on Larry's first night, his father said, they had not been able to stop talking until two in the morning. But apart from seeing his parents, one of Harvey's reasons for his visit to Johannesburg had been to persuade them finally to leave South Africa and settle in Israel. There was an immediate practical reason for them to make the change. Robert and his family were in Rangoon, Burma, where he had been sent by the Israel Labor Party to act as its representative on the Asian Socialist Conference for a two-year stay. In Tel Aviv, they had been living in a rented flat owned by a young South African who had returned to South Africa and wished to sell it. The flat was well built and in an excellent location and almost all their neighbors would be former South Africans. In Israel, Boris and Ella could catch up with friends long unseen and laugh at the follies of their youth and weep at the loss of other friends and relatives in the Holocaust.

The owner of the flat was only too happy to sell and the price was more than reasonable. It was a transaction speedily completed, settled by Harvey in one impulsive moment, as he settled most of his transactions. Once again he assured his parents that he would support them by sending a fixed sum every year. His parents agreed that this move would be the best thing for them, although it was hard on his mother to have to give up the glamour of being the mother of a famous film star and being invited to attend the premieres of his films, with all the accompanying publicity. What she would have liked best would have been to live in England, to be near him, but even she knew how impractical that would be. She knew about Margaret Leighton and hoped that nothing would come of that relationship. She never knew about his dual nature.

Before he left and throughout the five or six days of his stay in Johannesburg, he gave interviews published in the Johannesburg *Star* and in the *Outspan*. He did not mince words. His driving ambition, he impulsively declared, was to make a gigantic film within the grandiose natural scenery of South Africa, a film that equaled if not surpassed the greatest American Western ever made. "Johnny [John Huston] and I were toying with the idea of filming Stuart Cloete's *Turning Wheels* [a popular potboiler published in the United States about the Great Trek]," he informed reporters ebulliently—perhaps mischievously aware that this novel had been banned in South Africa. And only in remote South Africa, perhaps, could he airily call John Huston, "Johnny," and imply that they were close friends.

While in Johannesburg, he received a great deal of fan mail. Most had a single theme. He had worked hard and studied hard, and he had been lucky, he told a reporter, but to those asking how to become a star, he always replied, "There is nothing you can do to become a star. . . . It's the public who makes the stars. You can be a fine actor, or the best-looking man in the town—and if the public doesn't like you, you'll never reach the top. It's out of your hands. . . . There's only one thing you can do, in fact. Put yourself where people can see you, and where directors can spot you. If you're on the stage, or somewhere where you get audiences and you have this 'star quality,' you'll be noticed soon enough."

Even he, he admitted, had not won everybody's heart. There had been bitter criticism of him in Britain and the States. "It's upsetting," he said. "I can't understand it. Still, when I'm on the stage, the audiences flock to see me. My films are popular. The critics may be right—but I'm right too."

Speaking of his leading ladies, he was not always charitable. When the cameras are rolling, he said, their subjects have to "click." Sometimes it happens between people who just can't get on together at all offstage. He had "clicked" with Susan Shentall, his leading lady in *Romeo and Juliet*, although she was just a rank amateur who had no interest in pursuing an acting career. He had "clicked" with Mary Ure in *Storm over the Nile*, and certainly with the inimitable Julie Harris whom he liked and admired, and even with the tiny dramatic actress Rene Ray, with whom he had starred in *Women of Twilight* and who had also been in *The Good Die Young*. But in her case he was not generous. "She is one of those rare actresses whose successes can never kill a tremendous zest for the stage," he began blandly. Then he delivered his stiletto thrust: "Off the set she'll talk endlessly about the intelligence of horses and cats."

He was heading for Hollywood, he said, where he would be starring in *Diana* with Lana Turner and Jennifer Jones. These were plans that, as so often happened, never eventuated. Nor did a projected film titled *Joseph and His Brethren* in which he was to star with Rita Hayworth, and yet the purpose of his visit to Hollywood had been to discuss this film, to be made by Columbia.

Meanwhile, he returned to London for additional takes on *Storm over the Nile* and to attend its royal premiere. The film won universal praise for its fine photography and its battle scenes. The critics called Harvey's performance "polished"—when close-ups of his profile were not required. Seated between Harvey and Anthony Steel, the Duke of Edinburgh called the film "a whale of a picture." Greeting them with a hearty "Hello, you two chaps," (this according to Harvey) "he fired questions at us about production in the Sudan."

There was also another project that fell through. Before leaving for the Sudan he had agreed to appear on Broadway the following season in a play that had been banned from the London stage. *South* was a drama by the Franco-American novelist Julien Green dealing with homosexuality. Directed by Peter Glenville, it was, at the time, playing on the private stage of the London Arts Theatre Committee, which had encouraged the staging of distinguished works on homosexual themes in the past. *South* had played in Paris for two years. *Tea and Sympathy*, another play that had been successful in Paris, dealing with a lesson in sex taught to a teenage boy by a man had also been banned on the London stage, but with the man changed to a mature woman, the play was enjoying its second successful year on Broadway and later became a successful film. Still, Harvey doggedly retained his enthusiasm for *South*. "You seem to be more lenient over here," he told William Peper of the *World Telegram* when he arrived in New York. "I think it [i.e., the play] makes for a more exciting theater. I'm very anxious to act on Broadway. . . . We had a little censor trouble with my film [*I Am a Camera*] too. The play had to be cleaned up a bit for films, but Sally is just as outrageous as she ever was. Julie Harris is an extraordinary actress. Wait till you see her in this picture."

When he liked someone, his praise was genuine and unsparing.

But he had badly miscalculated. *South* was also banned in the United States.

In England, before leaving for New York, he had been scheduled to make *Her Chocolate Soldier,* a new film version of George Bernard Shaw's *Arms and the Man* with Claire Bloom and Alec Guinness, but filming had been postponed because the script was not ready. Unable to wait, he sailed to New York, where he was to star in a play called *Island of the Goats.* On board, he discovered a tearful Siobhan McKenna, who had just left her husband and small son in Ireland and was bound for Broadway, where she was to appear in *The Chalk Garden.* He appeared at her cabin door wearing a blue blazer, white ducks, and yellow bedroom slippers trimmed with white fur, a gift, he said, from his dear friend Greer Garson, and he looked so ridiculous that she could not help laughing. At dinner, he exuberantly charmed the guests at the captain's table, where, naturally, they were seated, and set them roaring with laughter at his wickedly funny stories and his sudden requests for exotic dishes that the chef had to prepare. He made close friends with two fabulously rich older ladies from San Francisco who owned a chain of newspapers and were sailing round the world, and the three of them concocted ridiculous toasts and drank the evenings away. Divine little dears, he called them. They adored him and might have granted him the moon had he but asked for it, some of the other passengers said, although he knew quite well that they were the kind of people who took rather than gave. As it was, he had a standing invitation to visit them whenever he chanced to be in San Francisco.

Island of the Goats, by the Italian playwright Ugo Betti, had been translated by the poet Henry Reed and had won the Italian National Drama Prize in 1950. Ugo Betti was the highly acclaimed author of twenty-five plays and was rated by his countrymen as their leading playwright since Pirandello. The play had been staged in Rome, Paris, and Berlin with great success. Peter Glenville, its director, had acquired the English language rights during its two-year run in Paris, and it was to be staged in London later in the season.

The play, in three acts, was about a widow who lives on an isolated Mediterranean island with her daughter and sister-in-law and herds goats. A young man arrives and upsets them all. In the end, they throw him down the well.

The play had every reason to be a hit in New York. Peter Glenville was the highly acclaimed director of box office hits like *Separate Tables* and its cast included Uta Hagen and Ruth Ford as well as Laurence Harvey.

"I am absolutely thrilled. . . . It is a most wonderful part. I would have taken it for nothing." Harvey gushed.

Staged at the Fulton Theater, in view of all its triumphs in Italy, Berlin, and its most recent two-year run in Paris, the play appeared certain of success. Yet the Parisians' enthusiasm notwithstanding, it made no impact on New Yorkers. Opening on October 4, 1955, it closed on October 8.

Harvey received thirteen curtain calls on its first night, but the reviews of the play itself were poor. Peter Glenville's production was called "monotonous." According to Brooks Atkinson, the drama critic for the *New York Times*, "As a versatile man, Laurence Harvey talks continuously and moves now and then," while Uta Hagen and Ruth Ford represented something "too deep for words."

After its one-week run, Harvey was less than enthusiastic about the play.

"It really should have been called *Island of Ghosts*," he told journalist Joe Hyams. We didn't think it would run like *Seven Year Stitch*, or whatever, but we thought it would have a fairish run. The big trouble was the play is ten years ahead of its time in America. It's in a style of writing your critics loathe and don't understand. Why, some of them even printed that I was supposed to be a symbolic devil in it. I don't know where they got that idea. If I was a devil, I'd have worn bloody horns and appeared in a puff of smoke. There was devilment but no devil, though if you'll pardon the pun, I was devilishly energetic in matters of love."

As always, he blamed the critics for failing to understand the play and his role in it, but refusing to be defeated by this setback, jauntily invited Noel Coward, who had become a good friend, to accompany him to applaud Siobhan McKenna in her Broadway debut.

He claimed that he was not bitter about the failure of *Island of Goats*. Bitterness was only for people with chips on their shoulders. He had enjoyed every minute of the production because of the brilliant people he had worked with. "At least they do creative things on Broadway," he sneered. "In Hollywood I spent more time discussing pictures than making them."

Obviously, the time spent vainly scouting for a good role on his first trip to Hollywood with James Woolf still sat heavily on his heart. What kind of parts was he usually offered in Hollywood? he was asked. "Most often they want me to play an English bore or else I'm asked to appear in a film with a poetic plot so that they can utilize my Shakespearean background. The feeling is I can be easily understood in Pottsville, whatever that is." What would he like to play, he was asked? "A Western," he answered. "I've done Westerns in England, but in eleventh century costume. The last one was *King Richard and the Crusaders [The Talisman]*. Actually they do make Westerns in England, too, but there they call them 'Easterns' and the Colonials fight the fuzzy-wuzzies [*sic*] instead of Indians." It was his ambition, he said, to make a real Western in England. "I can see it now," he enthused. "We call it *'Picadilly Pete'* and it would star Sir Ralph Richardson and Harvey Harrow. Sir Ralph, dressed in a top hat, striped trousers and spats, would ride in on a horse with a black Rolls-Royce lurking ominously in the background with Harrow the heavy. In the barroom showdown, Harrow throws champagne in Sir Ralph's face. Sir Ralph steps back and says, 'I say there, partner, go for your revolver.' And the battle's on."

At the age of twenty-seven he was still an adolescent.

On his return to England, he was met at the airport by Margaret Leighton, who was sporting the large sapphire engagement ring he had given her. Margaret had been granted special permission to meet Harvey in the customs hall at London Airport for a private welcome, but when Harvey left the plane, a gold-braided customs officer, an official from the ministry, and two film representatives stood by as they embraced and kissed. Advised to avoid the many reporters and cameras clustering outside, they came out of the arrivals building separately. Margaret Leighton attempted to do as instructed. Ever eager for publicity, Harvey, however, made no effort to avoid the questions shouted by the press and answered them all. Was he planning to marry Margaret Leighton? "I certainly hope to marry Miss Leighton, but how can I?" he responded. "She works at night and I work during the day. It's a job to arrange time. We're engaged. We hope to fix the date of the wedding next year. It has been difficult to decide anything so far because I have been filming or acting abroad—and Margaret has been in London."

Margaret Leighton did manage to put in a word or two herself. "Next year," she told the *Daily Express*, "I hope to be working in New York when Laurence is there and it will be easier to think about the wedding. When he is filming and I'm acting we see each other so little."

He talked about what interested him most: himself. Even in the short time he was in the States, he said, even though the play had been a dismal failure, he had been flooded with offers—to act in television plays, to star in films. He had received two acting awards, one of them for the most promising actor to make a debut on Broadway. He had no objection to the press taking pictures, he said. "You can take us together."

But here the film representatives intervened. They shunted Margaret into the back seat of a waiting limousine and stood guard, shouting that she did not want her picture taken. This was hardly what Harvey wanted.

Finally, both the stars were seated together in the back seat of the limousine and were whisked away.

He had brought her gifts from Africa, drums and a set of African figures, and to remember him by while he was in the States, had sent her—"wonderful" she called them—postcards of palm trees and sunny beaches.

She was, at this stage in their relationship, both generous and understanding. An actor, she told the press, had to live and work in close touch with authors, his fellow actors, managers, technicians, and every night, he had to tap the barometer of the audience. Larry was ideally suited to that life. He derived as much pleasure from an evening's conversation with his dresser as he did from an evening spent with a Hollywood potentate. Every facet of the business of being an actor was of intense interest and importance to him, and the audience was the most important of all.

During his stay in New York they had been in constant touch by telephone, she said, and he had asked her to find a play for him so that he could redeem his faltering reputation after the flop of *Island of the Goats*. He was determined not to succumb to failure, or to give up the stage and turn exclusively to making films. She had told him that John Clements, an influential friend, had become a member of the board of the Saville Theatre, and Harvey had asked her to go and speak to him. On route to his flat, she told him that she had done so and that John Clements had offered him a part in his forthcoming production of Sheridan's *The Rivals*.

He had not been well since his return to England, he wrote to his parents, and had been laid up in bed for a week. Their letters irritated him. Eternally dissatisfied, his mother complained that they had sold their furniture and lost money on the deal, that they had to purchase new furniture in Israel, and things were expensive. He reminded them that what he had sent them was more than thirty-five million people earned in a single year in England and that he was doing everything in his power for them. He had sent them a year's allowance in advance, though he could scarcely afford it. In fact, this allowance was on the small side—just sufficient to keep them in some comfort. "Please help me and try to understand," he ended his letter pathetically.

A week or two later, he was happy again, much better and up and about once more. "My doctors insisted I went [*sic*] into a nursing home, but managed to persuade them to let me stay at home and had an awful ten days in bed, but its all over now, thank God," he wrote.

He had started working on *The Rivals*, and planned to film it for television, and then he was to make a movie called *Three Men in a Boat*. In fact, he wrote, he had so much work for the following year he did not know how he was going to do it all.

The Rivals, which marked his return to the West End stage, also marked an unexpected triumph for him—unexpected, that is, by all his critics.

He had not performed on a West End stage since his unspectacular appearance in *Hassan* in 1951. The new play opened in Edinburgh where it enjoyed a tremendous success. There was a week's run at Stratford and then the company headed for London for an eight-week season. It was February, and the weather was terrible, with days filled with snow, fog, cold, and rain. The whole company had colds, yet he felt elated, sure of his London success. Such was his daring challenge to what he termed the poisonous pens of the London critics (they called this his "self-confidence," meaning, his brazen nerve) that he drove to the Saville Theatre where the play was staged in a brand new, newly purchased, gleaming black and sand-trimmed Rolls-Royce with Margaret Leighton, looking very beautiful and happy, swathed in expensive furs, seated at his side.

As Captain Jack Absolute in this Restoration comedy, he received rave reviews from the critics. Those who had, in his own words, "bashed, battered, mutilated and decapitated him," for his performances at Stratford were now extravagantly generous in their praise; he received what was described in theatrical circles as the biggest unanimous acclaim given to any actor in London in years. Romulus Films, his London headquarters, had to hire a special staff to deal with his enormous fan mail.

The change of heart by the critics was summed up by John Barber in the *Daily Express.* "Again and again," he wrote, "Laurence Harvey has turned his back on film fortunes in the hope of earning a crumb of praise from the English theater critics. And all he ever got was insults. He tried again in *The Rivals* and he was magnificent. Wildly handsome, decked in scarlet and white and gold, his cool gray eyes alight with humor, Harvey stole the play from such cunning artists as John Clements, Kay Hammond and Athene Seyler." "An absolute winner," the *Daily Mail* called him.

When the season ended, the play was filmed for television. Simultaneously, he began work on *Three Men in a Boat.* He was so busy, he complained in his letter to his parents, that he scarcely had a moment to himself. There were dozens of plays and scripts to read, there were the lines of his next film to read and rehearse, and ever new projects to think about. And for the first time, Margaret's name appeared in his regular letter to his parents: "she joins me in sending regards and love to you all," he concluded.

He wanted them to understand that he was serious about Margaret.

Three Men in a Boat, which he started filming only a meager handful of days after *The Rivals* closed, was based on Jerome K. Jerome's 1910 classic novel of the same title about the adventures of three young men vacationing in a boat on the River Thames and, when released, became a box office success, if not overwhelmingly received by the critics. This adaptation of the novel tried too hard to be funny, the critics said, despite the fact that one of Britain's most popular comedians, Jimmy Edwards, was in it, its costumes were colorful, and Harvey looked handsome and elegant in his Edwardian sports and white pants.

During shooting, the contrast between Harvey's well-publicized egotism and his private dedication to hard work was evident to his costars. At lunch in the studio's canteen on one occasion, Harvey, Jimmy Edwards said, twice sent back a plate of food on the grounds that it had not been prepared to his liking. Disgusted with this, Edwards, who was sitting opposite him shouted, "For pity's sake, need we have drama at lunch-time?" Yet, the next day on location on the River Thames, Harvey, Edwards, and a third actor, David Tomlinson, had to fall out of their rowing boat and into the chilly water and this took several takes. Edwards and Tomlinson were tired, cold, and grumbled a great deal long before the take was wrapped up. Harvey, Edwards told Francis Hitching of *John Bull*, did not complain even once.

He was working, he wrote to his parents, from six in the morning to midnight, six days a week on the film, acting in a play in the evening, spending his Sundays reading scripts, and, if that were not enough, was also in the process of moving into a new flat. It would not be ready for occupancy for some six months, but he was thrilled, at last, to have a home of his own, with his own furniture. It wasn't really a flat, he wrote, but what was called a small mews house, a converted coach house with its own garage. In this letter, Margaret, very much in evidence, sent her love.

He demanded that she share in that recognition and affection for his parents that he demanded of his next two wives.

Renovating and furnishing his mews house to his extravagant taste left him financially strapped, he complained, and above that he had to pay an additional £4,000 in income tax. He had been forced to borrow money and "God knows how I am going to pay it back." With his time taken up by the film and rehearsals for his next play, he did not have a moment, he wrote, to supervise the work on his new home. Deliveries of the bathroom and kitchen equipment, the wallpaper, et cetera, were maddeningly slow since most of these articles were being produced for export, not for home consumption and the government had imposed a big credit squeeze. Added to these difficulties was a spell of bad weather that delayed filming for weeks on the River Thames, where most of the action in *Three Men in a Boat* took place.

Although nothing was ready except his bedroom, he moved into what he called his new flat, at Bruton Place, Berkeley Square, in Mayfair. A cold, wet summer had turned into freezing winter. The BBC production of his play had been a great success and he had begun work on a new film, *After the Ball*, about the life and career of the famous music hall star Vesta Tilley. He played her manager-husband and while furnishing his new home, found himself deeply involved in the preliminary work on the script and the details of his costume, for this was a period piece.

He was alone again, for Margaret had left for New York to appear in the Broadway production of *Separate Tables* and would, he estimated, be away for at least a year. He was hoping to join her in New York to do a television play, or possibly a movie in Hollywood, if the right story came along.

Asked what the status of their engagement was, he told *Picturegoer,* "we are desperately in love with each other." But he set no date for their marriage.

On October 29, 1956, he attended a Royal Command Performance at the Empire Cinema in London, where, he wrote to his proud parents, he was formally introduced to the queen and Princess Margaret in a line of twenty international film stars that included Marilyn Monroe and Brigitte Bardot. A crowd of fans had swarmed outside the cinema to watch the greats of the time emerging from their limousines. The men—the late Peter Finch, the handsome Rossano Brazzi of *South Pacific* fame, among others—were in evening dress. The women were gorgeously gowned. Marilyn Monroe arrived swathed in a gold tissue toga cloak to shield her from the cold, clad underneath it in a skintight sheath of gold tissue hung from topaz shoulder straps. The aging and formidable Joan Crawford, in London to star in Romulus's production of *The Sins of Esther Costello*, in which Harvey had been slated to costar—another project that fell through—was resplendent in a white satin dress with a matching coat hung with crystal beads. Anita Eckberg, the tall, blond, luscious star of the marvelous Italian director Fellini's film *La Dolce Vita*, dubbed "the iceberg," who lived mainly in Italy, wore a dress—daring for the time—that plunged to the waistline in the back. No slouch herself on this glittering occasion, the queen wore a regal black velvet gown and her tiara sparkled with emeralds and diamonds. This was a very special and patriotic occasion: the film shown was *The Battle of the River Plate*, commemorating a famous naval battle during World War II, and officers from those fighting ships were also present. Even Harvey felt moved, as he wrote to his parents. As was not unusual with him, he took on the color of his environment and felt a surge of patriotism. When it was his turn to be introduced, the queen, who had something gracious and harmless to say to everyone, asked "Did you enjoy making *Three Men in a Boat* in the wet summer, Mr. Harvey?"

"It is a favorite tale of mine and I much look forward to seeing it on the screen," he smoothly replied.

The event had a bittersweet taste, for that week Israeli troops had marched into the Sinai desert and he was worried about the welfare of his family. "I only hope and pray that all will be well and that a speedy victory and peace will result," he wrote to his parents.

Margaret, he wrote proudly, was enjoying a most brilliant success on Broadway.

Later that year he was chosen as the after-luncheon speaker at a mammoth event given at the Savoy Hotel by the Variety Club of Great Britain, at which the annual show business awards were announced. Dubbed "King Rat of the Day" (in reference to a film made by Romulus in which he had no part), he said: "Honor still eludes me. The sooner they name a cigarette after me the better." His speech sparkled with wisecracks, and he presented awards to stars like Paul Scofield and Mary Ure with very good grace.

He had barely finished working on *Three Men in a Boat* and was rehearsing his next West End role in another Restoration comedy as Mr. Horner, the lighthearted seducer in *The Country Wife*, for which he again won high praise (he later starred in the Broadway production of this comedy with Julie Harris), when he moved into his new flat. Nothing was ready except his bedroom, he wrote to his parents, and "God knows how long it will be before I finally get the workmen out of the place." The workmen had been in the house for over five months and nothing seemed to be going forward. He uttered the usual complaints echoed at this time: people just did not seem to want to work anymore, to try to get them to do anything was like trying to get blood out of a stone. However, the bedroom was looking quite pretty and when everything was finally completed, he wrote, there would be some semblance of a home. But he had only a very short lease on the property and had to try to get an extension, for he had spent an enormous amount of money on it.

He only hinted, vaguely, of the habit he had developed of constantly getting new ideas for improvements, thus constantly adding to the expense and the delays, incessantly complaining about his mounting expenses and his fear that he was facing bankruptcy.

In his letters to his family, he always signed himself "Larry." They would have wondered who "Larushka" was.

He was very proud of his new house, of how he had furnished and decorated it, from the glistening fawn Bentley in the garage to his rather small bedroom that was reached by climbing a narrow staircase and looked, to a reporter from the *Sunday Express* like a cross between a sultan's harem and a window at an expensive furniture store. When they met, Harvey was wearing a track suit dated circa 1900 and shoes that might have come from some discarded Persian closet. And he looked extremely disheveled—as only a man owning a Bentley could look!

A four-poster Sheraton bed and a bar were all that could fit into his bedroom. He always needed "a drinkie" before dinner, he explained, pouring himself and his guest two hearty vodkas. After that he led the reporter on a tour of the rest of his new house. It was expensively furnished, and there was a super abundance of mirrors everywhere. The house was only big enough for one person, he sighed, although he could, temporarily, put up an occasional friend. What about his fiancée, Margaret Leighton? he was asked. Again he sighed. These sighs seemed like some hangover of a play he had been in. "My private life is just a disaster," he sighed, "a shambles." Marriage did not seem uppermost in his mind. "What can I say?" he sighed. "What can one say?"

He seemed, in this interview, to be morosely more concerned with the bad treatment he had received in Hollywood concerning *The Talisman* than with his vaguely prospective marriage plans. "They did all the wrong things to me in Hollywood. Put me in armor, the fools. I creaked and clanked all the way up Sunset Boulevard. . . . The people I had to act with were not much help you know. Puddings, most of them."

And following came an extremely ungenerous estimation of stars like Rex Harrison (whom, actually, he liked) and George Sanders (whom he did not). Speaking of his highly successful performances on the West End and the success of *Three Men in a Boat*, he said, "I think you can say I've arrived."

He might have been half asleep, or it might have been the morning after a night of heavy drinking—he drank a great deal—or some other cause that had made him groggy and rambling. One month later, however, he was much more lively in another interview. This time, he had invited the journalist to marvel at the results of his taste as an interior decorator, which had cost him some £10,000. This interview had been theatrically staged. The appointment had been at four-thirty in the afternoon. Harvey was still asleep in his Sheraton four-poster when the journalist arrived. Awakened by Mario, his smiling, dapper young Italian manservant—awakened with some difficulty, it appeared that he had to be convinced that it was teatime and not four-thirty in the morning—he appeared in his tiny living room, yawning, wearing a monogrammed dressing gown, Edwin Goring of the *Daily Mirror* reported. Mario, dressed in a white tunic, brought in the tea. After tea, his little mansion was exhibited.

He had decorated his house all by himself, he said proudly. Except the curtains, that is. "Margaret chose the chintz. I consulted her, of course." They were contemplating marriage as soon as possible, he said. That was his incentive for buying and furnishing his new home. They had made the decision to marry four years earlier, but there had been complications. There had been the complications surrounding Margaret Leighton's divorce. Their careers had to be considered. He had three films and two plays lined up. He hoped she would like the house, he said. She had exquisite taste.

Proudly, he displayed his sumptuous little palace. It was crammed with antiques, hung with silks, studded with glittering gilt.

"All junk," he said and dealt a casual kick at an expensive rosewood table. There was a mixture of Italian, French, Regency, Sheraton, Adam, William Kent—an overwhelming mixture of furniture, mirrors, marble, black wallpaper, and pink, bold-patterned curtains, Georgian cocktail cabinets, and the television stored in a Sheraton cabinet. There were twelve rooms in all, and three bathrooms and a kitchen, beautifully equipped with every housewife's dream. The basic theme of his house, he claimed, was simplicity. He felt happy in his new home, less happy about his career, for he hankered after more Shakespeare. He adored the fact that there was always work for him, and that money, which he claimed was the last thing he cared about, kept rolling in.

So did the bills, which littered the beautiful tables everywhere.

He had made his little house as gaudy as a brothel, as bright as a parrot's wings, the reporter wrote. Its pink front door led to his living room, done in startlingly black velvet. The dining room had a purple carpet, on which stood a white, black, and gold marble dining room table. The bedroom was in mauve and white and his bathroom was tiled in shocking pink. He loved showing off his treasure trove of a house to friends and journalists, giving interviews and guided tours, strolling through his rooms in black velvet slippers embroidered at the vamp in gold like those he had seen his aristocratic friends wear, elegantly clutching his ten-inch cigarette holder between his teeth, smoking incessantly, careful to let none of the ash spill on the carpets.

In order to pay the most pressing of his bills, he borrowed money heedlessly and recklessly from everyone: from wealthy businessmen who hoped to invest in his future films, from the ever faithful Jimmy Woolf, from ambitious producers, from rich friends.

In early December of that year, he flew to New York for three days to be with Margaret Leighton, who had broken three ribs in a fall during the run of *Separate Tables*. A real trooper, although heavily bandaged, she had insisted on returning to her role. For recreation the couple did a little shopping in Manhattan and talked, in general terms, of setting a date for their marriage. They had thought, they said, tentatively of June in the following year, but in the meanwhile, Harvey had to return to the final rehearsals of *The Country Wife*.

His leading lady was Diana Churchill, the actress daughter of Winston Churchill. The two of them giggled a lot together. He expected to stay in the play for five weeks, he said, and then he planned to fly to New York to do a television play, which, he hoped, would be Bernard Shaw's *The Doctor's Dilemma*, costarring Margaret. He needed to act on the stage, he claimed, in order to gain more and more experience as an actor. The pay was absurd for someone of his earning capacity: £30 a week. In fact, he held, it was actually costing him money to be in this play.

Waiting to drive him home every night was his outsized Rolls-Royce and his chauffeur in livery; the chauffeur, he claimed, was supplied by his studio. Dwelling on his lovely little house, he said he had a staff of two and two daily helpers. He had deliberately run riot, he claimed enthusiastically, in decorating his lovely little mews house, decorating its walls in green, black, purple, yellow, and red because he felt that color was so necessary in drab old London.

He was committed to act on Broadway, and after that, he announced to the press, he would be starring in a British film, *The Truth about Women*, to be made by Muriel and Sidney Box. Afterward he was to shoot a film in Bermuda, where he hoped to marry Margaret. And after the Bermuda film, he was to costar with Stewart Granger, another popular movie star of the day, in a film called *The Whole Truth*, and then he had the option of performing in two plays or making a film by the end of that year.

Only the first of these projects was realized. He did not marry Margaret Leighton in Bermuda.

13

Marriage, but Not Togetherness

He had become an established star in Britain, popular with the moviegoing public if not with the critics. Young women found him irresistibly attractive. People enjoyed reading about his antics, his larger-than-life image, in the movie magazines and the popular tabloids. It was said of him that he could have any woman he chose, merely with a glance. He had been so great a hit on the West End stage that even the powerful producer and theater owner Binkie Beaumont, who, when he had first arrived in London, had snubbed him as a foreigner who could never portray a proper Englishman, had opened his door to him. He stood an elegant six feet tall, was athletic, swam, fenced, rode, and boxed impressively. With his broad cheekbones, broad, high forehead, perfect nose, gray eyes, and clutch of brown hair tousled above his forehead, his lithe, tall frame, and broad shoulders, he seemed to his fans like some classical Greek god and to his detractors like some exotic butterfly. Even more attractive than his good looks was his voice, which, to American critics, had the rich, deep texture of velvet.

Graceful and slim, his clothes—and he was a perfectionist in that area—were meticulously selected to stun and amaze people, particularly staid and conservative Englishmen, who labeled his selections bizarre: pants as slim as gas pipes ("Larry is wearing ballet tights for trousers this year," a fellow actor joked), Edwardian-style jackets, shirts and ties that quite often deliberately did not match.

"I know," he told journalists, "that I'm regarded in some circles as a kind of King of the Mayfair Teddy Boys, but that's just a lot of hooey, believe me. I was wearing narrow trousers long before Teddy

Boys took them up. As for the jackets—well, it's a matter of expressing the personality. I'm different. I'm an actor. I'm not the boy from
next door. And never will be."

He loved, he candidly confessed, "all the trappings of being a film
star. . . . I like the caviar and the champagne that go with it. I want
to keep on being up there. I can't do without fame. People know it,
and I know that a lot of people hate me for it."

Attending a play, or the opera, he wore his distinctive scarlet-lined
opera cloak and Edwardian pumps—footwear that had gone out of
fashion before young people began dancing the Charleston—and his
handmade elastic-sided boots, made of the softest leather ("they save
a helluva lot in laces," he grinned) were great conversation pieces in
the West End bars he patronized. Acutely aware of the hail of gossip
about him, he took to claiming tongue in cheek that his clothes and
his mews house had been deliberately designed as "columnist fodder
. . . something to make them talk." He said that he preferred putter-
ing about in what he always wore: a pair of shapeless "off-duty"
jeans and a sweatshirt in the privacy of his house.

He loved the publicity that interviews brought. He loved showing
off his house with its walls filled with enormous mirrors and fine
paintings, allowing every room to be photographed, from its pink
front door to his shocking pink bathroom. He did not care if his
house was ridiculed as well as admired, so long as it was talked
about, and he proudly displayed its dining room with its black-
striped flocked wallpaper, its pink silk curtains, black velvet-covered
chairs. and its pièce de résistance, a candelabra that he swore had belonged to Lord Nelson and his lovely mistress, Lady Hamilton.

He talked to every reporter seeking an interview and fed every rumor, every bit of gossip about himself, even slyly quoting (admit-
tedly in a very cleaned-up version) the jingle composed by George
Sanders during the shooting of *The Talisman.*

"Hark to the tale of know-it-all Larry,
In pursuit of fame he will never tarry."

People said that he had made up this jingle himself. A lot of jabs
and jeers streamed, and continued to stream, his way, and he expected more. He had a truckload of jeers to direct at others. He at-
tacked the director of *The Talisman,* his first Hollywood movie, who,
he asserted in his interview with *Queen,* "had only worked with
Shirley Temple and Rin-Tin-Tin before and . . . couldn't decide
which I should impersonate. When he found I was neither sweet nor

carnal, he omitted to give me either a lollipop or a mere bone to chew on." At Stratford during his second season, the British press, which during his first season called him a "bright spark" and a "young hope," had "proceeded on a series of illiterate atom-bomb tests against me. Everything vile, cheap and common was done to bring me down." Not that he felt bitter about that; it had probably done him a lot of good, he believed. It had made him keep on working. An actor had to have the courage of a lion, the stamina of a boxer. England, he claimed, had not yet been ready for young talent, but since then a whole revolution had taken place. "But I must admit I do want fame. . . . And already I have had a fair share of it."

Only, it was not enough. It was never enough.

His public displays of unbridled extravagance and arrogance, his exhibitionism, his ribald jokes deliberately aimed to shock, all pointed to a determined drive to achieve a purely dramatic effect. The elaborate high jinks in which he indulged concealed the consummate professional. Never as drunk as he appeared to be, he played the heavy drinker staggering and throwing up at parties and functions in order to get laughs, and mocked people's mannerisms and accents not, particularly, in order to antagonize them, but more to test his audiences' reactions. People who really knew him found him not the arrogant bastard he publicly acted, but what Margaret Leighton had first discerned: a young man secretly lacking in self-confidence, always seeking praise and reassurance, afraid of failure, in short, eternally playing a role.

He owned a twelve-room house in the expensive heart of Mayfair, crammed with expensive art and antiques. He was a star, minting money even when acting in plays, spending it almost before he earned it. Yet a letter addressed to his parents and his brother Nahum in December 1956 reflected his deep-seated insecurity, his genuine fear of failure and poverty. Despite his quite phenomenal success in *The Rivals*, he wrote—it had been " the biggest hit in London and for me has added the sort of prestige I never dreamed of [but] . . . like all things in life one cannot rest on one's laurels and have now to work twice as hard to justify and improve one's position. Unfortunately there is no money in the theater and I am so badly in arrears financially that I hope my films next year will settle *this* year's debts. I feel very tired indeed, but unfortunately I cannot see myself getting any rest for a long time. I only pray that I can get through these coming months without physical incident . . . am busily preparing my next film which starts in March [1957]. . . . *Three Men in a Boat* . . . is also a great success. I am very pleased for my company as they have invested a lot of money in the film."

Constantly harping on his fear of impending poverty—however genuine these were—also served to keep his parents on a leash, ensuring that they would not risk the expense of flying to London to visit him, keep them meekly grateful for what he gave them, and keep them living in constant trepidation that he might cease to provide for them. He did support them, however, and it did not cost him much. As had been the case in Johannesburg, so also in Tel Aviv, they enjoyed the pleasure of receiving special invitations from the cinema managers to attend the premieres of their son's films when these were shown and basked in the applause they received when their names were flashed on screen identifying them as Laurence Harvey's parents, and they enjoyed the prestige that relationship brought. Only he never gave them the security of a modest annuity, which would have set their minds at ease and, therefore, like him, they lived in constant fear. They were always afraid that the annual allowance he sent them might not arrive and they would have to become dependent on their other two sons, who were struggling to support themselves. He was forever afraid that offers of work would dry up.

Margaret Leighton felt she understood his true nature. "Larry, is basically shy and insecure. But he's a perfectionist. He *must* have the limelight," she explained. It did not make him easy to live with.

Always in flight, he loved the ease and exhilaration of planes, and, for the rest of his life, always encased in the first-class compartments, drinking champagne, soared like a swift bird at the breakneck pace that his work demanded, crossing over from London to New York for a day or a weekend to visit Margaret or to discuss prospective projects in Hollywood.

That year, their will-they-won't-they marriage prospects were still just that—no more than prospects, although he protested fervently that they would marry—after shooting his next film. "Margaret is all women to me," he enthused to a reporter from *Everybody's*. "She is divine. I need women, but it is Margaret who is the love of my life. She is the most wonderful thing that has ever happened to me."

He had a good word or two to say about his old love, Hermione Baddeley, too, calling her "A great friend and teacher. We used to have long discussions. She is a dear friend."

Another of his "dear friends" was Greer Garson. "A wonderfully mature person," he called her. "We used to have long discussions," he reminisced nostalgically. She did not seem to have reciprocated these feelings—not after he termed her "mature." She hated being called "mature."

In 1957 he made *The Truth about Women, a* British version of a French farce, but without the wit and spice of a French farce and too staid to be effectual, a story of the five loves, in sequence, of a British diplomat. Julie Harris was in it along with Eva Gabor, Mai Zetterling, and Diane Cilento. It was in Technicolor, a major production, and its women stars were dressed by the great Cecil Beaton who later dressed Audrey Hepburn in *My Fair Lady,* and it was a box office smash, if soon forgotten. In it, looking handsome, young, and innocent, if with very little to add in the acting line, Harvey confirmed his position as one of Britain's leading film stars.

The Truth about Women was almost immediately followed by *The Silent Enemy.* Filmed in Gibraltar, it was perhaps the more patriotic than factual story of Commander Lionel Crabb, the frogman who had daringly sabotaged a crucial part of the German fleet during World War II. The real life Commander Crabb was a controversial and introverted personality. Harvey, for lack of an in-depth script, attempted to depict him as a very likable extrovert. With the aid of a natty beard, which he grew and dyed blond for the role, he managed to achieve a virile performance out of very little material. It showed, wrote his critics, quite subdued, a new positivity and maturity in his acting. Even the acerbic British *Daily Mail,* though severely criticizing the film as overdramatized and largely fictional, wrote that Harvey in his white uniform had "an upsetting resemblance" to Britain's late King George V, and faulted the script rather than his performance.

While working in Gibraltar, he finally married Margaret Leighton.

The family received his unexpected cable that same day: "Married Margaret Leighton today in Gibraltar. Ma, don't say anything. She is a great lady."

There was nothing his mother could have said. She was dumb-struck. Robert and his family had just returned from Burma and were staying with his parents while their new flat in the brand new suburb of Ramat Aviv was being readied. His father reacted bravely to the news, revealing his shock in flush-faced silence. To deflect his mother's possible hysteria, Robert was sent to the nearest liquor store and returned with a magnum of champagne. It was not French champagne, but Israeli champagne: the venerable product stored in the cellars of *Rishon Le'Zion*, one of Israel's earliest pioneering enter-prises, quite second rate in taste in those days, but all the same, champagne, and his mother could do no less than join in the toast to "Larry and Margaret."

Margaret had just finished her triumphant run on Broadway and was about to rehearse a new play in London. Ever publicity con-scious, Harvey had wanted to be married by a Royal Navy com-mander aboard his ship, which lay anchored at Gibraltar, but the Admiralty would not give its approval. The six-minute ceremony was finally performed by the Gibraltar registrar on August 8, 1957, on the *Gibel Derif*, a humble shipping tender that sailed from the naval dockyard into the bay with only a dozen passengers on board. Precautions worthy of wartime naval security had been taken to ensure that there would be no boarding parties of sight-seers and reporters. No sirens hooted, no naval guns boomed, no movie fans shrieked with excitement. With the film's director and screenwriter acting as witnesses, the ring was produced, and the ceremony proceeded. The usually ebullient Harvey, looking sub-dued in a dark suit, practically whispered his "I do," while Mar-garet Leighton, hatless, wearing a lovely pale pink silk dress and matching shoes and holding a single orchid flown in from Madrid as a bouquet, spoke her lines clearly. She was thirty-three. He was twenty-eight, but with his Commander Crabb beard he looked older, and they seemed to be a golden couple. Afterward, the party drove to the Rock Hotel for a reception, at which there were fifty guests and where the bridal couple were toasted with champagne.

Before ten o'clock that night the bride and groom slipped away, changed and drove across the Spanish border to have dinner in Algeciras. They returned at midnight to a flower-filled suite.

"We are very happy and this break for Margaret is doing her a world of good," Harvey wrote to his parents, meaning during the few days he and Margaret were together in Gibraltar. "Thank heavens I've survived," the bride told the *Daily Express* reporter the day after the marriage, "I wouldn't want to have another." They had planned to honeymoon in Minorca, but she received a cable saying that rehearsals for her new play were to start immediately and that, she said, "put a 'kibosh'" even on her honeymoon. Harvey, too, succumbed to the demands of filming, returning to work the very next day, shooting *The Silent Enemy*'s most difficult sequences, making a series of dives five fathoms deep with heavy oxygen equipment strapped to his body, and in the evening learning his lines for his next play.

Before she left Gibraltar, wishing to please her new husband—and complying with his wish—Margaret wrote a note introducing herself to his mother. Her note, penned in neat schoolgirl script on a sheet of yellow legal paper (it was all she could find) was received several days later. It read:

> Dear Mrs. Skikne,
>   I am very happy to be married to your son Larry. I look forward to meeting you and your husband one day.
>   Sincerely,
>   Margaret Leighton Harvey

It was a purely English middle-class thing to do, but to his parents it appeared to be extremely cold-blooded, and it was received in stunned silence.

Back in London again once the film was finished, her new husband was photographed carrying his bride over the threshold of their new home. Both were smiling with delight. But Margaret found that the charming little house Harvey had created was hardly a home. She had not been consulted about any of its features, barely even about the curtains, and little though she believed in her own taste, nursed a sense of resentment about this from the first. The workmen were still in it, since he kept changing the plans, holding that, as a former architectural student, he knew exactly what he wanted.

"It looks like a Chinese brothel," she once commented crossly.

Her reaction astounded him. He could not understand it. Did she not appreciate that he had built the house and designed every detail in it for their mutual comfort and pleasure? Meekly, she succumbed to his judgment. They were happy—most of the time. She wanted the two of them to become another Alfred Lunt and Lynn Fontanne, married stars with long and prestigious careers on the stage. He was enthusiastically in favor of this ambition, and dreamed, he announced, of bringing a production of the stage play of *Camille* to the States. He would play Armand, the lover, and Margaret would be the lady of the Camellias.

Publicly, theirs was a love affair filled with romance and exciting plans. But in the privacy of their home, she never knew what to expect, from one day to the next, sometimes even from one moment to the next. Bitterly, in a 1967 interview with Margaret Hinxman, she described how things had been during her marriage to Harvey. They had almost no home life. He was either working or looking for work. He preferred eating out and he hardly seemed to need any rest; he was always out trying to sell himself to producers and financiers. The harder he worked, the harder he pushed himself to do more. She could not fathom where he got the energy. Adding up the amount of time they had spent together since they had first fallen in love and then married, she thought it probably amounted to hardly one year.

Meekly, she allowed him to rule her in everything. He told her how he wanted her to dress and what jewelry to wear, took her to buying trips to the great couture houses in Paris, favoring the House of Dior, encouraging her to display wealth and fashion, demanding that she overdress for every occasion, that she dress smartly even when relaxing at home. When she lost the very expensive jewelry he had bought her to a burglar, he merely informed her, carelessly, that everything had been insured and bought her more. He loved her frivolous and expensive diamond-studded shoes. He insisted on driving her in his Rolls-Royce to the florist down the street to buy flowers and posing as her chauffeur, told off-color jokes at her expense to the employees while he waited. He dominated her but she felt grateful to him for it, because it brought her out of her natural shyness and reserve.

She sought his approval in everything. She did not believe he was calculating, only very ambitious and outspoken. In fact, his forthrightness earned him enemies in the press.

"I must say that there was never a dull moment with Larry," she told Hinxman. "He lived life at quite a pace. He spent money like water! He had tremendous zest and a wonderful sense of humor, but his moods were controlled by events. Whilst he could always put on an act in public, in private he was often elated or depressed. He could worry over the smallest personal detail about himself. His depression often preceded minor illnesses, especially digestive problems." Yet he refused to pay any attention to what the doctors advised, and insisted on continuing his irrigation treatments. And even when he felt ill, he could always get up and put on a front. "When he was happy the excitement was uncontrollable and he affected everyone around. That's when I loved him most."

What he hated most, she confessed, was what she liked best: a quiet, simple dinner at home prepared by the efficient Italian couple he had hired, and on some rare occasion, dining on a cheese soufflé that he cooked himself when the mood seized him. They were both dieting; she was obsessively thin and he ate only sparingly at best. Nevertheless, he preferred dining out, mainly at the Caprice where he had had a permanent dinner reservation and he paid for the meal whether they showed up or not—a custom she found outrageously wasteful.

On those nights when they dined there, they would order the finest steaks, chew out the juice, and spit the meat out into a napkin. Both of them drank all the time. She was a vodka drinker. He drank vodka and other hard liquor at night and generally sipped throughout the day the Louis Latour Pouilly Fuissé that a friend had told him about. He had it bottled by his own vintner and shipped to him in crates.

All too frequently he suffered from sinusitis, inherited from his mother, and once developed a painful abscess on his sinus, which he had to let a doctor treat under morphia. The pain would diminish a great deal at night, but during the day his medication gave him no relief and at length he had to visit a specialist. He returned, looking as pale as death, to tell her that according to this specialist, the pain from an abscessed sinus was the worst one could possibly have and out of panic and fear took to his bed until he was well again.

Their's was not a conventional marriage, even by Bohemian standards. They were both too different and, in the everyday intimacy of marriage, realized that they hardly knew each other; they had been so much apart, working in different countries during their courtship. He resented her cool formality toward his parents—she never wrote to them again—and her backbiting English actress girlfriends who, he knew, laughed at what they termed "his naïveté." He had no contact with her family. Neither of them appeared to have realized that they had been brought up so differently, she by a strictly religious, disciplinarian father, while he was the son of a Jewish mother, and both of them were full of flaws and neuroses themselves. They were not even exclusively faithful to one another. He had Jimmy Woolf, whom he sincerely loved, and also other, younger men, and sometimes the odd girl who caught his fancy. She had affairs with some of the men in the cast of a play she was in. She had always had affairs with her leading men.

Still, she tried to make this new marriage work. Outwardly they struck people as idyllically happy and head over heels in love. When they performed a rollicking dance number at the London Palladium's *Night of a Hundred Stars*, hamming it up in perfect coordination and with great style and verve, they seemed to the audience, an ideal couple, perfectly matched.

Like any other married couple, they invited friends to dinner when they had a free evening, seating their guests around their white, black, and gold marble dining room table with its legs resting on a purple carpet, making conversation while the Italian couple who were their cook and butler served delicious meals, eating their food on expensive black plates, and using gold flatware. At these dinners Harvey, as master of the house, liked to reign supreme, firing scathing criticism about the great stars of the day, pontificating about their acting styles—or lack of any. His friends and admirers listened to his critiques of all the great stars in seemingly acquiescent silence. But one evening, according to actor Robert Stephens, Laurence Olivier, who disliked Harvey but had accepted the couple's dinner invitation for the sake of his friend Margaret, whom he admired as a great actress, could bear it no longer. Harvey had just been criticizing the great John Gielgud when Olivier screamed, "How *dare* you. Call yourself an actor? You're not even a bad actor. You can't act at all, you fucking stupid hopeless sniveling little cunt-faced cunty fucking shit-faced arsehole," and left the house.

Regretting his outburst the next day, however, Olivier sent "the little bastard," two dozen red roses and a written apology.

A year after their marriage, things took a turn for the worse. Harvey's nightlife became even more neurotic. Going out to dinner or nightclubs was, to his thinking, an essential ingredient in selling himself professionally. But eventually this habit reached a stage when he stayed away for days on end. As Hermione Baddeley gleefully noted in her autobiography, Margaret took to spending a great deal of her time riding about in a taxi to his favorite haunts, putting her head out of the window and asking the doormen of restaurants and nightclubs, "Is he there? Is he there?"

Margaret suspected that he had affairs with both men and other women during their marriage. When she questioned him, he did not deny it—he was, she claimed, a very honest person, and he dominated her so completely that he did not care what she thought. All the same she still loved him and accepted everything he did. She would have liked to change him, or at least, make him understand how she felt, but she did not want to lose him. She was never certain of it, but he treated her with such complacency that she suspected that his love for her had gone. In public, he often referred to her disparagingly as his "mother," but he did not mind if she retaliated by insulting him.

Their relationship only went smoothly when they were separated by the demands of their work. Yet, to him, Margaret remained an extraordinary woman, a great actress, a great lady, as he had cabled his mother upon his marriage, although inevitably, they grew farther and farther apart. From being regarded as the happiest couple in England, only a year later there began to be rumors of their impending divorce. Even when they were on the same continent, they were rarely together. In 1959 Margaret was still telling journalists and friends how much they longed to be together, and what great plans they had to act together. Harvey, on the other hand, in an interview with the columnist Hedda Hopper, not much more than two years after their marriage, seemed more unsure of their relationship.

"In her class, she's incomparable," he said of Margaret. But, "It's terribly difficult to maintain a relationship on both sides of the Atlantic with two people being continually separated. . . . I blame myself. I've never really grown up in the way I'd like to have. My capacity for giving to the emotional needs of another person and giving it to the job too I feel is an impossible task at such a distance. In this business one becomes involved in a new circle of friends. I still love Margaret and it's sad."

At that time they were both in the States, but at either end of the country. She was making a film. Now and then he called her long distance, unexpectedly, but he was touring with the Old Vic and they rarely came together. When they were both free of their commitments, she said, they planned to have their first real vacation together—a kind of belated honeymoon.

This never occurred. In their increasingly rare meetings, they made public displays of affection that concealed their growing emotional distance. Most significant was the time, in 1960, when he was honored with Britain's Variety Club's Show Biz Award at a luncheon as the best actor of 1959 (for *Room at the Top* and *Expresso Bongo*). Since he was in the States when the luncheon was given and she was in London, Margaret Leighton was due to accept for him. Elegantly attired, she stepped forward to receive the silver heart that was the Variety Club's award. In her little speech, she apologized graciously for her husband's absence—he was filming in New York at the time. "If Larry were here he'd be cracking a lot of jokes," she said. "But I've never told a good one yet." Just as she began to conclude her little speech with "I am truly grateful to you all for. . . ."

"*Darling!*" yelled a loud voice, and Laurence Harvey made his appearance.

Margaret fell into his arms. The audience roared its approval. Harvey took over the microphone. "At 5:45 last night," he declared, "I was disengaged from a film in New York. Yesterday I was told I wouldn't be required until Friday. I was missing my missus so much that I caught the next plane for London." Did he tell his wife that he would be flying back to London? He said that he had reached their home just as Margaret was leaving for the luncheon.

"Well, I didn't know whether he'd get to the lunch or not—he had to shave and change his suit," she said.

Caught off guard by her husband's totally unexpected appearance, the highly professional actress made a joke of it to cover her confusion.

Later he declared that there had not been enough time to let her know he was coming; his decision had been made on a sheer impulse. But for her it must have been an embarrassing moment and marked the growing coldness of his feelings toward her.

In the final analysis, he blamed his obsession with work for the breakup of his marriage.

"Maggie and I split up because of my career," he explained to the London *Times*. "When we first met she was a big star and I was not so well known. . . . But I was on my way up. . . . The marriage was all right when we were both working; I suppose because we didn't see much of each other then. In the intervals between plays and films our temperaments often clashed. . . . For example, Maggie liked meals to be at a certain set time. Unless we were dining out . . . we always ate in the same restaurant and had a permanent table booked for which we had a special rate. Sometimes I didn't feel like eating until later. Or even not at all. There were terrible scenes about this. I felt we were both earning so much it didn't matter if we had to pay three pounds or whatever it was, to cancel a meal. So what if the steak got burnt? What was the point of having money? 'Throw it to the peasants!' I would cry. And that didn't go down at all well."

Once he ungallantly confessed in public that he had never wanted to marry Margaret in the first place, but had been practically forced into marrying her because "it was the gentlemanly thing to do." But once married, he said, she had very soon made the fatal mistake of trying to dominate him. Every woman he had known had made that mistake, but he had never let them make it twice. Worse still, he said, she had kept nagging him to devote himself exclusively to the stage, for she possessed the conventional snobbery that rated plays far above films. He had, on the contrary, been determined to star in both media. As a result, he declared, whenever she had offered him advice, he had done the exact opposite.

Margaret Leighton had a somewhat different story to tell. When her first marriage had collapsed, she said, she was bewildered, rather demure in those days and never took a drink—yet not so demure, it seems, that in the halcyon days before her marriage to Harvey she could tell Hollywood reporter Sidney Skolsky carelessly that she had married her first husband before a matinee and regretted it after the performance.

The fact is that because both Margaret Leighton and Laurence Harvey were workaholics, working nonstop, and that their work continuously separated them and they drifted farther and farther apart. Even before their divorce, he had found a new love interest, and coldly discarded his marriage to Margaret as unworkable.

When they learned of the breakup, the London press descended upon him like a pack of hyenas. Margaret Leighton was portrayed as almost a martyred saint, Laurence Harvey was called fiercely ambitious, sexually amoral, a ruthlessly self-serving bastard. The fact that she successfully sued him for some £7,000 that he had borrowed from her and won the mews house that he had so lovingly built and all its treasures was overlooked.

The extent of the ill feeling against Harvey is well described in actor Robert Stephens's autobiography. Margaret Leighton, whom he calls "terribly funny and terribly common," had begun an affair with him—he was eleven years her junior—in New York in 1959, at the time when she and Harvey were still regarded as one of the film world's happiest couples. Their affair had continued fitfully over the next two years. She was adorable, extremely beautiful and elegant, dressed exclusively (under Harvey's tutelage) by Yves Saint-Laurent, but had absolutely no self-esteem and desperately needed to be loved. Harvey, totally self-absorbed, had, Stephen writes, been entirely unaware of their affair, but had left Margaret because he wanted to marry Joan Cohn. (In fact, Harvey *had* been aware of their affair, and it had added to his coldness toward Margaret.)

He described Margaret as being devastated by Harvey's desertion, but seemed to think that Margaret was lucky to be rid of him. Harvey, he writes, was "an appalling man, and even more unforgivably, an appalling actor." Going to see him in *The Country Wife* (his next play upon his return from Gibraltar), he said, he "noticed something quite unusual in him as an actor. He had not a single nerve in his body." Most actors, he writes, make an adjustment in their nervous energy before going on stage. They "undergo a profound physical and physiological transformation" in the process of becoming another character, but this did not happen with Harvey. In his dressing room, before going on stage, he would smoke his Pall Mall cigarette in a long cigarette holder, sip a glass of Mâcon, stroll about, cough up some phlegm, which he would spit out on the floor, regardless of whom it hit, and then stroll on stage and start acting. Only, it wasn't acting in the sense that the greats like Ralph Richardson acted. They had technique, which fooled the audience into believing that they were watching natural behavior. With Harvey, nothing happened.

Several years later, Margaret Leighton married Michel Wilding, Elizabeth Taylor's second husband. "The English always marry the English," Harvey commented grumpily. She died of a debilitating disease in 1976.

But that was years later. When Harvey returned to London from Gibraltar and began rehearsals for *The Country Wife*, Wyncherly's classic Restoration comedy at the Royal Court Theatre, their marriage was still in its "honeymoon" stage. Once again, his performance earned him praise. "Laurence Harvey had the proper dash and flourish for the role of a gentleman who spreads false rumors about himself." "[He] has great sport pretending he's impotent," wrote the *World Telegram*'s theater critic. Following its success in London, he brought the play over to Broadway, where he repeated his original role as the wicked Mr. Horner who attempts to seduce the innocent country wife, played by Julie Harris.

Also upon his return to London from Gibraltar, he embarked on a venture that had appeared, at first sight, to be a sure-fire winner, but proved quite a trial. In March 1958 he went to Manchester to direct and coproduce, with Jack Hylton, a musical with an African cast titled *Simply Heavenly*. "I have been working sixteen hours a day," he wrote to his parents, "and have literally had no time to think of anything else"—anything else being his failure to send them their remittance. "I realize how awful your position has been and you know that I would not ever do anything to hurt you willingly and on my own accord."

The show, he complained, had proved extremely difficult to manage. Thoughtlessly succumbing to the reigning conventional wisdom, he complained that the temperament and discipline of the "Negro" artists left much to be desired and the strain of the whole venture had put him so near the breaking point that he had almost abandoned the whole production. He stayed, he wrote, because he had his investors' and his own interests to think of and was ready to fight to make the show a success.

When the musical opened, the wonderful voice of its star, the earthy Bertice Reading, set the first night's audience stamping their feet and roaring for encores. Earlier that day, Harvey and impressario Jack Hylton had paid this star's debts amounting to £335 to keep her out of jail. Her triumphant performance had been well worth it. But the story itself got off to a slow start. According to the critics, there was too much moralizing and too little singing. As Harvey was wont to do, he faulted others for it—this time, in a letter to his parents, he blamed the cast for their egotistic and neurotic failure to work together as an ensemble. European actors, he claimed, would have been more disciplined.

Nevertheless, there were marvelous moments that first night that set the audience roaring and clapping, and they would not let its star, Bertice Reading, off the stage until she had repeated her song, "I'm a Good Old Girl," until she was exhausted.

Once it had been licked into shape, *Simply Heavenly* enjoyed a triumphant run in London. Although he would never have admitted it, the responsibilities involved in the production had proved almost too much for him.

He was considering the offer of the role as a mentally unbalanced cameraman who murders a young woman because her image does not appear in focus to him in *Peeping Tom*, to be directed by Michael Powell. They were discussing how much of the story could be filmed and its shock impact when he got the lead in *Room at the Top.*

"The moment I have finished this production" (of *Simply Heavenly*) he wrote to his parents that same month, "I go to the north of England to a city called Bradford and start the film . . . it is one of the most exciting scripts that I have ever read and if done well should prove to be an enormous success and certainly one of the greatest stories ever made in this country."

He began rehearsing for this film and studying the North Country accent his character used while still entangled with *Simply Heavenly.*

14

Room at the Top Brings International Stardom

Room at the Top was a groundbreaking movie in many respects. Both in Britain and the United States, it brought the sex act out into the open. It showed men and women behaving as they did in real life: young people having sex in a public park, using foul language, making love naked on a bed—or at least, in this movie—little short of naked. It was a movie to which young people could relate. And in Britain, it snapped some hitherto rigid class barriers, opening the doors to stardom in serious movies to actors with regional, working-class and lower-middle-class accents, who had previously been relegated to playing minor roles as servants, country policemen, and quaint village characters. It was antiestablishment in many ways. There was nothing heroic about the hero: all he had was gumption and guts and a determination to climb out of the genteel poverty that, before the war, was all to which his class could aspire.

Room at the Top, John Braine's best-selling novel on which the film was based, was not the first to portray the rebellion of the young against the British class system and conventions. In the strikingly innovative French New Wave, filmmakers had opened up the screen to startling new characters and possibilities. The "British New Wave" in films, plays, and literature began in 1956 with a thunderously shocking (at the time) play, *Look Back in Anger*, by John Osborne (later filmed with Richard Burton and Claire Bloom).

Middle-class morality took its first fierce whipping in *Room at the Top*. The Old School Tie establishment was mocked. As a POW during the war, Joe Lampton, the cynical "hero" of this film used his time to study accounting while the Establishment heroes spent their days planning methods of escape. Adultery is shown without moralizing. Joe Lampton, the cynical climber is a rebel, but he is a rebel against the working class he was born into and its way of life and its behavior on the wrong side of the tracks. His overriding ambition is to clamber out of the working class in order to enjoy the ripe plums of the Establishment. Seizing his chance, he cynically pursues the naïve young daughter of a wealthy local industrialist and wins her by seducing her. She gets pregnant. He marries her and thus wins his place at the top rung of the social ladder. But on his wedding day, his mistress, an unhappily married older woman whom he genuinely loves, commits suicide. A tear is seen to rise in Joe Lampton's eye. His new wife thinks that this tear expresses his love for he. But he is really weeping for himself; he had been deprived of the mistress he can no longer enjoy.

This film was also innovative in its technique and style. It made the smoke- and soot-filled Yorkshire industrial town of Bradford (renamed Warley in the film) an integral part of the story. Its stars were filmed in enormous close-ups that magnified every detail of their faces, exposed the ripple of naked bodies delighting in the thrill of satisfied lovemaking, exhibited Simone Signoret's beautiful shoulders, arms, and one of her legs, which she defiantly lifts to show her jealous young lover during a quarrel.

John Woolf had first learned about the novel while watching the BBC's *Panorama*, featuring a group of Bradford women talking about this just-published book written by one of the town's former librarians. Woolf's brother, James, read the book and enthusiastically agreed that it would make a great movie and be a box office smash hit. He purchased the film rights to it while the book was still barely off the press.

However, Laurence Harvey, his protégé, was not his first choice to play the lead. He had been steering Harvey in another direction, into roles as the handsome, romantic, upper-class hero, and could not visualize him as the brazenly ambitious and cynical working-class Joe Lampton. With the box office in mind, his first choice for the leads were Stewart Granger and Jean Simmons, at the time a married couple and both of them enormously popular with the moviegoing public, but they were committed to other movies. It gave Woolf the opportunity to reflect that they might not have been able to give this unusual story the right range of emotion for which it called. Harvey wanted the part; he appeared to have had an instinct about it and, with some trepidation on Woolf's part, received it. Although he knew that Harvey was an excellent mimic, he also knew that the young actor was entirely unfamiliar with the peculiarities of North Country dialect and ways. Harvey was assigned a coach to train him in the proper regional accent and, always meticulous in his research, closely observed Bradford mannerisms, the way the citizens dressed, their down-to-earth talk. Yet, oddly, he was closer to Joe Lampton than Woolf believed: he, too, was a brash outsider battling to break into the Establishment.

His role in *The Silent Enemy* had required that he acquire a crewcut. This was the same style he wore for his role as Joe Lampton. Only, his crewcut was styled by an expensive London hairdresser and was hardly what the real Joe Lampton could have afforded.

As the innocent young woman Joe Lampton seduces, impregnates, and marries, Jack Clayton, the director, cast Heather Sears, his own protégé, a young actress who was, with Laurence Harvey, the only other star under contract with Romulus Films.

She was an extraordinary young woman. While still at school, she had taken to flying over to Paris whenever she had a break in order to join her "family," a group of artists, writers, and actors that included Picasso, the writers Albert Camus and Arthur Koestler, and the actress Simone Signoret, with whom she became close friends.

For the role as the young Joe Lampton's older mistress, James Woolf and Jack Clayton selected Simone Signoret. It would be too shocking for an audience, they felt, to cast an Englishwoman as Lampton's uninhibited mistress. Englishwomen, was the assumption, did not behave so freely. Frenchwomen were experienced in the ways of love and far more sexy, uninhibited, and worldly wise. A slew of wicked French novels and comedies appeared to reinforce this belief.

In her biography, *Nostalgia Isn't What It Used to Be*, Simone Signoret writes that it so happened that she had not worked in nine months, and at almost thirty-seven had begun to think of herself as a ripening old lady who was past it, that the future belonged to actresses who were young and fresh. When the telephone rang in her Paris apartment and the caller offered her the part of Alice Aisgill, she had never heard of the book and had no idea what her part was to be about. Given the novel, she read it with growing excitement and thought it was a wonderful story and a wonderful part. When the smiling, ugly little man with the bad teeth wearing an expensive, Savile Row suit and smoking an expensive cigar flew over from London to negotiate her contract, she was enthusiastic, but asked a cautious question. Were Americans involved in the production?

She had a reason, she felt, for her question. Only a short time before, she had been suddenly turned down for a part in a movie in the States and she thought she knew why. A year earlier, a revolution in Hungary against the domination of the Soviet Union had been ruthlessly crushed by Russian tanks, a brutal act that had been condemned by liberals everywhere, including Simone Signoret and her husband, the internationally popular singer-actor Yves Montand. Shortly afterward, to their astonishment, Montand had received an invitation to perform in the Soviet Union. Convinced that his presence would symbolize a Franco-Soviet people-to-people gesture of friendship, he agreed to go, despite warnings that his visit would be used by the Soviet propaganda machine. Simone Signoret had accompanied him. Montand had performed to overwhelmingly enthusiastic audiences everywhere, and they had met famous Russian artists and performers.

But they had indeed been used by the Soviet propaganda machine. At a reception in the Kremlin's great hall attended by 3,000 people including foreign diplomats and the entire Soviet leadership, an exuberant Krushchev had embraced and kissed the much-surprised Simone Signoret. The flash of cameras had recorded the event and newspapers everywhere published the picture.

Under the circumstances, she thought it only fair to warn James Woolf that no film she was in would ever be shown in the States. Senator McCarthy, who had wreaked havoc among the American movie and theater community with his witch-hunt for Communists, was dead, but McCarthyism, though weakened, was still alive.

Woolf, who became her good friend, firmly assured her that this was to be a British film and that as such Romulus could do as it pleased. Such was her trust in his word—and he never disappointed her even once during their years of friendship—that despite the fact that the script was still unfinished—and also because she knew that the part of Alice Aisgill suited her to perfection—she agreed to act in the film. Thus, on a spring morning of 1958, bidding good-bye to Yves Montand and her daughter, she took the boat train from Paris to London.

Bradford was, to the stars of *Room at the Top,* a boring provincial town with little or nothing to do in the evenings. Its only tourist attraction is an old Turkish bath, which has been visited by several famous stars in their time. The cast and some of the crew were put up in the town's Victoria Hotel. This was situated near the train station; trains could be heard shunting back and forth through the night and the hotel was better equipped for the needs of busy wool merchants and salesmen than for actors.

On the set, during the day, Harvey concentrated all his energy on his role, and *became* Joe Lampton. When work ended for the day, he found it hard to relax. He was stranded in his hotel. Rendered impatient with the gas rationing of the previous year, he had sold his rajah-sized, sand and sable-colored Rolls-Royce and had blithely roared about London in the pillion seat of a motor scooter behind his uniformed chauffeur. In Bradford, however, his motor scooter had no place and he was driven to the studio like the rest of the cast in a hired limousine.

John Braine, the author of *Room at the Top,* had been hired to act as consultant on the movie. Meeting him for the first time at the hotel, Harvey was like an exotic butterfly, Braine said: sophisticated, drinking French wine, gesturing with his long, gold-tipped cigarette holder as he talked while James Woolf hovered solicitously nearby. Conversation between the author and the actor was limited, however, to trivia. Harvey advised him to drink vodka for its purity instead of scotch. Invited to dinner at John Braine's house, he talked exclusively about himself. He had just purchased the rights, he told Braine, of a true account—even if it was not a true account, still it made a terrific story—of a Polish refugee's trek across Asia. This project would take five years to film. Cameramen and actors would have to endure all the hardships of the journey through the Gobi Desert and Tibet. He declared that no one would balk at this challenge: the purpose of human life was to accept challenges.

This was one of the multiplicity of Harvey's projects that never came to fruition, but he dreamed about it and talked about it all his life. It may have been an extension of the sense of safety and seclusion that he had experienced while sailing through the Suez Canal and seeing the endless mane of sand and the closed dome of sky of the Sinai Desert. He seemed always to be in search of this landscape.

He was called rude and demanding in his treatment of the hotel staff and patient and polite to his fans. Many of these North Country town denizens seemed to have regarded him as something akin to royalty. One fan, Doreen Kotroczo, now a grandmother, has never forgotten how, as a teenager, she ran to watch a scene in *Room at the Top* being filmed in her local library. Harvey was one of her favorite actors. "We especially admired that lovely voice!" she recalled. "He was very pleasant and signed my autograph book in the corner of the library where he was sitting. I was so thrilled. . . . I have always remembered it."

When an idle crowd of local youngsters teased him, he seemed not above enjoying a good laugh at his own expense. One of them remembered watching the scene in which Joe Lampton is beaten unconscious and wakes up the next morning to find himself lying in the road. When the cameras stopped rolling, a young man in the crowd of curious onlookers shouted, "Come up here on a Saturday night and we'll beat you up for free, Harvey." The actor got up and roared with laughter. Approaching the man, he spent time laughing and joking with him until called for the next take. He also went drinking with one or two of the locals. In response to a *Bradford Argus* call for anecdotes in 1998, Granville Jackson described Harvey's friendship with John Cliffe, a five-foot-tall professional drummer. He himself vaguely believed that Harvey had told him that he had been born in "Czechoslovakia—or something like that."

Still, succumbing to popular opinion, John Braine regarded him as being as ruthless as Joe Lampton; the actor and the character possessed that quality in common, he remarked. And he believed that Harvey appeared to have had not the slightest interest in women. Most men, Braine among others, commented, showed *some* interest upon seeing an attractive girl go by.

He did not make friends with Heather Sears, who despised his foul language, but he became very fast friends with Simone Signoret and in long chats with her, told her the truth about his origin and his family. She happened to be half Jewish. Her father had been a Polish

Jew and she had adopted the name Signoret, which was her French mother's maiden name. Despite the fact that her father had regarded himself as French, the Nazis had sent him to a concentration camp during World War II.

The two actors had many intimate chats about their parents. She told him that her father's mother had refused to recognize her father's marriage. Harvey told her that his mother was not thrilled about his marriage to Margaret Leighton. He praised his mother's cooking to the skies and declared that he had seriously thought of abandoning his career in order to go and fight for Israel—she was not certain during which war, whether the War of Independence in 1948 or the brief Israel-French-British attack on Egypt in 1956.

When filming ended, Simone Signoret and husband Yves Montand visited Israel, and in Tel Aviv, Simone Signoret met Harvey's parents and second brother. Harvey was pleased. "Simone," he wrote, "is a divine person and very real in this brutal artificial world."

At Harvey's insistence, his former lover Hermione Baddeley had been hired for the part of Alice Aisgill's friend, the woman who lent her apartment to the two lovers for their rendezvous. Harvey had not contacted Hermione Baddeley directly to offer her the part, but had left this to James Woolf to do. It was a small roll, but perhaps Harvey believed that he could, in some small way, repay her for the money she had spent on him. At least, that is what she suspected. A good deal of her dialogue consisted of berating him for his callous treatment of her friend Alice Aisgill. She must have enjoyed that.

No one seems to have foreseen the impact this film was to make. Harvey put it crudely. Films that add sex extraneously, he said in an interview published in *Premiere* in 1970, are "like . . . walking the streets of London on a shopping spree and stopping to take your dick out." *Room at the Top* made sex an integral part of the movie. Yet he assured a reporter that he had never been consciously aware of breaking down any walls or rules in making a film. "You make the film, play the role successfully or unsuccessfully, because you want to do it . . . and try and find a way of doing it with as much reality and in as good taste as possible."

While working on the film, he wrote to his parents, he was also trying to study the part of Henry V, "one of the longest parts in Shakespeare," which he was going to play in the Old Vic's tour of the States. He had so little time in which to prepare, he complained. The film was already running over schedule. He would not finish his part in *Room at the Top* before the end of August and he would have to leave for San Francisco on September 9 to join the Old Vic Company there. "Financially," he griped, as he always did, "this tour will be of no use but the prestige is something no money can buy." As to sending them more money that year, he wrote, he was in no position to help them any further, "but if you want to go back to South Africa I will raise *half* the fare." It was enough to keep them where they were. As he well knew, his mother had not really wanted to return to South Africa, but only to voice her abysmal dissatisfaction with everything.

He was feeling deeply depressed. "Nothing about shooting *Room at the Top* persuaded Harvey that it would be the hit it was," James Woolf told *Showbiz.* "I remember so well the last day of shooting. Larry said, 'Well, I'd better make the most of this day. It's probably the last time I'll ever see the inside of a studio again. Nobody's ever going to ask me to make another picture.' And he was convinced it was true."

Room at the Top had cost Romulus Films only £280,000 to make and brought in millions. The movie did not, however, meet with the unqualified approval of the critics.

Following its premiere at the Ritz Cinema in Leeds in January 1959, the film was called "not quite out of top drawer." It showed "seedy sex not honest passion" (this according to the local communist newspaper). At the other end of the spectrum, the Reverend Eric Treacy, archdeacon of Halifax, called it a story of sordid, sexual filth that may have done incalculable harm to the enormous number of young people who saw it.

Between the two, however, the more sophisticated reviewers praised the film and also all the performances, especially singling out Laurence Harvey and Simone Signoret.

By the time the film opened in the States, Harvey was in Washington with the Old Vic Company. Woolf called him when the American reviews were in and it was clear that the picture and Harvey were wildly successful, and that it had brought him transatlantic stardom. People were talking about this movie everywhere—even those who found the much watered-down North Country accent difficult to understand. Lines like "I hate you to put clothes on," regarded as pretty ordinary today, shocked and thrilled American audiences as it had British. Woolf had already heard from Alfred Hitchcock who wanted Harvey to star in *Alfie* in his TV series and in *No Bail for the Judge,* a movie with Audrey Hepburn, and there were three other movie offers waiting for him as well.

He was nominated for the Oscar as best actor for 1959, but lost out to Charlton Heston for his role in *Ben-Hur,* for which the studio had reputedly launched a public relations campaign costing hundreds of thousands of dollars. Simone Signoret won an Oscar as best actress.

Room at the Top brought admiration, praise, and movie offers, but it also fixed a Joe Lampton seal on him as a ruthless, ambitious, and self-seeking outsider. He left Joe Lampton far behind, however, in his portrayal of Shakespeare's *Henry V* on his tour with the Old Vic Company in the States. For this performance, too, his notices were extraordinary. Even so stern a critic as Brooks Atkinson wrote: "He is the most stimulating actor in the company, giving a performance of classic size. An actor of strength and intelligence in the best Old Vic tradition."

He played to packed houses throughout the tour. American audiences loved his accent, his voice, which they called mellifluous, his good looks, his tall, slim, lithe figure so handsome in armor. Even a Lithuanian newspaper printed his picture as Henry V, calling him "The Lithuanian actor." The big studios offered him long-term contracts, but he turned them down, amid cries of disbelief. Here was a new breed of actor, the columnists said. "Everyone in this country is surprised to find a young man playing Shakespeare," he told a reporter over cocktails, "and that's the principal reason why Americans avoid Shakespearean performances. They expect to find old men mouthing formal exercises in the tradition of the Japanese theater."

"Stylized Shakespeare is as dull and phony as anything in the theater," he told New York's *Morning Telegraph.* "The Bard wrote for his time, and to entertain people. Therefore, I try to make my characterizations come alive by foregoing the old booming Shakespearean delivery. Not long ago an American tourist approached me after a performance at Stratford-on-Avon [sic], amazed that he could understand the play and the actors. . . . Hollywood itself is falling into stylized performances. There seems to be a young group of actors making films here who specialize in mumbling their way through roles."

He also sounded off about British filmmaking, generally thought to be of so high an order. Those running this industry, he scoffed, were "a bunch of idiots." He expressed his open contempt of some of this industry's leaders, naming each one of them, and said there were only three who were any good: David Lean, Anthony Asquith, and Carol Reed—each famous for producing and directing remarkable films. Most of the others, he said, lacked imagination, and always set up the same old shots. Then he accused Renato Castellani of distorting Shakespeare in *Romeo and Juliet* and insisting that he say his lines sounding like a violin.

He seemed to be doing his best to antagonize everyone who counted.

Holding forth at a two-hour luncheon during a press conference on the eve of the New York opening of *Henry V*, shocking everyone with his iconoclastic views, he admitted, at the end of the conference that he adored conversation, especially his own.

He was still not quite thirty years old. For years the critics had mocked him and pelted him with their barbed reviews. One of them had sneered that Laurence Harvey would only know one way to play Henry V—as Flash Harry. That critic was wrong.

"You've been saying you were brilliant for years," one English reporter asked. "Have the critics finally caught up with you?"

Evidently, yes. But only temporarily. They soon reverted to their normal stance.

Much to his disappointment, a movie that James Woolf had negotiated on his behalf in Hollywood turned out to have an impossibly poor script, and he turned it down. Returning to London, he was again being driven around town on his motor scooter by his uniformed chauffeur—for purely deliberate effect this time: it made a striking contrast to the Rolls-Royces cluttering up the streets of

Mayfair. He was, also, living alone in his mews house. Margaret was not in London and their relationship was in its ice age. He gave no hint of any trouble in his marriage, however, in his letters to his parents.

Three days after returning to London, he had to fly back to New York to discuss future projects. "Like everything in this profession today," he wrote to his parents, "one cannot guarantee the future or the outcome of one's efforts, but it is essential to pursue every possible prospect and project."

Thrilled as he was with the enormous success of *Room at the Top*, he was now deeply immersed in taking singing lessons "which is a strange and new departure for me, because I have been asked to do a musical in New York next year and again am waiting for the script before any decisions can be made."

Harvey returned to London, where, he wrote to his parents, he had to go to the "tax people . . . and had a disastrous interview . . . and until the tax position is worked out I am preparing for the life of a pauper."

His was hardly the lifestyle of a pauper when he was interviewed by the *London Daily Express* reporter in what was glowingly described as "his beautiful drawing room" in his "exquisite house, furnished with great taste and care . . . [which appeared] to have every painting one had ever heard of on the walls and although I could not see 'The Adoration of the Magi' anywhere, it would scarcely have surprised me to find it skulking about somewhere upstairs." Harvey himself was wearing a mauve robe and sandals. He was about to fly to the States again for the sixth time in three months to make a television film for *Alfred Hitchcock Presents*.

"This TV film I'm doing is really delicious," he enthused, quite forgetting his low opinion of television. "I play a chicken farmer who murders his girl friend and grinds her up into chicken feed . . . when the police come, they can find nothing. Just a lot of well fed chickens. The best part is where I give the police inspector a couple of chickens—and he returns later to say they were so tasty he must know what kind of feed I used."

In England, he said enthusiastically, he was to star in *Expresso Bongo* and afterward he was due to return to the Old Vic. "That'll set my career back ten years, I expect," he said gloomily. "To say nothing of the fact that they pay no money. It will hardly keep my scooter in petrol."

Like Stratford, the Old Vic paid only £50 a week.

Then he was going into production himself, he announced, filming the novel, *The Long Walk*, which he owned.

He would soon be wearing green suits to match his money, the reporter suggested. And then he would flee abroad to avoid the iniquitous tax man.

"Not me," said Harvey with a steady stare. "You forget I struggled here via Poland [obviously an error] and South Africa, and I love the place. I would never live anywhere else."

A sentiment that really endeared Harvey to this interviewer!

Expresso Bongo brought the new young white working-class pop singers and their music to the screen. The script was adapted from a musical play written by Wolf Mankowitz.

This film is about a fast-talking, frenetically fast-moving, low-grade Jewish theatrical agent who scratches and scrounges up a bare living by trying to secure employment for his clients of second- and third-rate stripteasers, rock 'n' roll singers, and comedians. He rockets into the big time when he accidentally discovers a young working-class bongo drums player and singer, but sinks just as swiftly when he lets his protégé fall into more ruthless and experienced hands.

The very fact that he is a shady character, greedy, and a rogue, but not enough of a rogue to be successful and too much of a dreamer to be totally ruthless made him appealing to Harvey. Acutely sensitive to the gossip swirling about him—that he callously stomped on people's faces in order to get ahead—he went out of his way to explain to the press that his character in this film had redeeming qualities and that he would never want to portray a totally ruthless man. He had a failing for portraying the weak characters of the world. On the other hand, he told Pete Martin of the *Saturday Evening Post*, "If you go on the theory that society is composed of nice people, of whom you are determined to be one, you'll find yourself surrounded by persons far more ruthless and clever than yourself who will slice your feet out from under you at the slightest provocation . . . no matter who they are, they can cut you up."

Expresso Bongo had become a successful musical play on the West End stage and Harvey was eager to translate it onto the screen, also as a musical, and wanted James Woolf to produce. Woolf did not think it a suitable vehicle for Harvey. Despite the success of *Room at the Top*, he still persisted in his vision of the actor as a debonair matinee idol circa the 1930s. Harvey, however, insisted, and his mentor persuaded his reluctant brother, John, to lend Harvey out to producer-director Val Guest—on condition that it would not be a musical and that both he and Mankowitz became the film's directors and not Harvey, who longed to direct himself. Harvey reluctantly agreed to all these conditions, and such was his faith in the movie that he sank his salary into it.

The movie was made in six weeks, on a budget of only £130,000, practically peanuts even then. It was filmed in black and white for lack of funds to make it in color. Despite its handicaps of cheap sets and lack of color for its lavish musical numbers, it made millions. It also made a star of a very young, angelic-looking English working-class kid called Cliff Richards, who became the idol of the teenagers and whose records sold in the millions. Harvey had never lived among the English-Jewish lower-middle-class community. They were quite different from the South African-Jewish community in which he had grown up, but he adapted quickly, imitating their accents, their dialect, and the rhythm of their speech. Hermione Baddeley had a cameo part in this picture—perhaps at the instigation of Harvey and for the sheer fun of it portraying a cheap, drab, aging streetwalker. The minute or two she was on screen with Harvey created an electric connection that he did not have with Sylvia Syms, his leading lady.

Harvey won praise from the critics for his performance and was a smash hit at the box office.

As soon as *Expresso Bongo* was wrapped up, he flew to Texas to work with John Wayne on *The Alamo*, a beautiful movie, but not free from controversy.

15

The Alamo and *Butterfield 8*

Earlier in 1959 he had served as the narrator—replacing Marlon Brando—for *Power among Men,* a grandiose television documentary sponsored by the United Nations exploring four of the major problems of the postwar era: postwar reconstruction, raising living standards, providing power for industrial expansion, and using atomic energy for peaceful purposes.

He was also still shooting *Expresso Bongo,* completing his role in this movie in eight weeks, he wrote to his brother Robert, "where normally one would have taken 11–12 weeks." He had to finish shooting this movie on Friday, he wrote, and fly to Texas "to start work on Monday on *The Alamo* with John Wayne and Richard Widmark and director John Ford." This movie, he added, was scheduled to take about twenty weeks to complete and had a $10-million budget—an enormous sum in those days. "I only hope that the quality matches its extravagance," he added modestly. "These past 2 months have been a nightmare and looking back on it now I wonder I am still able to stand."

Starring with John Wayne, the fabled hero of his favorite cowboy pictures in Johannesburg was, for him, sheer ecstasy. Making *The Alamo* was the realization of John Wayne's dream. In Texas, he faithfully recreated a copy of the original Alamo, the little Franciscan chapel where the valiant two hundred men had, in 1836, held out for thirteen days against Santa Anna, the Mexican dictator, and given their lives in the fight for the independence of Texas from Mexico.

Although he had never fought in a war, John Wayne had, throughout his long movie career, come to epitomize the quintessential heroic American warrior. The idea of recreating the events surrounding the Alamo had fascinated him for years, ever since he had seen the letter appealing for help sent from the besieged fort by Colonel Travis, the commander of the garrison stationed there. No studio was willing to subsidize the movie he wanted to make and he was assured that it would have no audience, but he persisted in fulfilling his dream, using a substantial part of his own money to produce it.

Because of his triumphs in *Room at the Top, Henry V,* and *Expresso Bongo,* Harvey was at this time being wooed by practically every studio in Hollywood. In May 1959, while shooting *Arthur* in Hitchcock's television series in Hollywood, John Wayne invited him to dinner. John Ford, the greatest director of Westerns, had also been Wayne's guest. John Wayne was a great deal better informed than his deceptively blunt cowboy screen image projected. He was familiar with Harvey's work, as was John Ford, but at dinner the two of them had sat, poker faced, allowing a nervous Harvey to tell them about his movie credits and his approach to acting. He was holding forth as he usually did when Wayne laconically interrupted him and said, in his languid drawl, "Don't give me all of that shit about art. I'm up to my shoulders trying to get this picture together," and began explaining his conception of Colonel Travis, the character he wanted Harvey to play.

At this stage, Ford who had been watching Harvey closely throughout the dinner, turned to Wayne and said, "Don't bother telling him about the part, Duke. We haven't got much time. Just sign the bastard up." Wayne did.

Yet Wayne felt uncertain as to whether Texans would accept an English actor playing Travis, and delayed telling the press that he had signed up Harvey for three months. Then he issued a press release through Batjac, his production company, reading: "All Texans were 'concerned' over the fact that Harvey, an Englishman, would be playing Travis. But all Texans, in fairness, were taking a 'let's wait and see' attitude." He also talked Texas governor Price Daniel into proclaiming Harvey an "Honorary Citizen of Texas." Harvey received his citation on the Monday he arrived on the set. On Wednesday he was sworn in as a deputy sheriff of Kinney County. On Friday he was made a marshal of Bexar County. On Saturday he officiated as grand marshal of the Dallas Civic Opera Company's first annual ball. In all, he was made an honorary deputy sheriff in seven Texas counties.

The Alamo had been defended by two more American heroes: James Bowie and Davy Crockett. As James Bowie, inventor of the Bowie knife, Wayne signed on Richard Widmark, another of Harvey's youthful heroes. Wayne himself chose to play Davy Crockett, the wily frontiersman and politician from Tennessee. His sons, Patrick and Michael; his eldest daughter, Toni; his wife, Pilar; and his little daughter, Aissa, were all roped into the cast. John Ford joked that this was the most expensive home movie ever made! The whole movie, with its spectacular battle scenes, was shot in Todd-AO, the new gigantic wide-screen process introduced in the mid-1950s by Michael Todd, who shot the spectacular *Around the World in 80 Days* in this process.

Despite the physical hardships involved in making *The Alamo*, this was one of Harvey's good periods. He enjoyed a spell of good health. With the money coming in from his films, he was finally able to go ahead with his plans to coproduce, direct, and act in his own film. He had also finally succeeded in paying all his arrears in taxes, which had been threatening to overwhelm him and land him in serious trouble. Feeling cocky and on top of the world once again, he threw down the gauntlet to those who said that an Englishman could not play an American hero.

"How dare they!" he thundered to reporters. "Those who complained don't know a damn thing about United States History. Inscribed on a plaque at the Alamo site are the names of Englishmen, Irishmen and Scotsmen who took part in the battle. So you see, that's settled. I have every right to be in the picture."

Even if he was "a Lithuanian-born South African turned Englishman," as the press labeled him!

Some of the kinder critics pointed out that Travis himself happened to have been born in South Carolina and lived in Virginia before becoming the commander of the Alamo.

All the same, as Harvey told the press, he thought that Wayne had really been very brave to put him in the film with all the critics screaming condemnation. He also used this opportunity to announce that he longed to do a cowboy picture. "There's another type of film that Americans shouldn't think is all theirs," he told Joe Finnigan of the New York *Morning Telegraph*. "Do you know that somebody had to bring a lot of cattle to this country from abroad? It just so happens that Englishmen were among the first to come to America and they brought some cattle along, building huge ranches. Someday I want to film the history of English influence on the American west."

The only problem was lack of money. "I can't get the English producers interested enough to put up the cash. It's like getting Winston Churchill to run for Prime Minister."

Wayne had many obstacles to overcome, including the Texas climate, the constantly rewritten script, rattlesnakes, accidents, and tragedy. Harvey suffered a serious injury when, as Travis, his response to the Mexican demand for surrender was coolly to fire a cannon with a flick of his lighted cigar. The scene was thrillingly effective, but the moment Wayne yelled "cut" Harvey let out a scream of pain. As it recoiled, some of the thousand pound cannon had rolled over his foot. He did not reveal even the slightest hint of pain until the shot was over.

He developed a close cameraderie with Wayne and Wayne liked him, despite his belief that men must be men and his suspicion that Harvey was gay. In her biography, Pillar Wayne relates that Harvey kept them in stitches every night with jokes, stories, and speeches from *Hamlet* and *Romeo and Juliet* delivered with a Texas accent, and, as Travis, a South Carolina accent mixed with a Texas drawl. What appeared to stir Wayne's deepest suspicions most about him, however, was the fact that he drank only Louis Latour Pouilly Fuissé, the white wine bottled and shipped to him from France. And he had ordered dozens of bottles of this wine. Real men did not drink wine, in Wayne's opinion. Fully aware that Wayne considered him a sissy, Harvey leaned over the parapet of the chapel where he was stationed one morning and yelled "Hey, Marion!" to Wayne who was stationed on the ground below him. As everyone knew, Wayne's given name was Marion. Wayne joined in the general laughter.

Still, rumors and stories persisted. According to another story, some of the crew held that Harvey's "British-Lithuanian-South African accent" proved that he was gay. According to another account when John Wayne was asked whether it was true that Harvey had addressed him as "Duchess" he replied, "Only once!"

Although Margaret Leighton was still his wife at the time, and had paid him a three-day visit on the set, it was his aptitude for certain prissy English theatrical mannerisms and his use of hyperboles that made him suspect. Besides, there was always his intimate friendship with James Woolf who visited the set now and then.

On the whole, however, Harvey appeared to have won over the crew, who took to drinking his French wine with great enjoyment and who always laughed at the foul language he had come to use in everyday conversation. As his gift to Wayne on the latter's birthday, he thoughtfully ordered two cases of champagne, one vintage, the other not. When these arrived, reflecting that Wayne preferred hard liquor, he had the nonvintage case taken to Wayne and kept the vintage champagne for himself, mischievously charging both cases to Batjac.

Returning to London for three weeks after finishing *The Alamo*, Harvey became very ill (probably with sinusitis) and wrote to his parents, "but somehow kept going with two and three injections a day. Now thank God am feeling better & getting my strength back slowly. This continual running and working is I suppose catching up with me slowly, but on the other hand if I didn't do it, I would go raving mad, so am pursuing the best of two evils."

He longed for his mother to fuss over him and pet him, the kind of mother he did not have, like the kind sweet aunts, his father's sisters, all but one of whom had perished. Margaret could not fill that bill—and besides, she was always away, working. When he was ill he felt very much alone. When he was working he felt on top of the world.

Back in New York once more, he was interviewed by the popular columnist Sheila Graham. What primarily impressed her she wrote, was the brashness and the untamable quality she saw in him. He said very little about either *The Alamo* or the next movie he had come to make, but persisted in repeating his constant gripe against the heavy taxation in Britain. "I'm on the same level as a laborer. If I stopped working tomorrow morning, I'd be selling shoelaces." he told her. In Hollywood, he said, he had rented a house with the option to buy. "I can't purchase a house here unless I become known as an American resident. I'm now on a working visa, paying taxes both here and in England. If I'm here more than 103 days in one year I must pay tax here. But I don't mind as opposed to those people who run away [from Britain's taxation] and think they're going to amass high fortunes by going to various countries and not working in England and America. I'd rather give them the taxes and have complete freedom of movement. I do think it's a shame there's no law to alleviate the tax burdens of actors, however. Businessmen, manufacturers and what all are permitted to take a certain amount for depreciation of materials and equipment. There is no depreciation given on physique which is our sole trading."

It was true that the contracts James Woolf had helped him negotiate with M-G-M, Hal Wallis, and Romulus Productions, and the percentage he had earned on his successful movies would bring him more than $1 million within the next two years, as was pointed out, yet this did not reassure him. "People who made money before the war are living off it now," he claimed. "Whatever you earn in my income-tax bracket you have to spend. If you earn $1 million today, you end up with $50,000. It's disgraceful that neither the American nor the British Governments recognize that an actor's earnings fluctuate. Actors' salaries are publicized on a false earning basis, neglecting what they must pay out. Actors' salaries are too low. People envisage actors earning so much, when in fact they earn nothing because of taxation. I'd rather earn $50,000 tax free than $250,000 and be taxed. Working as I do between two countries, I have to live in a hotel or an apartment in New York or Hollywood. I tell you, honestly, I couldn't live on $50,000 a year. I always find at the end of the year that I can't afford anything. I have to work more. But who cares? I'm pursuing work I like very much. I've never had a holiday."

And reinventing his past yet again he added, "I've been working since I was 14. I ran away from home in Johannesburg after I'd whisked through school like a breeze."

Critics have claimed that Pandro S. Berman's *Butterfield 8* must have ranked high on everyone's list of favorite bad films of the 1960s. The original John O'Hara story was pretty much mangled by the script. The writer's conception had been based on the never-solved murder of a New York flapper named Starr Faithfull, and O'Hara had been obsessed with her story. M-G-M had bought the film rights, but the book had been gathering dust in the studio's library.

For Harvey, the prospect of costarring with Elizabeth Taylor, the world's most famous movie star, was very exciting. He was still staggered by the extraordinary success of *Room at the Top*, "which both baffles and pleases me," he wrote to his parents. *Expresso Bongo* had turned out to be another smashing success in the States, his fourth successful film in a row.

Butterfield 8 was plagued with many difficulties. Not the least among these was a strike that held up production and made him, Harvey wrote to his parents, "practically penniless," for he was forced to maintain houses in London and Hollywood and to live in an expensive hotel in New York. There was the problem of Elizabeth Taylor's frequent illnesses, causing further delays. He was having tax problems again. He had been forced to cancel a film he was to make and had signed up for three more films in succession without a break and did not know how he was going to manage to make them all, for they would all be filmed outside England. Living out of suitcases in hotels was expensive and was wearing him out, he complained in another letter to his parents. He did not mention that he always chose to stay in the finest and most expensive hotels, only that he was beginning to feel more and more "like a Nomad or 'Wandering Jew.'" He did not know what the future had in store and where, eventually, he would settle down, "but at the moment there seems no indication of either."

All these factors may have exerted some effect on his performance in the movie, in which he played Taylor's married lover. He appears to have deliberately underplayed his character, and this was not effective, although he had his moments. When, as required by the script, Elizabeth Taylor's stiletto heel appears to dig into his foot while he twists her arm, he seems to be in real pain. Without a twinge of guilt registering on his face, he tells his wife (Dina Merrill) that he does not know how her mink coat came to be missing, although he knows perfectly well that Taylor had walked off with it. There are other moments when his performance shows imagination and insight into the character, but these are too few and far between the general bland mediocrity.

It was on the set of *Butterfield 8* that Harvey and Taylor become lifelong friends. "She is wildly professional" he enthused to the *Saturday Evening Post*. "She's so wonderful to work with, I absolutely love her. When she comes onto a set, she gets on with her job and does it in the most extraordinarily professional way. There's a special sort of thing which goes on between her and the camera. She is no automaton doing what the director tells her to do. She *thinks*. She is imaginative. She starts little things going which help her interpretation of her role. With her there is never a lot of phony theatrics and clutching at herself to portray emotion. Nor does she need soft music to get into the proper mood before a shot. If you don't mind another superlative, I find her most enchanting to work with."

Despite her pet cats and dogs, never housebroken, spoiling her carpets, which the painstakingly clean and tidy Harvey would never have tolerated for a moment, he really loved and respected her, and his fond nickname for her was "fat ass."

He returned to England to make *The Long and the Short and the Tall*. This had been a successful play on the West End starring the newcomer Peter O'Toole, but he was still unknown to moviegoers and therefore was replaced by Harvey. Confident that it would be a box office success, he had sunk his own money into this production. As a working-class soldier trapped in an isolated jungle area with his platoon during the World War II, thoroughly scared, cursing, sneering at his comrades, quarreling with them, ridiculing the Japanese soldier they capture, and finally defending him against the others, he uses his talent for ranting and spouting filth and invective to convey his ultimately futile effort to stay alive, to remain human.

What becomes clearly evident in these last several movies was his determination not to be typecast. Offered the part, he could have succumbed to the temptation to make *Alfie* about a working-class youth who goes casually through life without much thought or ambition, but rejected this role, which rocketed Michael Caine to stardom. Instead, he constantly sought variety, playing the passive writer in *I Am a Camera*, the ambitious young working-class character in *Room at the Top*, the London East Side Jewish ponce in *Expresso Bongo*, the uptight American colonel in *The Alamo,* the discontented lawyer in *Butterfield 8,* and the acid-tongued Cockney in *The Long and the Short and the Tall.*

Months earlier he had told an interviewer that the roles he considered best for him were those in which he could play "an s.o.b." Though British producers could not match Hollywood money, he argued, "in the long run the role is usually more important to an actor than the money he makes for it. Careful selection of roles can extend your career by 10 or 20 years." He had loved playing Joe Lampton because this character was no angel; he possessed the same driving ambition and lack of scruples that most people occasionally had. On the other hand, Colonel Travis was a hero, but also human. "In one scene he gives a long tirade against Jefferson and democracy. It won't please many people, but it's a darn good scene dramatically. I don't agree with his sentiments any more than I do with Joe Lampton's, or the rat in *The Long and the Short and the Tall,* but if the characters are human and logically motivated, who cares? Certainly not the audience," he told Philip K. Scheuer of the *Los Angeles Times.*

While still in his practically moribund relationship with Margaret during the making of *The Long and the Short and the Tall,* the couple had gone out to dinner at a popular restaurant in Chelsea with Richard Harris, one of his costars and his wife at the time, Elizabeth. Rex Harrison happened to be dining there too and came to their table to chat. Elizabeth Harris promptly fell in love with Rex Harrison and left Richard for a brief marriage to Harrison.

It marked the prelude, in an odd way, to the open scandal that beset Harvey and earned him afresh the virulent hatred and scorn of many of Britain's actors and critics in January 1961, when Margaret Leighton was granted her divorce (on the grounds that he had committed adultery in a London Hotel the previous September). The action was not defended and the name of the "other woman" was not made public.

Returning to Hollywood—not without relief—Harvey cut a record of songs from *The Long and the Short and the Tall,* the ribald title song being "Hi Jig a Jig," with an all-male chorus. Following that he returned to Hollywood where he was under contract to Hal Wallis, negotiated by James Woolf, to do three movies, and to cool his heels. For once, he refused to talk to reporters. "Inasmuch as Mrs. Harvey was the first one to say anything about our private affairs, I will leave it to her to say anything else," he instructed his press agent to state.

Taking their cue from the British tabloids, the American tabloids played up the juicy scandal about this young British actor they had made so much of. They called him sexually immoral, unscrupulous, unprincipled, ruthlessly ambitious—even worse in reality than his portrayal of Joe Lampton in *Room at the Top*. Sickened by all this, he expressed his annoyance at the stream of "filth" about his relations with women printed in the tabloids while on a brief trip to Japan with Hal Wallis as a member of the advance team scouting locations for *A Girl Named Tamiko*, in which he was to star.

"I was completely and absolutely staggered," he insisted in an interview. "Everything was based on rumor and not on fact. The sad part of it is that it always hurts people unnecessarily. The press must get a great deal of pleasure out of it."

It had to be ignored, he said, but he was too angry to ignore it.

"I do wish they'd leave me alone," he snapped.

The treatment he received must have hurt more deeply than he chose to admit. He was still talking about that divorce as late as May 1971, when he was interviewed by Stella King in the London *Times*.

"What really upset me was that she got the house and the furniture: I just walked out and left it. And I really loved that house."

16

Scandal and Divorce

A new scandal revolved around his relationship with Joan Cohn, the widow of Harry Cohn, the late head of Columbia Pictures. Because his first wife could not give him the family he craved, Cohn had divorced her and married the pretty young actress called Joan Perry. What he wanted was a breeder, and she seemed to fit his demand.

When Harvey met her, Joan Cohn was a beautiful blond in her forties but looked a good ten years younger, and he was a handsome young man who had just turned thirty-two. He had grown accustomed to picking up a worshipful starlet or a young man here and there for a one-night stand; they mattered little to him. It was hardly love at first sight when he met Joan, but it was admiration at first sight, at least on Harvey's part. He was dining with James Woolf and friends at an elegant restaurant in Hollywood, his sinusitis had been troubling him, and he had retired to the rest room until the pain in his head, which he described as making him feel as if his head would blow up, had abated somewhat. On his way back to his table, he caught sight of this beautiful woman dining with a man he knew. He stopped to speak and to be introduced, but thinking her just another Hollywood socialite used such foul language in his conversation with his friend that she practically turned her back on him.

Yet she was so elegant and lovely that he could not resist, before leaving their table, tracing her arm gently with an exploring finger. She did not respond.

"Who is she?" he questioned James Woolf when he returned to their table.

Woolf informed him she was the widow of Harry Cohn and one of Hollywood's wealthiest leading socialites. He went straight back to her table, apologized for his rudeness, and invited her on a dinner date. Contrary to the general opinion, it was not altogether her money that attracted him, although this certainly carried weight in view of his ambition to produce and act in his own production company—he knew dozens of women with money who were ready to throw themselves at his feet. What drew him was her style, her elegance—things he cared about above all.

She refused to go out with him and thought him vulgar and rude, if not unattractive.

He persisted in asking her out until, tiring of the game, she consented. One of the diners at the restaurant he had chosen was the influential columnist Louella Parsons, so both of them knew that their date would be highly publicized—not that either of them cared. He told Joan that she reminded him of his wife, whom he loved so very much. It might have been his way of giving her a compliment. He also told her, once, that she reminded him of his mother—he adored his mother, he told her—and in fact, like Margaret Leighton, Joan had something of her coloring, if nothing else. After dinner they went nightclubbing. It was after midnight when he brought her home.

Would he like to come in for a drink, she asked?

He proposed that they go to "beddies."

She was not familiar with the word, but understood the concept, and turned him down.

Again he apologized, and they became good friends and, only later, lovers.

Margaret Leighton told the *Daily Express*, "Joan Cohn is not the reason for my . . . divorce. I am not jealous of her—or indeed of any other woman—where Larry is concerned. The marriage [came] to an end because of other problems which have nothing to do with another woman. . . . There has been a lot of talk about our separate careers pulling us apart, but when I was with Larry my career always came second to our marriage. No longer, I might add. Before I came to this decision about a divorce I made another. I had been in a successful play, *The Wrong Side of the Park*, in the West End. I decided to leave the play and take a year's sabbatical—a year off from work—so that I could travel anywhere that Larry went while HE was working. A camp follower, if you like. I had chosen to appear in *The*

Wrong Side of the Park, in preference to a new Tennessee Williams play, *Sweet Bird of Youth,* that had been offered me in New York, not only because I thought *Park* was a very good play but because at that time Larry was planning to work in London at the Old Vic and I wanted to be there with him. What happened? He came over briefly for a film here and then had to return to America to work there again. Those months apart were not my doing. In marriage, it is all right for the man to put his career first—but it does not do for the woman to do the same."

In a discussion of the mathematics of his marriage, Harvey had earlier confessed that he had only spent about 60 or 70 out of every 365 days with Margaret during their marriage. The remaining months he had spent living out of suitcases and flying round the globe building his successful career. "The advantage of not seeing your wife except for two months every year," he added, "is that when you do meet you are more like lovers than a married couple."

But not, apparently, in their case.

Margaret had no trace of bitterness in her voice when she talked of him. "I do not know what he is going to do, apart from his work. But I care what happens to him deeply. Still."

He was already living with Joan when Margaret Leighton divorced him.

Joan asked him to act as emcee at a ritzy fashion show she organized at her house for Janor, a designer friend. Joan had most of her clothes designed by Janor. She had decided to buy into the house, and to give the designer a first-class introduction to a select group of wealthy women friends through the fashion show.

A blow-by-blow description of the proceedings by columnist Lee Belser was vividly given in the *Los Angeles Mirror:* While the ladies and a bevy of columnists, including Louella Parsons, waited in anticipation, pad and pencils at the ready to make notes of the clothes they liked best, Harvey appeared, his cigarette, as always, in his long cigarette holder planted between his teeth, a glass of champagne in one hand, grinning at the huge vase of pink and white gladiolas that had been placed on the podium as a prop. He was in one of his inexplicably crazy moods, drunk and resentful, and began childishly ridiculing the designer's creations, cracking up the audience with embarrassing and often lascivious leers and comments that he seemed to think were cute and smart.

"It's veddy, veddy stunning, isn't it?" he chortled of one creation.

Striving to salvage the situation, actress Anita Louise, who acted as his assistant, asked what he thought of a blue chiffon lace gown a model was wearing.

"Well, it certainly speaks to me," he replied. "I love all that jazz that goes around." (These were ruffles.) "And it's so loose fitting. If there's anything I love, it's a loose woman."

"It says here that this is a beautiful wool and silk dress," he said, reading from the prepared script with exaggerated gravity, "so I think it's charming. But don't you think the belt would require a lot of untying?"

Each time a pink dress was exhibited he cried, "Don't you think it's teddibly chic? I think it's absolutely thrilling."

Between pauses in the show caused by behind-the-scenes glitches, sipping his champagne, drawing on his cigarette, unsteady on his feet, he sought to amuse the audience by scratching his chin and rubbing his nose. In imitation of a fluttery gay designer he declared that the still-famous star Merle Oberon had gone quite mad over one creation with a low slung back, and had ordered it in three different colors. And his comment on a dress that appeared to be the designer's favorite was, "If you have a neck as high as your waist you could wear it anywhere."

At this point, Louella Parsons and two other movie columnists walked out. Harvey had one parting shot left to those who remained. Asked what he thought of the collection, which was reminiscent of the 1930s, he said, "I don't really know how I feel about the thirties. I was just born."

He appeared not to realize how offensive this remark was to most of the women in the audience, who were in their forties and over, including Joan.

"This is my first and last fashion show," he sighed wearily in response to the questions of reporters and columnists who had remained in the audience. And he slithered weakly to the thick, expensive green carpeted floor, champagne and cigarette holder in hand.

The guests swiftly dispersed to find their chauffeurs and their cars.

He had made a shambles of her beautifully planned fashion show, yet Joan forgave him, and they were happy together. He loved her beach house in Malibu from which he could stroll across a small patch of sand for a swim in the ocean and enjoyed the magnificent French-style chateau that Harry Cohn had built in Beverly Hills, its thirty rooms tastefully and expensively furnished, its walls made handsome with fine paintings, its imported chandeliers, large swimming pool, cabanas, guest houses, and other standard Beverly Hills appurtenances like its large screening room, but he would not live there, even after they became lovers. It was not to his taste. He wanted to rebuild and redecorate it, but that was not possible. So he bought his own house, nearby, where he could keep his cellar of 2,000 bottles of his favorite French wine, furnish his rooms to his own taste, and have the privacy he craved whenever he wanted it.

He knew most of the "greats" in Hollywood by then. On December 31, 1960, he served as best man at the wedding of director Vincente Minelli and his flamboyant Yugoslav third wife, an elegant socialite who had friends in the international set. The wedding was at the home of Anne and Kirk Douglas in Palm Springs. Kirk Douglas was still a great star in the 1960s, and he was one of Larry's friends, with whom he said he could talk about the trials and tribulations of having been born Jewish in a world where Jews were still looked down upon.

He refused to be regarded as Joan's "boy toy," yet mean Hollywood gossips labeled him just that. One of the strangest stories came from Zsa Zsa Gabor, recorded in *One Lifetime Is Not Enough*. While married to her third husband, George Sanders, she writes, they dined at Romanoff's with Joan, Harvey, and Jimmy Woolf one evening. Harvey later married Joan, she holds, because he wanted to get some stock in Columbia. Joan, she asserts, adored Harvey and spoiled him immensely. Invited to a fabulous Christmas party at Joan's house, they encountered Harvey standing outside the mansion looking extremely cross. There was a new station wagon parked in the driveway. That bitch had bought him a station wagon when he had wanted a Rolls-Royce, he griped. There was no end to his arrogance, she writes. Once, at a dinner party at her own house, he complained about the wine and offered to send his chauffeur to fetch some decent wine from his cellar.

Before the news of his divorce by Margaret Leighton had broken, he had sent his parents on a vacation to Johannesburg. They were happy among their relatives, and enjoyed the fame brought by *The Alamo*, which was showing in one of the movie houses for whites in

that city at the time, and it also ended his mother's constant complaints about living in Israel, which she now realized she infinitely
preferred to the hardening features of white South Africa. He asked
them not to pay too much attention to the tabloids and what they
were writing about his divorce. This was the price an actor had to
pay for his profession, he wrote. Only the loss of his beloved little
mews house saddened him, and the loss of his beautiful furniture
and works of art. The house and its treasures had taken him eighteen years of concentration and hard work to create.

At this time he made no mention of his new love interest. They
had heard about Joan Cohn from friends in Israel who kindly translated the gossip for them from the Hebrew tabloids and were rather
gratified than otherwise: they believed she was Jewish.

His next film was disappointing. *Two Loves* (also titled *Spinster*)
sent him on location in New Zealand for a month, while the rest of
the movie was shot in Hollywood. In it he costarred with Shirley
MacLaine and the fine British actor Jack Hawkins. The movie was
supposedly based on the beautiful novel by New Zealand author
Sylvia Ashton Warner, but the final script, even when rewritten,
was a hodgepodge of confusion. Shirley MacLaine had a quarrel
with Hal Wallis, hated her part as an unmarried teacher in a Maori
village, and obviously disliked Harvey, to whom she was supposed to be attracted. Harvey thoroughly disliked her and hated
Wallis, whom he described as "the Eichmann" of the movie industry. Harvey, looking young, fragile, and vulnerable, appeared not
quite to know how to interpret his role, or, as he himself complained, to understand what it was. Apart from the magnificent
New Zealand scenery and the pretty Maori children, the movie
was hardly worth watching.

Almost immediately following *Two Loves* came his role as the
wild, hard-drinking, and untamed medical student in Tennessee
Williams's *Summer and Smoke.* He had confidently expected that his

role as the southern scamp who finally shakes off his wildness, finds his soul, and becomes a responsible physician would, at last, take him over the top and win him the Oscar he had not won for *Room at the Top*.

"With all my problems," he wrote to his brother Nahum in August 1961 (among these problems being the financial drain taken by the divorce, which, he claimed, "has practically ruined me and left me without a home or roots of any kind except in the world of the theater and films which is fortunately giving me a haven and a home where I can express my feelings and what little talent I have"), "with all these problems, I am very happy to say I saw a private showing of . . . *Summer and Smoke* . . . and I think, and I say this in all humility, it is without question some of the best work I have done to date and feel sure, although one never knows, that when it comes out towards the end of the year, it will confirm the reputation that I have taken so many years to establish."

It was not to be. Southerners have remarked that his accent was perfect. He had just the soft touch in his voice and manner of an authentic Southern gentleman, but his performance, carefully underplayed, was overwhelmed by that of his costar, Geraldine Paige, who dominated every scene. He was praised and admired for his work by people he knew, but hardly by the critics.

Following *Summer and Smoke,* he was scheduled to fly to London to make a television special on the history of the London Palladium and to appear for three months in a play about postwar Germany titled *Loser Wins.*

"Why a play now?" he was asked by columnist Erskine Johnson of the *Los Angeles Mirror,* especially since he had been openly lamenting that he wished the days were thirty-six hours long so that he could find time for a little fun.

"It's because I never want to lose touch," he explained. "The whole basis of acting is the stage. I need the continual experience. Actors must go on learning until they drop dead. I can't stand Hollywood actors crying and making announcements about their love for the stage—and then refusing to budge an inch from Hollywood while greedily pocketing money from movies and TV specials."

He had learned, slyly, the art of planting news items by means of sparkling little hints. For example, he absolutely insisted at this stage that he and Joan Cohn were "just friends," while in the same breath confessing that he had recently given her a five-carat diamond pendant. Her gift to him had been a pink Rolls-Royce.

He loved the simple life, he claimed, but his lifestyle contradicted this assertion. He designed his own suits and sent the most minute instructions to his Savile Row tailor, down to the precise placing of a button. When he wore denim jeans, they were custom tailored. After buying a string of Rolls-Royces, he claimed airily, he had acquired a Bentley, a slightly less expensive vehicle, but a more prestigious means of transportation, since it happened to be the car used by the British royal family.

With all the fame and publicity, his greatest and most enduring admirer remained James Woolf. Harvey, Woolf claimed, had the talent to go with his energy. He was the best example around of the "matinee-idol tradition," an "exceptionally well-trained and skilled all-around actor, with the extra dimension of enormous personal magnetism and good looks, which attract people, whether he's on stage or screen."

17

The Manchurian Candidate

Because Harvey kept demanding an ever-mounting workload, James Woolf had negotiated contracts with four Hollywood studios, committing Harvey to make twelve movies for them. What had he gained from this relentless, self-imposed pressure? he was asked. "A nervous stomach. Hangovers. Headaches [and to this may be added relentless dieting]," he responded. "And yet, when you put all these sorts of horrendous emotions together it adds up to something quite wonderful. I like more than anything to take a part—any character—and if I have succeeded in giving any sort of additional qualities, if I have created a living flesh-and-blood character out of nothing—then I feel I've succeeded as an actor."

This, he said, was how he had tackled his role in *Summer and Smoke*, working like a slave to create the character, while in *Two Loves*, which had been "the greatest dissection since the slaughterhouse," they had taken a script that had such character and beauty and cut it so much that in the end the boy he played made no sense at all. Sometimes, he snorted, an actor had no control, which is something the critics did not take into account.

The only good thing to come out of Hollywood in his opinion was that the competition presented by good foreign films was forcing the industry to move out of Hollywood to film on various locations throughout the world. "You might call it the broadening of the mind as opposed to the broadening of the behind," he told the *Los Angeles Times*. "I like that. The broadening of the mind as opposed to the broadening of the behind. That's what we mean when we talk about complacency. It's terrible to think that some people are just sitting around gathering fatty tissue."

He dreamed of taking a vacation and talked about vacationing on the French Riviera, yet never took more than a weekend trip with Joan Cohn to her luxurious house in Palm Springs, or spent a night partying with wealthy friends and famous stars in Manhattan or London. He loved dining out at some posh restaurant with his good friends, Elizabeth Taylor and Rock Hudson, or with producers and financiers whom he wished to persuade to back the movies he wanted to make. Now and then he would pay a flying visit with Joan Cohn to the flea market in Paris, making large purchases in swift decisions, constantly adding to his collection of antiques, but only his frenetic search for more and more work sent him jetting to Britain or the Continent.

Why did he keep running so much, he was asked? Because this, he explained, was partly the result of his early training in Shakespeare. "We would undertake a new production every day—and when you finally did one play a second time you took a different role. It is the only way for an actor to develop whatever talent he has. . . . For a film actor the parallel is obvious. Squeeze in as many pictures as possible."

But would that not result in overexposure, he was asked?

"Overexposure? Vastly overrated," he replied. "In the heyday of film making in the '30s, the Gables, Tracys, Lombards and other major stars would have felt they were loafing if they did less than five films a year. On TV, one effort will bring more exposure than three or four movies. The profit is negligible. Taxes take care of that. But the profit in exposure to audiences and in new challenges to the actor is incalculable."

In January 1962, recognition came for his work for the third consecutive year—he had been forgiven in Britain, or at least partly, and because of his star status, it appeared, for his bad treatment of Margaret Leighton—and was nominated for the British Academy Award for an unprecedented third consecutive year for his work in *The Long and the Short and the Tall*. The previous year he had been nominated for his work in *Expresso Bongo* and in 1959 for *Room at the Top*.

Ambitious to become a producer and director as well as a star, he turned to purchasing properties for development. His first purchase, *The Feathers of Death* by Simon Raven, a best-selling novel in Europe about the relationship between an officer and a private in a British

Guards' regiment sent to the trouble spot of British Kenya. The tension between the two men leads to a court-martial and the revelation of the emotional links between them. Harvey was to play the lead in this movie, to be made in Britain and Kenya, and the company that was to produce the movie, to be named L.H.P. Films, was his own. Harvey was to be joined by renowned actor-producer Richard Attenborough and the script was to be written by the equally famous Bryan Forbes. It was to be directed either by Jack Clayton or Peter Glenville, Harvey's close friend, who had directed *Summer and Smoke.*

Because of his other commitments, he said, this movie would not be made for some time. *The Clowns,* a second best-selling novel, was purchased at the same time and was also slated for development by his company. He had also formed a second company called Challet Productions. In all his transactions, the indulgent James Woolf was an active participant.

He was soon working in *A Walk on the Wild Side,* his next movie. Prior to making this picture, he had contracted to star in Jean-Paul Sartre's *Loser Wins* on the London stage, and Columbia Pictures had to pay a hefty sum of money to release him from that contract.

Nelson Algren's novel, *A Walk on the Wild Side,* had been widely panned by the critics, and Algren himself, who belonged to the "social protest" school of the "proletarian writers" of the 1930s, had been called sadly outdated. His first novel, *The Man with the Golden Arm,* had been made into a successful movie starring Frank Sinatra in 1956. Despite the critics' condemnation, *A Walk on the Wild Side* was also expected to be a hit movie. But if *Butterfield 8* was concocted out of a bowdlerized version of John O'Hara's novel and nevertheless became a box office success, the script of *A Walk on the Wild Side* trashed the original story by Nelson Algren even more thoroughly and proved to be no attraction at all.

Filmed on location in the Texas Panhandle and New Orleans, this story is about a penniless Texas farmhand who makes his way to New Orleans searching for a beautiful French artist who had spent several months recuperating from an illness in his hometown, where they had fallen in love. He finds her in a bordello, the property of a lesbian madam with a collection of vicious thugs. His attempts to rescue her only results in her death by a bullet intended for him.

This was a very young Jane Fonda's first movie, and she comes on very strong, guided by her mentor of the time, the Greek director Andreas Voutsinas, a young man wearing the regulation black pants and black turtleneck sweater capped by a black beret so fashionable among artists and liberal intellectuals in the 1960s. Laurence Harvey, the only male lead, speaks his lines with a quiet Texas drawl and an aloof style that clashes violently with Fonda's earthy presence. In fact, nobody's style matches. The cast including Barbara Stanwick, Capucine, and Anne Baxter do not constitute an ensemble and appear to have no intention of cementing one.

There were too many contending forces off camera and on. The first director was fired halfway through the movie, and was replaced by the brilliant Edward Dmytryk, but it was too late to rescue the movie. Jane Fonda held that all the women in the cast disliked Harvey and complained to everyone that acting with Harvey was like acting by oneself: she got no response from him. To which, no mean possessor of an acid tongue, Harvey shot back, "What a strange girl! She seems to be suffering from the Hollywood disease—get yourself a big name and there's no need to live up to it. . . . She has a few things written about her and she comes to the conclusion she's the biggest star in the movie business. You can't tell her anything. Two hours on the set and she's playing director and running the outfit." And of Capucine he drawled, that this "ghastly film," was made even more so "by that ghastly woman. I suppose it's not her fault she can't act."

Practically every actor had a sponsor. Harvey was involved with Joan Cohn and since the movie was produced by Columbia Pictures, he was regarded as a powerful force with which to be reckoned. Capucine complained that Harvey kept deliberately ruining her performance by spitefully chewing garlic and unnerving her with grimaces when his back was turned to the camera; consequently, she loathed him. To make matters worse between them, she was involved with the film's producer, Charles K. Feldman, and in each scene had the unfortunate tendency to exhibit her equine profile and her strong nose. Only Barbara Stanwick behaved like a total professional but could not salvage the picture.

Perhaps the only relief the audience had watching the movie anywhere in the world came in Tel Aviv, where, just as Harvey's character was being badly beaten up, the cinema manager had a message flashed onscreen announcing Harvey's brother's presence in the audience, and some wit yelled out "Brother, help him," and the audience got its only laugh.

No sooner had he finished shooting *A Walk on the Wild Side* in June 1961 when he started a new picture for M-G-M, *The Wonderful World of the Brothers Grimm.* Most of the film was shot in West Germany where, he wrote to his parents, the weather was wonderful. It was obvious that he thoroughly enjoyed working in this picture—an enjoyment that was not reflected at the box office.

While working in West Germany he received the German Film Art Institute's annual award for acting excellence. Presented to him in Munich, Hitler's original stronghold in August 1961, it made him feel somewhat uncomfortable, but he accepted it. He never denied being Jewish.

He finished *The Brothers Grimm* on November 22, 1961, and began a forty-three-day shooting schedule on *A Girl Called Tamiko* for Hal Wallis at Paramount the very next day. Although this movie costarred France Nuyen and Martha Hyer—two powerful box office draws of the time—it was not highly successful. Harvey plays a half-Russian, half-Chinese photographer living in Japan whose only objective is to obtain a visa to the United States. Filmed mainly on location in Japan, this movie's Japanese background is extraordinarily beautiful, but the story suggests an indictment of American immigration policy.

Only days after his return from Japan, in mid-January 1962, he began working on *The Manchurian Candidate.*

In the past, he had made many errors in judgment regarding his work. He had not realized what an impact his performance in *Room at the Top* would make. He had been convinced that his performance in *Summer and Smoke* would win him the Oscar he coveted and mark the apex of his career—yet he had not even been nominated. This time, however, his instinct told him that this would be a great picture, and that his performance would be highly regarded. Above all, he was thrilled about working with Frank Sinatra, whom he greatly admired. So keen was Harvey to act in it that he settled on receiving a lump sum of $250,000 against a percentage deal under which most of his other pictures were to be made. In this sense, he came comparatively cheap. Besides, he needed the money to finance his investments in his production companies and to cover his other extravagant expenses in clothes, antiques, cars, houses, and everything else his eyes fell upon and desired.

The Manchurian Candidate, based on the best-selling novel of that name by Richard Condon, is the story of a G.I. in Korea who is brainwashed by a Chinese psychiatrist and programmed to kill the American president in order to replace him with a communist puppet.

Frank Sinatra had learned of the novel and bought it for the screen. When he asked John Frankenheimer to be its producer-director and George Axelrod to become the producer-writer, they were both eager to cooperate. The snag, however, was United Artists, which was to distribute this movie as part of Sinatra's $15-million deal with this studio. Its president, Arthur Krim, argued that the movie was too politically dangerous: what if, for example, President Kennedy were to come to an agreement with the Soviet Union and end the animosity that was, as the time, besetting the two countries?

When George Axelrod, John Frankenheimer, and Richard Condon himself told Sinatra that this movie could not be made without the president's approval, Sinatra informed them, calmly, that while on a three-hour cruise of Cape Cod with President Kennedy on his ship, the *Honey Fitz,* when asked what his next project was to be he had answered that he wanted to film *The Manchurian Candidate.* Kennedy had immediately been interested. He had read the book and liked it. Who was to play the mother was all he asked? Sinatra asked him to call United Artists and tell them of his approval, and Kennedy had done so.

The film was shot in thirty-one days. An impressive group of stars was lined up for this film, including Frank Sinatra, Harvey, Angela Lansbury, and Janet Leigh. Ironically, neither Harvey nor Angela Lansbury had been Sinatra's first choice for the film. He had wanted Tony

Curtis in the Harvey role, and Lucille Ball to play the mother, but when he was shown a screen test with Harvey he instantly agreed that no one else could play this role so well. Lucille Ball was not available. Angela Lansbury's performance is so brilliantly authentic that it would be difficult to conceive of anyone else playing this role.

The Harvey-Lansbury relationship was especially interesting. Chronologically, Angela Lansbury was only four years older than Larry, and yet her performance is so polished and believable that she really does seem to be old enough to be his mother, and this remains freshly imprinted in the mind. She became, also, one of the handful of first-rate actresses whom Harvey genuinely liked, respected, and admired. Lansbury and her husband knew James Woolf, with whom her husband had business dealings, and they warmly liked and respected him as a friend and an honorable man. She had known and liked Harvey before, but they became good friends while working together in the film.

Frank Sinatra who was known to dislike retakes, always carefully rehearsed his role, and then did it in one take. The other stars usually took more than one take, Angela Lansbury related in an interview, but a brilliant exception stands out in her memory. In the last part of the movie, when her true identity is finally revealed, she makes a long speech to the brainwashed Harvey who remains hypnotically silent and motionless throughout the scene. This scene was done in one take. "Larry," she remembered, "had a horrendous cold that day, and kept coughing and sneezing. It seemed impossible to complete the scene that day, but as a true professional he knew how difficult the scene was for me and controlled his coughing and held out to the end of the scene without stirring."

It was her scene, and, sacrificing himself almost to bursting, he gave it to her.

She had met Larry while he was living at the Connaught Hotel in London. "He had a lust for life," she said. But he was also a very sincere and hardworking actor. Turning up on the set after a night of heavy drinking, he asked the makeup department for ice in order to remove the puffiness under his eyes: he would not spoil a scene for his fellow actors. "A charming man," she called him. He had the most wonderful clothes. She had gone to see him perform in *Henry V* during the Old Vic's tour of the States and was full of admiration for his performance. Several years later, she had flown to San Francisco to see him in the play *The Time of the Barracudas* with Elaine

Stritch. It had folded owing, she believed, to all sorts of unfortunate difficulties; these things happen. She admired Elaine Stritch and Larry as artists, both had been her friends, Elaine Stritch still was. Yes, she said, perhaps Larry did say things he should not have said publicly, but some of the things he said about the industry had been very perceptive and true, and needed to be said. "Above all else," she said, "he was a true professional. We had that in common. And also a personal friendship."

He had never told her the truth about his origins. He had never mentioned anything but the name, Larushka, which he had chosen to say was his real name, and that he was Lithuanian born. A Slav! She had believed him. She had not known that Lithuanians were not Slavs, or that he was not an ethnic Lithuanian. The subject had never come up.

What is rather surprising is the fact that Frank Sinatra had chosen Harvey as a member of the cast and liked him, although he knew that Harvey was well liked by John Wayne, whom Sinatra strongly disliked. But Larry was, although basically nonpolitical, possessed of a smattering of liberal values learned from his brothers as a boy. Angela Lansbury's grandfather had been the leader of Britain's Labor Party and would have become prime minister instead of Clement Atlee, only he was too old by the time of the Labor Party's victory in the polls. Her family tree must have reminded Harvey of his brothers. Without a deep interest in anything but acting, he did draw the line at rank conservatism, even to the point of boasting, once, that much as he liked Wayne, he would have smashed his face in if they had ever discussed politics.

The fact that Wayne was taller and stronger, or that he really liked him seemed not to have entered into the equation. At any rate, they remained good friends to the end.

Had he become a member of Sinatra's Clan (the "Rat Pack")? he was asked.

No. He had abandoned Hollywood and become a New Yorker and organized his own clan, he responded airily.

He had fun making this movie, he told famed columnist Earl Wilson over a bottle of his favorite Louis Latour Pouilly Fuissé in the bar of the Plaza Hotel where he was staying. Filming in New York, where the movie was made, he had great fun bamboozling the chambermaid with the various disguises he had to wear. One frigid Manhattan morning, the script called for him, in a hypnotic trance, to jump into the lake in Central Park. He had not shaved that morning and when he jumped into the lake, found to his surprise that his good English tweed suit was wrinkle proof. Frankenheimer told one of his people to jump on the suit and make a complete mess of it. He did not mention the fact that the water had been icy and that he had not even batted an eyelid as he hit it. He had jumped into the lake as a thoroughly brainwashed person: the slightest grimace would have spoiled the effect. Sinatra had noticed this strict self-discipline and admired it.

Leaving the hotel in his wrinkled and dirty suit to reshoot the scene, Harvey had encountered the chambermaid and wished her a hearty "Good morning." He said that he could just hear her saying to herself, "My God, they're letting some kind of bum in this hotel!" (As always, he loved to denigrate himself.) To make matters even worse, when he returned from his icy plunge with chattering teeth, wearing a terry cloth robe, long underwear, fur-lined boots, and drinking brandy, the wardrobe man joked, "The champ! He knocked him out in the 13th round." The same chambermaid overheard this and stopped vacuuming in shock, Harvey said. Or so he fancied.

Later that day, he left his room dressed as a clergyman for the next to final scene in the movie, in which he shoots his communist mother and her stooge and then himself.

"I blessed everybody from the front door of the Plaza to Madison Square Garden," he boasted to Earl Wilson.

He was very happy with his work in the film. It had been a long, hard, and consuming effort and an extremely difficult one, he wrote to his parents. "It isn't only making a film that eats up one's time, but there are also many other time consuming factors that one has to deal with in a very business like way for one has to survive this jungle like existence. Despite all this I feel a lot happier about this last film than I have ever felt about a picture in a long time. It should prove a very potent and important turning point in my career. It is always difficult to assess the exact value of one's contribution to a film, but I would say that here I have done some of my best work to date and I hope that when it is finally shown to the film going public they will share my views."

At the end of 1961, James Woolf had made a deal with Hal Wallis to star Harvey in *Becket*, and with Lawrence Weingarten in *Period of Adjustment* as part of a fourteen-picture deal with M-G-M to be distributed through Paramount, plus a two-picture deal with Seven Arts and Columbia, and one picture a year for the next four years with James and John Woolf, to be produced for Warner Bros. The deal with the Woolf brothers included *The L-Shaped Room* and *Councilman Lampton*. Only the first of these pictures was produced, but not with Harvey, who was busy elsewhere. The second never saw the light of day.

Busily wheeling and dealing even under the difficult circumstances of shooting *The Manchurian Candidate,* he was still intent on making the maximum amount of films. To suit his ambitious projects, he blandly proposed that production could be increased if the studios would cooperate with one another on their scheduled use of stars and that in order to facilitate his work—he wanted to make five pictures a year—cooperation was necessary between M-G-M, Paramount, and United Artists. He used as an example of this cooperation the fact that while filming *Butterfield 8,* M-G-M had cooperated with Sir Michael Balcon by paying the rent for the sets for Balcon's *The Long and the Short and the Tall* in England for six months while Balcon was waiting for him to finish. He approached the networks with a package deal on Shakespeare's *Othello* for which he said he would be the producer and the star, but this evoked no interest. If, the networks responded, he wanted to make this movie himself, they would look at the finished product. Refusing to be rebuffed, he set about seeking funding to finance a ninety-minute film of *Othello* at a cost of $375,000 and issued the following challenge in the form of a written statement to the networks:

> I find their attitude shaming and shocking, considering the tremendous profits they make. They are all so scared of anything which appertains to any degree of artistic aspiration. They have a lack of integrity, of wanting anything better. They are satisfied with the vulgar programs

now on, most of it canned imitations of humor and drama. . . . They be-
little the public by giving them this, because, fortunately, we have seen
a great exodus from the home, and back to the cinema.

He revealed that he had received an offer from David Suskind,
then a force in television, inviting him to star in any vehicle he chose.
"But when I said Shakespeare, he backed away."

At about this time, too, he had been approached to star in a series;
"the sort of thrillers where an English detective is running around
picking dead bodies out of the sewer," he explained contemptu-
ously. That did not interest him. If he became suddenly unemployed
in pictures, at the moment a very unlikely prospect, he would return
to the stage, he said. "I won't become a millionaire, as people with a
series do in TV. But I can make a very handsome living."

Asked to star in a remake of *The Prisoner of Zenda,* he said, "a
charming idea, but I've already seen the film."

He was adamantly opposed to remakes of pictures and plays, he
said. Yet, several years later when necessity beckoned, he changed
his mind.

He was determined, however, to produce *Othello* for the screen.
He planned to invite Jean Simmons to be his Desdemona and to
shoot the movie in Venice, where Shakespeare had set his play. "It
may be the biggest disaster in the world," he declared, "but I
should at least try to do it in the spirit of doing something good.
It would be better than the growls, yapping and monkeys you see
on TV."

If his *Othello* made the grade, he said, he planned to make an an-
thology series with a group of stars who took the leading roles in
rotation.

He flew to Paris, holed up at his favorite Georges V hotel, flew to
Spain for some location work on his next film, *The Running Man,* and
a few days later, flew back to New York and did the narration for a
television ballet presentation of Stravinsky's *Noah and the Flood.* Then
he flew back to Spain and plunged directly into work on *The Running
Man,* which was filmed on location on Spain's picturesque Costa
Brava on the Franco-Spanish border and in France and Ireland.

Interviewed on the set of *The Running Man* on location near the Rock of Gibraltar, he was asked how he managed to produce so much and at such a breakneck pace. The average major film took some nine months of shooting time, and yet he was ambitious to make six movies practically simultaneously. Even acting in three films a year involved some overlapping, some complex juggling of shooting schedules, necessitating travel by jets, fast cars, and fast legwork. On the set, there were no tantrums, no lost time (with the exception of *A Walk on the Wild Side*, that is, when he had spent so much time on the telephone and the other actors had been forced to wait for him in order to shoot a scene).

"Larry demands at least a half hour between films," one actor joked.

He had not even taken that half hour between finishing *The Brothers Grimm* and *A Girl Named Tamiko* to move on to his next movie; he had just nibbled a sandwich while driving from one studio to the next. Now, he told his interviewer, he was seriously thinking of purchasing his own $250,000 plane. "Scheduled airplanes seldom leave at the moment I want to leave, or arrive at the time I have to arrive. Oft times I have to rush out of the studio without eating, and with my makeup still on to catch a plane for Germany or some place."

Why, then, did he not make fewer pictures to ease the strain?

"I am only happy when I am working," he declared.

To him, the telephone was the most awesome invention of the modern age. "A thrilling instrument," he called it. "You can pick up the old blower and call Tokyo. Or get a divorce on it."

Also, he preferred dining out, he claimed, to dining at home. He had been eating away from home, he declared, since the age of fourteen. As he summed it up, "The mother image has been replaced for me by the restaurant image."

What was he running away from, he was asked?

"Not away from," he corrected. "Toward things—the good things in life."

Ironically, it was *The Running Man* for Columbia, released in 1963, that brought his wild dash from picture to picture and country to country to a halt for several months. Based on *The Ballad of the Running Man*, a novel by Shelley Smith, the script was written by John Mortimer, a best-selling novelist in his own right, and it was directed by Sir Carol Reed, one of Britain's top directors. In it Harvey plays a pilot whose plane crashes but he cannot collect his insurance because he missed renewing his policy by one day. He devises an ingenious plan to defraud the insurance company, hides out in Spain, disguises himself by growing a mustache dyed a deep yellow, steals the passport of an Australian businessman whom he murders, assumes an Australian accent, and waits for his wife to collect the insurance as his widow and then join him. An insurance investigator discovers the fraud.

The very pretty and talented Lee Remick plays his wife, and the English actor Alan Bates, then still young, good-looking, and a popular star in Britain plays the insurance investigator who falls in love with her.

This was not one of Harvey's best performances. As always, his accent was perfect, but he seemed bored with his role, and did not get along with Lee Remick, who thoroughly disliked his abrasive personality.

Nor had Harvey been very cooperative. Presumably unwilling to sacrifice the bulk of his high American earnings to the demands of Britain's high taxation, according to some reports, he had placed in his contract a clause stating that all filming had to take place outside Britain. Enchanted by the beauty of Spain's south coast, Carol Reed had not helped the movie either. He had done most of the shooting on the south coast instead of in Barcelona and, as he had first planned, worked up toward the mountains of Andorra.

In this film, the Rock of Gibraltar, where Harvey's plane crashed and he supposedly died, was the only location recognizable to audiences.

When Reed took the cast and crew for a ten-week location schedule to Malaga, Algeciras, San Roque, and La Linea on the Costa de Sol, Harvey began dimly to realize that the movie was doomed to fail.

The novel is a thriller. The movie version is a disappointing follow-up to *The Manchurian Candidate* and does little to enhance Harvey's reputation as an actor. In fact, everything about *The Running Man* was a disappointment to him. The locations were changed, causing delays.

Between April, when he arrived in Spain, and the end of June 1962, very little had yet been achieved, locations work was still going on. The constant postponements, delays, and general confusion acutely depressed and irritated him. He was forced, he wrote to his parents, to sue the company, involving himself in an expensive lawsuit.

"As one continues to work in this profession one finds it increasingly difficult as the whole economy & structure of the motion picture industry has, & is continually changing," he wrote despondently. "The people who run the companies today are no longer interested in films, but only in greed, lining their pockets and destroying what was once a great field of entertainment and sometimes even an art. In order to survive one had to be continually fighting their negativity and stupidity. Where one time we could spend all our efforts and energies on performance, we now have to watch every other aspect of the business. After all these years of intensive hard work and concentrated labors, I find myself no better off financially than I was ten or fifteen years ago, & one wonders whether it's all worth it. Unfortunately I am stuck with this business & know no other, so am forced to continue in this rat race hoping for survival."

By September the location had changed from the blazing heat and continual trek around Spain to Dublin, where the interiors were completed. The dramatic change in the weather from oppressive heat to cold came as a shock.

"Every member of the cast and crew seemed to have come down with a bad cold and sinus trouble, but the principal sufferer is me," he wrote to his parents.

The only saving grace was that in Spain, they had started filming at sunup and finished at sunset. In Dublin, it was a relief to return to regular studio hours.

He worried about the general depression that had overtaken the movie industry, especially in the States, and was determined to redouble his efforts to find increasing volumes of work.

18

"The Hottest Star in Town"

In late 1962, Harvey was back in Madrid shooting *The Ceremony*, his own property, for his own company. Despite James Woolf's apprehension that he would only jeopardize his career by tackling what was beyond his reach, he was determined to fulfill his ambition to take full charge and ownership of his own picture. He regarded his role as producer, director, and star of *The Ceremony* an exciting challenge to his self-confidence, a test of his abilities, and the opportunity to use his inexhaustible energy.

The story he had selected to film was a dark, rather pretentious political allegory from a novel titled *La Cérémonie* by Frédéric Grendel.

The script was written by Ben Barzman, with additional dialogue by Alun Falconer, but dissatisfied with the script, Harvey rewrote a great deal of it himself. Its hero, an Irishman played by Harvey, faces execution in a Tangier prison for a murder he did not commit. His brother engineers his escape, but when Harvey learns of his brother's affair with his girl, a fight and a car crash follow. His brother is captured and executed in his place. Its more than $1-million budget was financed by United Artists, which had its world distribution rights.

The film had a fine cast of English, Spanish, Irish, and American actors, including Sarah Miles, a young English debutante turned major film star with her first film, *Terms of Trial*, starring Laurence Olivier, with whom, despite his recent new marriage, she was enjoying secret trysts. James Woolf had recommended her for the role as Harvey's girl.

277

Faithful to his friend and loyal admirer, Harvey gave a decent part to John Ireland, whom he had known since they had worked together in *The Good Die Young*. Ireland appears to have lacked sufficient drive, or perhaps was more interested in the horses than in acting, and relied on Harvey for his film roles for much of Harvey's life.

The marvelous Spanish star Fernando Rey and a host of other Spanish actors were added to the cast.

Filming began outside the old city walls of Toledo with the highly reputed Oswald Morris as the film's cinematographer.

All did not go as well as Harvey had hoped. Two weeks before filming ended, he signed on Alfredo Matas of Jet Films as his Spanish partner and coproducer, expecting him to be able to pick up most of the under-the-line costs and to guarantee that the film would get a prestigious send-off in Spain. When this expectation failed, he shelved his deal with Matas and Jet Films, and with the aid of United Artists assumed sole control, although he was willing to sign up Spanish companies to handle the film's distribution.

By then, the budget had already risen to $1 million. All he received from the Spanish companies was $200,000.

Stubbornly, he tackled every production problem, aided only by a Spanish translator. All the same, handling every facet of this picture (this did not altogether displease him, he preferred doing everything himself) tested his patience as well as his stamina. There were innumerable obstacles to overcome. When, in an escape scene, Robert Walker, who plays his younger brother, had to clamber up an ancient Toledo city wall with the aid of a rope, the stuntman demanded that footholds be chipped in the wall for safety, Harvey impatiently grabbed the rope himself and clambered up the wall, barely saving himself from falling to his death but keeping the wall intact, as demanded by the city of Toledo. On another occasion, while directing Walker in a fight scene, urging him to make the punches appear more realistic, he suffered two broken ribs and had to work with his chest strapped up.

A totally unexpected blow came, which threatened to shut down production completely.

Harvey had approved publicity stills taken of Sarah Miles posing naked behind a trellis gate and these were published in several London tabloids. The staff at her parents' house saw the pictures in the tabloids and showed them to her parents. They telephoned their daughter to express their shock, as did her agent, who happened to be her boyfriend's father. Sarah Miles had raised no objection to having photographers on the set at the time, but she later claimed that they had "crept" onto the set without her knowledge and that the pictures had been published without her permission. Harvey immediately confiscated the remaining pictures and locked them in his safe. But there was no chance, he said bluntly, that the scene would be cut from the movie. "It is one of the most tastefully shot nude scenes in the history of picture-making," he insisted, "and anybody who thinks differently has a dirty mind." Sarah Miles herself said that she had agreed to do the nude scene after a lot of thought and long discussions. She had been very embarrassed, even though the lighting had been arranged so that very little of her could be seen clearly. She had not liked the idea of stripping and, "in any case, I'm too skinny for that sort of thing."

A story appeared in *Variety* implying that Harvey had lost his co-production status in *Ceremony* because of the nude scene. He responded that the nude scene had been in the original script, all of which had been translated into Spanish and had been submitted to all the appropriate authorities, and that the authorities had approved this sequence. The nude scene, he argued, was an integral part of the story and influenced the main character's behavior. It had not been a publicity gimmick and he could not be held responsible for the fact that the incident had been exploited around the world by "unscrupulous people." He explained that everything required by Spanish law, such as employing matching crews, had been done. He had lost his coproduction billing for quite another reason. His original deal with Jet Films had fallen through because Alfredo Matas had not been able to come up with the necessary funding, and as a consequence, United Artists had come up with a second deal. He insisted that he had behaved impeccably throughout the entire production and that he would not have done anything to prejudice his chances of filming in Spain again or, for that matter, in any other country. If the Spanish authorities had experienced a subsequent change of heart about the nude sequence he had not heard about this and had certainly not been so advised. "I cannot sit here and cater to the changing scene," he told the London *Times* testily.

"The work which I have put into this production has been the result of all the experience that I have gained over the years," he wrote, "and I am gambling everything I have on the success of this picture by not taking any personal financial benefits for myself. I

have been working under the most difficult and trying circumstances with the worst winter they have experienced in Europe in
over 100 years with a temperature below freezing and the studios
here are extremely crude compared to what we have been used to
but despite all this I am very excited about the results we are getting
on the screen. I hope to be through here about the first week in February, when I start on another film in Ireland. Again it looks as if I
shan't have any time for any personal activities and will have to con-
tent myself to a continuity of work without a break of any kind."

Despite the failure to benefit financially from *The Ceremony* (as
he complained), he did manage to send his parents their annual
allowance, and he succeeded, also, in indulging in his favorite extravagance: the purchase of antiques. According to Mike Hen-
nessey of the *Sunday Times,* it was said that half the art and antique dealers of Europe knew Harvey as a perfect buyer, and that
his shopping was not so much exclusive as exhaustive. He could
clean out an art gallery of all its paintings and the carpet off its
floor as well.

In her autobiography, *Serves Me Right,* Sarah Miles provides a flip
side to Harvey's personality. She was staying at a posh hotel in
Madrid in December 1962, and saw Harvey arrive on the set every
day looking the very image of a film director, down to his cigarette
holder and sheepskin coat, and obviously relishing his role as captain of the ship. Charmed by animals, she had impulsively kissed a
camel on the lips in the marketplace and was forced to get rabies
shots by the health authorities and a worried Harvey. There followed a night of watching haunting flamenco dancing with her
date, Omar Sharif, who had just finished shooting *Lawrence of Arabia*
(Harvey had coveted the role of Lawrence, which had gone to Peter
O'Toole). Omar Sharif had been very sympathetic about the camel
and the rabies shots. Accompanying her to her hotel room, they had
meant to make love, but when he had already stripped down to his
underpants and one sock, she experienced a change of heart. A gentleman of great courtesy, he never mentioned the subject of lovemaking again. Their friendship ended when the film crew moved to
Toledo for night shooting.

It was horribly cold there, too cold to snow. Harvey, she writes, found the cold a blessing, because they could then pretend it was spring in Morocco, and he demanded that she simulate being hot and make believe that day was night. She had to run endlessly up cobbled streets in a summer dress every night.

As the director, Harvey was relentlessly out of sympathy with her discomfort. Through the lens she resembled a dragon belching fire, he had complained, his cigarette holder gripped between his lips, his sheepskin jacket guarding him against the cold. Callously, he had ordered a member of the crew to find some ice for her to suck.

The sequence was repeated every night for a week. She even got a touch of frostbite, but he was not sympathetic.

In some of his scenes, he, too, had to appear half naked, wearing only an unbuttoned shirt in the freezing cold when his role demanded it. On other occasions, he had his sheepskin jacket and wore a black knitted cap over his ears. The crew tried to stop their teeth from chattering by covering their chins and mouths with woolen scarves, and the actors wore ski suits under their costumes.

Skimpily dressed while in character before the cameras, Harvey caught cold and became too ill to appear on the set for several days, but was soon working again, looking pale and ill. Influenza, was the doctor's diagnosis. He had a temperature of 102. Joan Cohn flew to Madrid to be at his side while the doctor stuffed him with antibiotics. He would not remain in bed for more than a day or two, however; he was terrified of the insurance claims that would result if he stopped shooting the movie.

He sacrificed himself, and he would give no quarter to his actors. Even when Sarah Miles's mother telephoned to tell her that her beloved dog was pining for her, he refused to grant his leading lady—whom he called "Smiles"—compassionate leave. Could she then send for her dog to join her, she asked? He remarked, offhandedly that Spaniards ate stray dogs, so that, whether true or false (she did not know which), it was not an option. She collected several half-starved stray dogs foraging in the back streets and brought them to her room at the Hilton. The manager asked her to leave. In the end, because she could find no other recourse, she had to take them back to their old haunts in the back alleys.

She did, after all, go home for Christmas. Harvey had offered his actors and crew hefty sums of cash to keep working during the five-day Christmas season, but the crew's contracts stipulated that they could go home and home they went. Harvey alone remained in Spain, where he was joined by Joan Cohn.

It was only after she returned to Spain to finish *The Ceremony* that Sarah Miles came to see Harvey in a very different light. Initially he had struck her as a frivolous playboy who used his charm to captivate Joan Cohn, an ultrarich woman, and James Woolf, a very rich protector. She had thought him weak at the core, but working with him had altered this impression.

Later, a special incident had reinforced her new respect for him. When *The Ceremony* opened in London, he had invited her to make up a foursome for dinner. He was staying at the Savoy and picked her up in his flashy, chauffeur-driven Rolls-Royce, looking very elegant, wearing black velvet loafers with his initials embroidered on them in gold, a plum velvet smoking jacket, and a cigarette attached to his black cigarette holder.

His date, a stunning blond model was driven home first. When the Rolls-Royce stopped at her door, they noticed that her glass front door had been smashed.

Despite her protests, Harvey insisted on waiting until she entered her bedroom before driving away. When they heard her screams he rushed upstairs to see a man with the build of a heavyweight boxer beating her up and cursing her for going out with "Jimmy Woolf's ponce."

Coolly removing his velvet jacket, Harvey challenged him to repeat the insult.

A furious fight between the two men ensued. Harvey fought valiantly, but his opponent was too powerful for him, until Sarah Miles hit the raging bully with a winkle-picker. There was blood everywhere. The blond model forced the two men reluctantly to shake hands before parting.

Upon reaching the Savoy, Sarah Miles wiped the blood off Harvey's face by spitting on his handkerchief. She told him that she had never thought he had it in him to fight like that. He said, modestly, that Lithuanians were known as lethal fighters and always had a trick up their sleeve—like a winkle-picker! He then suavely entered the Savoy like some well-bred socialite.

He cut and scored *The Ceremony* in Ireland and presented it in Venice and, like some second Mike Todd, a showman par excellence, screened it at a midnight showing for his "personal friends," including those who thoroughly disliked him. There were 1,000 guests in all, among them Elizabeth Taylor, Richard Burton, Robert Mitchum, James Mason, Dirk Bogarde, and Peter O'Toole. He had only planned to invite 300, he said, but the figure seemed to have snowballed.

The film itself did not enjoy the great success for which he had hoped. Yet, as one critic commented, despite its pretentiousness, it had the courage of its own oddity and remained, after a fashion, compelling.

He purchased the rights to a book by Slavomir Rawizc, called *The Long Walk,* but was unable to set up production as he had planned. Reluctantly, therefore, after he wrapped up *The Ceremony* in February 1963, he spent a week in Los Angeles then flew to Ireland to play the lead in *Of Human Bondage,* working on this picture during the day and editing *The Ceremony* at night.

If he had experienced the worst weather on record in Spain, plus spending literally twenty hours a day working on that film, working in *Of Human Bondage,* he wrote to his parents, "was, without exception, the most horrifying experience I have ever had in my entire theatrical career." The chore of filming it during the day and editing *The Ceremony* at night, he declared, "was the only reason for keeping me sane and prevented me from a nervous breakdown. The last four months I would rather forget and hope that nothing like that will ever occur again in the future. Needless to say, I was an absolute and complete physical wreck both emotionally and physically and so exhausted that I just wanted to run away and curl up in some grave. Unfortunately I am not even allowed to do that, as I now have to make preparations for a picture I am going to make next year and also start rehearsals for a play that I am going to do with an eight to ten weeks' tour in the United States before opening

on Broadway. . . . On top of all these problems this has been an extremely bad financial year for me, as I made my own film without
any salary of any kind and I am depending on its success commercially for any remuneration that I may receive."

Harvey had shipped back to Ireland his powerful white Jaguar
and the Irish chauffeur who had driven it both in Ireland when
Harvey was working on *The Running Man* and in Spain while he
was shooting *The Ceremony* and had made a great friend of him,
kissing and hugging him in public and inviting him to be his dinner companion whenever he happened to be short of his usual
friends. The ever-faithful James Woolf had reserved the best suite
at the best hotel in Dublin for him. On his bed there was a mink
spread, a gift that Joan Cohn had given him. They constantly exchanged gifts. He had given her fabulous baubles like a gold
Fabergé cigarette case adorned with the diamond-encrusted crest
of Czar Nicholas II of Russia and she had replaced the Thunder-
bird he had bought with the money he had earned from his role in
The Alamo with an opalescent Rolls-Royce, tied with a huge ribbon
and parked outside his house in Hollywood as a surprise that former Christmas.

Living for months out of suitcases, he had brought to Dublin
thirty of his suits and a dozen pairs of shoes custom made in Paris.
For his entertainment he purchased an expensive Sony tape recorder
and a selection of music tapes ranging from classical to pop, and
played these quite loudly in his suite when he could not sleep, causing the other guests to complain.

He had, while filming *The Running Man* in Dublin, patronized a
small restaurant called the Soup Bowl, and, despite his foul language spoken in a loud voice—until begged to stop, which he did
now and then—made it famous by his patronage, attracting stars
from the Abbey Theater and London to dine there and often, at dinners well supplied with caviar and Pouilly Fumé for which he paid
promptly despite his shortage of ready cash. He felt very much at
home in this restaurant and he would slip into its small kitchen now
and then to whip up the perfect bearnaise and other gourmet sauces
he prided himself on skillfully making.

Joan Cohn arrived and fussed over him, proudly calling him a boy prince and a genius, saw to it that he returned to his hotel and went to bed by midnight after a night's work or drinking and woke him up in the morning in time to go to the set. On his birthday she invited thirty-six guests to a dinner party, and they broke into applause the moment he walked into the room. He loved the dinner party, the applause. He loved the four-tiered birthday cake that was wheeled in. Dressed in his elegant beige polo shirt, his beige slacks, and beige suede jacket and suede shoes with the initials L. H. embroidered on the vamp, he loved everything about that evening. This was his way of relaxing from the tension engendered by working on the film by day and the nights he spent with his editor whipping *The Ceremony* into its final shape.

When Joan left, James Woolf, who had moved into another grand hotel, was his close companion. The friendship and sympathy between Laurence Harvey and James Woolf was, people noted, unique; they respected and loved each other and were extremely close.

But, smoking Churchill-like cigars, always draped in his heavy sheepskin coat, Woolf was obviously a sick man and was known to purchase quantities of barbiturates from the local pharmacies.

In *Of Human Bondage*, the film version of the novel by Somerset Maugham, Harvey plays the role made memorable by Leslie Howard in the 1934 film about a sensitive young medical student who saddles himself with a heartless prostitute.

Kim Novak had come to Ireland to play the prostitute, Mildred, the role that Bette Davis had made so marvelously her own in the 1934 version. She was a major star, groomed by Harry Cohn at Columbia who, disparaging her as he did all his stars, called her a piece of meat. This blond, statuesque, thirty-year-old Polish American beauty, was the diametric opposite of the flamboyant Harvey, and they loathed each other, practically on sight. He was, to the last degree, gregarious, loved dining out in company, being photographed and interviewed She was a loner, who preferred to dine alone in her suite. As the director Henry Hathaway was soon to learn, their acting styles did not match, and they made no effort to ease the strain between them. At sixty-five Hathaway had already made some eighty films, ranging from early silent features to big pictures like *How the West Was Won* and spectacular war movies. The incompatible acting styles and antagonism between Kim Novak and Harvey did not trouble him: "To be a good director, you've got to be a bastard. I'm a bastard and I know it," he said.

What did trouble him, however, was the tussle between the Irish and the British electrical unions as to which one of them should supply the larger number of technicians for the film. He was brusque with highly respected actors like Bryan Forbes, who had written the screenplay and also portrayed Harvey's student friend in the film, with Harvey's longtime friend, actress Siobhan McKenna, and with the seasoned, evergreen, ever overweight actor Robert Morley, as well as with important Seven Arts executives like Ray Stark and the ever present James Woolf.

The failure of Harvey and Kim Novak to create any rapport between them, the anemic quality of the repeated "takes" they made together infuriated Hathaway and snapped his patience. He walked off the set. Kim Novak had also had enough, and disappeared on a personal tour of Ireland. Idling in Dublin, Harvey's acquisitive streak was aroused when he attended an exhibition of paintings by modern Irish artists and he spent thousands of dollars, though advised against it by James Woolf, on the impulsive purchase of four huge canvases. Bryan Forbes was appointed the temporary director, but this only led to impassioned arguments between him and Harvey. A new director was imported: Ken Hughes, who had scored a great success with his first picture, *The Small World of Sammy Lee*. Hughes wanted to replace Kim Novak with Elizabeth Taylor, but she turned him down. Forced to stick with Kim Novak, hating the script, which he longed to rewrite, Hughes tried to shoot a love scene between a bored and disaffected Harvey and a seminude Kim Novak, and it turned out totally lacking in passion.

Even the patient and civilized James Woolf was made extremely miserable by the bad blood reigning on the set of *Bondage* and, for once, quarreled with Harvey and accused him of helping to ferment it. Regretting their quarrel, he called Harvey the instant he returned to his hotel, eager to discuss the problem, perhaps to explain himself better, but was coldly told by Joan, who was at the hotel that evening, that Harvey did not wish to speak to him.

Later that evening, Woolf was found in his hotel suite lying unconscious from an overdose of barbituates.

As soon as he learned of it, Harvey rushed to the hospital where James Woolf had been taken and remained there until he was told that Woolf was out of danger. Afterward, he told everyone that Woolf had taken some pills to reduce the pain caused by the major surgery he had undergone in the United States on his hemorrhoids. Torn with sincere emotion, he wept that Woolf was his life, his love. When Woolf recovered, they resumed their close friendship and fond mutual affection and were seen laughing and joking together.

In despair about the course the picture was taking, Harvey took advantage of the Easter weekend to fly to France with Joan to meet Somerset Maugham and to seek his advice about the character he was playing. Maugham was ninety years old and extremely frail, living in a lovely villa above Saint-Jean-Cap-Ferrat on the French Riviera and the proud owner of the only avocado tree in Europe.

In one version of Harvey's meeting with Maugham, he declared that he had gone down on his knee, like a medieval knight before royalty, in deference to the writer. More realistically, Maugham was pleasant, polite, but noncommittal. He had really known a character resembling Mildred (who had, in fact, actually been a young man), he said, but he had not read *Of Human Bondage* since its publication in 1915. He wished Harvey the best of luck. His youth had cheered him up, he said, but that was all the assistance he proffered.

Next, Harvey tried hard to get out of his contract with Seven Arts, but this would have meant paying the studio $750,000—and he could not afford to do that.

Once the editing was finished on *The Ceremony*, he threw a lavish party at his favorite restaurant and invited the guests to a midnight screening at a small art cinema on the Dublin quays. There were far too many guests, all of them rowdy and inebriated, to fit into the restaurant. To make matters worse, a rowdy crowd of onlookers had gathered around the cinema. Shouting at them to disperse, as Harvey tried to do, had no effect. It was a disastrous evening. He had a debilitating sinus attack, which the doctor, summoned from London, was unable to alleviate.

Aggravating his unhappy experience was his rage when he found that his precious Jaguar had not been cleaned to his exacting standards of spotless and shining perfection. The only two people he permitted to ride in his Jaguar were Joan Cohn and James Woolf, and even they were closely watched lest they mar the seats in any way. In addition, out of sheer frustration with the dismal problems of this film, he had begun drinking brandy, always a bad sign, as Hermione Baddeley had noted when they were living together. He accused the waiter at his hotel of having opened his bottle of brandy and sampled its contents. He had come from Lithuania, he yelled at him; he was a Jew and had known a rough life. He had worked hard to get what he had and he intended to keep it all.

Joan had returned to California. Hating every moment of working on *Bondage,* he refused to look at the rushes or the final cut.

Before starting work on *The Running Man,* Harvey had planned to appear in *Altona,* at London's Royal Court Theatre, but such was the ill feeling against him because of his messy divorce from Margaret Leighton that Terence Rattigan, the author, warned him that it would be unwise for him to make an appearance on any stage at the time. Harvey had boasted to his friends that the "noises of the jungle," as he called the voices of his critics, would not deter or frighten him but in the end was forced to buy himself out of his contract. Much the same problem had confronted him when he wanted to act in Terence Rattigan's play, *Ross.* Terence Rattigan had turned him down flat, certain that his play would be boycotted if Harvey appeared in it.

And yet the movie scripts sent to him seemed to him less and less appealing, and he kept turning them down.

In the States he found a play that intrigued him and happily took to the stage, doing what he liked best. "I've been under such pressure for the last two months as I have seldom experienced before," he wrote to his parents from San Francisco. "It's been very trying and difficult to readjust to working in the theater again after so many years away from it, and the circumstances which have surrounded this production haven't helped the play. However, the play is finally on and despite the fact that I personally got brilliant notices from the press and unanimous praise for the play there is still a lot of work to do before we go to New York. We play here for two weeks and then proceed to Los Angeles for three weeks and then to Boston for another three before going to New York. Naturally I am frightened and nervous as it's impossible to judge whether the play will have a successful run in New York or not, because so much depends upon the critic's reception, even though the audiences seem to love this play. I am personally praying for its success not only as an actor, but as a co-producer, as my company has a large investment at stake. Apart from feeling desperately tired and exhausted, I somehow seem to be getting on with it from day to day."

The play was a lighthearted comedy with a punch to it titled *The Time of the Barracudas* by Peter Barnes. In addition to his investment in the play (he had as his partners such heavyweights as producer Frederick Brisson, the husband of Rosalind Russell), Harvey also owned the movie rights. *Barracudas* seemed destined to become a hit. He had an excellent cast and his costar was the prestigious actress Elaine Stritch.

The play is about a middle-class couple who meet at a funeral, marry, and discover that each has murdered two previous mates in order to collect their insurance. The question becomes who would kill the other first.

On opening night in San Francisco, some of the critics were fulsome in their praise: "Laurence Harvey is absolutely marvelous; this young man is one of the most versatile artists we have today," gushed columnist Cobina Wright in the *San Francisco Chronicle.*

He was billed as the "hottest Star in Town" and he acted that way in public. Dining with a *Time* magazine interviewer at San Francisco's famed Trader Vic's, nibbling a tasty lamb chop and drinking his favorite dry white wine while the play was still in a state of chaos and changes were being made and lines were being rewritten, he said that his company had been "courageous and experimental" in opening on the West Coast instead of Broadway. He felt that audiences on the West Coast would be excited by something new rather than Broadway centered.

Why, he was asked, once more, did he rush into so many movies?

"I love it," he concluded, swinging his arm toward the ceiling. "I love it all. I do it because I love it. Not the money. What's money? I spend it as fast as I get it. Love the films. Love the stage. Love being an actor. Most of all, love the people, love all people. The terrible people, the boring people, the ghastly people. I love them. Love life. Eating its food. Drinking its grape. Love life until I can't get enough of it."

What would his life be like when he stopped running? he was asked.

There was a plate of fortune cookies on the table. Deliberately, he broke one open.

There was nothing inside, no slip of paper, nothing. Nothing at all.

After a two-week run in San Francisco, the play opened at the Huntington Hartford Theater in Hollywood. Here, as Cobina Wright commented, "Mrs. Joan Cohn, who is a very dear friend of Laurence Harvey, [gave] a supper in his honor at her luxurious Beverly Hills home."

All was not glitz and glitter, however. Harvey and Stritch were both strong-minded personalities who liked to have their own way. They could not stand each other. There were production difficulties. Somehow, the play did not quite click, and the audiences were not enthusiastic. In Los Angeles the temperature suddenly jumped to 110 degrees and they had to work in a hall that was airless, making everything doubly difficult. The play folded in Los Angeles with an enormous loss.

Harvey was extremely disappointed, but shrugged off the experience. "I love being an actor," he told the *Los Angeles Times*. "I love the theater. I can't say I love that hydra headed monster of an audience sitting out there every night, but I must get out and face it and test myself against it. I love it. Love it all. [I] love life until I can't get enough of it."

About the play he commented, "It's humanity. We're all trying to destroy each other."

He felt disappointed, but not shattered. He was, above all, a showman, with a consuming passion for work. As James Woolf said of him on one occasion, "I don't remember his being two weeks out of work in ten years. . . . Between movies there's always television, something, anything. Any form of exhibitionism, preferably the best paid. He's essentially an exhibitionist. I don't mean this in any derogatory sense at all."

"You're ruining Larry's reputation with that remark," director Jack Clayton interposed.

"Not at all," Woolf replied. "I think Larry would be the first to admit it himself. I dare say he's already talked *Time* magazine to a standstill. He has no capacity for being a supporting actor or a character actor in a supporting role. From his first day before a camera he was playing star parts and he can't conceive of himself as anything else."

That Joan Cohn and Harvey were a couple had by then long been established. Their favorite hangout was The Bistro, a restaurant that he owned together with several other financial backers. Together the two frequently held court there. All the walls were made of mirrors, and Harvey liked to sit facing a wall, where he could see himself and everyone else. It pleased him to make catty remarks about the clientele and then to hail each one with "Hello, you sweet son of a bitch," or "You absolutely sweet and adorable man," and to mimic people with devastating and humorous precision.

Playing the glamorous, great, and successful star with seemingly enormous self-confidence, he received an unexpected jolt in October 1963. The South African white Afrikaaner Nationalist government of the time had broken its link with Britain and wrote to him threatening to take his passport away in 1965 unless he returned to South Africa. He was not eligible to receive a British passport, since he had given up his residence in England. He was also a nonresident of the United States. "If I do not get a passport, I shall probably end up as a man without a country which, of course, would make my life and work impossible in the future," he wrote dolefully to his parents. Theoretically, his status was much like that of his second brother in 1950. He had not wanted to return to South Africa, even if permitted to do so. Like him, Harvey wished to have nothing to do with apartheid-ruled South Africa either.

His brother had found his solution by immigrating to Israel. Harvey found his by becoming a citizen of the Bahamas.

19

The Death of James Woolf—
Enter Paulene Stone

Harvey was thirty-two in 1960 and, as the decade unfolded, had become the star most in demand and most sought after by Hollywood. He belonged to both worlds: British and American, but although he grew his hair long in the British mod style, he still, like a matinee idol of earlier times, dressed in chic Savile Row, Italian-French suits, and fabulous silk shirts and maintained his fleet of handsome cars, his nonchalantly held long cigarette holder clamped between teeth at the side of his mouth with a cigarette always curling smoke. Crates of his special French white wine were regularly shipped to him by his vintner. His drug of choice was cannabis, although he preferred getting sloshed on vodka and brandy. By 1963, he had played opposite some of the greatest stars in the Hollywood firmament. Scripts were still streaming to him thick and fast, but he was becoming somewhat more discriminating in his choices. In 1962, he performed on television's top-rated *The Milton Berle Show,* in which Jack Benny also appeared. It was fun, and looking slim and tall and beautifully accoutered, he was fulsomely praised by both comedians as a consummate Englishman, which those who knew that, like the two comedians, he was Jewish, found deliciously ironic. Burt Lancaster and Kirk Douglas put in brief appearances, both in costume as Roman soldiers in deference to Douglas's successful movie *Spartacus.* It was Milton Berle appearing in drag as Cleopatra who stole the show, but the audience loved Harvey too. Only *Variety* took a dim view of this sketch. "Laurence Harvey," said the reviewer, seemed "ingratiating and more thespiating than comedying," a view not reflected in the ratings.

That year, he eagerly accepted the second male lead in *The Outrage*, playing Claire Bloom's betrayed husband in this American version of the famed Japanese movie *Rashomon*, this time set in the nineteenth-century American West and starring Paul Newman. It was filmed in Arizona, and was not a box office smash, mainly because the sharp bite of the original story had disappeared in its vastly different setting. Harvey's performance was good—he did not have much dialogue but, rather, conveyed his contempt and anger as the betrayed husband through the expressions on his face.

Despite the movie's disappointing reception and his second lead in it, Harvey was at the pinnacle of his popularity in the United States. The ever worshipful James Woolf declared that the actor, who had not had a vacation in twenty years and was basically an exhibitionist—a description of himself that Harvey was the first to admit was correct—would be even more successful than he already was within the next fifteen years. But he would always be the star in every one of his pictures.

For Harvey, quality parts had become increasingly important. One could not continue making one movie after the other, because there were not that many good movies. How many movies were really good, he asked rhetorically? One in twenty at most. Harvey found it boring just to do endless films. He was obviously madly keen on directing. Although Harvey had never liked the script of *The Ceremony*, he thought that he had done it "marvelously well."

In 1963 Harvey had talked about producing and starring in two more movies: *The Eddie Chapman Story* and *A Distant Trumpet.* Although he had many financial partners in his enterprises, these stories, to which he owned the movie rights, like the others he owned, were never made.

But it was on the stage where he really most wanted to perform; for the stage forever symbolized to him the highest form of artistic expression for an actor.

His opportunity arrived with *Camelot.*

In 1959, Alan Jay Lerner and Frederick Loewe were looking for a French actor who spoke English and had a large baritone voice to play Lancelot in their new musical about King Arthur and the Knights of the Round Table. It so happened that Harvey was on a publicity tour of the States at the time to plug *Room at the Top*. He eagerly offered to audition for the part. His voice was good, but it was a basso profundo and these voices had to be trained and developed, he was told. Understanding his problem, he asked Lerner to recommend a singing coach in England. If no Lancelot could be found within several months, could he audition again? he asked. Then, much to Lerner's and Loewe's surprise, he blithely announced to the press upon his return to England that he was to play Lancelot in the upcoming Broadway production.

Meanwhile, Robert Goulet was signed on to play Lancelot. He claimed to be French, but he was, in fact, an American who spoke the merest smattering of French, but his baritone voice was perfect for the part.

One month later, Lerner received a bill for £80 from Harvey's business manager for Harvey's singing lessons. Much amused, he returned the bill with a note advising Harvey to apply to the Ford Foundation, which had programs to train student singers. Unfazed, Harvey returned his note with a message scrawled across it in red ink saying that Lerner might wish to keep the note for his memoirs; it was so witty!

He had begun assiduously taking singing lessons. He was exploring a new field, he wrote to his parents in May 1964. He had been, he wrote, through a period of financial disaster and it had totally unsettled him: "The financial drain on me has been enormous and it will take me a good many years before I can get everything settled."

Instead of making up his losses by performing in movies, he signed up to perform in the British production of *Camelot*. The reason, he claimed, was because he had waited and waited to play the role of Lancelot in the Broadway production, as he was promised he would be by its writer and composer, and had finally lost patience and gone on to other things.

Lerner and Loewe must have been astonished to learn of this!

His persistence in taking singing lessons—and the help of influential friends—paid off. If he had failed to play Lancelot on Broadway, he won the part of King Arthur in the London production, which opened on August 16 at the Theatre Royal, Drury Lane.

There were four weeks of grueling rehearsals, sometimes in places as austere as the local YMCA (which he called "The Young Mod's Place") and in generally frosty rehearsal halls, and the cold had affected his feet and his tonsils, if never his acerbic tongue. "I'm a bit of a comedian," he modestly told the press. "Sometimes my tongue does run away with me. Of course this makes life complicated and doesn't endear me to some. At times I have so many assagais in my back that it hurts . . . when I laugh. But it's all very worthwhile. It adds a little excitement to life."

The assagais came in showers from the London critics when the show first opened. They praised it as a spectacle, but panned the words and the music. Only Barry Kent, who played Sir Lancelot, won praise. Harvey's performance was not even mentioned. These critics called the sets "magical." "To speak in favor one is driven simply into making a catalogue of visual effects—and these are splendid. The remainder of the production is almost a total blank," wrote the London *Times*. And the *Manchester Guardian* added, "if only it had been on color television with the sound switched off."

None of this criticism reflected the reality of what went on in the theater every night. The audiences loved Harvey.

Following the "nerve racking experience of opening the show," as he wrote to his parents, he played in *Camelot* for six highly demanding and successful months. From being the most despised and ostracized actor in London—that jungle filled with wild beasts, as he described it to his friend John Ireland, where he was forever regarded as the outsider and universally condemned for what was called the callous way he had walked out on Margaret Leighton—his portrayal of the regal and handsome King Arthur packed the theater every night with the cream of London society, old and new, the rich women in a glitter of diamonds, their men in formal evening attire, and the young set in the latest kinky designs from the newest couturiers and in treasures found on the lane behind the elegant stores of Piccadilly called Carnaby Street.

With all this triumph and adulation, why did he continue to complain so much offstage? he was asked by a reporter from *WeekEnd*.

"Because, my dear chap," he replied, "if I revealed my true self it would be dull, boorish, desperately uninteresting—and very limiting."

Apart from being a personal triumph, his performance in *Camelot* provided even his most virulent critics with the incontrovertible proof of his talent. On a visit to London, Lerner and Loewe found his performance stunning. One of the five great performances he had seen in his theatergoing life, Harold Hobson, theater critic of the London *Sunday Times*, dissenting from the majority of his colleagues, called it. No longer a basso profundo, Harvey sang his part in a "charming, light baritone voice, which made Fritz and me feel foolish and the audiences ecstatic," Lerner relates in his autobiography.

Despite the heavily embossed medieval costume and cloak he wore on stage every night and his painful back, which he had injured in a fall, he still appeared fresh enough after the performance to entertain his friends with champagne and kisses. Yet all he ate between the matinee and the evening performances were two freshly laid raw eggs and packages of laxatives purchased from pharmacies all over London brought to him by his chauffeur.

Joan had joined him during the last weeks of his performance in *Camelot*. *Camelot* was a triumph for him, the vindication of his talent as a performing artist. He might have continued in the show for an indefinite period, but his salary of £400 a week, which the London impresario Jack Hylton was providing, was far from adequate to support his extravagant lifestyle. Foreseeing this problem, he had insisted on inserting a clause in his contract enabling him to quit the show after six months.

He had pressing reasons for quitting. For one thing, he had moved, he told the press, beyond the stage of having an *ordinary* Rolls. His new car was a Rolls-Royce convertible priced at £11,000. In addition, he had purchased a £6,000 Maserati, in which he liked to take off when he had the time to shop in London's most famous— and expensive—antiques stores. He began dreaming of creating a spectacular new house in Beverly Hills, and hired one of the finest architectural firms on the West Coast to construct it in conformity with his ideas. He sent for the head of the firm periodically, paying all his travel expenses, to discuss his plans and also in this period developed an additional project or two. One was to open an antiques store on Robertson Boulevard in Los Angeles, where several expensive stores of various kinds already existed. Another was to open an even larger antiques store in Palm Springs where he had bought a house and, during his weekend excursions with Joan, who owned three palatial houses there, he had discovered a motel that could be converted to house an antiques store on the ground floor with an apartment block with penthouse suites, carports, and saunas to be erected above it.

He was told that this was a highly impractical project, but he did not agree. He had achieved the reputation as a sharp businessman—and he believed he was—able to corner and get the better of even the shrewdest Hollywood studio tycoon, to draw money from wealthy financiers whom he charmed into partnership with him. But it was, in fact, James Woolf who had won him his lucrative deals. Harvey knew how to spend money, how to scatter it like a profligate to the winds, how to buy impulsively whatever his eyes lit upon: objets d'art, paintings, antiques, novels to be turned into movies, plays, all the things he called his investments, how restlessly to fly from country to country to work in one movie after the other.

Riding high, flushed with the success of *Camelot* he was invited as a guest on a popular BBC live talk show hosted by Eamonn Andrews. Saying he wanted to tell a story, he sprang out of his chair and, to his host's total dismay, walked over to the orchestra, approached a camera and proceeded to tell a long and obscene joke involving a company of foreign legionnaires isolated for months in the desert who were eagerly awaiting the arrival of a herd of camels and preparing to compete for the prettiest ones.

Outraged viewers jammed the switchboard with calls. From then on, as in the United States, owing to Harvey's obscene joke, every program had to be prerecorded.

In October, while still playing to packed houses every night, he began working during the day on a new film, *Darling.*

The reason he gave for this double activity was explained in a letter to his parents dated September 9, 1964:

> I had a terrible thing happen to me on my return to England. The man who had been looking after my financial affairs during my absence in the last four and a half years had, to my horror, robbed me blind and left me with exactly 67 pounds in my bank account. There is nothing I can do about it now except send the man to jail but that would be very bad publicity and my lawyer advises against it, because he had spent all the money and left me absolutely penniless. This is one of the reasons I now have to work twice as hard in order to make up this dreadful loss. On top of it all I had a very bad back injury [on stage] which resulted in a slipped disc and despite the pain I have still got to continue to work every day. . . . The days seem to pass with such rapidity and there is so much to be done that I find it extremely difficult to keep up with myself. All I am looking forward to is getting over this very black period and finding a little bit of peace and quiet. It's difficult

working and feeling as I do, but under the circumstances there is nothing I can do about it.

Much to his alarm, this triggered his mother to write that she wanted to rush to his side to take care of him. He wrote back immediately to assure her that he was feeling better and that, much as he longed to see both her and his father, they would be all alone if they came to England, since he was far too busy to be with them. No, he wrote, it would be far better for him to visit them in Israel—the following spring.

In January 1965 he had another accident. During the Saturday matinee performance of *Camelot,* "I knocked my foot against an iron door coming off the stage and I have been in agony ever since and have not been able to do four performances," he wrote to his parents. "It seems to be getting much better, but I have to walk with crutches and have had a plastic cast made for my foot so that it eases the pain. I must say that this play has been nothing but trouble for me, first with my back and the slipped disc, then the scenery falling on my foot and now this."

Accident prone, he seemed to relish the pain caused by them, almost as if these were challenges or punishments for some deep sense of guilt.

The new film he was working on during the day while still playing to capacity houses every night was scripted by Frederick Raphael, a young writer who had caught the spirit of the new English hedonism and was very much in vogue at the time. John Schlesinger was the producer-director and Anglo-Amalgamated provided the funding. Harvey was so keen on being in this film that he offered to work without pay in exchange for 10 percent of the distribution profits. As a transatlantic star, he was the movie's box office "insurance," but this was risk taking with a vengeance. Nobody wanted to back the film. The girl around whom the story revolved was considered unsympathetic, immoral. As its critics had warned, the touches of homosexuality, the heroine's casual abortion, the petty thievery for thrills, and hint of lesbianism shocked many. Harvey plays a totally cynical advertising executive whose job is to manipulate the public's taste and sell a product to consumers, an elegant voyeur so corrupt and cynical that even a Paris orgy holds only a faintly amusing appeal. Even the very popular Dirk Bogarde, who plays the lead, is not altogether a sympathetic character in this film.

This was the beautiful newcomer Julie Christie's first film and it launched her into transatlantic stardom; she won an Oscar for her performance.

Darling was, as predicted, very much condemned in England and also in Italy, where the "heroine" and her homosexual photographer friend have affairs with the same young man and she then marries a boring Italian count with seven children. In England, since it was rated X, and could not therefore be shown on Sundays, it did, however, recoup some of its expenses. Made on a low budget of less than $510,000, it was very popular in Europe and the United States and netted a handsome profit of $10 million. Harvey's share was $1 million.

This was a period during which nothing in his career seemed to go wrong. His performance in *Henry V* had been a triumph in the States. *Camelot* marked his finest hour on the London stage. Despite his physical problems, he continued to play to packed houses throughout his stay in *Camelot*. And in the teeth of the hostility of some critics and the harsh innuendos about his snobbery and selfishness, he got along well with the cast. It was in an honest expression of their feelings toward him—at least of the majority—that the cast presented him, upon his departure, with a Georgian silver chalice and a scroll bearing the inscription: "Take with you, King Arthur, the gratitude of the court for your many benevolences and the certainty that your subjects will long remember your momentous reign."

Flushed with success, he coolly announced that David Merrick wanted him to star in *Hello, Dolly!* with Angela Lansbury.

The $1 million profit accruing to Harvey from *Darling*'s distribution rights in the United States and Europe enabled him to wrap up a deal to replace Maximilian Schell in a Nicholas Ray-Avala movie titled *The Doctor and the Devils*, from the play about a nineteenth-century body snatcher by the Welsh poet Dylan Thomas, to be made in Yugoslavia.

It had a budget of $1.7 million and involved sixteen weeks of shooting in Belgrade and Zagreb. Gore Vidal put the final touches to the screenplay. During the negotiations for this movie, Harvey began negotiating to acquire two additional film properties and also planned to appear in J. B. Priestley's comedy, *A Severed Head*. Frederick Raphael was to write the script and the film was to be produced by Romulus Films, with worldwide distribution by Columbia.

With the power of the studios at its lowest ebb, Harvey announced that actors could no longer rely on their deals with them, but had to assemble packages for presentation to film company executives, who no longer had extensive contract lists. He also announced that of two properties he owned, one had already been sold and he was negotiating for two more.

He claimed that he owned the rights to Cecil Woodham Smith's account of the Crimean War fought between Britain and Turkey in the mid-nineteenth century. Harvey's script bore the title, *The Reason Why*. It was widely reported that he had sold it to Joseph E. Levine, but Harvey claimed that the deal with Levine had never come through and that he intended to produce and star in it himself. He insisted that he retained the film rights to this property and had invested more than $200,000 in its acquisition and development.

Appearing on another BBC talk show, as if to prove his rights to this property, he suddenly whipped out a bugle and sounded a perfect charge. It turned out that this was the very bugle that had been sounded in the Battle of Balaklava in 1854. Harvey had found it in an antiques store and presented it to the Regimental Museum.

It then transpired that a very similar property was owned by director Tony Richardson and the writer John Osborne. This script, *The Charge of the Light Brigade*, was slated to be made in Turkey for United Artists. Harvey sued. He won a settlement upholding his charge that he owned the film rights to the story and the claim that the Richardson-Osborne script was, in effect, based on his own property. Richardson rewrote his own script. As a friendly gesture and in order to keep him associated with the film, John Osborne was offered and accepted the part of Prince Radziwill. However, the terms of the settlement of Harvey's lawsuit required that Richardson agree to give Harvey a part in the film at a fee of £60,000 plus a percentage of the profits.

Harvey had his own version of what happened. In order to show that he had no "hard cash feelings," he announced, he offered to appear in a cameo role in the Richardson-Osborne film. The only part available was that of Prince Radziwill. Osborne was asked to give up the part, which he did. Harvey showed up in Turkey in due course, played the cameo part in one day of shooting in dashing style, looking resplendent in his uniform.

He had just twenty words to say. Richardson repaid him by totally slicing his cameo appearance out of the film, making Harvey's face the most expensive one ever to fall on the cutting room floor.

Unfazed, he announced that he was developing several more of his properties: *The Long Silence,* scripted by Richard Condon; Alastair MacLean's novel, *The Golden Rendezvous;* and *The Assassin,* about the life and murder of Leon Trotsky, scripted by Mordecai Richter, all of them to be underwritten in part by the profits he had accrued from *Darling.*

The Assassin was especially close to Harvey's heart—not because he had any interest in Trotsky or his ideas, but out of affection for his brother Nahum, who had remained faithfully attached to his creed, and he wanted, fervently, to please his big brother, to demonstrate that he, too, was an intellectual and had not forgotten his aunt Hava who had actually heard Trotsky speak.

Again, none of these projects came to fruition.

His next movie, *Life at the Top,* scripted this time by Mordechai Richter, was, like its predecessor, filmed in Bradford. It lacked the shock impact of the first film and this realistic exposure of Joe Lampton's weak core dulled the character. In the first movie, Joe Lampton had climbed ruthlessly out of poverty and became a member of the Establishment. In *Life at the Top* John Braine, who wrote both novels, shows that this was as far as Joe Lampton could climb; he lacked the ability to become a leading power in the Establishment and had, however grudgingly, to accept his second-rate lot.

All he ate in this period, people observed, was soup with fish bones in it. He said he was afraid of putting on weight. He was very tall and very lean and did not look as if he had a weight problem. He put on no airs and was very generous, people said; he once gave a hotel employee £10 for bringing him a cup of tea.

Joe Lampton had been cut short in his endeavor to become a leader of the Establishment; he could not reach any further than he had gone. But the defeated hero was not a status to which Harvey was willing to submit. In 1965 he set up a company titled Laurence Harvey Productions, Ltd., with himself and John and James Woolf as directors.

One of the first ventures of the new company was to produce *The Doctor and the Devils*, taking as financial partner his ever faithful friend, John Ireland.

Harvey was the star in this film. When released, it proved to be surprisingly successful at the box office in Britain. Ironically, badly strapped for money, Dylan Thomas had hawked this play about for years during his life, to no avail; even his fellow Welshman, Richard Burton, was rumored to have turned it down for lack of money.

Harvey was delighted with the picture's success; all his future movies, he told *Variety* would fall into the category of the *"exposé* of sensation," since such pictures "attract attention."

By 1966 he had committed himself to making two more pictures in addition to his contracts to make one picture a year each for M-G-M and Columbia. Combined with his plans to make the four properties he owned into movies—this within the next two to three years, he assured the press—at least one journalist figured that without fully realizing it, Harvey had committed himself to working twenty-five hours a day for 365 days a year for that period. His projects might either pay off handsomely, or he might fall flat on his derrière, he announced airily to Abe Greenberg of *Hollywood Citizen News.* "But, as they said in Paris, "c'est la guerre!"

Yet now, despite the brilliant prospects that seemed to lie ahead for him as producer, director, and star of his own properties, Harvey had begun to feel the fear of becoming dated. The image of the handsome and debonair matinee idol who lived, as he did, like a careless millionaire who could spend money like water and recoup it through his films was disintegrating. Now he faced the serious competition of newcomers like Steve McQueen and Robert Redford, who were younger and whose casual displays of rough-and-tumble guts were more to the taste of the fans. In 1966, Harvey was approaching thirty-eight—an older man. Youngsters like Dustin Hoffman, starring in films like *The Graduate,* in which ambition to make money was looked down upon, were coming to the fore. The whole mood in the States had darkened as the war in Vietnam escalated. The young demonstrated their protest and opposition and ugly incidents accumulated.

One of the lowest points in Harvey's life came in May 1966 when, during a brief stopover in Saint-Paul-de-Vence, his secretary telephoned from London with the news that James Woolf had died.

Woolf had just returned to California from a trip to Japan where he had participated with director Lewis Gilbert in preparing locations for the ultimate escapist film, *You Only Live Twice,* starring James Bond, the film that Harvey had turned down as too boring, and that brought the first James Bond, Sean Connery, international stardom. Woolf was believed to be resting in his suite at the Beverly Hills Hotel when his colleagues arrived for a meeting with him. They were to discuss, among other business, plans for the upcoming Romulus picture, *Oliver,* derived from Charles Dickens' *Oliver Twist,* and the possibility, strenuously pushed by Woolf, of casting Harvey, who wanted it, as the villain: a red-bearded Fagin.

Waiting an inordinate length of time for their meeting, knowing that Woolf had not been well, Gilbert persuaded the hotel's manager to unlock his door, and they found him lying dead on his bed, apparently of a heart attack. There were a number of empty phials in his trash basket.

Shocked and heartbroken, Harvey called Joan Cohn with the news, although he knew full well that Joan had always disliked and been critical of Woolf. When John Ireland, who had tried to see Woolf to ask for work, called, Harvey asked him, much shaken, to bring

Woolf's body back to London. Woolf had asked to be buried as a Jew, and Harvey attended the funeral, which was conducted in accordance with the Jewish Orthodox tradition. Afterward, he remained alone in the graveyard for a very long time, staring at the plot of ground where Woolf—and perhaps his own orphaned future—lay buried. They had often had differences of opinion and, in the last few years of Woolf's life, had met less and less frequently. Although ever faithful to Harvey, Woolf had become somewhat more interested in promoting the careers of younger men like Terence Stamp. Joan had not trusted him, accusing him of being full of hollow promises of lucrative contracts and wildly successful movies still to come. But Woolf had been his beloved friend, companion, and mentor for fifteen years. He had treated Harvey like the prince Joan had named him, had bowed to his every whim, had seen to it that he was always given the best suites at hotels, arranged lucrative contracts for him, bowed to his wish to produce and direct even when he thought Harvey was acting unwisely, had taught him something about paintings and antiques even though Harvey essentially lacked the taste and the understanding of fine works of art that he himself had innately possessed and made up in the volume of his purchases what he missed in aesthetic vision.

Harvey poured out his feelings of loss to those who had known Woolf. He had loved him with a love surpassing the love of women, he told them, consciously quoting Oscar Wilde. He even expressed his grief to his parents: "I expect you read of Mr. Jimmie Woolf's death which upset me considerably. . . . I cannot believe that he is not here at his desk in the office any more . . . it was all so tragic and his untimely death will be a great loss to the industry."

Without him, Harvey felt lost, a man without a rudder. In his grief, he tried to fling himself into the new world of swinging London, playing Beatles tapes in the cassette player in his Rolls, dressing mod, patronizing the latest tailor in vogue who made clothes for the popular pop stars, keeping his hair longer in the latest fashion, dancing in the new discotheques where the young crowd danced, dining with friends—beautiful women and important financiers—on the bones of Dover sole and blackened potato skins or burned toast most of the time, now and then sucking the juice out of a prime steak or nibbling a morsel of French cheese or a teaspoon of beluga caviar or a morsel of an asparagus vinaigrette with Sauce à la Harvey, which he had created, always accompanied by a bottle of his favorite white wine, or with the finest French champagne, always with his long cigarette holder clenched between two teeth, and a long cigarette spilling gray dust, or with his English Dunhill pipe filled with his favorite mix of tobacco coiling smoke, holding forth to his dinner guests in the newly popular, most fashionable restaurants, on his favorite topics: how best to act and produce Shakespeare, et cetera.

While discussing marriage plans with Joan—they regularly exchanged expensive gifts and transatlantic telephone calls, and their relationship was written about by all the gossip columnists in the States and in Britain—he began an affair with a very beautiful young English model called Paulene Stone. "Redbird," as he named her, was thirteen years his junior, divorced, and the mother of a small daughter. She was the model most in demand, especially by the Hearst publications. They were introduced by a mutual friend. Their one-night stand—that was all it was meant to be—turned into a permanent affair. She taught him, she writes in her book, *One Tear Is Enough* (which, apparently, was all he had instructed her to shed), how to make love—passionate physical love—something he had never before experienced, she writes. She was enchanted with him, she had never met anyone like him and he basked in her boundless admiration. Joan was in Los Angeles—she hated flying—but their marriage plans were being concretized. He meant to marry her. He loved her. As a large stockholder in Columbia Pictures, her wealth and power gave him a sense of financial security and prestige, although he always strenuously denied that he had ever sought her financial help in any way. On the other hand, he also wanted to continue his affair with the worshipful Paulene. It seemed as if he had segregated the two women into two different compartments in his mind.

After completing *Life at the Top* and *The Doctor and the Devils*, there seemed to be little or nothing worthwhile in the way of good film scripts, he wrote despondently to his parents. He was reading many scripts and trying desperately to decide which he would choose. All his great plans to produce, act in, and direct his own films seemed to have dissolved into thin air. When he learned that his brother Nahum had undergone successful surgery for a slipped disc, he wrote to his parents, "I think I must have broken my finger in sympathy with him, which is also bound at the moment and it will be another three or four weeks before I can take the splint off." He longed to visit them, he wrote—this was a constant theme and he meant it—meanwhile he kept reading scripts and would let them know his plans. "The one consolation is that we are enjoying good sunshine here [in London] so I am able to take a little time to sit and relax, but even the fine weather cannot compensate for working, which, as you know, is very important to me."

He overcame the period of despair by contracting to play the lead in an old-fashioned British comedy titled *The Spy with the Cold Nose*. His leading lady, playing a Russian spy, was a lively, pretty young Israeli actress named Dhalia Lavi who had already made several movies in Britain and the States. There was good rapport between them; she was a snappy dresser in the latest miniskirt "mod" style with the figure to carry this off, and he looked thin and elegant and younger than his age. Since both their parents were living in Israel, they had something to talk about between takes. On a visit to England, her younger sister brought him his mother's gift of home-baked cookies, which, he wrote to her, he had "thoroughly enjoyed."

The picture was filmed on location in Yorkshire ("why do I always have to make films in the north of England?" he griped) and outside London at Shepperton Studios. In it he plays a fashionable veterinarian beloved of rich ladies with small pets, a bit of a fraud whose speech is pure Cockney in unguarded moments but whose accent in public is pure BBC. He is instructed by the Foreign Office to implant a listening device in a bulldog. This dog is sent as a gift to the Russian premier and relays all Soviet secrets to London. The Russians remove the device and return the dog with their own implant in it. Mayhem follows.

Bored with the trivial plot and his role in this movie, Harvey took to making spiteful comments about some of the actresses he had worked with, especially Kim Novak. The bulldog used in the movie belonged to a New York oriental dancer known as "jelly belly." Harvey had borrowed this dog in exchange for several kisses, plus the belly dancer's trip to England. At first, the dog proved uncooperative. "I'd rather work with him than with Kim Novak," Harvey was heard to say crossly, snapping his fingers at the dog. It paid attention for the first time.

His snide remark about Kim Novak was picked up by the press. He attempted to explain his remark to visiting columnist Earl Wilson over a lunch of kippers and his favorite dry wine. "I said I preferred working with her [Kim Novak] to the bulldog, not that I preferred working with the bulldog to her," he told him.

He also, during filming, began rehearsing his lines as Leontes in a new production of *The Winter's Tale*, to be staged at the Edinburgh Festival, rehearsing in the early morning hours and in the Old Vic rehearsal hall when shooting ended for the day. The play was due to open on August 22.

"I have arrived at a new interpretation of this play," he told the press enthusiastically, "from a small passage I read which had been cut from most productions."

He did not elaborate.

After Edinburgh, he told Earl Wilson, he would be starring in a movie in New York titled *No Way to Treat a Lady*, about a killer who kills in order to get his name in the papers.

Was it not too strenuous to work on a movie during the day and rehearse a Shakespearean role at night? he was asked.

"I did the same thing filming *Darling* by day and [playing in] *Camelot* at the Drury Lane Theater at night," he replied. "It's very invigorating. Who needs sleep, anyway?"

Paulene accompanied him to Edinburgh. He rented a house outside the city at an expensive £100 per week, but he encountered problems with his dressing room at the theater. It had no bathtub, or even a shower where he could wash off his makeup. It was like something out of a Dickens novel, he complained, antagonizing everyone. Civilization had apparently not yet reached Edinburgh! Finally he bought a monstrous Victorian zinc tub merely to wash off his makeup.

As they had done when he was in *Camelot*, all the royals came to see his performance, but his reviews were not good. For the first time in his career, he lost his temper with Ronald Bryden, the critic for the London *Observer*, in particular, and wrote the paper an angry letter:

"In a career that has spanned twenty years of the theater and films, I have been the butt and center of journalistic praise and emasculation," he wrote. "I had tried to remain impartial and unprejudiced, as I have always felt that the critics too must eat, even though they feed and profit in the barrenness and fruits of our labor."

Nevertheless, he continued, this time his compassion had been destroyed and he had been forced to respond. The critic had written that he preferred Richard Burton's performance as Leontes. That was all well and good, but "whatever contribution I have made as an actor, I have prided myself on originality of performance and concept. . . . I think what Mr. Dunlop [the director] had managed to achieve out of what is Shakespeare's most difficult play is remarkable. . . . All the subtleties, nuances and meanings in the play, which have heretofore been unexplored by Shakespearean critics and scholars alike, are brought out for the first time in this production. Mr. Bryden failed to notice them, or simply chose to ignore them, with what I assume can only be total ignorance."

While he was still in Edinburgh, the British newspapers published a report that the late James Woolf had left £31,241 net [£53,268 gross] before estate duty, which amounted to £11,972. The remainder of his estate was to be divided between Harvey and John Woolf. John Woolf contested the will. The case was settled out of court toward the end of 1967.

The Winter's Tale moved to London's West End, where it was highly successful. Harvey filmed this stage version for Seven Arts. He also began negotiating with Anthony Mann to make a Western based on Shakespeare's *King Lear*, tentatively titled *The Sierra Trail*.

In addition, he also wanted to make *Love on a Couch*, a comedy with a Los Angeles setting.

Returning to Beverly Hills, where he had purchased a handsome new house, he resumed his intimate relationship with Joan Cohn, his new girl seemingly forgotten in London.

A revealing glimpse of this life and thinking at this stage was provided by journalist Joe Hyams, who interviewed him for *Cosmopolitan* in September 1966.

Hyams had gone to meet Harvey in the latter's house and he found him, despite his rumored effeminacy, much taller and more masculine than he had expected. Harvey was, also, forty-five minutes late for the interview and arrived without a word of apology or explanation, speeding up his long driveway in a toylike Fiat decorated in Hawaii-Bermuda style with a pink body and a matching fringed awning. This he parked beside his black Rolls-Royce, and preceded by Jola, his handsome golden retriever (a far cry, this dog, from Rexy, his first mongrel pet that he acquired as a boy in Johannesburg), entered his living room, furnished in a mélange of styles and periods, the products of the antiques store he had opened in Beverly Hills. He was dressed in jeans, a pullover gold jacket, and desert boots. A gold identification bracelet embraced his left wrist and he wore a gold watch on his right. Sipping chilled glasses of Louis Latour Pouilly Fuissé to the taped background music of Barbra Streisand singing "Color Me Blue," he talked about Shakespeare's plays and other great stage characters who, he said, "have all been misfits of one type or another." Those characters who were bastards interested him most, he said. Because there was a bit of the heel in every man and woman. He was opposed to playing a character as all black or all white. To play a character in the conventional way was an unutterable bore.

Hyams was highly impressed. But his confidence was rather shaken when he learned that Harvey treated women with disdain and could clear out even a Hollywood party in four minutes with a vocabulary that a stevedore might envy.

This view seemed justified when Hyams and his wife at the time, the film star Elke Sommer, accompanied Harvey and Joan Cohn to a party given by Howard W. Koch, the head of Paramount and his wife for Britain's visiting Prince Phillip. Returning from the party for pizzas at the Koch's house, Harvey was rude to Joan, refusing to light her cigarettes or to include her in his conversation. And some of his language reminded Hyams of his time in the U.S. Infantry.

His last meeting with Harvey again took place in the latter's house. He was taken to Harvey's cellar, a vault below his living room, which was stocked with 2,000 bottles of French wine. Selecting a bottle, Harvey brought it upstairs. It was uncorked and poured into glasses by one of his three lithe young men servants.

Sprawling on a couch, his cigarettes and gold-banded Dunhill pipe within reach, sipping his wine, Harvey replied, when questioned about his treatment of women, that he had only played the heel, as he did on the screen, once—at the time of his split with Margaret Leighton. He had been deeply hurt when their marriage ended, but pretended that he was unconcerned—the cruelest thing he could have done. As for his failure to light Joan Cohn's cigarettes, he said, "I'm always kidding her. I'm as attentive as my temperament will allow."

His view of how men should treat women had, although Hyams seemed not to have noticed this, the strong flavor of a romance novel. He declared that he believed women preferred a strong masculine figure, a dominating man. When a woman found a man who dominated her, she had much greater respect for him. If the man failed to be the dominating one, the relationship was doomed. To live in peaceful coexistence with a woman, which was all a man could hope for, there had to be an area where they could talk, and that was hard to discover. Joan Cohn, he declared, came nearest to understanding him.

"We adore each other, though in truth, I can't afford to live up to her standards," he confessed. If one bought a girl who owned a thirty-dollar dress one costing fifty dollars she thought she was getting the moon. It was not so easy with someone as wealthy as Joan. . . . She's much cleverer than most women, though," he said admiringly. "She never interferes on a personal level as Margaret always did. Margaret loathed my being a film star. She wanted me to be a theater personality. Margaret did, however, influence me a lot. She was so definite in her opinions that I always did the exact opposite."

As a bachelor, he concluded, he was enjoying his freedom. He was going to London to make another picture—leaving without any emotional strings. "Just pack up and go—and that's the way I want it."

Only, that was not quite the way it turned out. . . .

20

Marriage to Joan

In 1966, swinging London had really begun to swing. Publicly, Harvey scornfully labeled the city "a dump," but while deriding it and claiming that he preferred lolling in the sun in Malibu or Palm Springs, he felt most at home there. He had been renting a suite at the swank—and ultraexpensive—Connaught Hotel in Mayfair for the past several years because, as he told the management, he liked their friendly service and he had furnished this suite with his state-of-the art stereophonic equipment, books, and antiques. In fact, he rented this suite all his life, even when his own home was only a five-minute walk away.

Whenever, briefly, Joan came to London during their marriage, they stayed in this suite. Now and then, when Joan was not in London, he slipped Paulene in to spend the night with him. Mainly, however, it was his ultraprivate haven from the storm of the world he loved, sought, and feared. It was as if he desperately needed to have this secret shelter, however rarely he used it.

But he also had a sense of anxiety about where his career was heading. In London, in February 1966, over a luncheon of smoked salmon and two bottles of Châteauneuf-du-Pape, he voiced this anxiety to Clive Hirschhorn of the *Sunday Express*, punctuating his opinions, as always, with expletives and the fashionable London thespian habit of using "darling," "dear," or "dear heart," in practically every sentence.

"In show business, it's folly to talk about what the future holds," he declared. "Things change so fast. Today's project so easily becomes tomorrow's disappointment. . . . The world of the film star is an obstacle race against time. The pitfalls and wrong turnings you can make are devastating. Often I fear for the sanity of some of my friends."

Despite his own many disappointments, he appeared to imply, he himself kept a level head.

He was not so levelheaded when he began harping on his main grievance of the time: his court-ordered annual payment of £2,500 to Margaret Leighton as part of the £25,000 ($70,000) divorce settlement he owed her. She had taken the lovely house he had built, and all the lovely things with which he had furnished it. She was happily married to actor-turned-agent Michael Wilding. She had a very successful career. Why, then, was she so demanding, he wanted to know? Did she think, he exclaimed rhetorically, that he was the Bank of England?

It had soured him on marriage, he complained. He adored Joan Cohn. She was a most intelligent and sympathetic woman, but he felt reluctant to spoil their relationship with marriage. He did not know too many happily married couples, what with the emancipation of women nowadays and the pressures of modern life. Margaret—and he, too (he did not place all the blame on her)—had changed completely after their marriage, and for the worse. Marriage was not "the greatest thing since Coca Cola." And show business being what it was, a star's chances of making a go of both his private and professional lives were very slim. "The dice are loaded against you. There's so much bitchery around, you really have to fight hard to survive. Everybody is against you . . . you have to fight for . . . success, sell your soul for it even," and when one finally achieved success, it was resented. Not by the great stars like Frank Sinatra, but by the little, frustrated people. "They're the ones to look out for, because brother, they're just gunning for you."

What, then, was the solution? he was asked.

"Simply, to get away. Take a boat and sail out into the setting sun somewhere, far away from humanity." And failing that, "to rise above it all."

Except that he did not sail into the sunset, or rise above it all. He fought. He had himself photographed relaxing in Joan Cohn's luxurious Beverly Hills home, and with the prospect of opening another antiques shop in mind, flew with her to Paris to scour the maze of its enormous flea market for yet undiscovered treasures.

He would, he said, probably be going into the antiques business in a massive way. He knew exactly what he wanted. The moment he saw the magnificent chandelier, stylish and graceful at the flea market, he snapped it up without a trace of attempted bargaining. It was such a lovely piece, he said, that he was tempted to keep it for the new home he was building in California. For him it was sheer murder, he said, to part with every beautiful antique he found. He did not expect to break even in his business venture; he loved the fun of acquisition. And, in his tour of the flea market, rejecting some pieces offhandedly as not even clever fakes, he found another tempting piece: a seventeenth-century refectory table. Joan Cohn, who knew a great deal about antiques, agreed that it was genuine. This, too, was purchased without the least attempt at bargaining. But the trouble, she explained astutely, was that he was his own best customer.

Although he professed to despise television, condemning it as a mediocre medium that relied on the mediocre for its existence and was the ruination of talent, he was planning to shoot a three-part color television pilot in Spain the following spring in partnership with John Ireland, to be made under the banner of Cherry Productions, Inc., in which he and Ireland were associated with several other investors. In the three episodes, Ireland was to star as a father who had abandoned his family and who, after his wife's death, returns to find that his son had become a member of a gang.

This property had been under development at Screen Gems and was recovered by the two actors. According to *Variety*, Harvey himself would not act in the series, but would direct one of the episodes.

He had also been planning to make *The Severed Head*, as previously announced, but that had given way to accepting the lead in an immediately more profitable film, *The Spy with the Cold Nose*.

The tragic death of James Woolf had cut him up deeply, but now he made a determined effort to snap out of the depression it had brought, to escape his grief and his fear of a future without Woolf's guidance and advice. In London, in keeping with the times, he modernized his wardrobe to include the casual clothes affected by the younger set, took to playing Beatles tapes on the cassette player installed in his Rolls-Royce, going to discotheques, and dining at the newly fashionable restaurants. Throughout this period, he continued his affair with Paulene Stone while making transatlantic calls and writing fond letters to Joan Cohn and seriously discussing marriage with her.

The year ended, in "swinging London," with the bill to legalize homosexual acts between consenting adults in private passing through the House of Commons on second reading. It relieved the tension of many, and parted the curtain for the staging of certain plays in which he had an interest.

In May 1967, he made good the promise he had been making for years, and flew to Israel to visit his parents. This was a time of great tension, with Egypt closing the Straits of Tiran and expelling the UN peacekeeping forces from the Sinai Peninsula, exchanges of fire between Syria and Israel, and Yasser Arafat's terrorist *fatah* active in southern Israel. His visit to Israel lasted no longer than a three-day weekend—and this included flight time. For its brevity he had a perfect excuse: he was already working on his next movie, *A Dandy in Aspic*. He did not stay with his delighted father and wildly overexcited mother, but was driven in style in a Columbia Pictures-owned car to the Dan Hotel, then the grandest in town, there to occupy a suite facing the frothy blue waves of the eastern Mediterranean Sea. In her pretty flat, kept so clean, people said, that one could literally eat off her marble-tiled floor—a cleanliness after his own heart—his mother had willfully prepared the gefilte fish and *kalfleis* that growing up he had loved, but could no longer eat because his guts were "buggered," as he privately told his brother Nahum, and to her horror, spat the food surreptitiously into his napkin. She worried about him. She forgave him. She summoned every available relative to meet him.

He was taken to Beersheba, some two-and-a-half- to three-hour's drive along the old road from Tel Aviv in those days. It was not a heartwarming sight, for this town was still much as it had been in the early 1950s when Nahum and Henya had first settled there: a sand and heat-clogged mushrooming of cheaply slapped together apartment buildings rising like ragged sentinels at the gateway to the southern desert. Here, Nahum served as an honorary city councilor and greeter to important foreign visitors, and half the town, if not more, came to the reception he gave for his brother at the newly built, stylish Desert Inn Hotel. There Harvey greeted old acquaintances he had known as a boy and who had created the South African kibbutz on land north of Beersheba.

The following morning, visiting Nahum and Henya in their flat at the southern edge of town, he told his brother, wistfully, caught up in a sentimental moment, that he wished that he, too, had a son just like Nahshon, Nahum's twenty-one-year-old son, who had made his home on another nearby kibbutz.

On his last night, returning to Tel Aviv, he discussed the possibility of starring in an Israeli-made film with the local Columbia representatives, and finally tearing himself away from his mother's clinging, hysterical arms, was whisked away onto his plane and was gone.

The experience had been a scalding one. It was not the threat of war that had affected him for, as Nahum had explained, everyone in Israel was inured to crises. He had not been made aware of the sirens that existed to sound the warning against air raids, or of the fact that plans were being made to turn hotels into emergency first-aid stations, or designated areas in the public parks into cemeteries. What he suffered from was the extreme depression he felt, induced by his mother's clinging hysteria and, above all, the fact that he lived in a totally different world; that they would never understand him and that he had to keep his family at a distance.

No sooner had his plane landed at Heathrow than he resumed his usual, hectic pace, his plan to purchase and develop film properties, his demands for frequent reports about the new house he was building, his ventures into the antiques business, the stringent standards he expected from the young chauffeur who maintained the fleet of cars he had accumulated and that he kept in Hollywood, Palm Springs, London, Italy, wherever his work led him: his three Rolls-Royces, his two British Coachbuilt Austin Cooper Minis, his two Maseratis, his Fiat, his two station wagons—one of which his chauffeur drove to Berlin for Harvey's use while he was shooting his next movie, *A Dandy in Aspic*—and the new Pontiac he received every year by arrangement with Columbia and which he used in his movies. And each car had to be kept spotless. He spied out even its tiniest flaws, the faint gray blur of cigarette ash on a floor, the speck of dust on a seat, the tiny spot overlooked in a corner of a window, and yelled at his chauffeur when he came upon it.

A Dandy in Aspic, adapted from a novel by Derek Marlowe, was, as it transpired, the last important movie in which he starred. He had some financial interest in it, but it was the joint property of Columbia and Anthony Mann, an important Hollywood producer and director. The movie was shot on location in West Berlin and in London. Harvey's leading lady was Mia Farrow and the movie also featured the fine British actor Tom Courtenay.

"Dandy," according to the dictionary, is defined as a man who pays the utmost and most minute heed to fashion and elegance. It also, to the author of the novel, meant someone who pays enormous attention to his clothes and summons peoples' attention to him in this way because he is a rebel against society and demonstrates it by his unique style. But this dandy is set "in aspic." He is jelled within his own luxurious elegance and in the end it smothers him.

To be dressed in the height of fashion, working with Pierre Cardin, at the time one of the finest French couturiers, was, for Harvey, a blissful experience. Harvey had been a regular customer of Pierre Cardin for several years. This couturier's fashions, he said, were "marvelous." Everything he designed had such flair, such style; his designs both for men and for women were truly revolutionary. He himself, he said, had to have everything he wore constructed to his own unique requirements: his handmade-to-measure shoes, because of his high instep; his shirts, because he had very long arms; and, of course, his suits. He was the first, he proudly reminded the London *Times,* to wear very narrow trousers, narrow lapels, and cuffs and four-button suits. He thoroughly condemned those people who had money but no taste. In his opinion, "Where you get one you hardly ever get the other."

The clothes Mia Farrow wore in *Dandy* were also designed by Cardin. She looked beautiful in the movie, and her clothes were breathtaking. But she was not enamored of couture clothes: "Larry Harvey was wonderful to me. I have nothing but the sweetest memories of him. He and Tony (our director) took me to Paris to be outfitted by Cardin for my role in the film. My own taste in clothes runs A LOT simpler (I'm wearing overalls—just cleaned the chicken-coop)" Mia Farrow wrote to this author.

Several months before accepting the starring role in *A Dandy in Aspic*, Mia Farrow had married Frank Sinatra amid a flurry of international publicity. Harvey admired and practically venerated Sinatra, and Sinatra had liked and admired Harvey for his talent as an actor ever since they had worked together in *The Manchurian Candidate*. One of Harvey's proudest possessions was a photograph of Sinatra and Mia with a dedication to him, which Harvey kept on display in a silver frame for the rest of his life—ignoring, it would seem, the fact of their divorce.

When, in Hollywood, Harvey had offered Mia Farrow the role as his leading lady in *Dandy*, she thought it would be fun to act in this film. Harvey assured her that her role would not take more than a stay of ten days in London and three days in Berlin, and Sinatra did not seem to object, although he did not accompany her when she flew to London.

The ten days in London went according to schedule. Harvey hovered over her like a parent with a small child, taking her to see plays, and to nightspots—inadvertently arousing the tabloids to shriek that Mia was deserting Sinatra for him. In Berlin, however, filming fell behind schedule. The three days of her stay became a week. Her work was still not completed, and Sinatra, who was waiting to start his own film, was becoming angry.

It was so cold that winter that, shooting on a racetrack outside the city, the vapor of their breath clouded the air and the actors had to chew ice before the cameras could roll. Only Tony Mann, who was in his mid-sixties remained cheerful: he was awaiting the visit of his young wife who was flying in from London.

That evening, after a hot bath, joining the rest of the cast at dinner in a restaurant, Harvey received a frantic telephone call from Mann's wife. Rushing back to the hotel they found that Mann had died in his bed.

While Mia stared, transfixed, at his corpse, Harvey and Mrs. Mann began discussing the fate of the movie. He wanted to finish it himself.

Finally he persuaded Columbia that he had the talent and the experience to do so, and Columbia agreed to let him go ahead.

Harvey gave his own account of the fate of this movie in two letters to his parents:

"I had to take over directing the picture," he wrote in the first. "It was a very sad occasion, but everyone rallied around and we finished the picture on time, and here I am back in London for two or three days. I will return to the States and then come back to cut the film in London. . . . I am looking forward to a short rest in America as I feel very tired after three weeks in Berlin, but I have great faith in the picture and I am sure it will be very thrilling and exciting. Now all that remains to be done is to cut it and we'll see what we have. . . . Mia Farrow is excellent and was delightful to work with."

The second letter was sent from Beverly Hills, and was addressed to his parents who were vacationing in South Africa. He wrote:

"I have been so busy traveling backwards and forwards on the picture . . . that I hardly have time to go to bed. If you remember, the director died ten days before the picture was due to be finished so I have had to finish it, and right now we are doing the musical score for the second time as the first score was wrong for the picture. It has been extremely difficult for me, but I hope that in the end we'll have something worthwhile. . . . I don't know where I'm going next.

"I have to return to London to finish the film and then back to America where I'll show it to the heads of Columbia and hear their approval or disapproval. I hope they like it, and it really looks as though we'll have a good picture. Mia Farrow is excellent in it and I enjoyed working with her.

"I can't tell you how marvelous those few days were that I spent with you. Let's hope I get another opportunity to visit you again in the not too distant future. I promise not to be so long in replying but I ask your forgiveness this time and I know you'll understand how time flies when you are working eighteen hours a day."

In Berlin, the picture came in under its budget of $1 million.

His relationship with Paulene Stone had been heating up. This was the first time he had formed a serious relationship with a younger—a much younger woman. She had red hair, and he called her "Red Bird." Between modeling assignments, she flew to Berlin for a meager weekend or two to be with him, and was deeply resentful of the time Harvey spent with Mia, not, it appears, understanding that Harvey was ready to devote all his attention to the actress in his charge. He had done the same thing for Sarah Miles in *The Ceremony*. As a result, as she writes in her book, *One Tear Is Enough: My Life with Laurence Harvey*, Harvey wasted one of the precious weekends they had together when he was summoned by a nerve-racked Mia and spent practically all night counseling her and cheering her up. Mia, according to Paulene, was only deceptively innocent looking, and in fact, was shrewd, smart, competitive, and ruthlessly ambitious—an opinion that is not generally supported.

Despite Paulene's opposition, Harvey who liked and understood Mia Farrow, remained protective of her. "She has incredible instinct and enormous depth as a person. She's kind of kinky, but then most people are, are they not?" he said of her to Mary Blume of the *International Herald Tribune*.

Harvey had somewhat reluctantly, it later appeared, signed on to costar with Rock Hudson in *Ice Station Zebra*, a blockbuster film to be produced by M-G-M. This was a Russian-American coproduction and both sponsors were frantically competing to outdo each other in offering financial backing. When the Russians said that they would invest £2 million, the Americans immediately offered to put up the same amount. It was to be an exciting, mammoth production; a giant that M-G-M was convinced the small television box could not contain.

While putting *Dandy* together in London, Harvey paid a flying twenty-four-hour visit to Hollywood to be fitted with his arctic clothing, then flew back to London and then to Turkey for one day for his cameo role in *The Charge of the Light Brigade*, the role destined to be viciously destroyed on the cutting-room floor.

Flying back and forth across the Atlantic, to Hollywood simply for a fitting for his *Ice Station Zebra* suit, to London to work on *Dandy*, to Turkey and back in a single day to shoot his cameo, was living the kind of life he loved. He was filled with exciting ideas for new projects. On a quick trip to the south of France, he met author Graham Greene and discussed the possibility of producing and directing *The*

Living Room, in which he wanted to costar with Mia Farrow. He wanted to produce a repertory season of classical plays in Los Angeles. He planned to open a Shakespearian theater in New York.

None of these plans came to fruition. He talked too much. He antagonized too many people in Hollywood with his careless, stabbing tongue and his kinky mannerisms. As was the case in Britain, he flouted all the rules and the studios appeared to turn their backs on him.

In Hollywood, the only role that had been offered to him was in *Ice Station Zebra.* Hudson was his good friend. Had he finally decided to accept it, he would have earned a quarter of a million dollars for ten weeks of work, but he decided to turn it down, because, he hinted to journalists, he wanted to play second fiddle to no one, not even his good friend Rock Hudson and could not stomach seeing his name listed under Hudson's in the titles. He could not accept that. Besides, he said, he did not think that the character he was to play had any depth. Ernest Borgnine got the part.

Halfheartedly, he accepted the lead as the husband intent on murdering his rich wife, played by Dina Merrill, in David Suskind's made-for-television movie, *Dial M for Murder,* a remake of the successful 1954 film starring Grace Kelly. It lacked the verve of the original Hitchcock film and his acting suffered for it.

Unable to find the work he wanted in Hollywood, too impetuous to wait for a decent role, he found a script, rewrote it, invested his own money in it, and signed on Ann-Margret, whose career also happened to be in the doldrums at this time—a has-been at twenty-five she was called then—as the female lead.

Rebus, or *Puzzle,* was shot in Lebanon and Italy. It concerns a casino croupier, who becomes entangled in an international conspiracy, and the girl who loves him. Harvey traveled to Beirut with his Italian crew for the location work, shooting the exterior of its pre-Lebanese civil war fabulous Lido casino in its beautiful island setting just outside Beirut. Only several months had passed since the Six-Day War of 1967, when Israel had resolved the crisis with Syria and Egypt by staging a surprise early morning air raid that caught Egypt by total surprise and decimated its air force. Lebanon's Mus-

lim population, and especially its volatile Palestinian refugee population, was yelling for revenge. As was the rule for anyone whose
passport carried an Israeli stamp, thus indicating a visit to Israel, a
new passport had been issued to Harvey, but the highly efficient
journalists of the Lebanese press speedily discovered that he had
visited Israel and published photographs of him and his family
taken from the Israeli newspapers.

Although he had a suite in Beirut's well-guarded, elegant Phoeni-
cia Intercontinental Hotel, where the rooms face the ocean and its
breezes cool the balconies, and only rich tourists and visiting Arab
dignitaries arriving in Beirut to gamble in the casino and enjoy its
spectacular shows could afford to stay, it was a frightening time for
Westerners, and he claimed to have been intimidated enough to lock
his bedroom door each night and, on the set indulged in childish
bravado puns like substituting "D'Jew" for "d'you" and almost, he
claimed, bought a gun.

Rebus was completed in Italy and had very limited distribution.
Ann-Margret overcame the doldrums in her career, but Harvey continued his hunt for movies in Europe. The only consequence of his
trip to Lebanon was the November 30, 1969, decision of the Arab Regional Bureau for the Boycott of Israel to ban his films in the Arab
states. The spokesman for the bureau announced that the bureau
"had received reports that Mr. Harvey was engaged in Zionist propaganda and was supporting Israel." The spokesman also accused
the actor of "urging people to volunteer for the service of Israel."

He felt pleased rather than otherwise, for he found himself in
good company: identical bans had been issued against Frank Sinatra and Elizabeth Taylor for their support of Israel. But it meant
that all his movies would be banned in the Arab world, in effect, a
loss of profits.

His next venture was to accept a role in an Orson Welles film that
Welles had been working on since 1967. Titled *The Deep*, it was based
on the novel *Deep Calm* by Charles Williams. Welles had filmed it off
the Dalmatian coast between 1967 and 1969, but it was still unfinished and, in fact, never was finished. Shot in Technicolor, the action
takes place in two small boats at sea. Welles's intimate friend Oja

Kodar was in it and its star was the prestigious French actress Jeanne Moreau. Welles had asked Harvey to act in it when his first choice could not break his commitment to a play in London.

With his customary flair for self-promotion, Harvey instantly informed the press that he had offered to do his part for nothing—such was his admiration for Welles—but that Welles had told him that he needed a week to think this offer over. To this Welles later replied that he had told Harvey he needed a week to think it over because Harvey had demanded a big piece of the picture, and that was what Welles wanted to think over. Apparently, Harvey got what he demanded, including $15,000 living expenses for two weeks' work—if only on paper!

In a dialogue with Peter Bogdanovich, Welles was not complimentary about Harvey, inferring that some actors should only be shot from the neck down. Harvey, on the other hand, raved about Welles's ability to shoot fast and with a sure hand, to know precisely what he wanted to capture on film. He also claimed that after he had completed his two and a half weeks of work and returned to Hollywood, Welles called him and asked him to return for an additional scene and assured him that he would pay his airfare. Collecting John Ireland in Hollywood and picking up Paulene Stone in London, Harvey flew to Zagreb with his entourage. There he found that no reservations had been made for them at the hotel and that Welles was on location, refusing to accept any calls.

Every hotel was full. They scoured the town and finally found a small boarding house that had a few spare rooms and could put them up for the night. Welles never surfaced. It turned out that he had locked himself in his hotel room in a sulk after a fight with his girlfriend. The scene was never filmed. Too impatient to wait for the plane to London, Harvey and his entourage took the first available flight, which happened to be bound for Rome. There he spent an idyllic few days with Paulene and she became pregnant.

He had left for California. When her pregnancy was confirmed, Paulene plucked up her courage to call him. The news pleased him. It was an affirmation of his masculinity. Little Domino's birth on August 7, 1969, filled him with pride. He sent the news to Nahum, and Nahum told his father. He now had three grandchildren, Nahum told him: Nahshon (his own son), Joshua (Robert's son), and Domino, Larry's little daughter. Shakily, his father accepted the fact. It was not told to Ella. Perhaps she had a suspicion of the truth, but said nothing. She was not an affectionate grandmother and she was ashamed of the new grandchild's illegitimacy.

In Los Angeles, Harvey moved his antiques shop to Antiques Row on expensive La Cienega Boulevard and opened a second antiques shop on Palm Canyon Drive in Palm Springs. Neither shop did as well as he had hoped. His large collections were expensively priced and not altogether to the public's taste. And besides, he kept taking choice pieces to his house because he could not bear to part with them.

From London he wrote to his parents in early May that he had just arrived from Rome, where he had been doing a few scenes from a film called *Sherry with Crème de Cocoa* and would be flying back to the States to finish this film, either in Las Vegas or in Reno. He would not remain in the States for very long, however, he wrote, since he was due to star in a picture to be made in Romania that would take sixteen weeks to complete.

This was his second film to be made in Bucharest. The first had been made some months earlier, and was titled *The Last Roman,* one of the panoramic blockbusters produced to entice audiences back to the cinemas. Little had been heard about it, but he had fallen in love with this country. Romania, he wrote to his parents, "is a very beautiful country indeed and quite an astonishing experience for me being behind the iron curtain. The people are extremely hospitable but very poor. What astonished me was that so many of my films have been shown in this country and indeed in all the iron curtain countries, as they do not have many English speaking pictures here. I have managed to find a little villa 35 kms. from the city and right next to the studio. It is getting very hot here and I am told will get even worse. . . . The picture I am making is called *The Struggle for Rome,* and is a costume film. I suppose it could be described as an epic, as we will be using over 100,000 extras from the Rumanian [*sic*] army. If I continue to make pictures here I will no doubt find myself back in Lithuania one of these days, as all of these countries are not opening up and begging for co-productions with the West. They provide all the facilities, studios, extras, crew as part of their cost and we, of course, provide actors, directors and script."

He was enthralled with the country, the variations in its climate and scenery, and he planned to return to direct, star in, and produce still another film there. This was to be his long dreamed-of project, the Western titled *The Sierra Trail* about a trainload of people making their way across America, experiencing good times and bad. Romania, he believed, lent itself perfectly to a semblance of the American West. "Of course," he wrote, "It is a much cheaper country in which to make a film," and the film people in Romania were as enthusiastic as he was about making it in their country.

To his brother Nahum he wrote enthusiastically about still another project. Nino Zanchin, *The Struggle for Rome*'s director, was writing a script about a love affair between an Arab boy and an Israeli girl, which Harvey had advised him should be shot in Jerusalem. Zanchin would be traveling to Israel and Harvey had recommended Nahum as his adviser.

In this period of renewed Arab-Israeli tension, it was not exactly an idea that caught fire in any quarters.

He was in charge of dubbing and editing *The Struggle for Rome* in Berlin, Harvey wrote, and he was really pleased with the movie. After eliminating a lot of the "slow" scenes, an exciting, visually beautiful Roman epic remained. Afterward he returned to London—and Paulene—to participate in the spectacular BBC tribute to Noel Coward titled "The Words and Music of Noel Coward." He did not move in with Paulene. She lived in a flat in Hampstead with her little daughter by her first marriage and he stayed in the posh flat at Grosvenor House that he had once shared with James Woolf and that he had inherited from Woolf.

When Helen Lawrenson, who came to interview him for *Esquire*, asked him if it was true that Woolf had left him more than a million pounds and the flat, he replied, "It would be lovely and divine, but it isn't true. He didn't leave me anything. His brother John got the flat for me, or, rather, Romulus Films bought it. . . . I've been under contract to them for a long time, but for the past six years I've had to pay them not to work for them because I've been so busy elsewhere. I had a house off Berkeley Square before, but this is quite comfortable, although it's small—just two bedrooms, two baths, living room and kitchenette."

All this he said, apparently without blinking an eye.

His interviewer described the splendor surrounding him: his silk apricot-colored walls; his green silk tie-dyed and cerise curtains lined with purple; his gold-hued velvet sofa heaped with cerise silk cushions; his tall, gilt-framed mirrors; his important antiques, including eighteenth-century English gilded chairs with cerise silk seats, the chair backs hand painted with landscapes and figures; the alabaster vase with classic Roman bas-relief figures; the magnificent eighteenth-century Chinese cabinet of black-and-gold lacquer; his sixteenth-century Moorish mosaic tile battle scene on a black marble pedestal; his gilded French chairs; and Arab mosaics.

To those who visited it, the flat seemed not much different, if containing more furniture, from the house on Bruton Street that he had lost to Margaret Leighton in their divorce settlement.

The next interview took place after he had flown to Antibes to try to persuade Graham Greene to let him produce, star in, and direct *The Living Room*, with such luminaries of the stage and screen as Dame Edith Evans, Dame Peggy Ashcroft, Sir Ralph Richardson, and Mia Farrow. Afterward, he had gone on a yachting trip with a friend, stopping at Monte Carlo, Saint-Tropez, and Cannes. This time, with a Mamas and Papas song on his hi-fi, he showed the interviewer his collection of prints and fifteenth, sixteenth, and seventeenth-century paintings. He had, he said, owned a Picasso and some "super" Chagalls, but these had all gone to Margaret.

Tea was brought in by a natty blond young man wearing a checked sports jacket over a dull-gold turtleneck.

There is another glimpse of him at this time: the rather warped view appearing in the published diaries of Kenneth Williams, a British comedian and homosexual who loved to tell anecdotes from his own unique point of view. In September 1968, he wrote, "going to Wembley for the [David] Frost Show, there was Laurence

Harvey, looking and moving and behaving like a 'raddled old queen,' telling tasteless jokes and pointless anecdotes, accompanied by an entourage consisting of a young homosexual, John Ireland and 'some bird' to make it look good, but it didn't kid me brother! I mean Sister."

As related by Paulene Stone in her book, Harvey's affair with her had been completely open; he had refused to conceal their intimacy. He had taken her everywhere and she had shared his hectic pace, accompanying him to meetings of prospective financiers, discussing film properties that were available, seeking acting assignments, accompanying him on his trips to various countries, that is, until Joan Cohn arrived in London. The inevitable publicity surrounding their relationship may have spurred Joan to decide to find out the truth for herself, Paulene surmises. Joan remained in England for what, Paulene writes, was an inordinately long time. But as soon as she departed, Harvey and she were back together again.

Filming the Noel Coward tribute took a month. On the day after shooting ended, Harvey was due to fly to Nassau, ostensibly to see to some documentation related to his citizenship. The last night of filming was spent at a gala dinner he had organized for some dozen of his friends at a chic Italian restaurant to celebrate his fortieth birthday.

She had an uneasy feeling that whole evening, Paulene writes, that something was wrong. Harvey seemed evasive. John Ireland, who was invariably there, kept staring at her with a solemn and secretive air.

She accompanied Harvey to the airport. He telephoned her from Miami that night and they had a long chat. All seemed well. The next morning a friend telephoned her with the news. On the front page of the *Daily Express* she read that Laurence Harvey had wed Joan Cohn the previous night. Announcement of the marriage was made in London by Columbia Pictures.

Her reaction was one of total shock.

Laurence Harvey and Joan Cohn were married at the exclusive resort of Lyford Cay near Nassau. Twelve people, including the bride's twenty-three-year-old son attended the ceremony, conducted by the island's magistrate. The bride wore a pale yellow coatdress with white polka dots and pearl fringes. The groom was resplendent in a red linen suit, white ruffled shirt, and a gold medallion dotted with sapphires. Though not rare in London, Harvey's outfit seemed extreme to the American public.

Why they had decided to marry at this point has not been documented. Perhaps he had a chivalrous impulse not to abandon her after so many years together. Or he needed to have the security that, in the somber days of looking for work, her wealth afforded. On the other hand, he always found money for his projects, somehow, and he was loud in his protestations that he was not Joan's ponce. Joan had always called their relationship "perfect" as it stood. Perhaps it was she who had demanded the change in their status. Whatever the truth, they appeared happy and comfortable with each other, and returning to her house on Crescent Drive in Beverly Hills, concentrated on remodeling two houses in Palm Springs that Joan owned and in adding to another belonging to him with the assistance of a leading architect who was flown to Palm Springs on weekends in either the twin-engine Air Commander that Harvey had purchased, or by helicopter.

In keeping with his grandiose ideas, the third house was to be enormous, containing a large dining room and bar, a master bedroom and study, two master bathrooms, two guest suites, servants' quarters, a large sauna, a gigantic swimming pool, Jacuzzis, fountains, loggias, garages, a tennis court, and a putting green.

Between planning his houses and sunbathing, he spent solitary hours in Joan's Beverly Hills mansion in the sauna and Jacuzzi, which he had remodeled out of a cabana some way from the main house. The new structure also included a living room and bedroom and toilet, which he had designed. It was a closed, private retreat that he appeared to need. Here, or rather, communicating with them as they stood outside, he would discuss movie projects and chat with friends. And he was invariably at least an hour and more late for dinner, keeping his guests waiting.

His failure to be offered leading roles in top-ranking movies only bolstered his determination to find a new property in which he could star, direct, and also produce.

When he came upon a script titled *He and She,* he felt enthusiastically certain that he had found what he was looking for and began negotiations with investors. When the original investors pulled out, he found another group of investors in Italy and sank his own money into the picture to the tune of 50 percent of the production cost.

He and She was to be the first of the projects he was planning for his production company. He had many other plans. One was to star with Paul Newman, Anthony Perkins, and Joanne Woodward in *Hall of Mirrors* for Paramount. Then his production company would be making another film in Romania and then one in England. *The Sierra Trail* would be followed by *Cockatrice,* adapted by Wolf Mankowitz from his own novel. He was also developing two more properties, both set in the States: *The Long, Loud Silence* by Richard Condon from a short story about a new civil war, and *To Kill a Cop* by Jesse Hill Ford, about a small-town policeman in the Deep South who is unwittingly used as a killer.

Mostly he talked with enthusiasm about *He and She.* This film, he explained, was based on an Italian play of the same title scripted by its author, Goffredo Pariso, with English dialogue. Harvey's leading lady was the fiery Italian beauty Sylva Koscina. This was the story of a romantic and rather staid poet who falls in love and marries a beautiful, earthy Italian woman who demands the physical love he cannot give her. She swims in the nude while a group of rough workmen watch and then lets them make love to her while he is forced to watch. In the end, he allows her to run him over in her car.

Making this movie, he told the press, had given him not only his fashionably long sideburns and natty mustache and short, trim beard, but also an ulcer, particularly because his Italian coproducers had insisted on taking the responsibility for editing the movie. Initially, he mischievously declared to a *Premiere* reporter, when this production was announced, he had wanted to play both parts, but later relinquished the woman's role to Sylva Koscina. He had worked with her before, in *The Struggle for Rome.* "She really does look like that woman. Big and sexy. A big monster lady!" he said. In this movie, "She is a woman who thinks man's sole function is as a stud," he explained. "He, although perfectly capable of performing the normal heterosexual functions, thinks there is more to life. It's a story of mental incompatibility. I call it metaphysical erotics."

Interviewed in his London flat by a *Los Angeles Herald-Examiner* reporter, wearing an old red bathrobe and matching scuffs, he announced, glazed eyed that he had put up $400,000 of his own money to finance this picture. He'd had to sell his house in Malibu—one of the greatest homes in southern California. "I had to come up with 50 percent of the production cost. But it's all my own money. I liked the film and wanted to do it and asked nobody for any help. . . . I take nothing from Joan, professionally or domestically. I ask for nothing and she gives me nothing. She has her money and I have mine. Of course, if I had married her for her money and her position, then I would feel guilty and rightly so, because it would mean that I was a ponce," he said angrily.

In fact he asserted, her connection with Columbia had made things more difficult. It meant that he could not approach Columbia with any project because that was what they expected him to do and his pride would not allow it.

Returning to a description of his new film, he stressed that it was so terrifyingly modern that instead of waiting until the end for the night of bliss, "the bliss comes at the beginning and then the trouble begins. And that," he declared to a reporter from the *International Herald Tribune*, "I'm afraid, is the way in 99 percent of relationships."

Shooting this movie had taken many months. On location in Tirrenia in Italy, he had been hampered by pounding rain, heat, fog, snow, sleet. He had brought two of his dogs to Italy, a golden retriever and a Great Dane, both of them puppies, and he had given them the run of the hotel. Working under the frowns of nature had been difficult. He had planned to make another film in Italy immediately after finishing *He and She,* but had been forced to abandon the project, and he had tentatively accepted an invitation to return to Romania to do a cameo role in a German-made film titled *Michael the Brave.*

21

Promises to Paulene, Married to Joan

Somehow, according to Harvey, the letter and telegram he said he had sent informing his parents of his marriage never reached them. They learned about it from the newspapers. He must never have been able to forget how badly his mother had behaved when Nahum had married, and must have feared that his mother would create a rumpus of some kind—this time reaching the newspapers and scandal sheets. To Joan, as he had to Margaret, he made no mystery of his real origin and what he expected from her was the same affectionate response toward his parents that he showed himself in his letters to them. She began addressing them affectionately as "Dear Mother and Father," or "Dear Mother and Dad," in her letters and appeared to be far more loving toward them than their two other daughters-in-law. This is what Harvey demanded and she happily complied.

She had accompanied Harvey to Italy and while he was deeply immersed in shooting *He and She,* decided to fly to Israel to visit his parents. Her three-day visit was wildly successful. Ella adored her. Joan's wealth dazzled her; the richest woman in the world was her son's wife! When she learned that Joan, despite her name, was a shiksa, she faced this truth bravely. There are photographs of the two beaming women walking arm in arm, looking like mother and daughter in their sleeveless summer dresses, both with much the same coloring, though Joan was blond and Ella white haired. Harvey was not wrong when he had told Joan that she resembled his mother. Joan also became immensely fond of Nahum and his family, and even smilingly tolerated Henya's admonitions that she drank too much, for she always had a small glass of vodka in her hand.

When she learned that the new, neat little "villa" they had moved into lacked air-conditioning, Joan insisted on buying an air-conditioning unit for it—the gift would be deducted from her taxes, she explained. She told Nahum that he looked ten years younger than his brother, which, seen at some distance, he did. He did not live a life shorn of care, but he did not have the dark shadows under his eyes that Harvey had developed, or his too-thin face. He seldom drank more than a little wine and ate plain, regular meals while Harvey drank too much, swallowed laxative pills every day, and barely ate. Most of all, Joan wanted to convince Nahum that a loving God existed. She was a good Catholic and could not understand why he stubbornly persisted in being an atheist. Harvey, she said, had at least, accompanied her to the beautiful cathedral where she worshipped, and had even knelt in prayer, although she did not believe he was sincerely bent on converting to Catholicism.

Nahum suffered from the digestive problems and bad backs that beset all three brothers. If he looked "ten years younger" than his youngest brother, this was because Harvey consistently avoided doctors despite his bouts of agonizing pain, fearing that they might insist on surgery, afraid to go under the knife, fearing that he might be hospitalized for idle months. The multitude of frustrations brought by producing *He and She* that seemed to drag on forever added to his pain. He had been wearing a brace for his back ever since he had seriously injured it during his performance in *Camelot*. While filming *He and She* he was rushed to a hospital in Geneva in almost unbearable pain. An inflamed pancreas was the diagnosis, and he spent a week in the intensive care ward being fed intravenously.

A quick trip to Los Angeles barely gave him time to recover from his illness. After that, he was off again to Italy, planning also to take a trip to Spain to discuss yet another projected film. He made light of his bouts of illness, writing to his parents that the press reports of his failed health were highly exaggerated, and rejected Joan's pleas to get a thorough medical checkup. Several months later, however, arriving home from Europe, he suffered another attack, this in the very early morning hours and was forced to submit to exhaustive tests. He was in such great pain that he was given Demoral for three days. The tests revealed that he had a diseased stomach, an ulcer-enlarged liver, a gall bladder that did not function properly, and an enlarged colon. According to the doctor, Joan wrote to Nahum, he may have been born with an enlarged colon.

Rest and simple food, however skimpily he ate, helped to put him back on his feet, if it did not cure. As soon as he was able to move, he flew to London again to fulfill his commitment to dub his speech in the cameo role he had done months earlier in Peter Sellers's satirical movie *The Magic Christian*. In this cameo, naked, all skin and bone, a perfect example of anorexia nervosa, he does a striptease while reciting Hamlet's soliloquy, "To Be or Not to Be," as one of the demeaning things people will do for money, on what appears to be the stage of the Royal Shakespeare Theatre at Stratford before a first-night audience seeming to include members of the royal family.

"I put the idea up for the film. It's an outrageous and hysterical business. I strip as I recite the soliloquy . . . completely in the buff. . . . But I have a Victorian velvet bow at the back of my head and at the crucial moment I pull the ribbon and the hair all comes down and covers me up. It shocks the hell out of the audience," he gloated.

Returning briefly to Los Angeles, Harvey accepted a minor, if significant part in Paul Newman's movie *WUSA* in which he plays a seedy confidence man masquerading as a priest for a corrupt fascist radio station.

March of 1970 brought the bad news of Ella's surgery to remove a cancerous breast and both his parents' increasing helplessness. Nahum suggested the possibility of placing them in a suitable retirement home. Harvey, ill himself and severely depressed, unable to relax, flew to London for ten days to give readings from Samuel Beckett's works at Oxford University. These were recorded and very well received, as was his recording of the song "This Is My Beloved."

His mother's new wave of hysteria added seriously to his depression. She wept bitter tears and was filled with bitter complaints every time he called. She could not resign herself to what had happened to her, and lying on her bed in her nightgown, would expose her scar to all her visitors and cry, dramatically, "Look what's become of the elegant Mrs. Skikne!"

He was torn, too, by his renewed relationship with Paulene, thrilled that she had given him a child. Ready to support her and the two girls, he bought her a pleasant house in the posh neighborhood of Hampstead. But he was determined to keep away from them for his wife's sake.

Joan was not unaware that he had other women—and young men, too. She knew the show business world, although she said, once, that she would rather he had women than men. She loved him and had never met anyone like him before and was very forgiving and ignored the gossip she heard about his relationship with Paulene. She admired him so much. He was a genius in her view and she did her best to be cheerful in his company and to give him all the freedom he demanded. If she gave him a long, slack rope, she told a friend, she could hold him all the more firmly. Her first husband, so much older than she was, was not faithful but had treated his young wife like a queen and left her the lion's share in Columbia Pictures. Harvey was no stay-at-home. On the contrary, he spent more time in Britain and Europe than in Hollywood, where work had become scarce. But he had youth, charm, elegance; he was hardworking and extremely ambitious; an actor, producer, director, a lover of antiques, who was not afraid to discuss his ideas for houses with leading architects; a witty raconteur; a man who could dazzle the guests at a dinner party.

They were happy together, she believed. She was older, but was so well groomed and beautiful that she did not look her age. He admired her slim, petite figure, her French designer gowns. Yet, only ten days after their marriage he telephoned Paulene and admitted, forlornly (she writes) that he had made a terrible mistake. It may be that his marriage had not brought him what he had expected or hoped for: an exclusive say in Columbia, perhaps disregarding the fact that her children were also shareholders in Columbia and had their own ideas. He always strenuously denied that he had wanted to run the studio, and Joan herself was never heard to say he had. The truth was that he could not tolerate a life of leisure, however voluptuously elegant, and like a racehorse restrained at the starting gate, he plunged and reared and champed at the bit. Scripts arrived in scores, but none that were as great as, perhaps, in his new position as an actor married to a powerhouse at Columbia, he had hoped they would be. Hollywood seemed, for him, to have become a closed volume and although he loved sunbathing and luxuriating in the clean desert air of Palm Springs on weekends, barbecuing the steaks himself for their dinner guests, exercising his handsome, thoroughbred dogs on the beach at Malibu, entertaining financiers and friends at Joan's house in Beverly Hills, buying new homes to relax in when he wished to be alone, he was restless, wanting much more.

Grandiose planning and hectic-paced activity soon replaced idleness. In March his company, Laurence Harvey Productions, joined forces with Wolf Mankowitz's independent film company, Wolfman Productions, with plans to produce a series of films to be made, for the most part, in Britain and Cyprus. This, by agreement, would not interfere with his earlier commitments, such as his negotiations with a U.S. distributor for *He and She* and his forthcoming appearances at the Chichester Festival in June and July in revivals of *Arms and the Man* and *The Alchemist.*

The new partners announced that they had six properties in various stages of readiness and that others were to be added from time to time. All would be independently financed.

"We'll leave the 'Not So Medium Cools' and 'Slow Riders' to others," Harvey boasted in a not so subtle dig at Paul Newman's highly successful *Cool Hand Luke* and Peter Fonda's *Easy Rider,* films that had brought a new, bold, modern look to the screen. This new type of film he condemned as doomed to become dated within two years, while he was certain that the films the new company would be making would endure. *Cockatrice,* adapted from the Mankowitz novel, in which Harvey intended to star and also to direct, would be one of the first of these projects. Also scheduled was a film version of Aristophanes's *Lysistrata* based on a new translation of the Greek classic, casting Orson Welles as Aristophanes, to be directed by Harvey who would also play a cameo role. The women in this play would have to be exceptionally beautiful, he thought, to be able to persuade the men to "make love, not war," as was the theme of the play. It would be filmed in Cyprus.

Another project to be filmed in Cyprus, was *Lovers of Miramdola*, from an original script by Mankowitz and based on a Hungarian folktale, to be directed by Harvey, who would also star in it as a ghost. Mankowitz and Harvey flew to Cyprus to discuss available facilities in that country.

Further productions were to include *The Chase*, an original screenplay, *Love on the Couch*, and *The Teller-Headed Summer*.

While performing at the Chichester Festival Theatre, Harvey also planned to film the stage productions of *Arms and the Man* and *The Alchemist*. With Mankowitz, he also became involved in the inauguration of the Samuel Beckett Theatre at Oxford University and attended the opening ceremony that month. The program, produced by Mankowitz, featured Harvey, Siobhan McKenna, Patrick Magee, and Richard Harris. *Breath*, Beckett's thirty-second play, was performed five times that evening. It was announced that Harvey's own company would foot the bill for five plays per year at the Beckett for the next seven years. This was not a purely altruistic gesture. In exchange, he was to receive first option on the film and television rights of plays staged in the theater.

Above all, the two partners insisted that they would keep artistic control in their own hands. "We don't want any dilettantes dictating to us," Harvey told *Variety*. And they were determined to keep costs down.

While rehearsing his roles at the Chichester Festival Theatre, he tutored an English class at Oxford's St. Peter's College. This he did as a favor to Francis Warner, a don he had met during his last stage appearance. It was during term time, and the don wished to attend a literary festival in Lebanon. Amid a blaze of publicity, Richard Burton had promised to substitute for him, but had failed to show up. Harvey quietly took his place, impressing everyone "by the intelligence and charm with which he dealt with undergraduates," according to a grateful Warner.

With his ivory cigarette holder, his gold cigarette case, chain-smoking, he conducted four two-hour seminars while Warner was away, making no pretensions that he was a scholar, but telling the students anecdotes about his personal experiences performing in Shakespeare and other plays, talking about his personal attitude to a particular part, and encouraging discussion. He said he found the students marvelously polite and charming, even when he taunted them a bit, as he did now and again.

His emolument, by prior agreement, was a bottle of sherry for each lecture.

He had a stroke of bad luck. While rehearsing *The Alchemist*—the scene called for him and a fellow actor to jump up and down with joy on a thin board simulating a four-poster bed—he bounced off the bed and landed on the floor with the board, and his fellow actor suddenly came down on top of him. His leg was bruised, he thought. He had not intended to have it x-rayed, but it was x-rayed nonetheless when he went to the hospital to have a piece of grit removed from an eye, and the x-ray showed that he had a cracked kneecap.

He underwent surgery in the London Clinic, stayed there for a week and turned his room into a hotel suite, filling it with flowers and stocking it with bottles of champagne, which the nurses served his visitors in champagne glasses. The accident had made him, he complained, for the first time in his career, miss an opening night.

But he was not to be kept off the stage for long. Six weeks later he made his debut in Chichester as Sergius in *Arms and the Man* and received good notices. Because of his bad leg, he was only able to play the lead in this play and had to give up his role in *The Alchemist*, which he knew by heart. He remained in Chichester, giving three to four performances each week until the festival ended on September 12 without pay, for the prestige of acting there, for the sheer love of performing. His health had improved and his leg, according to the specialists, showed a really remarkable recovery. It was as if he *willed* it to heal, they said, through courage and perseverance.

After Chichester, he returned to London to attend meetings and plan the development of his film properties. Joan had flown to London to be with him while he was hospitalized and returned to California when she was certain that the surgery had been successful, then flew back to London for his opening night at the Chichester Festival.

Harvey had rented a house for them in Chichester. They were sitting quietly, one evening, playing cards with his secretary when the telephone rang. Joan picked up the receiver. A woman's voice said that it was Paulene Stone speaking and that she wanted Joan to know that she had been Harvey's lover for five years. Joan responded coolly that she had been in a similar situation for eight years and had loved every minute of it and replaced the receiver.

Harvey had heard the conversation but said not a word. They did not discuss what had occurred. But their marriage, although both strenuously denied it, was on trembling ground.

She flew back to her beloved house in Beverly Hills, her weekends in Palm Springs, her ranch, her garden, her busy social life. He made a brief trip to California, then returned to London to star in the television version of the Chichester production of *Arms and the Man*.

Returning to California once more, he joined forces with Kirk Douglas to sign an agreement with the millionaire financier Bernard Cornfeld. The two stars were forming a new production company with Cornfeld's financial backing that would produce some twelve films. Cornfeld went bankrupt and the projected production company never saw the light of day.

Undeterred by failure, Harvey flew back to London, and with Mankowitz, presented Siobhan McKenna in a one-woman show titled *Here Are the Ladies*.

Against the advice of all his friends, Harvey took the starring role in a play in London's West End titled *Child's Play*. Making a last-ditch effort to save his marriage, he asked Joan to join him in London during the run of this play. She was hesitant, but eventually arrived, saw the play three times during the month she remained in Europe, went shopping in London, and paid brief visits to Paris and

Rome. The marriage appeared safe enough. As Joan explained to Nahum once, she liked to smooth things over with a sweet smile and gentle words.

Child's Play, by Robert Marasco, is about evil events at a Catholic boarding school for boys one frozen winter. It is a melodramatic thriller filled with blood, cruelty, pathos, and hints of savagery and sadism. There is a conflict between a neurotic and repressed teacher who is a strict and hated disciplinarian, played by Harvey, and a humane, jovial, popular teacher. In the end, Harvey is taunted into committing suicide.

The play had a two-week tryout at the Royal Theatre in Brighton where it was quite popular. Moving to London, it played more than one hundred times at the Queen's Theatre. Harvey, in steel-rimmed glasses, won praise for his role as the neurotic schoolteacher. Off-stage, posing for an advertisement in the London *Times,* the rigid schoolmaster was transformed into the smiling, debonair actor who was photographed modeling the very fashionable Italian designer Emilio Pucci's checked *bois de rose* and beige wool and silk jacket and roll-neck cashmere sweater, holding his long ivory cigarette holder with his long cigarette fixed in it, looking the epitome of international chic.

Audiences seemed to like the play, but did not flock to see it in great numbers. It closed in March 1971 after a three-month run and Harvey's heavy investment in its success failed to pay off. Ironically, seven years later, the play was made into a film that did well.

The play's failure did not deter him from hatching more projects. One of his properties was a trilogy of one-act plays that he wanted to open in Ireland and then take on tour in the States, and if all went well, bring to Broadway and afterward to London. He also planned to fly to Paris to discuss another film project and then to Madrid for still another. He was keen on starring in Shakespeare's *Coriolanus,* which was to be produced at the newly renovated Wyvern Theatre. The play was due to open in May. If he got the part, he would have less than two months of rehearsal time, but that did not deter him. And he also wanted to direct a new Wolf Mankowitz musical based on the life of real-life highwayman Jack Sheppard.

In London, he was seen everywhere with Paulene and with a maximum of press coverage. She was interviewed. The house he had bought for her was described. This was too much for Joan to take. She filed for divorce on the grounds of "irreconcilable differences" and Harvey was handed the papers as he stepped of a plane at Los Angeles International Airport on February 14, 1971. With his ivory holder and the cigarette fixed in it clamped between his teeth, and Paulene at his side, he received them laconically from the pretty girl from Joan's attorney's office.

To Paulene, to the press, Harvey complained bitterly that Joan had literally taken him to the cleaners and smashed his head into bleeding pulp. How this was possible when they had signed an iron-clad prenuptial agreement is difficult to fathom and can only be assigned to the realm of fantasy. But he had received a shock. He had not dreamed that she would ever divorce him, however badly he behaved. Dissolved in childish tears, he tried to plead with her, but she obtained a court order in Santa Monica to prevent Harvey from molesting her and another order was issued to prevent him from removing any furniture, paintings, or objets d'art from their homes in Beverly Hills and Palm Springs.

If both had wanted a quiet divorce, however, they did not achieve it. The proceedings bore all the earmarks of scandal typical of a Hollywood parting of the ways. He tried to justify himself to the press by giving his own version of the marriage. It had begun "promisingly enough," he asserted. "I adored her. In many ways she was good for me. But eventually it became an asphyxiating life. Everything had to be king-sized, the loving, the jewels. . . . You couldn't buy ordinary diamonds. They had to be like the Koh-I-Noor. I had to have four gold watches, not one. Seven gold cigarette cases, a television set in every room. We were surrounded by sycophants and parasites, a lot of phony gayety sustained by booze," he told interviewer Donald Zec.

To the public, Joan, for her part, maintained a dignified front. But she was heartbroken. She loved him still, she said, weeping over the telephone in a long-distance call to Henya. She would always regard Henya as her sister-in-law, she said. After that she called Nahum and Henya several times more, sounding somewhat tipsy, unfortunately disregarding the difference in their respective time zones, generally waking them up at odd hours between midnight and dawn. But the marriage was dead.

When his brother Nahum wrote him that their parents could not really take care of themselves in their flat any longer and agreed to move into a nursing home, he responded that he was doing his utmost to help, but he had no money. He was heavily involved in a court action "which," he wrote, "could leave me destitute. . . . My sojourn into the theater has not even covered the rent and my dearest, about to be ex-wife, is making life extremely difficult and has threatened to put me on a rack that makes Chinese torture seem like a busman's holiday. It is amazing how wrathful vengeance can be and, of course, the richer the party the greater the scorn. I, personally, have been living on borrowed money. . . . I am being torn financially, emotionally, physically and mentally in so many different directions that, quite honestly, I don't know whether I am coming or going. The film industry . . . is in a very serious state of collapse, and for any work an actor does he is paid a minimal amount of money and given percentages of profits that he never sees."

Nevertheless, he wrote, he would try to send them the means to move into a nursing home—provided their father did not change his mind and leave him stuck with putting out some $2,000, which he could not waste.

His parents did not move into a nursing home.

Unexpectedly, though he had vowed never to marry again, he suddenly proposed to Paulene. She had flown to visit him when he was in West Berlin shooting his next movie, *Escape to the Sun*. The city was very cold and heavy with snow, when, at dinner in the hotel's restaurant, while barely picking at his asparagus vinaigrette, he asked her to be his wife. She said "yes," of course, and that she wanted a large fake diamond engagement ring—something to stir Elizabeth Taylor's envy. Much amused, he agreed. But a large fake diamond ring was not to be found in West Berlin, so she settled for a ring with sixteen brilliant-cut quarter-carat diamonds set in gold.

Both of them looked radiant when they got off the plane at Heathrow, she wrapped against the cold in a gorgeous and very fashionably mod fur coat, he in his fashionable heavy sheepskin three-quarter-length coat. He was sporting a "mod" mustache, which made him look quite young, and in a jubilant mood, kissed dancer Lionel Blair and embraced writer Wolf Mankowitz, who had both come to meet him, and breezed over to the bar to buy himself a drink.

For his luncheon interview with Donald Zec the following day, he arrived wearing huge dark glasses to conceal a black eye, the result of an accidental collision with Paulene's right hand, he laughingly claimed.

In Paulene he had finally met his match, he proclaimed, but he was not through tongue-lashing Joan. "I've no idea how much money Joan has, it never came up," he related. "Except once. We were sitting at dinner by ourselves at the 36ft. dining table—at either end, of course—and she said: 'I've been wondering what to do with my two million dollars worth of jewels. Should I sell them?' 'Only if you need the money,' I said. And that was that. Then a little while later, it cropped up again. 'I've decided to split them up. On my death half will go to my children and half will go to you. The only thing that worries me is that you'll pass them on to your next girlfriend.' I was so furious, I shouted: 'Oh no I won't. I'll wear them myself.' I don't know why she's so bitter. . . . I was with her for ten years, all told. I took her everywhere. I introduced her to everyone. I gave her diamonds and rubies and emeralds; gifts as good as any millionaire could give her. And more important, a live name instead of a dead one. And what happens? In the end she hates me and starts going out with Tab Hunter."

He could abuse his ex-wives, tell the world that the only person who ever understood him completely was not a woman, but a man—James Woolf—and sue a journalist who said nasty things about Paulene, but he really cared for nothing but the chance to work.

Escape to the Sun was a French-German-Israeli production based on a story by the Israeli writer Uri Dan and directed by Menahem Golan. It could have been an exciting film, but its script was mediocre at best and its characters stereotypes. The story is about a group of Jews attempting to escape from the Soviet Union in order to reach Israel and is roughly based on the true story of a group of Jews in Leningrad who attempted to hijack a Soviet airliner. In it Harvey plays a KGB agent who finds the group, and in a change of heart, guides them safely across the border instead of forcing them to return to the Soviet Union. The cast included Josephine Chaplin, Lila Kedrova, and, inevitably, John Ireland. Harvey was so certain of this film's success that he wrote to his parents, jubilantly, that he would be coming to its premiere in Tel Aviv and, determined to win their acceptance of his new family, would be bringing Paulene, her older daughter, and, above all, his delightful little daughter to visit with them. "You'll love her at once," he assured them. Like his first two wives, Paulene was also expected to write to his parents and to address them, fondly, as "Dear Mother and Father." It seemed not to have occurred to him that they would find it more than difficult to accept the fact that they were not married and Domino was illegitimate. With Paulene, after what he termed "seven grueling weeks" of shooting the movie, he took a flying trip to Gstaad, Switzerland, not to ski, or to relax—he was incapable of relaxing—but to be seen in Gstaad's glamorous nightspots. Afterward he flew to the States for several weeks to deal with the problems engendered by his divorce, complaining bitterly in his letter to his parents that the American divorce laws had made the divorce a "costly and emotionally draining experience."

At forty-three, slim but as yet hardly showing in his features the inroads made by his increasingly bad health, he began working on *Night Watch*, costarring Elizabeth Taylor, on what he termed his "silver jubilee in films." Financing this film was his new, intimate friend and ardent admirer, George Barrie, the director of Fabergé, in partnership with Joseph E. Levine.

Night Watch, filmed on location in a house in Bayswater and adapted from a thriller by Lucille Fletcher, is about a wealthy widow whose new husband attempts to frighten her to death.

For Elizabeth Taylor, *Night Watch* was what Richard Burton, to whom she was still married at the time, termed one of her "sadly deteriorating" movies.

"I adore her," Harvey told *Photoplay:* "She's one of the few people I've ever worked with who really gives me something in return. One of the very few. With a lot of actresses I just have to imagine them being what I can read into the parts they play. . . . With Elizabeth it's different. When she speaks and behaves like Ellen in *Night Watch,* I know that it *is* Ellen. There's no question about it being anybody else. It's because of her absolute concentration on what she is doing."

In the midst of shooting, Elizabeth Taylor had an accident, falling from a platform on the set and fracturing her left index finger. Two days later, the movie's director, Brian Hutton, contracted bronchitis and the set had to be shut down for a week. The cast had become accustomed to seeing Harvey experiencing almost unbearable bouts of pain, but he always insisted, stubbornly, that it was only his nervous stomach acting up; he was used to the pain, he'd had it all his life. When the director returned, the son of the supporting actress, Billie Whitelaw, was rushed to the hospital with meningitis. When he was well once more, and Billie Whitelaw returned to the set, Martin Poll, the producer told her that Harvey had been rushed to the hospital in the middle of the night with acute appendicitis. Filming came to a halt once again, this time for more than six weeks.

Appendicitis was the original fictitious reason announced for his surgery. It soon became apparent, however, that much more was involved. Harvey himself could not resist displaying the great welt that ran right across his stomach, and explaining, rather gleefully, that twenty feet of his colon had been removed. "Now they can call me semi-colon," he joked. Later he told Paulene and the press that he had been operated on for a twisted colon. All his friends came to believe that the incompetent London doctors had botched his operation and twisted his colon. It may well be that he played on their anti-English bias by introducing this belief himself.

"I'm not all that sick," he assured the *New York Post* a month or two later. "As a matter of fact, I went to treatment today—and it wasn't a cobalt treatment. . . . It was an injection."

"It's shrinking," he said, looking down at his shoes, "everything is fine. Of course, I'm in agony all the time. . . . The head job I think I've done. Now it's purely physical and there's nothing I can do about that. . . . I don't understand why it hit me, because I'm such a heel. I thought it only happened to good people. . . . All I care about is the ability to work, the ability to function, the ability to create."

Holed up in his suit at the Warwick Hotel he showed few signs of discomfort or fatigue during an interview in his hotel room with *Women's Wear Daily*, yet he claimed that before his surgery he had hardly ever even taken an aspirin (there was no mention of the five or six laxatives he had been in the habit of taking before every meal) and now he was required to take pills. "When you are in good health, it is easy to take for granted such things as jumping out of bed. . . . When you are sick, even the most routine responsibilities make you feel like you've worked a 24 hour day. For a person like me, who has been used to working 18 or 19 hour working days, this has been quite a switch."

Shooting of *Night Watch* ended in September 1972. Two days later he left for California, both to arrange for the showing of the movie and to discuss other projects. When *Night Watch* was finally presented at Radio City Music Hall it was a pitiful flop. As always, Harvey placed the blame on the critics. "The reviewers and the previewers and the deviewers are all gone, those who put poison pen to paper are all gone and I'm still here," he boasted to the *New York Post*. "All the things I created were copied, and then the critics went wild and discovered all these wonderful new techniques which I had invented. You can never please the critics. Never. I don't read them. If somebody rings me up on the phone and tells me about a good notice, I let him read it to me."

On one of his trips to Hollywood, he starred in a segment in Rod Serling's popular *Night Gallery* at the end of its 1972 season. Titled *The Caterpillar* and written by Rod Serling, this was about an Englishman in Borneo who attempts to have a flesh-eating earwig placed in his business rival's ear. It is placed in his own ear. After a night of excruciating pain he miraculously recovers—only to learn that the earwig lays its eggs twice. It was *Night Gallery*'s most watched segment, shot in three days. Harvey had taken it like a trooper when shown his small, drab dressing room. "Now I know that I've reached the bottom," he joked. Although in excruciating pain, he had deliberately gone off his painkillers for the final take so that he could portray the agonizing pain of an earwig's sting.

Several months later, he starred in a *Colombo* segment as a deaf master chess player who murders his competitor and is trapped by his deafness.

He finally married Paulene in Los Angeles on New Year's Eve 1972. To the *Sunday Mirror* that same day, he explained why. He had simply decided to succumb to the inevitable, he explained. It was fate. He was forty-three. She was thirty. "I'm an eternal optimist," he said. "I've been let down so many times, I've had so many knocks that I'm quite astonished by my own resilience—or naivete. But in Paulene I've found a woman capable of being a real mate. Till now I've always preferred older women, I've admired and learned from their experience and judgment and worldliness. Now for the first time in my life, I'm involved with someone younger. I feel I can pass on some of that knowledge. I can be the teacher, the educator."

Marriage would also legitimize his daughter. He wanted that most of all: to know that his daughter was his parents' legitimate grandchild, together with his brothers' children. The couple was married at an all-star New Year's Eve party given by author Harold Robbins in his Beverly Hills home. Judge Brand, who had terminated Harvey's marriage to Joan that February, officiated. "One likes to keep things in the family," Harvey murmured.

Three days after the wedding, Paulene left for London with the children in order to place her oldest daughter in a boarding school. For the rest of Harvey's life, she flew to Los Angeles whenever he summoned her, but not to stay. Depending on his mood, she appears to have been summarily called to Los Angeles and just as summarily sent back to London.

In his new mansion on Cabrillo Drive, he read scripts by the dozen, supervised his antiques stores, busied himself planning a new wing to accommodate the children but, as with Margaret, would not permit Paulene to have any say in planning or decorating this new house, as he had not permitted her to have any say in renovating the new house in the well-to-do London suburb of Hampstead in London that he had bought before their marriage and where he had startled the well-to-do bourgeois neighborhood by putting in a swimming pool, the first there, on its grounds. There he had dreamed of creating a special room with round corners cut out of concrete, where floors, walls, and ceilings were to be sprayed with black velvet flocking. Stereo music was to be piped into this room, but there would be no telephone. It would be a room where he could live as a recluse, his refuge from the world when he needed one. He hired a top London architect and told him what he wanted. Only, he kept changing the plans, and in the end, the architect left for other assignments. Harvey flew to California and the place of refuge he had longed for was never built in his London house.

Instead, he planned to build it in the handsome house on Cabrillo Drive. Here its large living room contained a fifteen-foot bar, pale, and honey-colored furniture, expensive antiques, and silk curtains. Stereophonic music was piped in. Well out of the way was his own bedroom with his private bathroom and the essential toilet attached to it and there he was reputed to spend many hours. People had to speak to him by standing on the lawn outside this toilet. But it was a wonderful house, those who visited it said, filled with exquisite antique Chinese objets d'art.

Because the surgery had left a thick welt across his stomach that did not seem to heal, the doctors in Beverly Hills prescribed cobalt ray treatment in order to shrink it, but the benefit was minimal. In London he had visited quack healers recommended by friends, but to no effect. He hardly slept, barely ate, lived on painkillers, and was becoming as thin as a stick, but he was full of enthusiasm for his new project: a movie titled *Welcome to Arrow Beach*, in which he was to star, and for which he would serve as the director, producer, and coauthor of the screenplay.

It was to be a horror movie, a purely commercial enterprise, not an artistic one. This was to be a movie showing extreme violence; that, he believed, was what the public wanted—people eating one another's flesh. "I'm not about to demean myself after twenty-six years in the business with a revolting little picture," he told Earl Wilson of the *New York Post.* "It's shocking and sad, but it's done in good taste."

Holding a drink in his hand, his cigarette fixed in its long holder, relaxing in the handsome offices of Brut Pix and Fabergé in the Burlington Building, he declared, "I'm trying to make it as romantic as possible."

Earlier, he had scouted locations in Vancouver, but decided that Santa Barbara was a more suitable location and sank some of his own money into the enterprise, hoping to be richly recompensed with the profits this movie would make. Most of the money for this film, however, was put up by George Barrie.

The film was a failure, and for many reasons. Harvey ran into difficulties with the unions, with the script, with the cast. He had money problems and he was in constant pain. With his cast as often before, he was infinitely patient, despite his acute pain, talking for hours over the telephone to his discontented star, Joanna Pettet, and calming ruffled feathers. "He was very considerate, a perfect gentleman," Meg Foster, then a very young ingenue remembered, some twenty years later, her extraordinary blue eyes lighting up as she spoke of him during a chance encounter in Santa Monica with this author one cold and rainy Christmas Eve.

Working for sixteen to eighteen hours each day, finally having to kneel, bent over with gnawing pain, on the cutting room floor to edit the film, he finished it in March 1973. He had not wanted Paulene to be with him in California while he was working on the film; presumably he did not want her to see his agonizing pain. The faithful John Ireland was the only friend he could really trust, and he helped Harvey onto the Fabergé jet loaned to him by George Barrie for his flight to London.

Upon arrival, he appeared, Paulene writes, to be too thin and somewhat overtired but well, and very happy with the just-completed film. People had seen the rough cut and were enthusiastic. Impetuously, he decided that they had to fly to Paris to celebrate.

They flew to Paris on the Fabergé jet, took a suite at the ultrachic, ultraexpensive Plaza Athénée, flew to Rome for lunch, dined at the greatest Paris restaurants, danced through the night at the finest Paris nightclubs, living like the very rich, the jet set, and he told her anecdotes and gossip he had learned from Jimmy Woolf about the mistresses of French kings and dishes named after famous writers.

But that night she discovered the Pethidine he was taking for his pain. He told her that he only rarely took it and stubbornly refused to discuss it further. It turned out that, ignoring his doctors' instructions, he had decided when to take the medication and when not to take it.

During the flight back to London, a friend prompted her to the realization of how very ill Harvey looked. After Paris, she was supposed to return to London while he flew on to New York, but he wanted her to accompany him and she did. Before returning to London a week or two later she begged him to get a checkup from his doctor in Beverly Hills. He promised, but she saw that he had no intention of doing so. She called his doctor herself when she returned to London. When Harvey returned to his house on Cabrillo Drive the pain had become so excruciating that he was instantly admitted to the UCLA Medical Center for a series of tests. When she called the next day she was told that he was to undergo immediate surgery. The stomach cancer that he had denied having had metastasized. Further surgery was impossible. He did not have long to live.

Word of his condition had spread. His room was filled with flowers, cablegrams, bottles of wine, scripts to read. Weak as he was, he wanted no tears. He had such a rage to live that, plugged into machines as he was, he asked for the proper wine glasses with which to serve his visitors and a glass of his favorite white wine to sip.

To his brother Nahum he wrote,

"fate has dealt us a bitter blow in striking this poor, battered body yet again, and laying it low. . . . I don't know whether there have been any reports in the newspapers about my condition. Needless to say, the journalists do tend to dramatize these incidents, although I must confess that this time what I have gone through has shattered even me. I have been forbidden to work for at least six months, which for me can only cause economic disaster. Despite all this, please reassure the parents that every effort will be made to continue their allowance. . . . I intended to come to see you all at the end of May, at the invitation of the Israeli government and the Prime Minister [the occasion was intended to honor him for his work in *Escape to the Sun*] but regrettably have been forced to cancel because of this unexpected problem."

Discharged from the hospital, he returned to his house on Cabrillo Drive. Publicly, he appeared unchanged, for even though he looked gaunt and ill, he was also alert, seemingly ready to go to work and read scripts. He discussed new projects, entertained friends and business associates, paid the most minute attention to the new wing he was building to the house, making decisions about every detail and strenuously excluding any input from Paulene. She was with him when journalists from practically every country called requesting interviews. Was it true, they wanted to know, that he had terminal cancer? He refused to speak to any of them.

Paulene was sent back to London. Left to himself, he was rumored, by the spiteful gossips of the gay community, to haunt the rest rooms of the great hotels, accosting rising young stars, practically clinging to their backs as if to drain some of their health for himself, jealously demanding to know what movies they were shooting. These may have been simply vicious rumors manufactured by idle tongues, but his despair must have been real enough. Even if he got the chance to act in a movie, let alone to direct one, what producer would take the risk and which insurance company would sign him on?

One week after she left Los Angeles, Paulene received the startling news that he had embarked on a world tour with George Barrie and several others in the Fabergé jet ostensibly to promote *Night Watch* and *Welcome to Arrow Beach.*

The group visited some fourteen cities, including Sidney, Honolulu, Hong Kong, Singapore, Teheran, Rome, and Paris, but while the others went sightseeing, Harvey remained on board in the superbly outfitted plane, for he felt too weak to exert himself. The tour had been a drain on him, he wrote to Nahum upon his return, but it had also been therapeutic, coming as it had at a time when he had most needed to get away. "Apart from the physical pain that one has to endure from day to day, the biggest problem is overcoming psychological pressures. The weekly treatments [he had been undergoing chemotherapy] and depletion of one's strength continually serve as a reminder, plus the fact that the doctors have forbidden me to do any work. Having been so active all my life, I find it extremely difficult to be suddenly so inoperative and helpless. I am trying to prepare various scripts for the future, and to keep as busy as I possibly can under the circumstances."

He returned, not to the house on Cabrillo Drive, but to his family, to his wife and the children in the house in Hampstead. In London he received a blood transfusion but discontinued the chemotherapy treatment, which he found too debilitating. Rising, weak from the transfusion, which had been massive, he cabled friends everywhere in the world inviting them to a champagne dinner party and Elizabeth Taylor, Kirk Douglas, Peter Lawford, Rex Harrison among many others flew to London to be there, arriving to salute him for his defiance and courage in the face of looming death.

In his house in London he tried to live as he always had, dragging himself to his usual haunts—or at least some of them when he felt strong enough—dining with a friend or two, planning to produce and act in films and on stage. He wanted to direct a film to be based on a Wolf Mankowitz novel and called a writer in Hollywood and asked him to fly to London to work with him on the script. He wanted to star on Broadway in a play by Alun Owen. He insisted on going to lunch with John Ireland who came to London to see him and, asking him to order fish, nibbled on the bones and sipped some wine.

Harvey died, quietly, on November 25, 1973, at the age of forty-five, not two months after his forty-fifth birthday.

22

Aftermath

His death was reported on the radio and television news and in newspapers in the United States, Britain, and Europe. In Hollywood, there were scandalous overtones. From her bed at the UCLA hospital where she was preparing for abdominal surgery, the heartbroken Elizabeth Taylor impulsively arranged a memorial service at an Episcopalian church just across the street from the hospital and her physicians permitted her to attend the service.

John Ireland, Harvey's close friend of more than twenty years, whose career he had aided and to whom he had given parts wherever he could in his movies, delivered the eulogy in the presence of the one hundred invited guests.

> We who have been pricked by the sharpness of his wit, comforted by his abundant generosity, warmed by his humor, feel the void left by this dear person. Thank you, Larry, for caressing us with your friendship and your love. . . . Although he never reached the pinnacle of success in this country his outstanding talent deserved, he was a colorful and exciting man. He said and did many outrageous things. Few men ever faced the knowledge of death more courageously or gallantly.

That the memorial service had been conducted in a church, deeply outraged Rabbi Max Nussbaum of Hollywood's Reform Judaism's Temple Israel. He had himself converted Elizabeth Taylor to Judaism prior to her—what turned out to be brief—marriage to Eddie Fisher. That Friday evening he said kaddish (the prayer for the dead) for Harvey before some 700 members of his congregation that included many of Hollywood's most prominent personalities and dashed off a letter to the *Los Angeles Times* stringently condemning Elizabeth Taylor: "I'd like to thank you for the entire Rabbinate [i.e., for conducting the memorial service in a church]. It was an utter scandal. At a party some years ago, Laurence Harvey started singing songs in the most classic beautiful Lithuanian Yiddish I've ever heard."

Elizabeth Taylor made no comment. Peter Lawford remarked, "I never thought about it. . . . Come to think of it, Larry, who was hardly a practicing Jew, would have preferred the room at the Bistro. . . . But it was taken."

Harvey was cremated at the Golders Green crematorium in London on November 30, 1973. War had just broken out between Syria and Israel: Syrian tanks had invaded northern Israel on Yom Kippur (The Day of Atonement) when most Israelis were either attending synagogue services or at home. Joshua, Robert's son, who had been spending a year in Israel and was due to fly back home to the States, was deputized to stop over in London to represent the family at the funeral. He was a little startled, he said, to find that the funeral service was conducted by a priest—something he would *not* be able to report to his grandparents—but Paulene reported proudly to Nahum in a letter that the service had been nondenominational "to fit Larry's international status." The press was there in force, but kept respectfully at a distance. Tributes were delivered by Wolf Mankowitz and composer Leslie Bricusse. Beautiful floral tributes had been sent from all over the world and were arranged outside the chapel. After the cremation his widow invited Joshua to share in a handsome funeral meal at her house, he reported, but he belonged to the wrong generation to recognize most of the guests.

The memorial service was conducted in St. Paul's Church, the parish church of Covent Garden and the headquarters of the Actors' Church Union on Friday, January 4, and a plaque was dedicated in its sanctuary in Harvey's memory. It reads, simply: "In memory of Laurence Harvey. Actor. 1928–1973."

In a letter to Nahum, Paulene stressed that the memorial service had not been a religious ceremony, but one of tribute. The music played was from *The Alamo* and the ceremony had ended with Harvey's recording of the song, "Camelot," from the musical in which he had starred. There were readings by Rex Harrison and John Standing, a hymn, a reading from Jeremiah, psalms, followed by a sermon by Father John Hester. After the dedication of the plaque had come the offertory hymn and the communion hymn.

She added with pride that she was planning to have the children baptized and hoped to name them Larushka and Mischa respectively in order to perpetuate Harvey's name.

Thus, a new myth was added to Laurence Harvey's name.

In the first of her two autobiographies, Zsa Zsa Gabor confidently states that Harvey had left a will written in the purest Hebrew—a language he did not know. In her second autobiography, this will was written in Aramaic, a language only a few scholars can read.

As far as is known, however, he left no will. Perhaps he thought that in this way Paulene would inherit everything; perhaps he thought that everything would vanish with him; perhaps he could not bring himself to make a will because he could not face the ultimate reality of death, however valiantly he struggled to maintain his courage. "I'm rather good at living in abject luxury," he had once declared. Perhaps because, having spent money so heedlessly throughout his life, he thought he had nothing much left.

However, there was the house in Hampstead, the house on Cabrillo Drive, the antiques stores that did not make money; one or two other properties here and there that had not yet been frittered away. He appeared never to have paid any attention to his expenditures. If he liked a painting or an antique he spotted he would buy it, regardless of the price, or whether he could afford it. It turned out that he had continued to retain his suite at the Connaught and to keep his possessions in it, and had been paying the rent for it all his life, even though he never so much as visited it in his last years.

Both Paulene and Domino were certainly his heirs, but without a will it took at least five years before the estate could be probated through the courts. Elizabeth Taylor offered to take the Cabrillo Drive house off Paulene's hands. Since Hollywood is essentially a very small town, full of gossip, Joan came to hear that the will, if there was one, was missing, and telephoned Nahum to ask whether he had any information about it. Paulene learned about the call and

reportedly believed that Joan wished to cut herself a piece of the estate. The London *Daily Express*, which appears to have spread this
rumor, received an angry letter from Joan denying any implication
that she put forward a substantial claim to Harvey's estate. "I have
money coming out of my ears and have no interest whatsoever in
his money. When I divorced Larry that was the end of it," she told
the *Hollywood Reporter.*

Paulene was also reported to have been furious at the "invasion"
of her house on Cabrillo Drive by John Ireland. Ireland had driven
to Cabrillo Drive from his home in Santa Barbara to pick up his
wine, claiming that Harvey had promised to make him a gift of part
of his famous cellar, but at the absent Paulene's strict instructions, he
was denied entry to the house by the staff.

In London, Paulene was described as being "less than amused"
about the incident. She had reason to be angry with him. Like Peter Lawford, he had believed that she was not competent to look
after Harvey and that the English doctors were killing him. Treating her as a mere cipher, he had made arrangements to fly a specialist from Los Angeles to London to take Harvey back to the
States.

"Here come the sharks," Paulene had remarked to Harvey's longtime secretary Sandi Stubbs and Joshua at the funeral meal as cred-
itors and friends swearing that Harvey had promised to let them inherit all kinds of treasures flocked to her door. Beset by mounting
debts, Paulene returned to modeling just six weeks after her husband's death. She was only thirty-one, and had spent months in the
London house watching over her husband. Nine days after his
death, she announced her engagement to Justin de Villeneuve, the
former fiancé and manager of Twiggy, the famous model and actress. Their engagement was broken off a week or two later. She said
that he was the one who had broken it off, and that she loved him.

Her professional name perpetuated Harvey's fond nickname for
her: she called herself Paulene "Redbird" Stone.

In 1975, it was revealed that Harvey had left an estate of £34,349
in England. Letters of administration had been granted to his
widow, Mrs. Paulene Harvey.

As one of the sponsors of the Western Institute for Cancer and Leukemia Research, Joan Cohn Harvey honored Laurence Harvey (and primarily John Wayne) at the December 1973 dinner given by the institute in the ballroom of the Beverly Wilshire Hotel. Friends of the actor established a Laurence Harvey Cancer Research Fund at UCLA in January 1974.

In June 1974, George Barrie recorded a tribute to Harvey with Lou Rawls who sang the two songs, "Who Can Tell Us Why," and "The Night Has Many Eyes," from Harvey's last two movies. Barrie had always believed in and admired him. He had taken him on a joyride around the world in his private jet. He had invited him to succeed Cary Grant as the Fabergé spokesman when Grant retired. There would always be a place for him, Barrie had promised. He was heartbroken when Harvey died.

With his death, both his parents lost the will to go on living. Alzheimer's disease descended swiftly upon Ella; she spent the rest of her life in an empty daze. Boris moved to his son's house in Beersheba. He had always been interested in sculpture and began carving figures out of wood. But he died within months of pneumonia.

Harvey had maintained his ties with his parents all his life—above all, since he had left home and began to live in a totally different environment at so young an age—to reassure himself that he was not alone in the world. In character, he was much like his mother. He had inherited her need to be admired, her obsession with cleanliness—his friends claimed that despite his many servants, he would clean, dust, and polish his beautiful houses himself after they had finished, although he always strenuously denied this charge. He had been their mainstay and their pride, although he had lived a life that was light years away from anything they knew or understood.

Uneasy with his bisexuality, wanting to be seen as a man's man, he invented tales about his past, coolly telling one interviewer that his education had been poured into him in a back alley in the toughest part of Johannesburg, and that at the age of fourteen, he had spent months with his jaw in traction in a South African naval hospital.

This piece of "rough stuff" as he had appeared to some, had early become interested in acting. In 1970, Percy Baneshik, a playwright and columnist for Johannesburg's *Star*, remembered that he had met Harvey in 1942. He had written a short play about Shakespeare that was to be produced for the Johannesburg Repertory Players. Harvey, who looked sixteen but was only fourteen at the time and "a rather cheerful puppy, a rough fellow in those days," as Baneshik described him, auditioned for a part as an Elizabethan sailor on the grounds that he *had* been a sailor (after all, he *had* run away from home and spent a handful of weeks in the South African navy before his mother had come to bring him back home) but he was turned down.

This had not stopped him. In England, he was rejected by the reigning thespian establishment and derided as a foreigner and he had defiantly reinvented himself in reaction as a Lithuanian, a country he knew nothing about, named himself Larushka, which meant nothing, and Mischa, and called himself a "Slav," unaware that the Lithuanians were neither Slav nor Greek Orthodox but ardently Catholic. Combined with his fresh, blond good looks, his height, and good physique, this had given him, brilliantly, a mystique that distinguished him uniquely as an actor.

Determinedly swimming against the current, he became a contract player, earning a minimum salary, and starred in a cheaply made movie. He might have continued in obscurity if, by sheer chance, he had not met the brilliant James Woolf. For Woolf it was love at first sight. For Harvey, it was the start of a new life.

"Jimmy was father, mother, mentor, brother, lover—I don't mean in the homosexual sense—everything to me. When he died, I found myself very lonely, empty, vacant. I did a few films in remote places, everything to run away. . . . You search and search for a small percentage of the kind of relationship in your adult life, and one . . . one never finds it," he had told the New York *Post*.

It was Woolf who had given him his starring role in *Room at the Top*, the film that made him famous, and who nurtured his career and got him his best deals in Hollywood and London. At the height of his fame Harvey was the busiest actor in Hollywood. But he also had a rage to live high on the hog, to drink too much, to wear the finest clothes, patronize the best restaurants, occupy the best hotel suites, build the most luxurious homes. All this required a great deal of money, yet despite his reputation as being greedy for money, he threw away the opportunity to earn millions on at least two occasions in order to act on the stage, for the stage was his first real love. He was called self-centered, ruthless, and arrogant, yet to those of his fellow actors he liked he was generous, and as a director he gave his all to his stars.

Above all, he lived life to the hilt, said and did outrageous things, and wanted to command a vociferous response and reaction. He wanted to become a notorious public personality, he said. "When they write my obituary," he told the London *Evening Standard* in 1970, "I hope they'll say, 'L. Harvey, actor-director, he brought a bit of life and fun into his profession.' That's the greatest tribute I could wish for. As far as my work goes, I know I've done a lot of rubbish but I'd hope I would be remembered for some of my stage performances and for films like *Room at the Top, Expresso Bongo, Darling, The Manchurian Candidate.* And four films—four really good films— isn't a bad record for any actor in this business."

He could have added several more.

Ironically, his finest work was on the stage. But only those who saw him performing on stage can know that. At school, he had displayed no interest in any subject and had scraped through with only a sketchy education. He became keenly aware of his lack of a good education, and it showed in his often silly remarks and acute misjudgments. If he lacked depth, his sheer acting ability earned him critical praise for his roles in Shakespeare and Restoration comedies as well as in modern plays.

Despite his excesses, the waste of his talent by acting in minor films, his childish behavior toward actresses he did not like, his sharp tongue and flawed judgments as well as his insights, he was a true professional, with an impeccable BBC accent, a sense of style, luxurious in taste and habits, not a man of culture or education, but providing an excellent facsimile of one.

Laurence Harvey's Films

House of Darkness (1948)
Man on the Run (1949)
The Black Rose (1950)
Cairo Road (1950)
The Man from Yesterday (1951)
The Scarlet Thread (1951)
There Is Another Sun (also titled *Wall of Death*) (1951)
I Believe in You (1952)
A Killer Walks (1952)
Innocents in Paris (1952)
Landfall (1953)
Twilight Women (1953)
Romeo and Juliet (1954)
King Richard and the Crusaders (also called *The Talisman*) (1954)
The Good Die Young (1954)
I Am a Camera (1955)
Storm over the Nile (also called *None but the Brave)* (1956)
Three Men in a Boat (1956)
After the Ball (1957)
The Truth about Women (1958)
The Silent Enemy (1958)
Room at the Top (1959)
Expresso Bongo (1959)
The Alamo (1960)
Butterfield 8 (1960)
Summer and Smoke (1960)
Two Loves (also called *The Spinster*) (1961)
The Long and the Short and the Tall (also called *Jungle Fighters*) (1961)

A Girl Named Tamiko (1962)
A Walk on the Wild Side (1962)
The Wonderful World of the Brothers Grimm (1962)
The Manchurian Candidate (1962)
The Running Man (1963)
The Ceremony (1963)
Of Human Bondage (1964)
The Outrage (1964)
Darling (1965)
Life at the Top (1965)
A Winter's Tale (1965)
King Lear (1966)
The Spy with the Cold Nose (1966)
The Doctor and the Devils (1967)
A Dandy in Aspic (1968)
The Last Roman (1968)
The Struggle for Rome (1968)
Rebus (also called *Puzzle*) (1969)
He and She (1969)
The Magic Christian (1969–1970)
Arms and the Man (1970)
WUSA (1970)
Escape to the Sun (1972)
Night Watch (1973)
Welcome to Arrow Beach (also called *Tender Flesh*) (1973)

Bibliography

Andrews, Eamonn. *Forever and Ever Eamonn: The Public and Private Life of Eamonn Andrews.* London: Grafton, 1989.

Baddeley, Hermione. *The Unsinkable Hermione Baddeley.* London: Collins, 1984.

Brown, Ivor. *Shakespeare Memorial Theatre, 1951–1953: A Critical Analysis.* London: Reinhardt & Holt, 1953.

Clark, Donald, and Chris Anderson. *John Wayne's The Alamo: The Making of the Epic Film.* Secaucus, N.J: Citadel Press, 1960.

Collins, Joan. *Past Imperfect.* New York: Simon & Schuster, 1984.

———. *Second Act.* New York: St. Martin's, 1996.

Farrow, Mia. *What Falls Away: A Memoir.* New York: Doubleday, 1997.

Forbes, Bryan. *A Divided Life.* London: Heinemann, 1992.

Freedland, Michael. *Jane Fonda: A Biography.* New York: St. Martin's, 1988.

Gabor, Zsa Zsa. *One Life Is Not Enough.* New York: Delacorte, 1991.

Goodwin, Cliff. *Sid James.* Rev. ed. London: Virgin Books, 2001.

Heymann, C. David. *Liz: An Intimate Biography of Liz Taylor.* New York: Birch Lane Press, 1995.

Hickey, Des, and Gus Smith. *The Prince.* London: Frewin, 1975.

Isherwood, Christopher. *Diaries, 1939–1960.* New York: HarperCollins, 1979.

Kelly, Kitty. *His Way: The Unauthorized Biography of Frank Sinatra.* New York: Bantam, 1986.

Lerner, Alan Jay. *The Street Where I Live.* London: Hodder & Stoughton, 1978.

Miles, Sarah. *Serves Me Right.* London: McClelland & Stewart/Tundra Books, 1995.

Shipman, David. *The Great Movie Stars.* New York: St. Martin's, 1972.

Signoret, Simone. *Nostalgia Isn't What It Used to Be.* New York: Harper & Row, 1978.

Sperling, Cass Warner, Cork Millner, with Jack Warner Jr. *Hollywood Be Thy Name: The Warner Bros. Story.* Rocklin, Calif.: Prima, 1994.

Stone, Paulene. *One Tear Is Enough: My Life with Laurence Harvey.* London: Michael Joseph, 1975.

Sutherland, Douglas. *Portrait of a Decade: London Life, 1945–55.* London: Harrop, 1988.

Vanderbeets, Richard. *George Sanders: An Exhausted Life.* New York: Madison, 1990.

Wapshot, Nicholas. *The Man Between: A Biography of Carol Reed.* London: Chatto & Windus, 1990.

Wayne, Pilar, with Alex Thorleifson. *My Life with the Duke.* New York: McGraw-Hill, 1987.

Additional material can be found in the Margaret Herrick Library of the Academy of Motion Picture Arts and Sciences in Los Angeles and the Billy Rose Theater Collection of the New York Public Library.

Index

About the Author

Anne Sinai was born in Lithuania and grew up in South Africa. She studied English and history at Witwatersrand University and received a postgraduate degree in social anthropology and native law and administration. She enrolled at the London School of Economics and Oriental Studies, but since they had never become South African citizens, she and her husband had to leave England as aliens. They lived in Paris and then Israel, where she worked as a journalist, writing about new immigrants, and spent two years in Burma (Myanmar), where her husband was sent on a diplomatic mission.

In the United States she was editor of *Middle East Review,* a quarterly with articles by American and international academics exploring the problems involved in attaining peace between the Palestinians and Israel. She has coedited books on various Middle Eastern states and also Jerusalem.

Widely traveled, she has lived in the United States since 1964 with her husband, a political scientist and author, and her son and his family, and is a U.S. citizen.